The Admiral's Baby

The Admiral's Baby

Laurens van der Post

Most Immediate. En Clair.
CS5 to SACSEA:

We can continue to rock the baby to sleep
only if you people outside the house would
not make so much noise.

Signal from Admiral Sir Wilfred Patterson, commanding
the Fifth Cruiser Squadron, to Admiral Lord Mountbatten,
Supreme Commander Allied Forces South East Asia.
22.30 hrs. 19.9.1945.

JOHN MURRAY
Albemarle Street, London

© Laurens van der Post 1996

First published in 1996
by John Murray (Publishers) Ltd.,
50 Albemarle Street, London W1X 4BD

Reprinted in 1996 (three times)

The moral right of the author has been asserted

A catalogue record for this book is available from the British Library

ISBN 0-7195-5742 9

Typeset in Baskerville by Servis Filmsetting Ltd
Printed and bound in Great Britain by
The University Press, Cambridge

*This story is told also as a memorial
to my 'CS5', Admiral Sir Wilfred Patterson,
and 'Christie', General Sir Philip Christison,
of Burma, the Arakan and Java*

CONTENTS

FOREWORD

IT MAY WELL be asked why I have waited fifty years to write this story of *The Admiral's Baby*. At the request of Gilbert MacKereth, the British Minister in Java – to whose staff I had been transferred in 1945, at the express wish of Lord Mountbatten who felt my presence in Indonesia would be needed – I had written an official report for the Secretary of State for Foreign Affairs in London and had taken it for granted that this official account told the story sufficiently.

I had written it reluctantly, and only on the condition that I could write it not in the conventional pattern, but at the length at which I felt the story deserved to be told. It was, therefore, one of the longest reports ever written for the Foreign Office in modern times. The British Minister in Java, in his covering note to the Secretary of State, explained why he felt that I was the person most suitable to write such an account, and ended up with an explanation of why the report had to be so long. It was, he said, the only way in which those 'astonishing happenings' during the British occupation of Indonesia could be properly understood.

Within hours of completing the report, which MacKereth received with the highest praise, I left on a long tour of interior Java. By the time I returned, my report, together with others and MacKereth's own report and covering note, had already gone off to the Foreign Office. My own copy remained with my personal papers in my office and, after my final departure from Java in June 1947, was sent with my heavier baggage to my home in England.

I did not see the report again until recently, when we closed down our home by the sea at Aldeburgh and moved its contents to London. There, still unopened, was the parcel that had followed me from Java. During all those intervening years I felt that, having written the report, I had done my duty to my years in Java and that there was nothing more quintessential to say. But I had not reckoned with the fact that those eventful years, all experienced on active service in the field, and in the jungles of Java, had not yet done with me. Memories of those years had been at work in my unconscious self and now were surfacing and urging me to retell the story, revealing the part that these experiences had played in my life and in the life of my time. This was to be a truly human story which, set beside my official report, would give a unique picture of those extraordinary months after the surrender of Japan.

It is perhaps not surprising that when I reread my report of the occupation after so many years I did so with astonishment, feeling as if someone else had written it. I was amazed as much by the 'someone else' aspect of the account as by its complete objectivity and the fact that it seemed to me to be written as living history of the best kind. And yet, far from satisfying what I had thought was this feeling of having done my duty by Java, it aroused in me an acute guilt that there was a tremendous story still to be told – far more important than that in my report – and an important and scandalously neglected history to which I hope this book will make a worthy contribution. In order to give *The Admiral's Baby* its full perspective I have included my official report as a separate element within it. One without the other would be incomplete.

It is important as history because this was the first and most graphic instance of how the emergence of Japan from 1854 onwards, and the terrible war in the Pacific which she inflicted on the world, had caused a rude awakening in the subject races of the great empires established by the West all over the world. One of the principal tasks of the Western world henceforward would be to come to terms not only with the realization that empire in the old sense had vanished for ever, but also with the fact that an enormous rescue operation had to be mounted to save the awakened from the passion of their awakening.

ACKNOWLEDGEMENTS

I owe a great deal to Jane Bedford for her help in the writing of this book, and to Louise Stein for a number of reasons, but here most particularly for her fastidious revision of the manuscript.

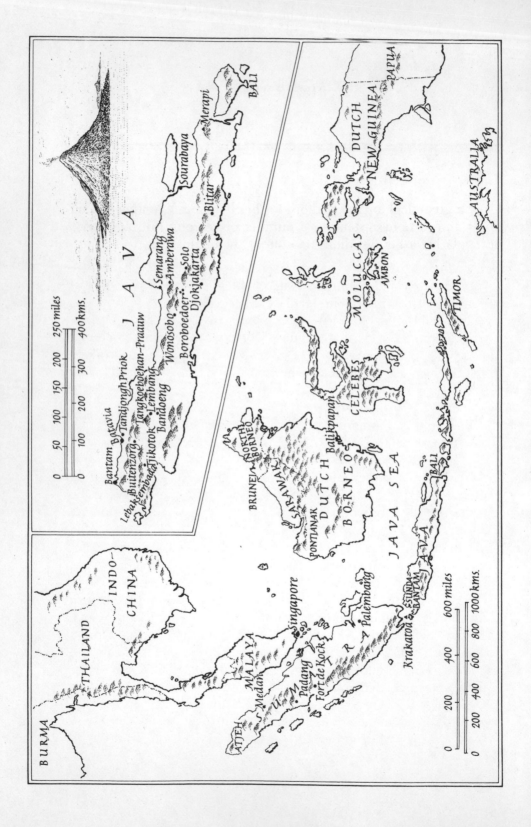

PRELUDE

IF I HAD to choose a point where my life suddenly changed course, it would be in the Western Desert, some days after Pearl Harbor. I was engaged on a plan for raising an Arab-Senussi commando which had been allotted to me after an important reconnaissance along the frontiers of Syria and southern Turkey. I had taken with me on this reconnaissance Wilfred Thesiger, and his Djebel-Druze orderly, and had then left him in Syria to pursue his own plan of raising a Djebel-Druze commando. At that moment Hitler's armies were sweeping through the Ukraine and the Crimea, and there was a growing concern that they might reach the border of Turkey and, as in the 1914–18 war, persuade the Turks to join them and so create another flank for the hard-pressed British forces to defend.

I had not been long in the Western Desert when I was suddenly ordered to report to Terence Airey in Cairo. He had been on the staff of General Wavell and was now in command of combining all our operations behind the Italian lines in Ethiopia. He told me that he had had a request from the General for me to join him in Java, as he foresaw the need for working behind enemy lines, as we had done in Ethiopia.

So in January 1942 I found myself reporting to General Wavell at his headquarters in Lembang, on the outskirts of Bandoeng in Java, on the slopes of the sleeping volcano of Tangkoeboehan-Praauw ('The Ship Turned Upside Down'). There, the Dutch and the British had already grouped themselves under a single command, which now also included the Americans, to gather their unprepared forces to counter a long-planned invasion by the Japanese of the Pacific and the countries of South-east Asia, not least the oil-rich islands of the Dutch empire. So dynamic and fanatic had this invasion become that the Japanese had already struck through Siam and into Malaya, and were rapidly advancing down its long peninsula.

This meant my assignment had to be varied almost from day to day, even at one stage involving me in a mission to find a backwater in southern Java from which General Wavell and his staff could be evacuated by submarine in case the Dutch decided to surrender. I do not think this was a serious proposition in General Wavell's mind, but it was felt by many of his staff to be a possibility for which they should be prepared. After the precipitate Dutch surrender, I was captured by the Japanese in the jungles of the Sunda lands of Java. I have described my three and a half years of brutal captivity as a Japanese prisoner-of-war in my book *The Night of the New Moon*, and *The Admiral's Baby* takes over where that story left off.

I had all along thought it most strange that the atom bomb was dropped on so moon-swung a people as the Japanese, in the phase of the moon when the old had died and the new was not yet born. The feeling of strangeness and awe throughout the last two weeks of my captivity, to the moment when I was standing free in the street – watching all my fellow prisoners disappearing on their way to Batavia, and home – with the new moon fulfilled in the full moon rising over the wide plateau of Bandoeng, was to make the general specific and awesome also to me.

The Admiral's Baby

HISTORICAL NOTE

The Dutch East Indies Company was established in 1603 and was to become one of the most powerful and ruthless chartered companies in the history of empire. By the time of the Napoleonic Wars the Dutch had largely replaced the Portuguese in the Far East and dominated trade in South-east Asia. To the wealth and power they had achieved from their trade in spices and silks, things coveted by a hungry West for centuries, they added enormously by developing the fertile soil and exploiting the climate of Indonesia to grow coffee, tea, sugar and, ultimately, rubber.

At the heart of this flourishing empire was the island of Java, closely linked with the island continent of Sumatra. Strategically situated as they were on the trading routes of the China Seas and the Pacific, the Dutch exercised their authority from the northernmost tip of Sumatra across Java, Bali, Seram and Timor, to Papua in New Guinea, and north from Java to Pontianak and across to south-eastern Borneo. By the time of Pearl Harbor, the Dutch empire was the third largest in the world, enriched beyond the dreams even of the chartered company by the discovery of oil in Sumatra, Borneo and their outer islands.

The whole world regarded the Dutch empire as a model empire, one which the British and the French could not match. But in truth all through their occupation of Indonesia there was great unease, rebellion and civil war which, as the centuries progressed, transformed itself increasingly into political unrest and agitation. However much the ruthlessness of the company had been ameliorated by the change of climate in world opinion, the Dutch still governed Indonesia with an iron grip and their governor-general exercised the power of arrest, imprisonment and even exile on an increasing number of rebellious subjects merely by declaring that he was acting in the public interest. As a result, when the Japanese invaded in 1942, the most prominent of Indonesian leaders like Soekarno were in prison, and men of the calibre of Hatta and Sjahrir were in exile, like so many of their country-men, in the outer islands. The Australians at the end of the war were shocked to find on one island alone some 1,700 political detainees.

The form of the place names used is that current at the time the events described took place. Their modern equivalents are given as cross-references in the index.

CHAPTER ONE

Full Moon

AND SO THERE then I stood on the night of 21 August 1945, in the street in Bandoeng where my book *The Night of the New Moon* ended, watching a long column of my fellow prisoners-of-war, brought up in the rear by the sick, the wounded and the near-dying on stretchers carried by men themselves so enfeebled that they could hardly keep upright, on their way to the railway station, to Batavia, and ultimately to their homes.

As I stood there, it was almost as if the fullness of the moon, so overflowing with light, had a message in code from Providence that the bomb that had fallen on Hiroshima had brought not only destruction but also new possibilities of light and being to the human species, as the light of new life was now being granted to me and all my fellow officers and prisoners. At this moment I was possessed by a feeling of fulfilment such as I have never known.

The experience itself was, of course, of the most intensive form of subjectivity of which I was capable; and yet it was also utterly objective – so objective that I could only point to its meaning by drawing on one of the mathematical axioms which, in a surprising love of mathematics as a boy, I had found (as Pythagoras and Euclid did) to be more like religious statements than scientific observations. The axiom which has stayed with me in connection with that moment is the mathematical assumption of infinity as 'a reality so great that it can neither be increased nor diminished' – which may sound nonsensical to the rational minds of our time and yet is of such absolute truth that it transcends all contradiction. I thought of the outstanding examples in history of other men caught up in the extremities of life and of their time and, with a strange sense of healing, uttered thanks to a power beyond all life and time for at last being able to say 'It is fulfilled'.

As I stood there watching my men, the crowds which had filled the streets (so dense and eager that at times they burst through the Japanese soldiers lining the route) were so touched by their wasted and infirm appearance that they felt compelled to show their compassion by embracing them or even just squeezing their arms affectionately as they passed. Yet it was significant how, in spite of the immense compound of emotions surging through them all, they kept their voices low. The moonlit air stirred with a strange excited murmur, trembling like a tuning fork with an excitement that was, however, not rid yet of the feeling, after years in the hands of a tyrant as ruthless and unpredictable as the Japanese, that it was wise to keep one's voice low and not raise it to a level where sound could be provocative.

As this long, slow column of men rounded the bend on a steep incline to the railway station, the crowd began to withdraw, and finally I seemed to be standing there alone, as the last of the dark column merged with the greater dark of the shadow below the hill.

Speechless as I was, I turned to the imagery of the moon to speak for me. I had learned from reading my beloved Dante in my youth that the images which come to one unbidden, of their own accord, are images one has to follow, and on this occasion there was not only the imagery of the moon in my mind and experience to speak for me, but there was the moon itself, the most beautiful, the reddest of full moons, rising over Bandoeng.

In this regard I had no wish to make an astrological point. But as that terrible day of outer and inner turmoil and hope of 6 August 1945 had come to its end, and the details of the horror of Hiroshima emerged, I had felt compelled to say that it seemed most strange, 'too strange for misunderstanding', as T.S. Eliot put it. It was as if, out of the depths of life and time, from the vast, expanding perimeter of our universe and its beaches of galaxies, white with star foam, some overwhelming impulse had come to synchronize the extinction of the moon with the event at Hiroshima, so that its extinction and imminent rebirth could act on the limited awareness of man as an unmistakable announcement that the past was dead and a new phase of meaning was about to begin on earth.

This feeling had been confirmed in the fortnight since that

moment of moonlessness by the absolute and instant change that occurred in the Japanese, a change which could never have been accomplished in the normal course of even such a devastating war as the one now behind us. For them, as for me, the terrible cataclysm which had overcome them, the feeling of a new power at work in life, combined with the sense of renewal which the moon had always represented to them, demanded a clear acceptance that all the old ways, laws, conventions and creeds that had brought us to this terrible confrontation had been judged invalid by life. The challenge now facing us was to renew ourselves and our societies, or perish. My memory of those men who had just vanished into the night as if rounding a corner of Fate – men who had endured so much but had never once failed to respond to the worst with what was best in themselves – and of the dark experience of imprisonment made me certain that, in this challenge for renewal, men like those would not fail.

And then, with the realization that the street around me was suddenly empty but for a few stragglers, and that it was getting late, I turned about to return to what had been my prison, with the moon in my eyes. As it rose in that clear receptive air, which stood at night over the plateau of Bandoeng like crystal water in a deep and dark well, my prison-fulfilled self seemed to fall from me, and I felt on course as I had not since I was first captured by the Japanese.

I had remained behind in Java and not left for home with my fellow prisoners-of-war because of a request I had received that morning from the Japanese to help them, a request which seemed imperative and which I felt I must obey. Following their surrender they had strict instructions from the Japanese High Command of Field Marshal Terauchi in Saigon that they were now totally responsible for the lives and well-being of all ex-prisoners-of-war and internees, and they desperately needed help to achieve this. They turned to me, as the most senior British army officer, explaining that the senior prison group commanders – in our case two RAF officers – had already been summoned to the prison headquarters and ordered to prepare their camps for immediate evacuation that evening to Batavia.

For the first time since my capture I felt free that evening to give my mind entirely to myself, ready for a renewal in my own right. This feeling was so immediate and far-reaching that it reminded me of a day after the fall of France when, during a break in manoeuvres on an historic plain near Camberley, I was resting with John Marne, our company commander, and the rest of my men, and we were speculating how the war would end. Something in me made me say, without conscious forethought, 'It will all be decided in the end by the split of an atom.' Everyone laughed and said I should read less H.G. Wells.

That memory led me swiftly back, through memories of other intimations, to a night in Tokyo in 1926 when I saw my first Noh play. It was, like all Noh plays, profoundly symbolic, and led to a singular, unmistakable point. It was about a woman, strangely tormented, full of fear, doubt and anguish, and presented on the stage looking over the rim of a well as though it were the dark pit of her own stricken soul. As she gazed, the moon began to rise behind her with measured and effortless calm, until its light found the edge of the well, slid over it and slowly began to creep down the inside of the well itself. It was extraordinary how the lack of physical and external drama went unnoticed: the actors, the words and the ancient music on wooden instruments created an intense feeling of identification and involvement in all those of us watching, with increasing and fearful excitement, as if the anguish of the suffering woman on the stage would be too great ever to be overcome. So when the moment came, and the moon at last found the water of the well and filled the darkest deep of the woman herself with its light, the relief was almost unbearable and I found myself in tears.

Her recovery of a moon-heart and her moon-illuminated self, and the full moon now spreading its light wide and deep over the Bandoeng plain, so distinct and clear that it threw shadows on the sleeping volcano of Tangkoeboehan-Praauw, and what the moon had always represented in me myself, all became one.

I remembered far back to my own beginnings, to my Bushman nurse Klara telling me the moon stories of the first people of Africa and how the moon looked down on the people of the early race and saw how afraid they all were of dying. So the moon chose the fastest animal it could find, the hare, and sent it with the message: 'Do not be afraid of dying. Look at me. As I in dying am renewed again, so you in dying will be renewed again.' It was the same message that the Japanese told their children through one of their legends of the Lord Buddha who, when he was dying, told all the weeping men and animals around him to look at the moon and likewise to know that in dying they too would be renewed again.

So the feeling of renewal in myself was instant and total. I was, as the poet said, 'without past regrets and future fears', and I arrived at the gates of what had been so grim a prison to us all as if it were some hall dedicated to a new liberty of person and spirit. Even the sentries at the gates seemed to confirm this because they instantly sprang to attention, summoned by a corporal with the loudest '*Kerei!*' I had ever heard, the sort of '*Kerei!*' I think reserved for royalty or the highest command – whereas only at dawn that morning if I had not deferred to them in some ritualistic manner they would have beaten me up as badly as they had so often done in the past.

I knew that I was readier in spirit than I was in body, and this new freedom in what had been my prison for so long brought with it the realization that I must see to the needs of my body as soon as possible. I was physically so weak that the short journey by car that morning, when I had been taken from this prison to the Japanese headquarters, had almost made me sick. I had felt on the verge of collapse as I listened to the Japanese offering me a glass of wine and announcing their surrender.

So now I made for what had been the office of the Japanese prison commander. I was not too tired to notice that already it had been scrupulously cleaned and all traces of Japanese occupation removed. There was a long, comfortable couch (from which the commander had often interviewed me, without even bothering to sit up) and I stretched myself out on it. I had some hours to wait for the arrival of a senior Dutch military officer from Batavia whom I knew and for whom I had asked that morning. The Japanese had told me that ever since 12 August (I do not know why the 12th, except that I think it was the day on which, on our secret radio in prison, we had heard that the Emperor himself was suing for peace) the Dutch – of whom 69,000 had been interned when the Japanese took over the island – had been breaking out of their internment camps. This had become a grave problem for the Japanese now that they had been ordered to be responsible for the lives and well-being of all prisoners-of-war and internees. They would try their utmost to fulfil the order, but it was going to be impossible if the scale of self-release which the Dutch had started to practise was not contained.

There was, they said, a great 'unease' (I shall come back to the word and the special way in which they used it) and a spirit of 'wilfulness'. This last word I also knew well because when I was captured I was accused of showing such a spirit in not coming in immediately to surrender to the Japanese as the Dutch Commander-in-Chief and all the armed forces at his disposal in Java had done. It was, in their code, one of the gravest of crimes subject peoples like prisoners and others could commit, and I myself had been condemned to death for it.

In the midst of all the turmoil that followed my return to prison from the Japanese headquarters that morning, and while helping to prepare the camp for instant dissolution and evacuation by train to Batavia that night, these words 'unease' and 'wilfulness' kept coming back to me, as also did the fact that the Japanese had asked me for help. In particular this request for help kept nagging at me, and as I now lay down on the couch these three things were in my mind simultaneously.

First of all, the help. For some strange reason I linked it with one afternoon when as a young man in Pretoria, in my native South Africa, in 1926, I had gone to the assistance of two distinguished Japanese journalists who were being refused service by the proprietress of a café where I was enjoying a cup of coffee and some real Afrikaner waffles. She was shouting at them: 'No niggers are allowed in this establishment!' I had immediately got up from where I was sitting and invited the two Japanese to join me for coffee, and waffles. I came to refer to this incident as 'The Parable of the Two Cups of Coffee', because this small, spontaneous act had momentous consequences, including my journey soon afterwards to Japan, which had a profound influence on my life and, above all, enriched my perceptions and enjoyment of the diversity of cultures, races and non-Western societies.

When I came back from Japan the experience remained with me as something that would never repeat itself again, or so I thought – a fairy-tale event in my life that would be locked for ever in its own place and time. As I had no opportunity for speaking Japanese (and although I had acquired a fairly good patter of Japanese, I had not learned nearly enough characters to read it), the conscious aspects of what I had acquired seemed doomed to diminish and fade over the years. And yet on the morning in 1942 in the jungle in western Java when the Japanese ambushed me and charged with their bayonets, I had called out to them, as if I had used the phrase all my life, one of the highest of the many polite expressions available to the Japanese: 'Would you gentlemen please be so kind as to condescend to wait an honourable moment?'

The Japanese had been prepared for grenades, machine guns or rifle fire, but not for the highest degree of politeness. The effect on them was electric, and the officer in charge immediately beat back his men with his sword, and my life was saved. Once the Japanese hesitated, we were to discover, we always had a chance. This knowledge saved my life not only then but thereafter, and led to all that was basic in helping us all through those three and a half years of imprisonment.

The call to help them now – which on the face of it appeared so reasonable and perhaps not so difficult – I felt, somehow, was going to have even greater consequences than that of merely saving my life. It was as if these two forms of help had straddled the calamities of war and the brutal eruption of medievalism in the spirit of Japan. With it now spent, all that had attracted me so in my first era in Japan was still there and signalling its return to business.

Meanwhile, this intuitive awareness of how great the need for help was, not only for the Japanese but also in Java and perhaps in all of us, came in the way in which the Japanese referred to 'unease' of spirit. There seemed an unease of spirit in the Japanese themselves. I knew, from the moment we established radio contact again after the news of Hiroshima, how divided the Japanese army must have been before they could agree finally on the surrender into which the Emperor had led them. I knew that the Emperor himself had had such difficulties in imposing his wishes that he had had to send his brother Prince Chichibu to confront Field Marshal Terauchi, who appeared to be inclined to disobey the order to surrender.

I knew, too, that the Japanese army had not yet been tested in the defence of its home country. Their invasion forces had been confronted and ultimately defeated and pushed back at the far perimeters, but they still had some four million men on the continent of Asia who, judging by their kamikaze pilots and other evidence of their determination, would fight even more fanatically for their homes. I suspected that the debate and the division among the military themselves must have been profound, but that ultimately the command of the Emperor – not as a man but as an ancient symbol to the Japanese – had taken over, and that the disaster of Hiroshima and Nagasaki had awakened their energies of renewal, so constant and heroic a feature of their perpetual battle against volcanic eruptions, tidal waves, typhoons and earthquakes.

I had no doubt that all this unease would now be contained safely in Japan, but what of this Japanese army in the secluded and, from their point of view, privileged theatre of war in Indonesia? They themselves had done much to provoke the unease to which they referred and which, I was certain, could only mean the spirit of Indonesian nationalism.

All through my imprisonment I had accumulated as much intelligence as I could about what was going on in Indonesia outside the prison walls. I had a group of Dutch and English Malay-speakers sifting carefully through all the official Malay newspapers that were allowed our way, as well as my own contacts with the Chinese outside the prison, and above all with Koreans in charge of the Japanese military bureaucracy at their headquarters, and the Australian accountants who from time to time helped them. They were all singularly well-informed about events in Java. For instance, through them I was to know all about the prophetic rebellion of Javanese officers trained by the Japanese, which showed that nationalist feelings in Indonesia were not directed solely against the Dutch, but just as fiercely against the Japanese. What would the Japanese do now about that kind of manifestation of unease? What indeed were they going to do about all the many ways in which they had latterly hastened to encourage a pro-Japanese nationalism?

As I lay now on the Japanese general's couch, I reflected on something which had happened to us in prison and which was to be the cornerstone, as far as I was concerned, of everything I tried to do throughout those interminable years. One had to express it in terms of the paradox that it was, and 'find our power in our powerlessness'. In prison there was no hope of help from the outside, no physical help of any kind to which we could turn to confront the Japanese in that terrible dimension. We stood there in that regard as naked as we had been born. Yet it seemed that somewhere within us, in that very nakedness, there came something, an experience of how life over and over again had enabled living flesh and blood to triumph over that helplessness and that nakedness. The more I turned to my instincts, the more I found the strength of a vast memory incorporated into my imagination and spirit which suggested that if I confronted life from minute to minute, without any pre-conditioning of teaching or ideas of conduct instilled in my boyhood, there would be an answer to the problems that confronted us.

I have often referred to this aspect as the 'war within the war' that we had to fight. Somehow, whether we knew it consciously or not, we came to expect that the power that was in the keeping of life and creation would enable us to be as creative as it was possible to be, even in such a moment of denial of creation and of life in death. Many of us did not survive, but those who did not went to their end with dignity and honour. Those of us who did survive were changed and transformed. We had become so utterly wrapped in the power of sheer life within ourselves, of life just for life's sake, that we had gone out of our prison that night able to leave the experience totally behind us.

Group Captain Nichols, the great prison commander with whom I had shared the command of some thousands of prisoners for those three and a half years, was to write to me later from England that he could count on one hand the number of people whom he had taken home embittered and sour. It was true. But they had found the world to which they returned not a world redeemed but one inflicted with profound unease. Yet, apart from that handful of exceptions, they themselves came to the unease at ease with themselves and with life, and had left all negations behind. In our powerlessness in all worldly senses, we had been invested with another sort of power, a timelessness that never left us again.

I too, tired as I was, felt at ease with myself and with this call for help that I had received from the Japanese. I turned on the radio to hear what the world outside had to say and tuned it to Perth, in Australia, the station on our secret wireless that we had found had the most news of South-east Asia and, in particular, Indonesia. It was the first time in more than three years that I had listened to the news from the outside world myself. Tuning our secret radio had been a difficult and barely audible exercise which only the specialist officer and his chosen helpers could perform properly. But, as I found the relevant station, my head began to reel. The noise and the welter of a world busy with the outbreak of peace and its consequences, all the events that had to be marshalled to a common end, and all the many voices and dimensions in which the external reality was manifesting itself, made me wonder at my capacity to contain it all and absorb it into a pattern by which I could direct my behaviour.

Fortunately it was ultimately more intoxicating than unnerving, and the excitement of our liberation gripped me and added to the feeling of content that was seeping through me – until I heard the announcer introduce a special message from the Dutch government-in-exile to the peoples of Indonesia. It was the voice of Mr van der Plas, the former governor of East Java, who had gone with his government into exile. He was already known to me by reputation as a man of intelligence and knowledge, particularly of Java, and with a real love for the Indonesians.

But when he began to speak I became more and more perturbed.

What he had to say made me feel that he was speaking from a totally different planet. It was incomprehensible and frightening because the gist of it was that soon the Dutch and their allies would be back in Batavia to deal with all the 'war criminals' who had collaborated with the Japanese, to hang 'traitors' like the nationalists Soekarno and Hatta, and to restore Java and its chain of islands to the peace, prosperity and happiness that they had enjoyed under the Dutch before the war. There seemed to be no suspicion on the part of Mr van der Plas that the Dutch presence in the old pre-war form would be unwanted in Indonesia, and that everywhere the peoples of those islands were rising in revolt not only against the Japanese but also against any hint that the Dutch might come back as the lords and masters they had been for so many centuries.

The longer I listened to all the patter that followed, the more my feeling of dismay grew. It was as if the lessons of the war which had just ended had failed to strike home into the spirit of man, even after so much killing and destruction.

I had, long before the war started, ceased to see the manufacture of armaments and other forms of economic and political villainy, or the lust of commanders of armies everywhere, as the causes of war. Nor, for me, were wars born out of some form of spiritual and spontaneous psychological combustion. Rather they grew directly out of the inadequate and partial nature of the patterns of life imposed on our rulers and establishments in so-called times of peace. My feeling of certainty that our men who were now on their way home from imprisonment in Java would be equal to any challenge that could confront them, was suddenly threatened by this intrusion of official Dutch comment. These intimations of intent showed that nothing really fundamental had been learned from either the kind of peace which had brought the war about, or the war itself.

And it seemed to me ominous that in so short a space of time the men broadcasting on behalf of the Dutch government-in-exile had forgotten the black hats of Soekarno and his nationalist followers which had appeared all over Indonesia on the morning after they had all flown off secretly to exile in Australia, Ceylon and India. They knew about those black hats and what they meant. How could they possibly talk as if they were about to be welcomed back with joy, as if they would be able to resume the comfortable way of life they had enjoyed in Indonesia before the war? My own memory of the alacrity with which a population of millions had discarded the batik turbans they wore by severe prescription around their heads and had overnight donned those black hats, suggested to me not just a sudden change of heart but also the revelation of a spirit that had long glowed like the coals of a great fire ready to be blown into flame when the first storms of change that were blowing reached them.

All these considerations were given a singular point by what had passed between the Japanese commanders and myself after they had told me of their surrender earlier in the day. Although they did not say so outright, it was obvious that even they were deeply disturbed by the reaction of the native Javanese to the act of surrender. They told me that they had also been ordered by radio to take extra precautions to protect prisoners-of-war and civilian internees against any hostile act by the local population. They would do all they could to carry out this instruction, but they could only do so effectively if the prisoners, particularly the Dutch prisoners and civilian internees, would cease breaking out of their prisons and internment camps which exposed them to the risks of violence and even murder by these elements to which they had referred. The Japanese had thought, therefore, that they would appeal to me to accompany one of their senior staff officers to all the camps in the interior to order their inmates to stay in their concentrations until the Allies came to relieve the Japanese of the task of protecting them.

I could not, I felt, say no to what was almost a cry from the heart for help. I made only one stipulation and that was to instruct them to send immediately for the senior Dutch military officer in Batavia, whom I knew and liked, to come with us. While waiting for the military officer I fell asleep on the Japanese general's couch in spite of the inducements to continue listening freely to all the news from the outside world, and was still fast asleep when he arrived some three or four hours later.

We immediately got ready to leave and, as we did so, he told me that four days before the Japanese surrender, Admiral Maeda had summoned Soekarno and Hatta and their Indonesian nationalists to his headquarters, and with them had declared Independence for Indonesia. Together they had hoisted the nationalist Indonesian flag over the flag of the 'Rising Sun'. Admiral Maeda was one of the most enigmatic, strange and yet powerful of the senior Japanese officers in Java, always with a secret agenda of his own, however much that agenda was incorporated within the overall ambitions of his military overlords who had begun and conducted the war. He suffered most from the general delusion the Japanese had about themselves in Java, that they were putting the Javanese and other Indonesians to their

own use, and he seemed unaware that men such as Soekarno and
Hatta were a front for a deeper, more measured and more lasting
urge for self-determination being skilfully prepared by people like
Soetan Sjahrir.

In fact, to this Dutch military officer, it was just proof, if proof was
wanted, of how all the trouble fundamentally was trouble instigated
by the Japanese. He told me, with rather a boastful expression, that
they would soon deal with this handful of intellectuals and other
fanatical, Japanese-trained followers. His attitude seemed to me to
be another sign that there could be an alarming return to the
imperviousness of the Dutch in Indonesia that I had already noticed
before the Japanese invasion.

What was even more surprising in that attitude, as it had been in
what I had heard on the radio, was the absence of any understanding
of the impression that the surrender of Java by well-trained and well-
organized Dutch forces, without any fighting of consequence, must
have made on the indigenous population. I felt the Dutch should
have realized that any subject race whose lords and masters have
failed in their first duty of protecting them from foreign invasion and
domination of the kind they suffered under the Japanese, would
resent and even despise those lords and masters, and reassess them
accordingly. Instead of a real battle for the European way of life, the
Indonesians had seen island after island, the island continent of
Sumatra itself and the teeming and beautiful world of Java, fall ignominiously without more than a skirmish or two – and those fought
principally by the Australians under Brigadier Blackburn. The
populations of these islands would have had no idea of what the
gallant Dutch airforce, and the Dutch navy under Admiral Doorman
(who went down with his ship in the Battle of the Java Sea), had done
to redeem that picture of an apparently abject surrender to the
Japanese, followed by total collaboration by the civilian population
with the Japanese military in running the public utilities, plantations
and industries. In fact, during the occupation the complex social
pattern of these rich and well-governed islands was allowed to continue almost without a stutter.

We left at once, with a Japanese staff officer, for Semarang, the first
of a number of journeys to the camps where Dutch civilians were
being held, principally those for women and children. The main
concentrations were in central Java at Amberawa and Semarang, in
that part of the island where the nationalist eruption was to manifest
itself in its most severe, deep and stubborn form. As a result, these

camps were the most exposed and the most in danger. After talking
to the camp commanders I realized how urgent and real the problem
of their protection was, and we hastened back to Batavia and gave
instructions to the Japanese to summon the heads of all the camps to
Batavia for a conference where we could decide on the best means of
working with the Japanese, until the arrival of the Allied forces who
would take over the government and administration of the country.

This decision seemed to me all the more important because at that
moment we had no idea of how and when the Allied forces would
arrive. In fact our lack of information was illustrated by a remark the
Dutch military officer made to me as we returned to Batavia. After a
sentence or two of understandable horror about what we had seen
in the camps, he said, in a tone that was quite strange to me: 'Well,
it won't be long now before the Americans get here.'

'Why the Americans?' I asked.

'Because they are the only ones with enough power and enough
guts to deal with these yellow apes.'

He was able to say this freely because we were speaking in Dutch
and the Japanese staff officer who was with us, and other Japanese
around, could obviously not follow what he had said. But what struck
me most was that he uttered the remark without, I felt, finishing all
he had wanted to say, and the sentence was broken off rather than
ended.

I knew instantly what he really meant; he meant that the
Americans would be unlike the British. One of the most difficult
things for us all in the prisoner-of-war camps had been the unspoken
accusation of the Dutch that we had run away from the Japanese in
Malaya and that that was why it fell so quickly, and that really all the
horrors that had been inflicted on them in Java were the result of
British cowardice. Even the nicest and best-disposed Dutch, of
whom there were hundreds with us in camp, displayed this extraordinary, pathological obsession, and their emphasis on the
Americans was always there. All the rumours were of great
American landings in and around Java, and always there was this
unuttered comparison with the behaviour of the British in Malaya.

I remember that in one of a series of talks on history that I used
to give to the officers and men with me in the prison camp, I told
them of an account that I had had from Wavell himself about the
last days of the British in Malaya. Wavell had gone in a flying-boat
from Java to Singapore for a long conference with General Percival,
who was in command, and arrived back in Java at midnight. It was

so dark that he slipped on the wharf and fell some distance, break-ing a couple of ribs. The next morning, when he called some of his intimate staff to talk to them about the situation in Malaya, he was obviously in pain. I thought he also looked exceptionally tired but the calm and measure with which he spoke were most impressive. As an illustration of the quality of the resistance which had been put up against the Japanese he told us of the arrival in Singapore, in the late afternoon of the day he visited the island, of the remnants of the Argyles and Sutherlands, one of the most distinguished of the many distinguished Highland regiments in the British army.

On the far northern border of Malaya, the Argyles had been the first to go into battle against the Japanese but they were steadily forced to withdraw, fighting always with order and tenacity as they fell back, simply because they had no air cover and had lost control of the seas with the sinking of the British battleships *Prince of Wales* and *Repulse*. The result was that the Japanese could always land wher-ever they chose behind whatever front the thin British forces had created, forcing them to fall back so as not to be cut off from their base in Singapore.

They were the last of the British troops to arrive. They did so towards evening, crossing the causeway which joins Singapore island to the long peninsula of Malaya. It seemed the whole population of Singapore turned out to see them. With just a hundred or so left of the original battalion of some seven or eight hundred fighting men, they marched in full possession of their arms, carrying their wounded on stretchers, and with their bagpipes playing them across the causeway. Wavell said the whole of Singapore was in tears at so brave a sight.

It was a moment bright in the darkness which seemed to cover the whole of the earth at that time; a darkness so great that I always felt whenever I woke up in the morning that, no matter how light those wonderful equatorial days were, they were only a thin veil over an almost cosmic darkness. These moments, as I look back on the years of war, were like those flashes of sun that break through typhoons and hurricanes at sea and, at their height, herald a moment when even the voices of hurricane and typhoon are hushed and are inter-penetrated and interwoven with blue and light before the storm closes in again.

This achievement of the Argyles was one of those moments. It had been an enormous comfort to me and my men, and it made me resent this Dutch officer whom I knew so well and liked, in a way, so well. I was to wish on our return, when we were met by Captain Nakamura (appointed by the Japanese to be my liaison officer), that he had not hastened off to his camp and that he could have heard Captain Nakamura tell me with great satisfaction that they had now established direct contact with the British forces who were coming to take over in Indonesia, and that they were commanded by someone called Lord Mountbatten. The Captain wondered if I knew him.

Meanwhile, I had been deeply impressed by the way in which the Dutch women had managed their camps. I think on the whole that their treatment at the hands of the Japanese had been better than that of their menfolk, but their plight was much more harrowing because they had not just themselves to think about but also the children, from new-born babies to adolescents. Having seen these camps in the early days after the Japanese capitulation, I felt more than ever how right had been the instinct of the British and Commonwealth soldiers in their continually expressed determination to come back to Java when the war was over and raise a monument to the women of the island.

The Japanese staff officer who had been to Semarang with the Dutch military officer and myself had returned for the moment somewhat reassured, but not for long. The rumours that had come from the interior in our absence had shown that the task of protecting the ex-prisoners-of-war and internees was going to be far more difficult than even the Japanese had anticipated.

First of all, the Dutch male internees' camps proved a more intractable problem for them than the women's camps. From the moment these Dutch men had heard on their secret radios of the Japanese surrender, their long-suffering bodies and spirits had rebelled and they began to leak out unseen from their camps in ones and twos and threes. This leak had grown into a steady trickle and the trickle threatened to become a stream. Japanese evidence was that they were being picked up by the insurgent nationalist groups forming all over the island and in many cases murdered by a population bewildered and rebellious, their sense of resentment against the Dutch heightened by what the Japanese had exacted from them as well.

What is more, I found at my headquarters a rumour going round that a Javanese schoolmaster had gathered a considerable force in western Java and was in the process of cutting off and surrounding the Japanese forces in the interior. I immediately got the Japanese to arrange a meeting at my hotel with one of the most respected of the Dutch civilian leaders in the island, a young aristocrat and business-man called Herman van Karnebeek, and secured his co-operation in impressing on all the men of influence among the male internees that they must stay in their concentrations until Allied forces arrived.

I also had a meeting with the Japanese general and again impressed upon him that, if necessary, he would have to use force to suppress any insurgence that threatened the safety of the internees, particularly the women in their remote and isolated camps. He seemed appalled by the thought that he might have to fight against the Javanese nationalists, and asked how he, as a man of honour, could now take part in a campaign to suppress something that the Japanese themselves had initiated and encouraged.

I remember clearly my reply: 'You will have to learn that there is a way of losing so that it becomes a new way of honour, as I have had to learn in all those years in your power.'

At that a hiss of emotion, so characteristic of the Japanese when deeply stirred, escaped through his lips like steam from a safety valve. As if by some spirit of an ancient reflex, he bowed to me and then, coming out of his bow, his eyes wide and moist, he exclaimed: 'That is a very Japanese thought!' And with that Japanese thought he initi-ated the spirit in the whole of the Japanese command which made them fight, when it became necessary, as hard as they had ever fought, to protect the women and children of Java in their captivity.

As for the Dutch businessman, Herman van Karnebeek, I know that he too kept faith. After the official meetings with the Japanese were over he stayed with me for a while in the little office at the Hôtel des Indes where I had now made my headquarters, and we talked about the future and the values of life that we should now more than ever have to bear in mind. It was then, as he said goodbye to me, that suddenly he broke off and, addressing me as '*Overste*' (the Dutch for 'Colonel'), remarked: 'You know, the British are an extraordinarily lucky people, because always, no matter where and in what situation they find themselves, life never fails to throw up someone specially qualified to serve their needs. Look how even here, in all this mess, where one would have betted that for once their luck would fail them, someone like yourself, who knows the Japanese, the Dutch, the Javanese, and not just Britain but also its Commonwealth, and has experienced all that we have gone through in the last few years, has turned up to help them and their allies.'

He can have had no idea how that helped me. It was confirmation and encouragement to me that I could perhaps perform this role which had been conferred on me by fate, since that moment of full moon in the streets of Bandoeng. For, faced with the orchestration of violence and evidence of disintegration that was accumulating around us, I had begun to doubt my own capacities. His remark was the first objective sign I had had that I might not do too badly. I have always felt grateful to him for that remark, because it was an act of recognition of the kind one cannot give oneself but which can only come from an individual who holds up a mirror to enable one to see something in reflection.

Liberal and broad-minded as he was, I think even van Karnebeek did not suspect that the Indonesian rebellion and signs of insurrection went any deeper than something seized upon by the Japanese and blown into a fire for their own purposes, a fire that could quickly be controlled and quenched the moment the Japanese left and the Dutch took over.

The very next day, in the midst of the conference between all the leaders of the Dutch women's internment camps, the Japanese and myself, for which we had returned from Semarang to Batavia, came the first positive proof that we were urgently in the mind of the Supreme Allied Commander and his advisers. Captain Nakamura arrived in a high state of excitement and reported that a group of four British soldiers had just been dropped by parachute at the main airport and were being brought to the Hôtel des Indes to join me and the Japanese Command. As ambassadors of the peace and relief to come they were, of course, infinitely more convincing to the Dutch women than the Dutch senior officer and myself, however welcome the news we had brought from the world outside. They took immense heart from the event and hastened back to their various camps to continue their difficult task of containing the natural impatience and longing for instant release of their cruelly tried countrywomen and impetuous adolescents.

This little airborne reconnaissance unit was under the command of a young English major, Alan Greenhalgh, who had seen a great deal of active service in the battle for the crossing of the Rhine and the invasion of Germany. With him was a young Dutch captain, Baron John van Till, who was serving in the Princess Irene Brigade, and two signallers with equipment to give them independent and reliable communication with the outside world. They were quickly installed in the Hôtel des Indes across the courtyard from the pavilion

in which I had made my own small headquarters. In the early afternoon of that momentous day they were already in touch by radio
with Allied Headquarters at Kandy in Ceylon, and at eleven o'clock
that night the two officers and I left for the threatened civilian internment camps again.

We visited all the camps we could in central Java. Since Alan
Greenhalgh and John van Till represented a special organization
that had been set up for the 'Recovery of Allied Prisoners-of-War
and Internees' (RAPWI, as it soon became known all over South-east
Asia),* they had a specific programme of their own to pursue which
made it necessary for them to stay longer in the camps than me.
Wherever we went I took advantage of the opportunity to make the
Japanese take me out on a wider reconnaissance of the countryside,
so that I got a far more detailed impression of the spread of unrest.
Already the atmosphere had changed. In the beginning, as on the
night of the full moon in Bandoeng, the indigenous population had
seemed to have a sense of identification and involvement with us in
our common subjection under the Japanese, and had shown an
almost affectionate and friendly sympathy towards us. Now they
appeared openly hostile to the Japanese, more unfriendly towards the
Dutch, and remote towards Europeans in general.

We were on the point of going on to Sourabaya when we were
summoned back to Batavia with the news that a British cruiser
squadron was on its way there and was expected within three days,
on the morning of 15 September. The Japanese were becoming
increasingly dismayed at the situation in Java, and news of the
impending arrival of British warships seemed to please them almost
as much as it did me. They clearly had not been exaggerating when
they spoke about the necessity of containing prisoners-of-war and
internees in their camps if their capacity to protect them was not to
be gravely impaired. It was not three weeks since my first visit to the
camps. Yet the speed with which new forces were stirring everywhere
in the native populations of the islands was more rapid than even I,
who had lived through it all from the appearance of the first black
hats to the ultimate capitulation of the Japanese, could have anticipated.

All sorts of small illustrations pointing to the great change which
was occurring remain in my mind, as for instance a glimpse of a

*Its full title was the Combined Services Organization for the Relief of All
Prisoners-of-War and Civilian Internees.

railway junction at dawn from the sleeper in which we were travelling. I had woken at first light and, when our train came to a sudden halt, looked out of the window and across the rails to another platform. There I saw a large group of Javanese wearing the uniform of officers of the nationalist army. This army had been trained by the Japanese until some twelve months before at a place called Blitar in East Java where the Japanese had one of the largest of their military training establishments. There an extremely well-organized group of Javanese soldiers had rebelled. The Japanese put down the rebellion with difficulty and extreme ruthlessness, beheading eighteen of the ringleaders, but the real organizer escaped and, despite the efficient Japanese secret police, found safe asylum among peasants in the hills and became a legendary figure in the island.

Now, for the first time, I saw what Javanese officers such as those who had taken part in this rebellion looked like. They all wore Japanese samurai swords which, as they were a race of slender, delicately made people, nearly touched the ground. But what was most striking was that, one and all, they had grown their thick, shining, black hair right down to their waists. It all made an extraordinary dreamlike impression on me, as if I were seeing a rehearsal of what a drama of Cavaliers and Roundheads reproduced in those islands might have looked like. And there came to my mind, too, the unsurpassed symbol of Samson, whose secret of strength lay in the unimpeded length of his hair; and I found, as so often, how only the most common and travel-stained of human platitudes could express what happened to the human spirit when it turned to its full, instinctive male self and 'let its hair down'. I had no doubt after seeing this that, at long last, the Indonesian spirit had let its hair down and was determined to be its natural self.

Even more poignant to me in that dawn setting was the awareness of the paradox of earth and people which these young men evoked in my spirit. No scene on earth could have looked more beautiful. The light was beginning to find the paddy fields, with the women under their broad hats already moving across them to sow and to reap all in one day, as they did in those fertile plains with harvests three times a year. Nothing could have been a calmer and more natural portrayal of all that Thomas Hardy meant in his universal lyric about a man, a horse and a plough:

> Yet this will go onward the same,
> Though dynasties pass.

Dynasties not only of the West but of the East were passing in this land. Those distant hills and mountains all carried ancient Hindu names of eras and gods old in human memory, like the peerless Ardjuno of the *Mahabharata* and the epic princedom that inspired the Hindu dynasty of Modjo Pait. So deep-rooted were those distant memories that they remained rich in associations in the dreaming unconscious of Indonesia and, despite the brief Dutch intrusion, and an even briefer Japanese interlude, they were still celebrated in the drama of the *wayang*, the profoundly symbolic shadow show of the common people of Java.

Deeper still, I had myself caught a glimpse of it in the dark jungles of Bantam in the secluded zone of the Badoeis, the aborigines of Java, still inhabiting a corner of their native home and living their animistic selves with such authenticity and authority that Bantamese, Javanese and Madoerese regarded them almost as people in Arthurian England would have looked at their druid predecessors ruled by Merlin himself. This Badoei element played the same role in the underground of the Javanese spirit as Shinto plays in the various layers of Japanese culture.

There was something in the atmosphere of the moment in which we were all so fatefully enveloped that suggested the stirring of the elemental unfulfilled passion of the earth itself in the underground of the Indonesian spirit, and it was as if not only the people of Java but the earth itself was in the grip of this immense paradox of outward calm and peace and beauty, and inward fire and unrealized passion of unlived life. Even that great empire of Modjo Pait was found ultimately inadequate, and was followed by a Buddhist empire; the Buddhist in its turn was overthrown by Islam; and Islam became overlaid by the movement of the West into Asia and the appearance of the ruthlessly competitive and avariciously commercial Dutch East India Company.

All these sorts of things were implicit in those moments, and scenes like the one that I have just described combined to make me fear that, in this dynamic passing of dynasties, unless the powers who came back to rule these islands made the most imaginative reappraisal of their own history and their inadequacies, and changed their plans and future course accordingly, there could be no peaceful outcome to what I felt was so profoundly in preparation around us.

And then at other stations, and at other approaches at other times of the day, I was amazed to see things that made me realize how all these primordial forces were near to conscious eruption. Revolutionary slogans appeared on billboards in that ancient countryside, and groups of men gathered, no longer in uniform but more ominously in sarongs and often in rags and tatters, holding up their banners to every train passing through to remind their passengers how often the things they were demanding had been claimed with blood and revolution by the people of the West.

The favourite among these slogans seemed to be from the preamble to the American Declaration of Independence which begins with those resounding words: 'We hold these truths to be self-evident, that all men are created equal, that they are endowed by their Creator with certain unalienable rights . . .'. But, with a versatility as remarkable as their frequency, there also appeared quotations drawn from people like Rousseau, and the rhetoric of the French Revolution, and from *The Rights of Man*.

All this, of course, was food for the most disturbing thoughts because clearly here the instinct of an unlived self crying for recognition in the heart of the saronged millions had found inspiration and support in the slanted rationalism of the Western day.

Most of all, Batavia itself had changed almost beyond recognition since I had first seen it a bare three weeks before. The streets were no longer quiet and orderly, with people going about their obsequious Japanese-approved business. They were instead crowded with thousands of men bearing slogans like those I had first seen at railway stations and other public gathering places. Moreover, these people seemed to cluster and congeal, presumably around some rumour or untoward incident, freely and uninhibitedly in a way I found alarming, because I had learnt from years of war that these things were an infallible symptom of men and their systems broken from their moorings and cast adrift.

Back at my desk I found all sorts of messages waiting for me from the military prisoner-of-war camps. Already groups had been organized from among our soldiers waiting for embarkation to help protect the Dutch women's camps in Batavia at night from the Indonesian nationalist mobs that threatened to invade them.

I remember that when Alan Greenhalgh, van Till and I returned to our headquarters and were in the midst of drafting messages to Ceylon, the telephone rang. An officer who had been very close to me throughout our imprisonment, a young English major called John Denman, was on the 'phone asking if we knew what was happening.

Some Dutch soldiers whom he knew had released themselves and gone back to their pre-war offices to reclaim them. Denman had just seen, with horror, these soldiers attacked by a mob, dragged into the street and their throats cut. He was anxious to know when our own forces could be expected, and hoped that they would come in time to prevent what he saw as the spread of disorder engulfing all.

Denman said that he and his fellow Britons had never felt threatened. In the freedom they were given to go out of their own pre-embarkation camps, they found they had only to say that they were British for whoever had accosted them to become friendly (though with a nuance which suggested that they would have been friendlier still had they been able to say they were American). It was most noticeable, he said, in the detachments detailed each night to go on duty at the civilian internment camps. If a crowd collected at the gates, a deterrent as effective as any Japanese display of force was the British officer in command showing himself to the crowd and asking in a clear voice in Malay: 'Does anyone here speak English?' Invariably an English-speaking Javanese would materialize and become an active go-between for the occasion, helping to make it clear that the officer was British and, like all the British, friendly to the Javanese, and advising the crowd to disperse. Invariably they did, well before the Japanese guards arrived on the scene.

I was glad to be able to tell him that it would not be many days now before relief of some kind came. I could not, of course, say more.

I had no idea of the composition or the specific mission of the approaching British cruiser squadron, but I spent the two days and most of the three nights before its arrival preparing a report on the situation in Java for its commanding officer. From all I had been hearing on the radio (not only from Perth but also from San Francisco and Delhi and, to an extent, from the BBC), I now realized that he would be arriving grossly misinformed about what he had to expect.

The dismay I had felt on that first night listening to Mr van der Plas had by no means diminished. The sound and the fury of the Dutch against so-called collaborators in the islands had grown, and Queen Wilhelmina's broadcast of 1942 (which had apparently promised the peoples of the Dutch empire, the third largest empire in the world, a measure of emancipation which they had never enjoyed before) was referred to with increasing and almost desperate frequency and insistence.

It seemed to me more urgent than ever that I should put down in writing all that was needed for an appreciation of the purely military aspect of the problem that confronted us, and then a wider and more strategic appraisal of all the many forces that were interweaving and manifesting themselves and that would have to be confronted in the future occupation and administration of Indonesia. Where I could, I did this in the manner of the 'situation reports' I had learned to make at staff college in Britain.

The background to the report I knew not only from my own experience in the last three and a half years, but also from the history of those islands. For South Africa, where I was born, had for many generations after the Cape station was founded in 1652 been ruled not by the Dutch in Holland but from the Governor-General's office in Java. I knew from our South African history what it meant to be ruled by a powerful and ruthless Dutch charter company and not, as was still supposed, by the elected government of the people of Holland. That alone gave me an extra understanding of how, like ourselves in South Africa, the peoples of Java could have smarted from the moment of their conquest at the beginning of the seventeenth century to the present.

I had also lived and experienced the whole of the Japanese interlude from its beginning to its now imminent end. It was an experience which in its ultimate meaning totally contradicted, in fact as well as in potential, those broadcasts I had heard from Australia. Perturbed though I had been by the evidence of insurgent nationalism in the islands, my concern sharpened by the anxiety I felt in the Japanese over their inability to handle it properly without incurring the displeasure of the victorious Allies, I did not at that moment feel that it was inevitably going to turn into a major revolution of liberation. What was happening could still be a natural consequence of the evolution of empire which could be dealt with, once the immediate disorder had been contained, by the contemporary adjustments all empires had been increasingly called upon to make in the twentieth century in their far-flung dominions.

I wrote this report under great difficulties because the news of my office had spread, and more and more people of all kinds, Indonesians as well as officers bringing me news of the pre-embarkation camps, came to disturb me. I have already mentioned Major Denman and the vital information he had conveyed to me. Now there were visits by many others, two of which have remained unblurred in my mind.

The first was a visit late one night from a Dutch lady in her early forties, a gallant commander of one of the smaller internment camps for women. She came to talk to me about the importance not of political and military necessities but of more fundamental difficulties that would face them all in taking up relationships that had been so brutally and for so long interrupted. I remember in particular a moment at the end when she said goodbye, and she began to cry. When I asked her why, she stuttered and said it was because she was so afraid of the future.

'These years have changed us all profoundly,' she explained, 'but what that change is precisely I do not know, and it is the not knowing that frightens me. And what about our husbands and our menfolk outside the camps? They too will have changed. We have all talked about the tremendous political changes that might await us, but what about these changes inside ourselves? At the moment I still feel close to these changes, and I feel it is important not to forget them. But all the talk I hear is as if people think they have just to go back and rejoin one another and carry on where they left off before, and that frightens me because this experience tells us something. There is something for us not to lose again, and I fear that we shall lose it, and fail, and just be back in our comfortable, sterile old patterns.'

I cannot vouch for the literal accuracy of these words but that was her meaning. Again it was another sort of confirmation for me, and I was grateful to her for caring so deeply about it and for her tears, because it was a fear that I shared myself. Yet I found comfort in the fear because I thought that it would help to preserve us from losing the things we had found in those years of captivity.

She had hardly gone when the figure of a man came striding from the main building of the hotel towards the door in which I was still standing, watching the woman going back to her car. I knew that figure, and yet I did not know it, and even as it became recognizable I could hardly believe it, because it seemed not so much something that was happening to me there and then, but something being re-enacted out of my past.

I think recognition came to us both at once. In Dutch with a deep, guttural Swiss accent my new visitor said: 'Thank God, Colonel, it's you at last!'

'Paul!' I called back. 'It can't be true. It can't be true!' And we embraced each other.

I had last seen Paul Vogt on top of Djaja Sempoer ('The Mountain of the Arrow') in the valley of Lebaksembada ('The Valley That Was

Well Made') in Bantam, on the morning when I had walked off to my capture by the Japanese. I did not really know what had become of him after that, except that he and my other officers when captured in turn by the Japanese were not executed but were taken off to other prisons.

The first time I had ever seen him had been more than three years before when he had appeared, as he did now, out of a dark night into the light shining over the veranda of a club for the civilians who ran a gold-mining enterprise in the remote hamlet of Tjikotok in Bantam. It was a dense black night, hot and sweltering, of the kind Joseph Conrad describes in *Victory*, and there was a flicker of lightning some-where in the distance, bright enough to extinguish all the incredible stars that glided in multitudes over the vast equatorial night.

I was tired and had sat back to listen to the civilians behind me at their little tables near the bar talking, of course, about nothing but the impending Japanese invasion. And then, across the fringe of light where the dark of the jungle stood like a wall, it was as if a secret gate had opened and the man whom I was now embracing emerged, walking with a staff in his hand. He was broad-shouldered and not very tall, and had the figure of someone raised from generations in mountain country. He had thick, black unkempt hair. His shirt appeared to have no buttons and was pulled wide open across his chest, and he wore a thin pair of cotton trousers of some kind and sandals, looking almost as if he were a part of the jungle itself. He was immediately greeted from all sides by a loud and welcoming 'Hello, Paul!', a greeting which he answered in that gruff Dutch of his. He gave no other acknowledgement, walked up to the steward in charge of the bar and asked for a beer, and went and sat at a table all by himself, quietly sipping and watching us all intently, and obvi-ously listening intently too.

He must have sat there for nearly an hour, drinking perhaps three bottles of light ale, and his behaviour seemed to me so unusual and eccentric that I watched him on and off, fascinated, as intently as he watched the rest of us. It was obvious from the behaviour of the other men in the little club that this was not at all unusual and nothing to be specially remarked upon, but to me it was as compelling as it was strange. And then he had stood up, called out a gruff goodnight and walked over to where I was sitting and asked me in English if he could have a word with me alone. His English surprised me as it made it obvious that he knew of me. I got up and he took me to the edge of the light, with the jungle black beyond.

I have not forgotten a word of what he said to me, so deeply was it grafted into my hearing and being: 'You do not know me,' he said. 'And I do not know you. But I know somehow that your fate is joined with mine. If ever you need me, do not hesitate to send for me. You have just to ask anywhere for Paul, and they will tell you where I am. Goodnight!'

He turned and went through the exit into the night out of which he had come.

Some ten days later I found how precise had been his hunch that his fate and mine were joined. It was a lovely Sunday morning. At exactly nine o'clock, everyone was summoned to that same club-house to listen to a broadcast on the national radio from the head-quarters of the Allied Commander-in-Chief, General Ter Poorten. He announced that he had surrendered himself and all the forces under his command to the Japanese, and that all unit commanders were to establish contact with the nearest Japanese forces and surrender themselves and their arms.

I found myself and my three English officers instantly unwelcome in the little mining community because, when asked what we were going to do, we had said that we were not going to surrender. My own mission, in a sense, only began with the surrender, and I had orders that when it came I was to establish myself somewhere in the jungles of Java where I could collect and turn into some kind of resistance all the men who felt compelled to disobey the order to surrender. I could not stay in a European civilian outpost which had announced its intention of carrying out this order to the letter.

All this had been foreseen by me and my superiors, and because neither I nor my officers knew Java at all (we had originally been destined and selected for operations behind the Japanese lines in Malaya) we had been allotted two experienced officers of the Dutch colonial army who knew the west of Java and Bantam extremely well and, of course, spoke the language and dialects. It had never occurred to me that these men, who had been especially sworn in for this assignment, would disobey my orders, but when I told them to help us pack up our trucks and get ready to move off into the jungle, they asked me for a postponement of a day or two to think over what they called 'the new situation'. When I refused and said we had to leave as soon as we could, and that they must get ready and join us in loading the trucks, they disappeared, and I was never to see them again.

So we had to move off, deprived of the human element and expertise both my General and I had insisted on as vital to our mission, and for the moment all of us felt singularly abandoned. We knew that we had to find, somewhere in the hills and valleys of Bantam, some area where we could establish ourselves until we made contact with stragglers. With luck some would be men who knew Java and its people, and who by nature and spirit were determined to go on resisting the Japanese as long as humanly possible.

We set off along a road which we had reconnoitred before. It led to the edge of the jungle west of Tjikotok which intruded in depth between the mining area and the more remote and thinly populated areas of Bantam. At the junction of a side-track we were startled by the sudden appearance of a squadron of mounted native infantry. They were commanded by a Captain Dont, and were a well-equipped unit of the Royal Marechausee. For a moment I thought how wonderful it would be if they, who spent most of their duty patrolling the remote areas of Java, would join us. But the thought perished when their commander heard the news, for which he asked like a parched man for water, and his open and friendly manner changed. He instantly became formal and made it quite clear that he wanted to be rid of us as soon as possible. After a brief conversation they set off at a fast canter in the direction of the main road to the capital.

An hour later we came to the place I had in mind, a deep gorge where there was a rest-house and a parking place for trucks and vehicles, and then nothing but a well-trodden and broad footpath into the jungle, of the kind which served as the only roads for the Bantamese in the extreme west. We were busy unloading when out of the jungle Paul Vogt appeared, greeted us warmly and asked us if we could tell him the news. When I told him of the surrender, he exclaimed in a passion of anger: 'I knew it! I knew they wouldn't fight! I knew the Dutch would just abandon the locals to the Japanese! I've not lived and worked among them for nothing. Well, I'll fight! I'll join you.'

The prospect of having someone who by all accounts knew the country and its people, and particularly the jungles which he as a geologist and geophysicist had explored for years with the gold-mining company, could not have been more welcome. But he was Swiss and, like all Swiss, was bound to preserve his country's neutrality. Perhaps this was a problem which in the end might defeat the chivalrous impulse which made him volunteer to become one of us. When I raised this point he brushed it almost angrily aside, and said that if I did not want him he would search elsewhere for people who would take him – it did not matter who, anybody who was going to fight to preserve the country and its native people from the Japanese. For his own safety then, I told him, I would have to commission him formally in the British army. And so, within minutes of meeting him again, I had commissioned him as a Second Lieutenant in the British army and annotated his commission in my dispatch book. Four days later I promoted him to First Lieutenant, and four days after that to Captain, to make him of the same rank as my other officers.

With him to guide and advise us we came, after a story far too long to relate here, to the moment when we had established a base in the jungle and were beginning to collect stragglers from the Australian and British armies to build up the sort of unit we had planned. In the intensity of those circumstances and the difficulties and dangers with which we were confronted, I got to know Paul as one of the most exceptional human beings I had ever met, not only superb as a geophysicist but also at heart an artist and a sculptor already established in the valley of Lebaksembada, loved by all the indigenous peoples there, and living with the very beautiful and remarkable daughter of the local Bantamese sultan.

My untimely capture did not allow me to use what I learnt from him about Indonesia for the purposes for which it was intended, but it was invaluable for the rest of my time in prison, and now, when the native voice of Java was to count for more than it had done for centuries, it was essential.

We sat and talked in my office not only about what had happened to him and the others after my capture, but also about what was happening in Indonesia at that moment, and what it was likely to become. The interest taken in him by the Swiss Embassy in Batavia from the moment the Japanese discovered that he was a Swiss subject, and the lengthy debate between the military and the diplomats over this extraordinary matter of a Swiss fighting against them, led to his early release from his Japanese prison into the Embassy's keeping. With access to all the Embassy's sources of information, he knew all about the upsurge of nationalism in Java and told me that already in a place called Wonosobo in central Java a schoolmaster named Soedirman had raised a force and attacked a Japanese division. The latest rumour, which was believed by the Swiss, had it that the Japanese were surrendering themselves with all their arms to the Indonesians.

Our meeting ended in agreement that he would pack up as soon as possible at the Swiss Embassy and join me in my quarters. My delight and relief at such a conclusion were almost as great as they had been on that Sunday morning when he joined us in the jungle in Bantam. When I went to bed, before turning out my light, I heard again one of those Dutch radio voices from Australia threatening to hang Soekarno and all his followers in the very near future, but I was used to it by now and did not let it perturb me as much as it had done in the beginning. What did disturb me was a report in the news that, some forty-eight hours before, the British naval forces sailing into Hong Kong to take the Japanese surrender there were attacked by some kamikaze naval patrol vessels. Fortunately no ships were damaged. I just hoped that the gunnery officers of the British naval force due in Java in a few hours' time would not have become trigger-happy as a result of the incident, since we were due to go out into the roadstead and meet the British warship in just such a naval patrol vessel as had been used in the kamikaze attempt at Hong Kong.

CHAPTER TWO

CS5

IT WAS VERY early when I got up to prepare myself for the day ahead. It was dark, and Batavia was unusually quiet, so still that I could hear, far away along the fringes of the city, the last exchanges on the bamboo gongs of the night-watchmen in the outlying hamlets signalling to one another that all was well. It was almost as if in these sounds and the peculiar quality of the stillness there was a pre-knowledge of how immensely significant the day was going to be for the people of these islands – and especially for people like ourselves after years in the hands of the Japanese.

I felt it even as I looked at my simple uniform, laid out for me on the couch in my office by my Javanese servant the night before. I had had it especially washed and ironed, and it was the best of my two sets of prison clothes. The only difference between them was that this was not patched like the other one. Nonetheless, it showed the hard years of service it had already performed. My official badges of rank – which had vanished, along with my military hat, within days of my capture on Djaja Sempoer – had been replaced by Australian soldiers of mine, who made new ones for me out of some metal they found in the workshops. To an expert eye the badges had a home-made quality that was unmistakable, but they had the merit of showing my rank convincingly enough at a distance. The badge for a home-made hat, also made for me by my Australians, was not that of my regiment, which had been too difficult and convoluted for them, but was taken from what they remembered of the badges worn by South African officers with whom they had served in the

Western Desert. It consisted of the head of a springbok, and it endeared itself very much to me because one of its horns was crumpled and made it seem, therefore, a more proper symbol for service in the distorted and twisted circumstances that we had to endure. And yet somehow I felt that for someone who was representing not only himself but also, for a moment, those thousands of men of the Commonwealth who were now collected in Batavia for embarkation to their homes all over the world, and especially all those who had died, it was more fitting than the most immaculate of uniforms could have been. Indeed, so much more than themselves had my clothes become that I had to smile inwardly at myself for having paused to stroke my military shirt as if it were a favourite household pet. It was rather a telling illustration of one of the paradoxes of our time in prison, that the fewer our possessions the more they meant to us, so that even such a brutal simplification of life, which appeared to deprive us of things people value most, became to us a source of enrichment. Accordingly, as I joined Alan Greenhalgh and John van Till in their fastidious, tailor-made uniforms, I knew I would not mind any comparisons that might be made during the day to come.

I had no idea on our journey in the Japanese staff car to the harbour of Tandjongh Priok, some twenty kilometres away, and on to our meeting with the British naval force, that this was the last time I would be working closely with Alan Greenhalgh and John van Till. Their special RAPWI mission was to part them from me within a few hours, but at that moment, as we drove through the slowly awakening city of Batavia, we talked as if the event to come were a mere part of the routine of our duties, and not the historic day of emancipation it in fact was. We discussed, among other things, the Hong Kong incident, and as we got out of our car and walked towards the offices of the Japanese port captain we looked searchingly for any signs of unusual preparations in and around the naval patrol vessel which was there, tied to the quay and made ready for our journey out into the roadstead. Alan in particular was so unperturbed that he joked about the incident and, touching his pistol, remarked that if the Japanese had any desire for a kamikaze outing it would not be necessary for them to commit suicide: he would render them that service himself.

However, when the time came, some hours later, for us to embark, we felt certain that nothing untoward had been planned and that if anything were to go wrong it would only be as a result of the warship misreading our presence, which we felt could easily be avoided by approaching her in the slowest and most respectful manner possible.

As we left the harbour the day was still of an incredible beauty, perhaps at the peak of the beauty that those Javanese mornings achieved before the sun took over and burned them into a feverish, blinding heat-haze, which was its preparation for the temples and palaces of cloud it invariably summoned out of the sea and which by afternoon had formed a cathedral city in the sky. It was as if there was just sufficient moisture in the air to lead to an all-round refraction of light which imparted a subtle rainbow glow to the day and made an opal of the light. For me there was always magic in that moment and no light could have been more evocative. Then, suddenly, in the haze gathering on the far horizon in front of us, a darkening of this opalescent glow began to assert itself; and then, as if it were not substantial and real and made of steel but rather a coloured photographic print emerging from its negative, the outline of a great ship appeared. At our orders the pilot immediately reduced speed and slowly, as this ship became increasingly clearly defined, we went towards her and she approached as if not under her own power but, to my heightened senses, magically drawn towards us until there was, distinct and clear, a British cruiser, hardly moving at all. The absence of a wake showed that her engines had been stopped. There was no ripple across her fine-cut bows and clearly she was gliding in this dignified and elegant way into the moment when her anchors would be dropped. Watching through a pair of German military glasses we had obtained from the Japanese, there came a moment when the ship's guns, on which I had concentrated most of all, seemed to me to be slowly turning in our direction. At once I climbed on to the foredeck and, with the pilot flag in my hand, began to signal the ship in the semaphore that was still being taught in our classical army training at the beginning of the war:

'British officers approaching. Repeat. British officers approaching.'

Almost at once I saw how right we had been in anticipating that the watch on us from the ship would be intense, because the response from her gunners was instantaneous. Like the fingers of a hand stretched out in a gesture of peace the guns did a brief waggle, and I knew our message had been received.

Soon we were alongside and there was a ship's ladder ready with an able seaman to help us up. The bosun, seeing my home-made badges of rank, immediately began to pipe me on board. It was one of the most wonderful sounds I have ever heard in my life. I was so deeply moved that I did not know quite how I was going to contain myself, feeling rather as I imagined horses feel when they hear military music for the first time, not knowing where to hold their heads and a shiver going through their skins, and it brought me close to tears. But I must have contained myself, because there I was stepping on to the quarterdeck of HMS *Cumberland*, the flagship of the Fifth Cruiser Squadron, and giving her the best military salute I have ever given anybody or anything.

What Alan and van Till felt I could not tell because I was immediately taken aside by the officer of the day. They presumably were taken in charge by another officer to deal with their own RAPWI business, and I did not see them again that day. I was conducted below and found myself in a room full of men in uniform, mostly the uniform of the Dutch forces, as at the Allied headquarters in Bandoeng.

And then there was Admiral Patterson, the CS5 himself. His tall figure made him look slender and elegant in comparison with the assembly of robust officers packed into his room, and his features were clean-cut and unusually defined. His wide, intense blue eyes darkened, I thought, for a moment with a shadow of concern as his hand came forward and he took my own and shook it warmly.

It had been a good three weeks since our release from captivity and first access to normal food, and I was getting physically stronger. Nonetheless, I must still have looked ill-fed and prison-worn in that context and the Admiral, in a voice rounded with natural feeling, urged me to sit down at once, beside him. The sudden cancellation of all the years of human and physical denial and the inrush of spontaneous humanity were so overwhelming that I was not even certain the chair in which I sat could hold me. I steadied myself and looked around at this room crowded with officers. They were, with one exception, large men for whom, whatever the war had imposed on them, denial of physical sustenance had not been one of their trials.

There was only one small person in the uniform of the Dutch civil service whom I recognized at once from the many descriptions I had had of his person and character from officers in prison who had served with him in the course of his long career. Slight, bearded, obviously tense and highly strung, he was the embodiment of the voice I had heard so often on the radio, railing against Soekarno and Hatta and all the Indonesian collaborators and warning that they would be hanged: Mr van der Plas. He was almost over-eager to begin whatever was in the minds of himself and his fellow officers.

I do not remember the words with which Admiral Patterson took charge of the occasion then, though I do remember being grateful that I had prepared myself for this moment by writing those long and meticulous reports on Indonesia. I presented them immediately to the Admiral, explained what they were and asked him if they could be read first, before I made my report and answered any questions. This made immediate sense to the Admiral, and I remember him smiling and saying something to the effect that it would give me a chance to have a good warm drink of some kind, with which he was sure I could do.

There followed some hours of intense interrogation. My intelligence report astonished even the Admiral, but the Dutch contingent of high-ranking civil affairs officers and representatives of other services were filled with disbelief. I in my turn was astonished that their ignorance of what had been happening in Java, not just since their capitulation but over the past three weeks, was even greater than I in my most extreme anxieties had presupposed from listening to their radio. But gradually the interrogation and my answers penetrated, the atmosphere became more sombre, and for the moment Mr van der Plas suppressed his eagerness to go ashore and hoist the Dutch flag over the government buildings in Batavia. I can remember how startled and aghast they were when I told him there could be no question of hoisting flags at the moment because only the day before I had received a report from Sourabaya that some Dutch prisoners, who had left their camp against orders and had hoisted the Dutch flag in the city, had been set upon and murdered by an incensed Indonesian mob. Somehow I knew already, from my experience in Java and my feel for the concealed volcanic element in the character of the people, that the more collective the social patterns to which they conformed became, the more easily they were inflamed by the simplest of symbols. It was always a source of comfort to me that, in the fierce little skirmish fought in *Cumberland* over this issue that night, with Admiral Patterson's support I emerged the victor, because hoisting flags of one's own and pulling other people's down was, over the months that followed, to become about the most dangerous and provocative sport in which Javanese and Dutch could indulge.

It was late afternoon when I finished. The Dutch were astonished to discover that Java was not, as they had expected, a piece of scorched earth. There were no bridges blown, no factories burnt, no power stations out of electricity. Trains and communications services were still running in a surprising measure, and the Javanese subordinate services, challenged to do all that their masters had done before, had risen to that challenge in a remarkable way.

I remember almost the last question I had to answer was from one of the tallest and biggest of the men there, a Dutch airforce officer of high rank, who asked me if I had by any chance on my journey round the women's internment camps come across his wife. He broke down when I told him how, by some extraordinary coincidence, she was the lady who had just visited me in my office at the Hôtel des Indes, and there was no reason why he should not be able to see her the moment he went ashore.

I had a feeling of guilt at my unaccustomed cynicism and apprehension that their reunion might not be permanent (and indeed it did not last beyond some six months). I thought of the fine-drawn features of the woman's face, deeply etched, as in a Rembrandt sketch, by the shadows cast by the electric light of my office, and her sense of foreboding, joined to the expression of three years of suffering and deprivation which took over as soon as she ceased to speak. And I looked at him, so exactly like the dozen or more Dutch officers I had seen at Wavell's headquarters on my arrival in Java at the beginning of 1942. I had been quite shocked by the appearance of all the Dutch officers on his staff: not one of them was not overweight. At eleven o'clock on a hot tropical morning they were all served with large plates of thick pea-and-ham soup, and again at lunch they all began with gin, followed by beer, and a rice table in the highest Javanese fashion. If differences of physique could convey the truth, I could see how justified was the fear which she had expressed intuitively of the difficulties there would be between all like herself and the world they were about to meet, which had gone through the war safe and well-fed in Australia.

I must hasten to add that only a few of the women in the internment camps had husbands who had been flown out with essential Dutch staff, leaving them behind. Those whose husbands had been commanded to leave the island when the Dutch surrendered to the Japanese understood very well that this was necessary, and in the national interest. The example for these women had been wonderfully set by the American wife of the Governor-General of Java,

Lady Tjarda van Starkenborgh-Stachouwer. She had refused to accompany her husband when, in his role as head of the new Indonesian government abroad, he was ordered to leave Java, preferring to throw in her lot with all the other women in internment camps – and of course she deserved a monument for staying on. What the women did deeply resent was the example of a few officers (among whom the most outstanding was General van Oyen, the head of the Dutch airforce) who flew out their mistresses and left their wives behind.

I finished my part in the early evening, with Commander Charles Hart, the senior signals officer. He had already sent my reports as 'Most Immediate' to the headquarters at Kandy, and we now drafted a signal for the Admiral to send, summing up the events and intelligence of the day. When we had finished, the duty Commander in charge of the ship came in to see us and we sat down to a cup of real ships' chocolate, which I thought one of the best brews I had ever had to drink, and talked in general for a while. But, general as it was, one – to me most moving – piece of information emerged. The *Cumberland* had been on the point of sailing home to Britain when she was suddenly diverted for this advance mission to Indonesia. All the men had been stocking up for months with souvenirs and special presents to take home for their wives and children and friends. But today, said the Commander, when they had gone ashore and seen the plight of the women and other prisoners, they had hastened back to the ship in droves to plunder their little hoards of stockings, underwear, nightdresses, and all else of nylon and silk, still strictly rationed at home, and had given away almost everything they had bought.

'At one point,' he said, 'the traffic of the liberty boats between the ship and the shore had me foxed. As I saw them setting off from the shore to return to the ship long before their shore leave had expired, I knew that something unusual was going on. I soon found out that the men were coming back to fetch things they had been collecting for months, to distribute to the prisoners and internees they had met.

'Most of the silks and nylons they'd bought for their wives and sweethearts out of their wartime pittances will never reach home because they were given away to those poor women in the internment camps. But I could weep for the women at home!

'As for beer, the men's weekly ration was soon given away, and I had to put a stop to it before all the beer in the ship was gone. "Look at them, sir," the Coxswain said to me. "There they go – they look like a lot of Port Said pedlars!"'

That reaction of the ship's complement to what they saw of the suffering people on shore seemed to me to illustrate the natural goodness and generosity of ordinary people. But it also demonstrated how sudden had been the transfer of Indonesia and all its problems to the Supreme Commander's post-war obligations. That and the lack of information and preparedness which had emerged from the Dutch contingent I had met that day, made me fear for the future even more than I had begun to do before *Cumberland*'s arrival.

By this time, I realized that I was truly exhausted. All the surplus energy generated by the excitement and relief that at last we were in full contact with our own people was gone, and I could barely face the bath the Admiral had asked his steward to draw for me in his own quarters. He had insisted on me occupying his cabin for the night, saying that he preferred to doss down on deck. In retrospect perhaps I should have protested more than I did, but somehow I felt that the demands of protocol were irrelevant and would blur the mood and spirit which a great, but typical, warship had brought to these starved and deprived islands.

I slept that night a sleep that was far beyond the dimension even from which one imagines dreams to come, and I woke with reluctance yet with a deep happiness that was like a kind of sweetness which seemed to be in all my senses. Even the morning seemed to stand there like a comb of translucent honey. I had no feeling of being in a ship at sea, I had no feeling in fact of being anywhere at all. It was quite a long time before it became important to realize precisely where I was. It was enough for the moment to be in a spirit of an everywhere, an everywhere of goodness, kindness, order, beauty, harmony and security. And then gradually the sweetness lost something of its ultimate perfection in acquiring the limits of a shape and a form. At first I felt as if I were somewhere else, in Africa at dawn listening to a vast flock of sheep and their lambs leaving their kraals to graze in the care of their shepherds on a wide plain on a cloudless day, bleating with joy that now the darkness had gone and they were free and unafraid and could go out calling and leaping, overwhelmed with a sense of re-beginning not only in themselves but in the earth as well. That then passed into a feeling of being somewhere in an English country house, one of those country houses of which there are so many in

England and which belong so organically to the green and the trees and the gentleness of the land as if they were not imposed upon the earth in stone and brick so much as grown into being, aglow within the steady flame of care that had gone into their creation over the centuries. It was no coincidence, it seemed to me as the days went on, that I should have had, and indeed still have in my memory, the feeling that all the country-house atmosphere within the ship was expressed in having the name conferred on it of Cumberland, one of the most unspoilt of Britain's counties.

And then I was back in Java and I knew at once that the truth as far as I was concerned was in that deep, deep world of joy from which I had woken myself and which enclosed all the values that I had to serve. I sensed too that those values were in danger, not from a foe like the Japanese any more, but from something in us as Europeans which the war had not yet totally erased. The anxiety I had been feeling intuitively was not just because of the rising tide of violence which was already breaking out in Java and the rest of Indonesia, but because those who had now recovered power seemed in danger of repeating a pattern of the past which had already been declared utterly bankrupt. The uprush of an archaic nationalism amongst the Javanese, and the determination of the Dutch to quench that nationalism in a retrogressive and dishonoured way, would between them cause us to lose the immense opportunity which the end of the war had given us to start afresh.

If this were a matter for the Dutch alone, perhaps I would not have been so anxious. But the British, who had been so perilously over-stretched for years, had yet undertaken to accept the surrender of the Japanese and for the time being to make themselves responsible for the consequences that followed. I felt that from this moment on there would be pressure on them to be the instrument of the Dutch in a way which, if we were not careful, would involve us in fighting a colonial war, and in fact repeat a past which we had already renounced for ourselves in India, Burma and Malaya. That, I resolved, was something that had to be prevented if this special moment of innocence in history, as I called it, were not to be violated, as a similar moment was violated after the 1914–18 war when President Wilson, with his principles for peace and a new world order, and a League of Nations to express the potential brotherhood in all men, was betrayed at Versailles.

I was still in the midst of letting all this into my mind and imagination when there was a knock on the door, and the steward came in with a tray of tea and biscuits. The tea and biscuits, which are almost a banality of life wherever the peoples of the British Commonwealth take them, somehow did not spoil the sense of meaning. Almost in a trance I heard the steward say: 'The Admiral's compliments, sir. You are not to hurry, but when you are ready he would be glad if you would join him in his cuddy.'

I found the Admiral at the head of his table in the cuddy, and my heart sank at the sight of the signals piled on the table between him and Charles Hart, and at the thought that I would have to go in for a round of signalling before I could get back to my office in Batavia and all that would be piling up for me there. The Admiral, however, relieved me immediately by waving his hand dismissively at the signals and saying, with that lightness of spirit which those who did not know him might have taken as flippancy: 'Take them away, Hart, take them away. We can look at all those this evening when no doubt we will know better how to deal with them. We shall have to watch out that, for all those with no war now to occupy them, the joy of dis-covering some employment here with us doesn't drive them to make even more of our problems than they merit.'

As a much relieved and weary Charles Hart gathered the pile of signals together and left the room, the Admiral explained that the reports which had been sent off to the Supreme Command in Kandy had obviously caused as much if not more agitation, questioning and searching for answers in that exalted circle as they had done in the ship the day before. There was, no doubt, an even greater clash between sceptics of the van der Plas kind and the true believers on the staff who were not interested in proving any preconditioned or preordained attitudes, but wanted nothing but the truth in order to know how to fulfil their mission of securing the total surrender of the Japanese in Indonesia and preparing to take over the administration of the islands on behalf of the Dutch.

He then looked up at me from the papers in front of him. It was a look that moved me very deeply, a look almost as if he and I had been friends since the beginning, and which was one of welcome without reservation of any kind in the company he would most like to keep. He had obviously been thinking in the night about the whole situa-tion. He and I would have to talk at length about it. He was going to postpone the real talk until the evening when he wanted me back in the ship, but for the moment there were certain things that must take priority. First of all he would need a presence of his own on shore. He had already issued orders through the Japanese liaison officer that the Japanese were to vacate their headquarters in the Konigsplain in Batavia. He wanted me to take it over and establish an office for his Command in it. Therefore, as soon as I had had breakfast, I was to go ashore and transfer myself to the Konigsplain, establish what would be required for such an office and report back to him on what I saw as my needs.

'Laurie,' he said, startling me by the use of a diminutive only the people who had known me in my youth in Africa used, 'from now on consider yourself, for all practical purposes, my Military Governor of Batavia, and no longer the freelance governor you have so admirably been.'

I might have known that in a navy which had such close connections with South Africa, there was certain to be someone who knew about me and my family and would provide from my past what was to be the name by which my intimates in the forces would in future know and call me. In this world of the services everyone had a special appellation by which they were known, quite regardless of their rank, high or low. All the Murphys immediately became 'Spud', the Wilsons 'Tug', the Whites 'Chalky', the Clarks 'Nobby', the Millers 'Dusty', and so on. I was even to have a distinguished Brigadier-General as my opposite number on the staff who, because his surname was Wingrove, never heard himself called anything but 'Pooh'. And General Dempsey, who was to come to us briefly after his command of one of Montgomery's victorious armies in Germany, was known as 'Bruiser'. For me this use of nicknames was another reason why in the services I always had the feeling of being either in some sort of monastic order, or in an increasingly closely knit family.

The Admiral went on to say that there was one priority that could not wait and he expected I knew what that was. I did, and with relief agreed that most necessary of all was to set about collecting accurate intelligence as to what was actually happening in Indonesia. Without it we would not be able to direct the Japanese properly, and I emphasized how much – indeed more than they may have readily envisaged – we would have to depend on the Japanese until our own soldiers arrived to take over from them. And we needed to fill the vacuum of information about what had happened in the islands during the war, and about the completely new and potentially revolutionary situation all over South-east Asia which from now on would confront us in increasing measure. In fact it was more than intelligence in the ordinary sense of the word; it was almost a process of re-education of both ourselves and, through us, the Dutch if we were not going to have a colonial war on our hands. These two things were for me in the same dimension and neither could wait.

I said the Japanese would willingly and conscientiously continue to protect the civilian population in their concentrations as they had been ordered to do, but that there could be no question of ordering them to put down their arms, which I feared the Dutch might want us to do.

I had already, of my own accord, taken some steps to gather all the intelligence I could. In fact I had several people in mind for gathering information about what was happening in Java beyond the intelligence supplied by the Japanese. So I would like, as he had suggested, to get ashore as soon as possible, do what I could do immediately in that regard, and return to *Cumberland* regularly to elaborate on what I had already told them the previous day, because there was still much more to tell and do.

As a result I was back at my office in the Hôtel des Indes within an hour. I found Paul Vogt waiting for me there as if he already knew in his intuitive way that I needed him as much as I had needed him in Lebaksembada. It did not take me long to establish myself in the Konigsplain. I got the Japanese to send immediately for Jongejans, the young Dutch lieutenant who had acted as our main interpreter in all the prisons in which I had been. He was the son of a Dutch colonial civil servant who had distinguished himself in taking over the administration of the remote province of Atjeh in Sumatra where the Dutch, right up to the outbreak of the war, were still encountering fierce resistance from the Atjehnese, by temperament and history as fierce and volcanic a people as the Bantamese of Java. He was intelligent, sensitive and brave, and never lost his balance or his temper. There was no one whom I respected more, and within a few hours he had joined me. When he told me that he had discovered that his wife was also in a women's camp in Batavia, we sent for her to join us.

Although I had been out of Batavia for barely a day, again, as during all my absences from the city, the rapid orchestration of the pattern that had had so small a beginning when I had first visited it some three weeks before seemed to be increasing in volume and range with geometric progression. There were even more banners carried through the crowded streets. The fact that many of the people who carried the banners did not speak a word of the English in which they were written made no difference to the pride and ardour with which they carried and waved them, not only in squares and main streets but down side streets and alleys, where one would suddenly be confronted with: 'WE HOLD THESE TRUTHS TO BE SELF-EVIDENT . . .' It was obvious that these slogans were intended for the eyes of the Dutch, the British, the Americans and the rest of the outside world, and that the crowds were not there just as a random and impulsive mob, but were summoned, prompted and guided by an educated and sophisticated organization.

Already in the night the Japanese had had to put down several small riots and skirmishes with the crowds on the fringes of the internment camps, and as the day went on I had to order them not to allow people to assemble in numbers but to disperse them wherever a crowd showed signs of congealing. I was soon to learn how right my instinct had been. There was only one way of dealing with riots, or a tendency to riot, and that was not to allow them to happen. As a result I was more concerned than ever with the rumours coming in that Soekarno and Hatta were planning to set up government in Batavia itself, and that a call had gone out for a mass meeting to be addressed by Soekarno the following day. I immediately called upon my Japanese liaison officer to tell his commander-in-chief that no such meeting was to be allowed. I could see nothing but trouble coming of such a meeting, not only in the streets of Batavia but also in the hearts and minds of Mr van der Plas and his associates, and governments beyond.

There were disquieting reports too of the murder of more Dutch civilians who had left their concentrations, both in Batavia and in the larger world of the islands beyond. I was also dealing with Paul Vogt's 'more than a rumour' which he had brought from the Swiss Embassy: not only had Soedirman, the schoolmaster, been completely successful in getting the Japanese division in Wonosobo to surrender with all their arms and equipment, but in the area between Semarang, Amberawa, Solo and Djokja the Javanese insurrection was growing in numbers and appeared to be organizing itself in a surprisingly sophisticated manner. This was of special concern to me because it was the area in which there was perhaps the largest concentration of interned Dutch women and children and I immediately sent a message to Alan Greenhalgh and van Till.

The Japanese surrender to the Indonesians in Wonosobo was the most serious of all from the point of view of the future, not only because it had given the nationalists access to a considerable quantity of arms and equipment, but also because it was an indication of the general morale of the Japanese. I could not believe for a minute that the Japanese could have been induced to surrender so quickly had they not been more than ready to lay down their arms.

In the midst of this period came the day of the formal surrender of the Japanese Command in Indonesia. The pressure from Mr van der Plas's contingent on the newly arrived Admiral Patterson to make the surrender an occasion on which the Japanese all over the islands would lay down their arms and Dutch authority be proclaimed, was intense. But by this time I had communicated intelligence to *Cumberland* of the steady deterioration of what was still loosely called law and order. News had come from Sourabaya that some more Dutch people who had again tried to raise the Dutch flag, this time over a hotel there, had been killed by an angry mob of Indonesians. To people like myself it seemed desirable that the Japanese should not be further demoralized by having their arms taken from them. It was also quite clear that the suppressor must now change his role to that of protector if the erosion of whatever social structure there remained was not to accelerate.

Fortunately Admiral Patterson, coming as he did from a large Irish family, had an innate awareness of the power of nationalism, and a nostalgia which all Irish people have for the vanished world of the Celtic civilization which preceded our Roman pattern. Hence he instinctively recognized similar forces at work in other cultures and nations. It was as if from the start he knew what all the trouble was about in Indonesia. Armed with such intelligence as he had, he stayed firm and refused to comply with the extravagant and unreal demands made upon him, not only by the Dutch in Batavia but increasingly by the Supreme Allied Command.

From that moment was born the Dutch legend of British one-sidedness and refusal to carry out, as they saw it, the contracted policy agreed upon at the time of the sudden transfer of power at the end of the war from the Americans to the British. I heard again and again the suspicions and complaints that the Dutch had against the British: 'The British are at their old game again, trying to prevent Holland from taking over her legitimate powers in Indonesia until they can see that they themselves are safely reinstalled in Malaya and Burma.'

So the actual ceremony of surrender did not produce the

pronouncements, assumptions and transfers of power into which the Dutch wanted to rush the Admiral and, through him, the Supreme Command. Elsewhere, judging by what one heard on the radio, wherever there were concentrations of Japanese to surrender, the ceremonies were conducted with colour, show and the participation of representatives of all the Allied nations. The greatest of all was, of course, the surrender to MacArthur in Tokyo Bay, but it had its full dress rehearsals in other parts of the vast area the Japanese forces had overrun in the course of the war.

This at least was the impression that I had, an impression that made me extremely uncomfortable and again made me fear for the peace to come. It was as if, out there in the limelight of the great theatre of the world, we had witnessed the conflict of two great opposites that had been at war ever since human beings first came down from the trees and walked upright, a conflict always ending in the apparent victory of one opposite over another. Now this victory was once again being celebrated as a final resolution of this recurring decimal of confrontation in the human spirit, and not recognized as another failure, in splendid disguise, to achieve a heightening of human awareness sufficient to transfigure this everlasting clash of opposites into something more than the sum of themselves.

There seemed to be nothing new in these celebrations, nothing that had not been tried over and over again at the end of all the major and minor wars, the revolutions, skirmishes and battles in parliaments, drawing-rooms, boudoirs and even the kitchens of humanity. All seemed ultimately to be found wanting, and slowly and steadily to lead back and grow into an ever more disastrous repetition of a failed pattern of the collective human spirit. For this reason something in me rejoiced that the surrender was to take place in *Cumberland*, a solitary ship under the unique command of an unusual individual, and not only out of the glare of the limelight but even out of sight of the peoples of the islands.

Also, all those things that imprisonment seemed to have made an essential part of the climate of my spirit were, in the nature of themselves, physically present in that day of days. I do not know what it was about all those long afternoons in Indonesia, but, in a very pronounced although inexpressible way, each ample afternoon was special after its own fashion, each had not only a singular beauty but also almost a power and glory of its own. This day of the surrender was no exception. The rise of the day to its full stature, in an afternoon of clouds of a singular height and glory, was of a measure that I had never experienced before. This was something in its own nature and specific place in the heart of creation, measured and utterly bespoke to wrap the day and light in its very own greatcoat against the dark and cold of night.

In prison I had never had any idea of how the end of captivity, let alone the end of the war, would come. It had always seemed a matter not for my imagination but, as it were, for the cosmos, one that would only be decided when all in life and time, with its infinite diversities and complexities, would be ready for the occasion. I had always known I would recognize the moment when it came, but I had not known how to present it to myself. Even on the day of the surrender I did not wake up with any expectations of what the ceremony on the deck of *Cumberland* would be like. It was as if, although still to come, it was already part of a spent era. I had taken no conscious interest in it; I did not know how it was going to be organized and had too much to do to find out. I did not know who was to be there. All I did know was that the Admiral wanted me to attend. And as I repeated the journey from Tandjongh Priok to *Cumberland* in the very same Japanese vessel which had taken Alan Greenhalgh and van Till and myself to greet *Cumberland* on her arrival, the extraordinary dimension of what was happening all around me came over me.

Although it was fairly early, the day had already taken aboard its full load of eventfulness, and everywhere the galleons of cloud and dreadnoughts of thunder had slipped their moorings and set sail. *Cumberland*, great ship that she was, looked in that immensity singularly small and alone, too small for all she had to symbolize that day.

Obviously the physical substance of that setting had not changed, except in so far as change in the observer can change the observed. The ship no longer seemed strange to me. The able seaman who helped me on to the ladder was the same who had helped me on to it the first day I boarded. The bosun who piped me aboard was the same bosun with the same whistle; and the quarterdeck which I had saluted with a rush of emotion was the same quarterdeck, but I myself now brought on board what I had obviously not possessed before – a feeling of belonging. I needed no guide up the ladder to the quarterdeck where the surrender scene had been arranged. I joined the group of senior officers who were gathered there to await the appearance of the Admiral, and looked at a modest table covered with a white cloth which had been set out for his use during the ceremony of surrender, so immaculate in that noon-day sun that its stainlessness hurt my eyes. Therein lay a striking difference. All around had been cleaned and cleansed so that the abiding intent of its design for battle was gone, and it was there as if prepared for a wedding.

It was part of the Admiral's immensely chivalrous nature that, in every way, for him the occasion did not belong only to the 'now' of the living and the future but even more to those who had suffered so acutely and died in so many thousands to bring it about; and I expect it was because I was the nearest survivor of that vanished world of the dead and the suffering under the Japanese in Indonesia that I became its representative on that long and enigmatic afternoon. I felt this aspect of my history had already been amply acknowledged by the Admiral's announcement the evening before that he expected me to attend the ceremony on the quarterdeck the next day, so I was both moved and amazed when he appeared and asked me to sit next to him, still dressed in my prison uniform, as he received the surrender.

There appeared from the far end of the quarterdeck a little procession of Japanese officers, small men, who under that immeasurable expanse of cloud and sky and sea and sunlight seemed smaller than ever. They looked to me a pitiful sight, and provoked no sense of triumph and glory or anything other than Shakespeare's cry: 'The pity, O, the pity of it!' And, as always when confronted with my own portion of irrevocable fate, I felt that flesh and blood were too slight for the weight of the reckonings sometimes imposed upon them.

There was just one moment in what followed that had a uniquely personal import for me. I had not seen the Japanese General since that extraordinary day when I was taken from my prison to his headquarters, where he and his Chief-of-Staff had stood up, bowed to me, and raised glasses of wine to announce their surrender with a toast: 'We drink sincerely to your victory!' Then the General himself had added, 'We Japanese have decided to switch, and when we Japanese switch, we switch sincerely.'

As he noticed me now, with my prison clothes and close-cropped head, he appeared startled if not shaken to see me sitting beside the Admiral. Above all it seemed to me that he was in the grip not just of his own powerful emotions but of all the eruptive and cosmic energies of the earthquake land of Japan, and was containing himself with immense difficulty. When he came nearer and I could see his face distinctly, I saw in his eyes what I had found in the war was a characteristic Japanese sign of emotion controlled with tremendous difficulty, a quivering at their corners almost like the quivering of a tuning fork.

He and his tiny following of officers drew themselves up in front of the Admiral, came to attention, saluted and bowed deeply to him. As the General came out of his bow I heard the interpreter ask if he had anything to say to the Admiral.

'Yes,' the General said, with profound respect, his voice taut like a violin string with all these inexpressible feelings which were in torment and turmoil within him. Yes. If the Admiral would permit it, he had only one request. He was certain the Admiral would know what their swords meant to Japanese officers like themselves. He would be grateful if, in the act of surrender, the Admiral would allow them to retain their swords.

A hush fell over *Cumberland*: the moment of greatest crisis that now faced the General, not to mention the Admiral, had arrived. I held on to my belief in all that was positive in my experience of the Japanese and their culture and, somewhere behind the tension, had a glimmer that all would be well – but I was not sure. I knew too much about the role of the samurai not only among soldiers but also among the ordinary people of Japan. Above all I knew so well the profound imagery associated with the sword.

Every sword in a Japanese samurai family has a name and a history. Each sword is not just a sword, in the sense of the swords turned out in foundries in Birmingham and Sheffield and, for that matter, Toledo. Each sword is more than a sword. For that reason, added to the name by which it is known is the profound suffix '*maru*', with all its Shinto associations. The West knows '*maru*' principally as an addition to the names of ships (as for example the *Canada-Maru* in which I sailed to Japan as a young man) without realizing that it is also attached to other things that man, by an unusual thrust of inventiveness and cosmic inspiration, is able to make for his needs; a physical something which is more than physics and is in fact a manifestation and a visual reminder of something far beyond the world of matter. Thus every maker of swords is known by name, and the most notable are ranked with the highest artists and sages of the spirit, because into the making of the sword they will put not only the experience of certainties passed from father to son, but all that they have of value or spiritual awareness in themselves; and they will die happy if, after a whole lifetime devoted to making swords, they have accomplished a bare score of swords.

Even to this day I know of a traditional sword-maker in Nara, once capital of an inspired epoch in Japanese civilization when some of the greatest swords in history were made, who still makes swords in the way his family did in the ninth century. When he prepares himself to make a sword and has to draw the steel from the best ore available, the area in which he is going to work is marked off with sacred cords. He and his sons and helpers have special baths of purification, and the kimonos they are to wear are washed white and blessed for the labour. He will then, once the sword has been drawn and shaped, spend not less than a year on the refinement and the nuances – not only physical but spiritual – to be worked into the sword. During this year he imparts to the sword what they all think of as the soul of the sword, the '*maru*'. And even then it is not uncommon for him, after all that labour, to find only one out of half a dozen of the swords so fashioned worthy to bear the seal of his family and his art.

I did not dare look at Admiral Patterson because I knew what the answer had to be. There was nothing on earth or in heaven that could prevent it. I only prayed that the manner of its deliverance would redeem it. I did not doubt the unusual quality of both heart and mind that I had already experienced in the Admiral in the short time I had known and worked with him. But I did doubt the extent to which even his intuitive sense would be aware of the earthquake spirit which would assail the Japanese General, and which would subject him to a trial that, even after Manchuria, China and the horrors of the Pacific, he could not have experienced before.

Yet the Admiral did not fail. His voice was firm, clear and utterly made to fit only the truth, not as an inert fact but in its full meaning, alive in the ongoing processes of time. Even now I can find in what he said no excess of triumph, gloating or presumptions of the future. Like a single note lifted from a symphony, clear and precise in arriving at its own special moment in the score, elevated above all the other instruments in the full orchestra of Providence, I heard him say: 'It is the irrevocable command of the Supreme Commander of the Allied Forces in South-east Asia that you will surrender the swords you have done so much to dishonour.'

In the stillness that followed, the sound of the voice was taut like the string of a violin still quivering from the stroke of the bow which has delivered it of its note. Even in me the emotions evoked by the inrush of all the associations created around the sacred symbolism of the sword were almost overwhelming. I knew how all these associations and more would be at war within the spirit of the General, and I prayed that he would be able to contain them. I even had a swift and terrible fantasy of him not surrendering his sword but disembowelling himself and throwing the contents of his body in the faces of his conquerors, as – at the beginning of the Meiji period – a Japanese had done in the face of the British envoy who had humiliated him and his people. I am certain I could not have felt these things if that terrible option were not prominent in the spirit of that cluster of little men, seeming so small on this quarterdeck of a British man-of-war.

And then suddenly it was as if the grace which Providence grants to fallible humanity after it has undergone cleansing in the dark waters of suffering, was suddenly let in. The ship regained its sparkle and suddenly felt newly alive around me, fresh and immaculate as if it had never known any stain of dishonour itself but could lie there naked and unashamed beneath the equatorial sun and whatever had observed it from beyond that vast, deepening blue of the early evening. A mass of those cloud ships gathered slowly around it, as if part of the ordained witness needed to make that moment truly part of the eternal wheeling systems of creation.

At that moment I was reminded of the occasion when Excalibur became the sword of all swords in my imagination, when I first heard the story of how the young Arthur drew it out of the stone in which it was stuck, when all others before him had failed. And I remembered the ancient myth of the Round Table, and all that had happened to the knights who had dedicated their own swords to be of the company of Excalibur, up to the last moment when it had to be returned to the waters of Avalon where a hand rose out of the deep, clothed – as the poet tells us – in 'white samite, mystic, wonderful', and drew it slowly back into the dark waters, into the keeping of the great memory of life that had gone before, to be kept from rust and human abuse for another new and more meaningful purpose to come.

And in the swiftly rising shadows of this equatorial night, like the night on which the wounded King Arthur was about to die, it was as if the voice of Arthur himself were speaking and saying once more: 'I have lived my life, and that which I have done, may He within Himself make pure!' Those words of the dying King, full of the anguish of his own inadequacy, were redeemed with a certainty that, inadequate as the search for a Holy Grail had been, it could now at some distant date in the future be fulfilled as it would never have been fulfilled had they not all begun and suffered for it.

And there seemed to me no distance between that first experience of the story of King Arthur and what this scene evoked in me on the quarterdeck of *Cumberland* now. And then somehow I knew that the '*maru*', the soul of the first maker of a Japanese sword, had been so quickened by the gravity of the Admiral's spirit that the General could step forward and with a moving dignity lay down his sword, and the '*maru*' could, like Excalibur, be decently committed to the deep of the history of man.

I have never really tried to recall what happened thereafter. All I know is that when Charles Hart and I sent the signals of the day to the Supreme Commander to tell him that all had been fulfilled, the Admiral added a characteristic personal note of his own: 'All done and all ready and prepared to hasten home when you give us the word.' Neither he nor I knew there would be no question of hastening home, or that for many agonizing months *Cumberland* and her accompanying ships of the Fifth Cruiser Squadron would have hard, hard work to do. I almost wept for *Cumberland* and her crew when I thought how full she had been of gifts for sailors to take home and how empty she now was of anything that was surplus to the role she had to play.

As I went ashore, before the clouds closed over the last of the blue, and the rain and thunder came, I looked at *Cumberland* as she lay there, and I thought of all that she and the Admiral had contained and accomplished that day. She became one of the dearest ships in my memory. I have sailed the seas almost more than any professional sailor. All my voyages have been memorable to me but there are a few that still glow with a numinous light in my memory: the first whaler in which I went whaling and its strange commander Thor Kaspersen; the *Canada-Maru* and its knightly captain Katsue Mori (who remained my constant and devoted friend, despite the war in between, until he died at one hundred years of age in Tokyo not long ago); the wonderful little *Gloucester Castle*, which also served as an auxiliary to the navy in two world wars (in the last of which she perished), and her philosopher engineer in whose charge I worked my passage as a trimmer/stoker in the engine-room; and then *Cumberland* and the exceptional human being who commanded her and the fleet she led to war. Later was to come the last of the Union Castle line, *Windsor Castle*, on which I sailed on the last ever voyage between Europe and the Cape of Good Hope. All are there in my memory now, with *Cumberland* sealed in the proudest of places.

For some days after the surrender I watched subtle but steady changes in the island, which gave me some cause for alarm without destroying my hope that our forces would come in time to prevent what was valid in Indonesian nationalism from leading to war with the Dutch. I knew my Admiral felt it was a war which we must do all we could to prevent, though not to the extent of going into battle.

I spent some days getting the Japanese to take me on a quick reconnaissance of the interior, and there I found more signs of change. For the first time I saw young men enrolled in the beginnings of what was to become the formidable youth organization of the Pemoeda (the Javanese equivalent of a kind of Hitler Youth), and young girls in gymslips marching with sticks for rifles.

What I saw confirmed my fears of a slow escalation, but still made me feel that we had a chance if we acted quickly and decisively in bringing about a reconciliation between all that was best in the Dutch and all that was potentially valid and good in the Indonesians after so horrendous a war. All that was necessary was to have a calm period under a power that was interested only in maintaining law and order, to give us all a chance to come to our contemporary senses after so cruel an isolation from the outside world.

The rumours that Soekarno and Hatta, and others like them, were going to be arrested and tried, and possibly hanged, were still doing the rounds, causing an increasing sense of apprehension among the Indonesians and encouraging hostility to the Dutch. I had heard that Soekarno and Hatta had been sent for safety to central Java, because of fears that they would be assassinated by the Ambonese.

And here a word about the profoundly Christian Ambonese is essential. The island of Ambon is really where the story of the Dutch in these South-east Asian waters began, and began in a very nasty manner. It was on Ambon in 1623 that the Dutch slaughtered the English traders they found there, cutting their throats like dogs. The Ambonese themselves had something in their character, something open and of unusual quality, which made them accept what was good in the Dutch religion. And, because of the extent to which they began to identify with Christianity through the Dutch, they became their most loyal and brave subjects, so much so that when the native soldiery were disbanded by the Japanese, the Ambonese were interned with us and often even more cruelly treated than we were.

I have a memory which sums up for me the special qualities of the Ambonese: first in the jungle, and above all in prison on Sunday evenings, we would hear them after their self-conducted service singing in their deep voices 'Abide with Me' in the High Dutch version of the hymn. The memory remains undimmed and, though more than fifty years have passed since I heard that sound, it still echoes and re-echoes in my mind.

Escaping as the Ambonese now were from the camps in which all were supposed to await the arrival of the British forces, they began to fall under the influence of the Dutch returning to the islands and also to build on their own innate sense of resentment towards the Javanese, whom they imagined had lived privileged lives during the war. They knew nothing of the thousands of Javanese who had endured forced labour on Japanese military projects everywhere in Java, Sumatra and the outer islands, and who had died in great numbers.

I kept the Admiral fully informed of all these developments because there were things we could and had to do to mend the destructive trends of the day. I was very soon able to increase the scale and scope of our intelligence. This was due entirely to the presence of Paul Vogt in my quarters. When I came back from my excursion into the interior I found him talking to an Indonesian dressed in the uniform of a colonel in the Dutch army. He was of slender, almost frail build, like all the Javanese, and possessed a head of wonderful black hair. As he turned round, I was met with a face and features composed, I felt, of all that I liked in human beings, particularly the breadth of his forehead and his wide and open eyes. His name was Colonel Raden Abdul Kadir Widjojoatmodjo, which was typical of the rolling Sanskrit names of so many Indonesians, from sultans, through the vast *petite noblesse* to which this man belonged, to the ordinary people of Java. I came to know him as ''Dul', and he was to be with me in all I had to do in my time in Indonesia.

'Dul had been flown in a few days earlier from Australia, where he had been serving the government-in-exile since the Japanese invasion. I was soon to find out that he read the situation as I read it, but at that moment we had no time to talk properly because he had come on a very urgent mission. He told me that one of his old officers, a Major Santoso, had been captured by an Indonesian rebel command which had established itself on the outskirts of Batavia. 'Dul knew exactly where Santoso was being held and, to his knowledge, interrogated. He had already suffered much at the hands of the people who had captured him, and 'Dul was certain he would be shot. It was typical of 'Dul, and of the sense of veracity that he conveyed, that I instantly trusted him without question. I merely asked, 'Are you certain you know where, precisely?'

'Yes,' he assured me.

I had a jeep at my disposal, which was standing in the keeping of a marine nearby. I said to 'Dul: 'If you are armed, will you please leave your weapons behind. They won't help if we're going to do what I have in mind. Come along.'

We went out immediately and climbed into the jeep. He directed me, and after driving for about fifteen minutes we came to a large building. Outside on duty were four guards with pre-war rifles and long bayonets. We jumped out of the jeep. I announced to the bewildered guard: 'I have an urgent message for your officers from the British Admiral. We are British officers under British command.'

Without waiting for a reply we walked straight through, as if we took it for granted that we could. The guards were so astonished that they stood there gaping as we vanished through a door to the right and then moved quietly along a corridor to a room with its door ajar.

Behind the door we heard the sound of urgent voices. We walked in, and there was a group of Indonesian officers in uniform and, to one side, looking bewildered and as if he were in pain, an Indonesian in the same uniform as 'Dul. 'Dul whispered in my ear, 'That's Santoso!'

I went up to the officers and apologized for the way in which we had rushed in. I said I had come directly from the British Admiral in *Cumberland*. He had been looking for days for Major Santoso, whom he wanted to interview. I was very grateful to see that they had found him, and I was taking him at once to *Cumberland* to present him to the Admiral, and would let them know what the Admiral decided about him. Again I offered my apologies for my unannounced intrusion.

Astonishment seemed to paralyse them. I walked over to Major Santoso, held out my hand, and said: 'Major Santoso, I am so glad to meet you. You are to come immediately with us, as commanded by the Admiral in charge of the British Forces in Java.'

Before anybody could come out of what seemed to be a total hypnosis, we went smartly out of the room, down the passage and into the jeep, and drove off without looking back. When, two minutes later, we realized we had not been shot at, I stopped the jeep.

'Dul and I let out all the breath which had gathered under the fear with which we had done what we had done, while Major Santoso sat there like someone just woken from a nightmare, dazed with physical pain and fatigue as well as with overwhelming relief.

After that rather desperate incident 'Dul and I became the best of friends.

With the relief of having returned successfully and safely came the knowledge that now there were two factors emerging which could be a menace to law and order in Batavia: the emergence of a nucleus of the nationalist forces which had already incarcerated a Japanese division in the interior; and its opposite in the reorganization of the Ambonese. These would have to be part of all the Admiral's reckoning.

The following day 'Dul gave me a long report that he had already written for Mr van der Plas who, after his time ashore, far from moderating the picture he had formed for himself of Indonesia and what was to come, was more extravagant in his demands than ever. The interpretation I had made of what I had seen was not only matched by 'Dul's report but greatly enriched by it. He had spent his short time in Java so far meeting as secretly as he could (because anything else had become dangerous in his uniform) old friends and officers of his, and many men – like Sastro Mulyono – of the Boediardjo clan, who were of such notable help to me in the months that followed. At the heart of his report lay the message to the Dutch government in Kandy, in Ceylon and in The Hague: 'The Japanese may have been the midwife of Indonesian nationalism, but the child is pure-bred Indonesian.'

I should add that, in addition to what he was by nature and birth and education, 'Dul had served the previous government of Indonesia with distinction and commitment in the Muslim world, so important to the millions of Muslims in Java. He had, for instance, spent several years with the formidable Ibn Saud, the Bedouin founder of the Saudi Arabian nation and traditional trustee and keeper of Mecca. He was afterwards, in quiet intervals in the storm that was brewing, to keep my small dedicated staff fascinated with his accounts of service not only in Abyssinia but, above all, travelling in Saudi Arabia with Ibn Saud himself.

But at present he and I had too much to do to think about our past history. He was from that moment my liaison officer, in the first instance with the Dutch, and also at first with the Indonesian people, though to the latter his commitment and loyalty to the Dutch made him more and more suspect. I became his principal contact, his only real contact for the Dutch with my Admiral, with Lord Mountbatten in Kandy and finally with the British government.

In due course, when I had my own mess, 'Dul and his wife were to come and live with me. But all that lay in the future. Here it is only necessary to stress the instant bond, the trust and the loyalty with which we were committed to the same course: to provide the Dutch and the Indonesians with a truly contemporary relationship without spoiling the future by fighting one another with preconceived notions.

At the same time, another difficulty was developing for the Admiral and ourselves. Our channels of communication were becoming increasingly difficult, and subject to a strain which must be understood if what follows is to make sense. The signalling facilities on *Cumberland* carried a growing load of urgent as well as routine communications with the headquarters of the Supremo (as we all referred to Lord Mountbatten). As our intelligence began to spread and to penetrate, there was between Mountbatten and the War Cabinet in London a formidable volume of exchange of questions and answers, and instructions imposed on him, which raised the complexity in width and depth of his demands on us in *Cumberland*.

In addition, the Dutch began to communicate independently from The Hague with their government-in-being under Dr van Mook, the Governor-General-designate of Indonesia, and his advisers; and the reactions and instructions on high policy from The Hague were extremely ill-informed as to what had happened in Java under the Japanese. Moreover, thanks to Philips, the early explorers of radio communications, telephonic communication had already been established and now enabled the Dutch in Java to speak easily to The Hague and to pass on their version of events (consisting mostly of complaints against *Cumberland* and us) before the Supremo's staff at Kandy had even decoded our urgent overnight signals. Indeed, the Foreign Office in London was already being bombarded from The Hague by the Dutch version from Indonesia before the Supremo and his staff had absorbed what I think were truly objective and valid reports from us. The confusion and the trouble that followed can be readily imagined.

But one thing had already emerged in those few days since the surrender – the urgent need for the Admiral to recognize the fact that there was a valid nationalism at work in Indonesia which could not be ignored and which was already being extremely well-informed by a body set up quietly and unobtrusively under the leadership of a remarkable Indonesian called Soetan Sjahrir. They had listened throughout the war to broadcasts from all over the world, and were better informed about what had happened outside than even a person like myself, despite our secret radio. They heard in particular the vicious radio propaganda from Australia and elsewhere, and all the talk about the Dutch coming back to deal with collaborators, in particular Soekarno and Hatta. Now, with the swelling Dutch presence in Batavia, rumours were growing by the day that soon the nationalist leaders (who were all 'collaborators' in the Dutch mind) were going to be arrested and dealt with.

I could not urge on the Admiral more than I did, and really he needed no urging, that these rumours were increasingly dangerous in Batavia. I told him, too, of the rescue of Major Santoso, a sign that the nationalists had a small but significant military presence in Batavia. We also knew that Soekarno and Hatta had been rushed off to central Java – the heart and soul of traditional Java – to be kept there in safety. And somewhere in Batavia I had already identified the men who were forming the nucleus of a nationalist government of Java. I knew this particularly because I had established contact – although I had not yet met him – with someone whose name had been given to me as a possible guerrilla contact during the war, an Indonesian liberal but also a loyal servant to the Dutch, Amir Sjarifoeddin. He was not a Muslim but a Christian. An unusual man, he was a lawyer, and played the violin beautifully. He had endured imprisonment under the Japanese and, like all their prisoners-of-war, would certainly have been killed had it not been for the atom bomb and the consequent surrender of Japan.

I suggested, and the Admiral readily agreed, that I should try and meet a representative gathering of these people, and explain to them precisely why we were in Java and what our immediate policy was.

It did not take long for word to get back that the representatives would meet me. So, one rainless afternoon, I set out towards the most purely indigenous (and potentially most dangerous) area of Batavia. I had to go through streets which I knew to be unsafe for the Dutch, and not at all comfortable for Europeans of any kind, so I arranged for a car in which the hood could be put down and the occupants made clearly visible to anyone in the streets. Instead of taking one of my armed marines with me I took a sailor called Cooper – curiously enough born in Port Elizabeth in South Africa – who was dressed in the conspicuous and easily recognizable uniform of the able seaman he was. I, too, was obviously unarmed, and my British uniform plainly visible. Moreover, I instructed our driver to drive normally like a car going about its daily business in the streets of the capital and with none of the provocative assertiveness with which official cars tend to rush and force their way wherever they go. Our car flew the White Ensign and we drove through streets that became more and more crowded, mostly with the sorts of people who walked behind those banners and slogans from dawn to sunset. The feeling of an unconscious congealing and conformity of a collective spirit became almost tangible, and yet the crowds never turned hostile.

In due course we arrived at what looked to me like a well-found middle-class bungalow on a little rise, with steps coming down from it and with a path through a little garden to a gate with a latch, giving on to the street. As I got out of the car with Cooper at my side, the door on the veranda opened and out of it emerged one of the most beautiful women I had ever seen; she was an Indonesian lady, slender and delicate, dressed in an antique batik to which only the aristocracy of the interior would have had ready access at that time.

As she came towards me, her sarong brilliant in the light, it was extraordinary that a Japanese *haiku* flashed through my mind, a *haiku* written by a wonderful Japanese woman poet centuries and centuries ago, which had nothing to do with human beings and yet whose vision so corresponded with what I saw:

> I thought I saw the fallen blossom
> Returning to the tree
> But, lo! it was a butterfly.

This blossom, with her feet hidden in her batik, seemed to float down the steps towards the gate. Before she reached us she lowered herself on to her knees and bowed her head to the ground in the formal tradition that ruled good manners between well-bred Javanese women and their men. She then stood up and said something in Malay, to which I responded in my simple soldiers' Malay, then led us up the steps and showed me into a room where a group of men were seated around a table.

I do not remember exactly how many were there, perhaps fourteen. Most of their names would not add to what I have to tell, but some I should name. There was Amir Sjarifoeddin, of whom I have

written. There was Hadji Agoes Salim, whom 'Dul always called
'The Wise Old Fox'. He had before the war performed valuable services for the Dutch government in Java, had of course been to
Mecca, as the 'Hadji' in his name showed, and as a kind of elder
statesman had represented Indonesia at important conferences in
Geneva. There was Darma Setiawen, as robust in spirit as in frame,
who may not stand out like a peak in the events of the time but who
became a friend and was a constant and steady representative of
nationalism, with whom I was to communicate freely. There was one
woman, Maria Ulfah Santoso, an instinctive, natural and pure
Javanese equivalent of the suffragettes in Britain. She had a formidable intellect, and was a woman of character and courage who,
though battling in a world of men, lost none of her femininity.

At the head of the table sat Soetan Sjahrir. I had already heard of
him in my prison, because he was one of many Indonesians who had
been judged without trial by the Dutch Governor-General and condemned to exile on an outer island before the war. There he and
Hatta lived for some years and in their loneliness adopted two little
children, on whom they spent their love and to whom they passed on
their background and wisdom. The two men were regarded as of
such importance that before the Japanese landing they were flown
from their island exile by the Dutch military back to Java for internment, and only released when the Japanese took over.

Soetan Sjahrir it was who inspired the decision to appoint
Soekarno and Hatta to deal on the best possible terms with the
Japanese. He himself retired with some chosen and trusted friends to
a discreet and apparently private life to prepare themselves for the
future.

Sjahrir, like so many of the nationalists – indeed like Soekarno
himself – was born in Sumatra. He, like his close friend Hatta, had
studied in Holland and had left a Dutch wife behind in Holland; he
had also written a great deal in Malay as well as in Dutch, and was
universally respected for his intellectual stature. As he stood up to
welcome me I felt that something passed between us, something of
the kind Paul Vogt had referred to when he came out of the jungle
that night in Tjikotok in western Java and uttered in broken English:
'I do not know why, but I feel your fate and mine are joined together.'

And so the moment had come when I had to speak to them. I
could, of course, have spoken to them in High Dutch. High Dutch
was the official language of the South Africa into which I had been
born (and not yet the Afrikaans which was to replace it). I had

spoken it with fellow Dutch prisoners in captivity and I knew that everyone at the table there spoke and understood it probably better than I did. But I wanted at all costs to avoid doing that. I had already found that most Indonesians seemed to distance themselves, and even withdraw utterly in spirit, at the sound of Dutch. It was a sign of how rapidly the change I have commented on was taking place. But more than that I knew that my surname could not be more Dutch than it was, and that it would not convey what I had in fact become by birth and education and South African tradition: something I could only call British, and above all English. It was important that they should know me for what I was, a British soldier, with no trace of the kind of Dutch they had experienced in Indonesia. My rough grasp of Malay, which was already the unofficial language of Indonesia, was not adequate for the sort of thing I hoped to say. I therefore asked in English if I could speak to them in the English that was natural to me, but said that if that was not possible for them to follow, I could give them a choice of French, German or, what I was certain none of them would like, Japanese – but somehow I felt that between us that would not be appropriate. I was instantly aware that the end of that sentence in particular had changed the atmosphere. It was almost as if, somewhere at the far end of the corridor of their spirit, a switch had been thrown and a glow of light appeared. For the first time there was a glimmer of a smile on many faces, and on the wide, robust and frank face of Darma Setiawen a shameless grin.

Sjahrir spoke for the first time and said in a measured voice, whose sound I liked as much as the appearance of the man, 'We all at this table understand English and some of us, as you may notice, now even speak English.'

I spoke then at some length. I thanked them for having come to meet me. I had an important message for them from my Admiral, Sir Wilfred Patterson, who was representing Lord Mountbatten and who had been delegated by the Allied High Command – in which, as they knew, both the British and the Americans as well as many European allies were fully represented – to prepare for the coming of British forces to take over for the time being the administration of Indonesia.

British troops had driven the Japanese out of Burma after a long, hard and savage war, and had been about to land at Port Swettenham and drive them out of Malaya when they were relieved of yet more fighting by the collapse of Japan after Hiroshima and

Nagasaki. Now the British had been given this unforeseen task in Indonesia, and therefore had to regroup and organize themselves to come here and take over from the Japanese. I assured them that they were doing this willingly and as quickly as possible and that, in a matter not of months but of weeks, they would arrive and the Japanese, who were now under very strict Allied orders and discipline, would be disarmed and leave these islands for ever.

I said I would just like to add something personal, and that was that I had shared to the full the terrors of the Japanese occupation for more than three years as a Japanese prisoner-of-war. I therefore felt that I had a unique bond with them all and a special incentive in wanting to bring peace and order to Indonesia, and to give all those communities who had become very special and dear to me the harmony and relief which they had so richly earned. I thought it important to remember those years of isolation that we had all had to endure, and that even at this moment we were not free of the consequences and not yet clear of the terrible shadow that had been thrown over us. I begged them all to remember that, although we were relieved of starvation and malnutrition, and the Javanese people especially of seeing their men sent to work in their thousands on nightmare Japanese projects in the outer islands, I knew that thousands of them had perished, as our soldiers had perished in the same cause, and I honoured them for that.

I myself had come straight from prison and been chosen by both Lord Mountbatten and the Admiral to take charge of the office they had established on land. I was in daily contact with the Admiral, and through him with Lord Mountbatten, and what I had to say was in my capacity as their representative in Batavia and elsewhere in Indonesia. The immediate task of the Admiral and the British forces that were coming was to accept the Japanese surrender which, as they probably knew, had already happened a number of days before. Then – as soon as we had the military capacity and the proper civilian personnel – we would disarm the Japanese totally, relieve them of all the duties they were carrying out now under Allied supervision, and get rid of them as quickly as possible.

Another important task imposed on the British was to see that all the military prisoners and all those interned in whatever capacity were freed; and in particular that the women and children, who had suffered far more cruelly than the civilian population outside, could be gathered together and evacuated to homes of their choosing.

The Admiral and Lord Mountbatten knew that there were

rumours going around, and that a lot of people thought we were also there to arrest the most prominent of their people, out of ignorance of what had really happened in Indonesia. All these rumours were false. The Admiral wanted them all clearly to understand that his overall aim was simply to bring peace and harmony to Java, Sumatra and the whole of Indonesia. We were not there in any way to do anybody else's bidding. People were free to think and talk and do as they liked – with the usual democratic provision that they would do so without harm to any of their neighbours, even those with whom they might violently disagree. I wanted them all please to bear that in mind. Nothing else that they heard was true.

When we were more organized we would try as far as possible, by use of radio and other means, to keep the people of the islands fully informed of our intentions. We had no secret agenda. We only wanted to further the progress towards peace and, we hoped, a new world, a world without war and violence. I was certain that in that we were all at one, and I asked any of those present who had influence in the islands to spread that message and to make certain that, just as our bodies were beginning to be made well and whole after years of malnutrition, our spirits also should be made whole after being so abnormally deprived of a life in which these values could be taken for granted. I had my office in the Konigsplain, which was the office also of my Admiral, and I asked that if they had any serious misunderstandings they wanted to clear up, or any quarrel with what we were doing, to let me or members of my staff know.

Above all, I asked them to bear in mind, as I always did, a saying of Anatole France (he spoke with an eloquence I could not match since I spoke from memory only): 'Men', he wrote, 'frequently quarrel over the words that pass between them. They even kill one another over the meaning of the words they exchange. If only they realized what the words were trying to say, they would embrace one another.' Would they therefore see, in my words and those of the British and Allied Command, not only what we were trying to say but, in all we did, bear in mind what we were trying to do?

The silence as I finished became something almost tangible. I think it was a silence of surprise, but also of a very deep emotion which I felt myself because I spoke not like a soldier but out of my own inner self. I did not wait for a reply but thanked them and said goodbye, excusing myself by saying that I had a lot to do. I left with Able Seaman Cooper at my side. But I believe it is essential to add that this summary that I have made of what I said then sounds, after all these years, totally inadequate for all that was expressed on this occasion.

I do remember also another powerful emotion that came to me as I got into my car, a feeling of something fulfilled. When I had obeyed my instinct to go straight from prison back to military duty, there had also been a feeling of guilt that I was not rushing back to my home in England where I had been reported 'Missing' and then 'Believed Killed'. I had not been home for more than five years, and had not seen my mother and my two children in Africa for ten years. I had often wondered how my daughter had developed from the wonderful giggling little girl I remembered into someone who must now be growing up into a young lady. And still I had put this strange prompting before reunion with them all. Not only did this emotion become conscious in my car on the way back, but all feelings of guilt totally vanished, and I felt an absolute certainty that I had to serve on in Indonesia. It was a return in a deeper way to the feeling I have described on that night in the streets of Bandoeng, and now it seemed immeasurably more profound.

I returned to my headquarters to find the Admiral there, and at his side his Flag Lieutenant, 'Flags' as he was known, a person of quality with a total understanding and appreciation of his Admiral. There were also – what was to become an increasing worry, almost a horror – the representatives of world news agencies and two Dutch special correspondents. As I walked in, the Admiral broke off what he was saying and greeted me: 'There you are!' I had the feeling that I could not have appeared at a better moment, for he looked at the group around him and said: 'Gentlemen, Colonel van der Post. He has just come back from a meeting of great importance that you ought to know about, and I will ask him to tell us what he can about his mission.'

It was impossible for me to summarize or to censor what had happened between me and the Indonesian leaders. I just had to apologize to the Admiral and the press and say that I might be rather long in telling them what had happened, but that it could not be helped, as it was very important that I convey not only an account of the events of the afternoon but also the atmosphere in which it took place, and what it conveyed to me. I thereupon reported in some detail and, I believe, with a continuation of the feeling with which the afternoon with the Indonesian leaders had ended. Also I told them the names of all the men in the group who had met me, but devoted special attention to those among them whom I was certain would be known at The Hague, and even perhaps to the people of Holland – Soetan Sjahrir, Amir Sjarifoeddin and Hadji Agoes Salim.

When I finished speaking, I thought the press and the others there seemed to be looking at me in some bewilderment, but the Admiral just said: 'Gentlemen, I think we have cause to thank Colonel van der Post. He has done something today of great significance, and I hope you will convey it to your agencies and newspapers in the way in which it has been reported to us here. Thank you, gentlemen.'

He then turned to me and said, 'I want you to come at once with me to *Cumberland*,' and we handed over the meeting to the care of Jongejans while we went to send a 'Most Immediate' signal to the Supremo.

But I left with an indefinable feeling of unease about the men we had met there. They looked a decent enough group of people but I feared what was happening already on the radio and in the cables they exchanged with their employers. Somehow the impression conveyed to Holland was qualified and guarded, and was indeed the first intimation of the slanted view with which all I did was henceforth to be perceived and reported, and of the attribution to me of a singularly diabolical role. In all these reports, even on Russian radio, I was beginning to be seen not as a fallible human being doing his best but as a dangerous person, undoubtedly a villain.

I left *Cumberland* early the next morning, just as soon as the Admiral had completed the naval equivalent of Reveille in the army, the hoisting of the White Ensign. It is perhaps my favourite version of the flag of union which incorporates the crosses of three national saints, and is a twin almost, in my own associations, with the flag of Australia which incorporates the Southern Cross under which I was born. As always on these occasions the marines performed the ritual in the unique manner which is in their special keeping. The Admiral too always had, at dawn, and at sunset at the retreat of the day and the striking of the ensign, a look in which he was not seeing the immediate physical world of his ship and all that it contained around him but rather the long history which ships like his had served. I thought of Mozart saying that he saw his music like a landscape laid out before him, but then he had had to travel it for days before he could express what it was that had been evoked in him by it. Somehow I always felt less incomplete when I had witnessed the ceremony with the Admiral conducting it; and I more and more needed that sense of completeness because on land the situation we had to face was becoming not only more fractured but also more dangerous.

It started that day for me when, back at my office, I was contacted by Mr van der Plas and his associates who said they thought it would be rather a good idea if the Admiral invited some of the leading nationalists to a meal in the ship, and then quietly arrested them and shipped them out of Indonesia. I instantly rejected the idea but said I would also report it to the Admiral. I had never seen and was never again to see him so angry. He went very still, his voice full of tension and yet controlled: 'What sort of people do they think we are? Do they really think that I would see one of His Majesty's ships put to so ignominious a use?'

The message, I must say, when I repeated it to them word for word, went home and, of all the exacting and extreme things that came from the growing number of Dutch in the islands, nothing of the kind was ever asked of us again and many shame-faced explanations to the effect that it was never seriously intended came my way. But somehow I could not help feeling increasingly sorry for people like Mr van der Plas because there was no doubt that they loved Java, and indeed the Indonesians. Yet they did not seem to know (as I am afraid most of us do not) that it is important not only to love but also to know how to love; that it is not the emotion of love in ourselves that is important, but the experience of it as something that remains the total and true objective expression of itself.

One incident at that time illustrated how even the Dutch who had been through captivity with me, and whom I liked, had not yet acquired an awareness of what the grace of Providence – which had released us alive from the Japanese terror – demanded of us. A captain of the Dutch police, who had been a real source of help and courage in prison, appeared one night at my office not only to greet me but also to tell me something which he thought I would welcome. We had in prison a handful of Eurasians whose joylessness and tendency to a form almost of collective manic depression continually surprised me. When I thought of the wonderful Cape-coloured peoples of my native country, their zest, their enjoyment of life, their sense of dance and music and poetry as well as of humour, and the gaiety of their culture, these Eurasians were a truly depressing people.

The origin of it all, I believe, was to be found in something which is important to the understanding of the history of Indonesia, and even of what was happening around us. The world – and the Dutch

themselves – always regarded the Dutch empire as free of the colour
and racial prejudices to be found in other countries. It is true that the
Dutch who served in Indonesia were physically attracted by the
indigenous people, who are generally comely and beautiful, and it
had become a habit that the men sent at a young age from Holland
to serve the government in Indonesia, who felt they could not as yet
afford to marry a woman of their own kind on the pay with which
they started their careers, would contract a marriage with an
Indonesian woman of their choosing and would even have children
by her. But then, when the moment came and they felt they could
afford it, they would divorce their native wives and leave them and
their children, and contract new marriages in which these liaisons
were never acknowledged or discussed, although their wives and
indeed everyone else knew what had happened. I think this was in
some ways worse than an honest colour prejudice because it was so
rational, so calculated and without heart, that it really hurt.

It was not surprising to me that the Japanese had introduced these
Eurasian offspring into our midst to spy on us in prison. They were
always a danger, as this captain had known: he had warned me that
if we were not careful they could easily cause a massacre among us.
The captain now came to tell me, among other things, that he, and
presumably some helpers, had taken six of these people out into the
night and shot them. He justified this by saying that he was sure that
that was what the courts would have demanded of the police if there
had been a proper court of law in the land.

That he could tell me of this with nothing but a sense of duty fulfilled and, what was more, expect me – whom after all he had come
to know quite well – to be glad of it, shocked me deeply. The memory
of these sorts of ghosts who walk about in the underground world of
what we call peace has continued to haunt me.

Meanwhile the task of collecting the intelligence that we needed
was becoming increasingly difficult. I was very glad that van Till and
Alan Greenhalgh were there to do what was necessary in preparing
for the coming evacuation of all the prisoners-of-war and internees,
and that I could concentrate on what was going to be the real priority, the establishment of peace and the prevention of another cycle
of violence and war in Indonesia that would make a proper solution
of all outstanding problems impossible.

On top of all this our communications had become so over-
strained that we were not surprised when an emissary appeared from
the Supremo's staff at Kandy. He was an elderly colonel, a very dear

and nice man who, I think, must have been retired from the army when the war broke out and who immediately presented himself for service. He seemed from the beginning appalled and, when not appalled, deprived of the gift of truly perceiving and understanding what was happening around us. At the end of some days the Admiral had him to dinner on *Cumberland* before sending him back to his headquarters with a special report for Lord Mountbatten. The report in outward appearance consisted of a pile of documents bound in the shape of a fat book. The colonel was told that, as was his custom, the Admiral would like the messenger to look at the message before it was sealed for delivery. So the colonel opened the book at the first page. On it was written: 'The following report is the considered appreciation of Rear-Admiral Sir Wilfred Patterson, CS5, of the situation in Indonesia.'

Page 2 began: 'I believe there are three towns of importance in Java: Batavia, Bandoeng and Sourabaya.'

And then there followed blank page after blank page, to the last page of all which read: 'I regret that owing to the complexities of the situation this despatch could not be shorter.'

The colonel of course was horrified. He was even more horrified when the Admiral told him: 'Colonel, this is an order. I am sealing this report now and you are to deliver it to Lord Mountbatten himself.' The colonel writhed with protests but the Admiral was clearly in earnest about his command and it had to be obeyed. I do not know what happened between the colonel and the Supremo. I can only say that all those he left behind in the Admiral's cuddy somehow felt immensely the better for it.

On the drive that morning from the harbour at Tandjongh Priok back to Batavia I had already noticed an unusual stir and press of people heading towards the city. I had a nose by now for changes of atmosphere in Java, and I arrived to find my office in the Konigsplain already extremely busy, and all my staff waiting somewhat anxiously for my return. It had been a night of alarms and excursions for them all. The intelligence coming in suggested that there was going to be a dangerous massing of people. There were rumours that the Ambonese had taken revenge on the Javanese, against whom they felt they had grievances. Almost overnight Batavia had become a city full of grievances, which I thought of as a porridge of negation.

I sent immediately for Nakamura, my brave and intelligent young

Japanese liaison officer. He was equally concerned, and we agreed – as we had already long since agreed – that the only way of dealing with riots was not to let them happen. All day long he saw to it that the Japanese, as quietly and restrainedly as possible, broke up the little crowds on street corners and in alleyways where they tended to be massing, and in this way we got through the day without a major riot.

In the midst of all this, as if the day had decided to present us with a single symbol of the general situation, two Japanese officers quietly brought an Australian RAF officer, whom I had known well in prison, to see me. They confessed that they no longer knew how to take care of him without damage to himself and dishonour to their pledge to protect all internees.

He was an unusual person, because for nearly two years he had succeeded in hiding in the house of his Eurasian mistress and her family until eventually he was found out by the dreaded Kempetai, the Japanese equivalent of the German Gestapo. He was not tortured, but was badly beaten and then thrown like a post-office parcel into our camp, where he shocked us all not by his physical condition – because we saw many of our members every day in that state – but by the length of his hair. Ours was not only clipped short but often, as in my case, totally shaved. The camp in general was indeed as shocked by this as socialites giving a smart party in the Mayfair of pre-war London would have been scandalized by a guest who turned up with three days' growth of beard on his face. One of our officers, my second-in-command in prison, a very special and dear, brave and efficient professional soldier in Churchill's old Hussars regiment, was so disapproving that he called this poor man's appearance 'obscene', and Nichols, our prison commander, rushed him off to have his hair clipped to prison standards before releasing him for general circulation. He was always unusually quiet from then on and did all that an officer was expected to do, but I always had a feeling there was an extra measure of melancholy in him.

There he was now, and on seeing me his face, which had been set and sombre, was suddenly lit by a wide smile, and he exclaimed, without any formal address: 'Ah, at last! One of the truly wise men of the East!'

I had been called many things in my life, but never that, and was somewhat startled. He then added: 'I have come to settle some very important points of dogma with you.'

I took him from the Japanese, and gave him some tea and food with my marines. At all sorts of odd moments of the day, he broke away and wanted me to explain difficult biblical references he had in mind. This continued until late in the afternoon, when at last a message came from *Cumberland* that a boat would be waiting at Tandjongh Priok to take him aboard as soon as we could get him there. The petty officer who had been placed in charge of him came to me with apologies that he refused to go until he had seen me again.

He came into my office and in a stern voice that I hardly recognized said: 'Take this most immediate message and see that it is transmitted most immediately to all the kings, potentates, rulers and leaders of the world. Quote: I command you all to see that peace shall reign immediately through the whole of the world. Unquote. And sign it Jesus Christ.'

And then, as if his order could not possibly be countermanded or changed, he turned about and was on his way to *Cumberland*.

At the moment of this disturbing happening came another event which was to be the means of sending this Australian RAF officer back to his native continent. It was now possible to communicate daily with the headquarters of the Commander of the Allied Forces in South-east Asia (ALFSEA as we came to call it), and thus request flights to Australia. I then found to my amazement that such a flight had already been arranged. It had come about because of something in itself rather ludicrous, and yet it fell into the realm of those strange happenings that come winging out of the mysterious nature of things to make substantial and to confirm the phenomena that human beings used to dismiss as 'just coincidence' but which both physicists and psychologists today refer to as 'synchronicity'.

Almost at the same time as this officer had been presented to me on land, a senior midshipman in *Cumberland* had summoned a marine on deck and sent him down to the Duty Commander with a message which I am told turned the war-stained marine pale with shock and confusion, and made him for the first time in his life hesitate to obey an order. The midshipman is reported to have said to the marine, in an unmistakable voice of command, 'Go down and tell the Commander to report to me immediately on deck.'

The marine, shaking at the knees, had gone below, quickly came back, stood to attention and said: 'Sir, I have been ordered to convey to you the compliments of the Commander, and to tell you that he wants to see you down below at once, on a matter of urgency.'

This made the alarmingly quickened mood of the midshipman almost uncontrollable. He replied: 'I do not think you could have conveyed my order to the Commander properly. You are to go back immediately and tell him that I want him up here at once. I cannot waste my time going down to him.'

By this time the Commander had realized that something was wrong and appeared on deck. But even before he could speak, the midshipman said: 'Ah, there you are at last. I am extremely dis-satisfied with the state of this ship. I cannot understand how an officer of your experience has allowed it to come to this pass.'

The Commander knew, as I had known in my office with the Australian officer, that this young man, who had been torpedoed twice in the war, was no longer sane and arranged the flight to Australia for him. Both men were duly flown to Singapore the next day, and on to Australia.

Instantly several things came to my mind that I could not pursue until I was alone that night: one was a most disturbing recollection of the Russian Koteliansky in London, who with the help of Leonard Woolf was translating some of the stories of Ivan Bunin, whom I thought – and still think – the greatest short-story writer of the century. Koteliansky told me that in Russian the word for an idiot, even a lunatic, was the same as the word for a saint. Hence Dostoevsky's *The Idiot*. I remembered that in the Middle Ages in Europe, when every village and city which had not exceeded its pro-portions had idiots and lunatics at large as part of their normal life, they were regarded as 'good Christians', which in time became debased to the derogatory word 'cretin'.

I wondered then, as I wonder now, who and what it was that I had helped to send to internment in a lunatic asylum in Australia. What was it that caused what we call 'madness' in them? Was it that the madness of the collective state of the spirit, which had resulted in the war, had determined to make itself explicit in these two, perhaps unusually sensitive spirits?

I could not have been more ready at the end of such a day for my own return to *Cumberland*, to find the Admiral, his Captain and Charles Hart already gathered and looking ruefully at the signals that had been coming to them all day from everywhere, but mostly from the Supremo's headquarters in Kandy. Many of them need never have been sent. To reply to them individually was impossible, and a collective reply would make no sense. It was something that could not be allowed to go on. We sat for a moment in silence, think-ing of what to do. Then the Admiral leaned forward and pushed all the signals aside: 'Gentlemen, we shall look at these again tomorrow, if necessary. But now I want you', turning to Charles Hart, 'and Colonel van der Post to draft the following "Most Immediate" message to the Supremo himself.'

Charles Hart and I went off and sent the following signal speeding through the ether towards Lord Mountbatten in Kandy. I remember the wording exactly to this day:

Most Immediate. En Clair.
CS5 to SACSEA:
We can continue to rock the baby to sleep only if you people outside the house would not make so much noise.

I promised the Admiral that night that, if I lived, I would one day write a story about all that had happened and was happening to us in Indonesia, and call it *The Admiral's Baby*.

After sending the signal, I thought of a moment behind the Italian lines in Abyssinia, when the rains had broken and my little tent was too light to keep out all the heavy 'drip drip drip'. I was talking to the great and tragic Orde Wingate – who had an extensive knowledge of military history – about how, in all exceptional military careers, the future was decided by the capacity of the commander to use the appropriate words. We went over examples like Henry of Navarre, barely out of adolescence and about to go into his first battle, addressing his knees and saying to them: 'That's right, tremble! Tremble! You would tremble even more if you knew where I was taking you!'

I thought of Frederick the Great, at the crucial Battle of Rosbach against the forces of the cruelly persecuted Maria Theresa, riding up to a ridge under the heavy bombardment of the Austrian artillery (supposed to be the best in the civilized world at the time) and seeing the wavering young recruits, whom he had been forced to call up after the heavy losses incurred in his Seven Years' War, and calling to them in his faulty German with a heavy French accent: 'Don't tell me, chaps, that you are afraid to die!' The irony of it was enough to rally those potentially stout young hearts.

I thought too of Marlborough at the opening of the fateful Battle of Malplaquet, finding his officers already in hasty retreat from the French. He rode up to them and said: 'Gentlemen, I think you are going the wrong way.' Turning in his saddle and pointing, he went on, 'The enemy is over there.' They turned about and went on to join the battle and, what is more, to win it.

It seemed to me that the Admiral's signal was of that quality and in that tradition, and that however much of the Germanic may have been inherited in the spirit of Mountbatten, he had enough English-ness in him to know that an Admiral who liked him enough to have the confidence to tease him could be trusted in a way which even the best and most committed of his many first-rate Admirals, whatever their merit, could not have been.

CHAPTER THREE

Christie

IT SEEMED TO me another form of synchronicity that for a few days we had a relative calm, both in *Cumberland* and on shore. This brief freedom from signalling enabled the Admiral, Flags, Charles Hart and me all to go down one evening to the officers' wardroom and spend an hour or two sharing stories and drinks and great enjoyment. The evening ended with the Admiral and Flags doing something which others may have thought a decline into familiarity of the Admiral's dignity as a commanding officer. The Admiral and Flags took each other's feet in their hands in such a manner that their bodies were formed into the shape of a ball. Then they threw themselves along the floor and rolled like a ball to the end of the wardroom, and back again. It was a feat that was acrobatically most exacting and demanded a physical fitness and qualities of stamina and exertion quite out of the ordinary. At its end they stood up, did a quick brush of imaginary dust from their persons and, to an enthusiastic round of applause, the Admiral said goodnight and took himself off to bed. Even now I can see dignity not diminished but made more accessible and human.

Then one afternoon a special 'plane brought into our midst Lady Mountbatten, her military ADC (a major in the kilt of an illustrious Highland regiment), and a young lady who was already known on the wartime stage in London but of whom I had not heard before.

Lady Mountbatten, in whom courage was as natural as it was in her husband, had already flown, weeks ahead of any organized Allied intrusion, into zones all over the crumbling Japanese empire where there were prisoners-of-war and civilian internees. She had just come from Medan, in Sumatra, where a thousand or more prisoners-of-war who had been with Nichols and myself in prison in Bandoeng had been sent some eighteen months before. She had already been briefed by Alan Greenhalgh and Baron van Till.

It was already evening by the time I got to *Cumberland*. The quality of that evening again brought Conrad to my mind, not only because it seemed so like the atmosphere which surrounded the tragic unfolding of his moving story, *Victory*, but also because it reminded me of the other great stories he wrote about that part of the world, especially *Lord Jim*.

I was to meet Lady Mountbatten, elegant and utterly at ease with herself and her mission, and her lady companion that evening in *Cumberland*. After supper in the Admiral's cuddy, she, her lady, the Admiral, Flags and I sat on the afterdeck and savoured the peace and calm of a lovely evening and the night that came out of it. As we sat there, Lady Mountbatten's companion gave Flags and all the officers and men a description of England, and above all of the West End wartime theatre and its emergence into peace, that was real food to spirits starved by years of war.

I, too, wanted to listen and was surprised at a longing I felt to be among those things they were talking of, but Lady Mountbatten was interested in Indonesia in a deeper way and obviously had a feeling that I could help to fill in an area of her knowledge and her understanding of what was going on.

She began by saying that in inspecting these various camps, from Burma and Malaya to Sumatra and Java, she had been amazed at the impression she gathered of a totally new mood and unforeseen world-in-the-making behind the prison walls. Surely it could not be anything as serious as her immediate feelings suggested? Such major changes could not be thrust on life so suddenly. After all, she said, take the Dutch empire in Indonesia alone; it was one of the best-governed empires in the world and if there had been a serious sense of rebellion and rejection of empire at work, surely the Dutch would long since have spotted it and known all about it?

As she was speaking I felt myself back in the troopship in which I had sailed from Liverpool to a destination and an assignment of whose nature I was then unaware. The ship was one of a convoy of twenty of the finest passenger liners in the world and I was the only officer unattached to a unit of my own, and singularly alone. The military officer in command of all the soldiers in the ship therefore

asked me if I would take charge of entertainment for the officers and
men. We were shadowing the coastline of Africa and the moment
came when we saw the lights of Dakar and ultimately reached Sierra
Leone. This nearness of Africa aroused such an interest in the men
that I started to talk to them about the continent, its history, its
present and its future. These talks became mass meetings and the
greatest and most popular feature of the voyage. I remember a
Guards officer whose nickname was Jupiter coming to me and
saying: 'I find it so interesting that you seem to have such a gift and
obviously a desire to re-educate all of us. I cannot tell you how much
we value that.'

Suddenly the conversation starting between Lady Mountbatten
and myself struck the same instinctive response in me to pass on
whatever I knew of life and time to others.

So I began to tell Lady Mountbatten that it was not surprising how,
over and over again in history, major events would seem to erupt or
explode in unsuspecting societies and cultures. It was one of the most
marked and most difficult of processes to understand. This had been
no more demonstrable than in South-east Asia and in the Java which
now confronted us. To the Dutch experts on Java, who had come in
with the Admiral and whose number was growing so rapidly, the
nationalism of which she had already caught an inkling in Sumatra
and Java seemed to have appeared with an almost sinister
miraculousness, if not by a process of spontaneous combustion.

I laboured the point somewhat, because this unawareness seemed
to carry the most providential warning not only for the British and
the Dutch in Indonesia but for all the powers concerned with the new
world that was springing into being even beyond South-east Asia,
and particularly in Africa and South America. It was most urgent
that we should realize this – that history mobilizes its energies
inconspicuously, almost secretly, and with unfailing patience over
long, apparently uneventful years out of just the sorts of things that
the contemporary man rejects as trivial and insignificant. An unawareness of this process is one of the inadequacies of democracy
and it results in a failure to deal with events at their beginnings when
they are so small and apparently trivial. They then have a certain
innocence, a lack of a history of their own, and are flexible, pliable
and easier to deal with. But democracy, always preferring its comfort
of spirit and being to any change that may disturb it, watches them
grow, small bit by small bit, until they are enormous, and impossible
to handle and contain.

It is rather like the avalanche in the Himalayas which creates itself out of light, fluffy little snowflakes all winter long and then in the spring, when the winter is forgotten, suddenly rolls down on to the plains, sweeping cities and temples to their doom. It is as if history, like biology, conforms to a law whereby great mutations are brought about not so much by slow and orderly evolution as by a series of sudden eccentric and apparently inexplicable jumps.

Through what agencies historical mutations cease to be potential and suddenly become kinetic is probably one of the most difficult things for an historian to decide. It may be something trivial or capricious, just as the casual hooves of a chamois are enough to start the avalanche or, to take another example, the 'Boston tea party', which resembled a university rag rather than an authentic discharge of history. Or it could be a single shot and the death of an Austrian prince, as at Sarajevo in August 1914, which started the greatest of all world wars and brought about the deaths of millions of Europeans and hundreds of thousands from India and America before it came to an end.

Take the war from which we had just come. The build-up was already obvious in the 'twenties as far as South-east Asia was concerned, in the moment when the Japanese Foreign Secretary cocked a snook at the League of Nations, which was more than the act of disdain and rudeness which the world seemed to take it for. It was a clear sign that something far more profound was already stirring in the Japanese spirit, marking retrogression into the archaic era that was to produce Mussolini and Hitler, and confirm Stalin.

And then there had been the sudden appearance at the beginning of 1942 of black hats in Java. Did she know about that? She did not, and I went on to tell her what had happened when Wavell and all his headquarters staff suddenly left Java in the dead of night and slipped off and away to India. Early the next morning I had walked through all the offices littered with things discarded in haste, and out of the window had noticed that overnight all the Indonesians had cast away their traditional batik headgear and had donned the black hats of the Soekarno nationalist movement. This act seemed to me of specific importance, and a frightening omen of something having vanished for ever, and of something new and powerful to come. One of the last things we had discussed with Wavell's vanished staff was the question of organizing resistance in Java once the capitulation to the Japanese had taken place. How could I possibly carry on resistance in Java if the whole population were turned against the Dutch and, ultimately, ourselves? We had been able to do it behind Italian lines in Abyssinia only because everywhere in that vast country eminent nobles and the greater part of the civilian population had never surrendered to the Italians.

This sudden appearance of black hats was all the more significant because there could have been no detailed organization, however widespread and clever, to produce such a phenomenon overnight. No one could possibly have spread the news of Wavell's departure, and organized the whole countryside in the small hours of the night.

The Dutch, who even the day before would have reprimanded their Indonesian servants for not wearing the batik, now behaved as if they had not noticed the black hats, and that seemed most sinister of all to me. What was more, the singing of the refrain '*We Zijn Niet Bang*' ('We Are Not Afraid'), which among the Dutch had resounded over drinks and food, in bars, cafés and restaurants all day long, suddenly ceased.

And then the next day, on a reconnaissance far into western Java, sitting on the veranda of a hotel at a luxury hill-station packed with Dutch refugees from Sumatra, all rather elderly, and young couples and wives with their children seeking safety in Java, I suddenly heard a man behind me complaining: 'What upset me most before we left was that the head of my workers came to me and asked me to give him some condensed milk! Can you imagine such effrontery? I tell you, I do not like it!'

I heard it all as in a dream, and thought: 'But why on earth is a tin of condensed milk so upsetting?' And instantly it became a dream image to me, wherein nothing is false and everything is chosen by the dream because it alone will serve its purpose: what that worker was saying to the Dutch on behalf of the collective unconscious of Indonesia was: 'You have never given us the milk that we needed, the milk of human kindness. But you are to do it from now on!'

I was going to leave it there, but not only did both Lady Mountbatten and the Admiral ask me questions, they clearly intimated that they wanted more. By now, too, a number of officers on deck had, at a sign from Flags, drawn in around us to listen and I found myself compelled to talk about the Dutch spirit of empire, and how it had never been a true expression of the people of Holland at their best.

The chartered company that was formed to conduct Dutch trade by way of the Cape of Good Hope and on through Indonesia to

Japan was one of the most rapacious and ruthless in history. And that infamous massacre of the British traders on the island of Ambon in 1623 was indicative of the company's nature. In Japan, their total preoccupation with trade and with making money was demonstrated by the way in which the Shoguns of Japan allowed them to succeed the Portuguese, who were despised and expelled from Japan because, through missionaries like Francis Xavier, they had converted the Japanese to Christianity in vast numbers. The Shoguns felt so threatened by this that not only were the Portuguese expelled but thousands of Christian converts were massacred.

When the Dutch East India chartered company made its approaches to the Shogun, it was granted a base at Nagasaki for the purposes of trade on one condition – that its principals would parade at least once a year in Tokyo, where they were to cut capers all through the main streets dressed as fools and clowns. The charade must end with them trampling and spitting on the Cross. They did not seem to find this too high a price to pay, and continued to comply with this condition and perform the ritual until 1854 when Commodore Perry forced the Shogunate to open Japan to the West.

I told them how we too had suffered under the enormities of that chartered company in South Africa; how in the emergence of a truly South African nation, France and French culture had been forbidden to the Huguenots as a condition on which they could have the freedom of conscience for which they had fought and been driven from France.

I recalled how for many of us (and indeed for the administrators in Java too) significant changes had come, not from a group but from the solitary and individual spirit of a writer who wrote under the Latin pen name of Multatuli ('I have suffered much'). His book, *Max Haavelaar; or the Transactions of a Coffee Merchant*, had been translated into all European languages and had even become part of Lenin's reading. Indeed it had influenced Lenin in seeing to it that the Bolshevik charter, written in exile for the administration of Russia's vast landlord empire, would, when the revolution came, avoid the mistakes made by the chartered company in Indonesia.

I could not help contrasting the fate of Indonesia with our luck in South Africa when the British took over permanently. Soon the chartered company spirit vanished and we experienced government that understood the lessons of the American War of Independence, and followed them through in a process of transformation of Empire into Commonwealth. We had, even in the dreaded Lord

Charles Somerset who was the first governor, a 'something else' which expressed itself more particularly and to a greater extent in a series of remarkable governors. At the same time it was already manifest in the highest degree in the young Englishman, Stamford Raffles, through his creation of Singapore. I thought of how moving was the open letter, which he wrote when he was only in his twenties, to all the men who would serve under him, telling them what England expected of them. He was not yet thirty when in the Napoleonic Wars he was sent to govern Indonesia. His impressive book on Java is a testimony to the depth of his knowledge and his affection for the Indonesians and their country. His reforms were so enlightened and so far in advance of anything under chartered company rule that, when Indonesia was handed back to the Dutch, and they quickly reinstated the spirit and even the letter of chartered company rule, they pilloried him for all he had done for the Indonesians.

Years later, when Raffles decided to return to Britain, the only ship available was due to sail by way of Java and to call in at Batavia for several days. Knowing how the Dutch felt about him he tried to find another ship, but failed. He then wrote to the Dutch Governor-General, an aristocrat from Holland, and told him what was happening, saying that while he was in Batavia he would not, of course, leave the ship. But at the same time he asked if Lady Raffles, who was pregnant and not well, could be allowed to go to the nearby hill-station to avoid the discomfort and excessive heat of a ship tied up in so notorious a cauldron of a harbour. The Governor-General refused his request and (something which I think was worse than the refusal) told Raffles that he had been surprised that he had dared to make it. Though this may seem a small thing it is an indication of the basic lack of humanity which was so deeply embodied in the spirit of the Dutch East India Company.

Inevitably, when Raffles' reforms were modified or abolished the Javanese rebelled and a war broke out in 1840.

My story led on to 1926 (the year, incidentally, when as a young man I sailed past Java aboard the *Canada-Maru* on my way to Japan), when the crew of the cruiser *De Zeven Provincieen* mutinied and took over the ship (their mutiny coinciding with a revolt in Bantam) – a mutiny which provided the first occasion on which air power was used to bomb a warship.

Talking of these and other things the evening passed. When asked by Lady Mountbatten what she should read I said that perhaps best of all was a book by Louis Couperus, the greatest Dutch novelist I think of all time, which reveals the imperviousness of Europeans in their treatment of subject races. It is called *De Stille Kracht*, rather inadequately translated as *The Hidden Force*, and is a wonderful story of how a first-rate Dutch public servant in a remote province, doing his company duty correctly, is seen through and despised by his Indonesian servants.

Early the next morning Lady Mountbatten and her two companions flew off. I was never to see her again, but I have always been grateful to her for the way in which she quickened in all of us a feeling of the women waiting for the return of their men from war, and for her elegance which matched her courage.

Soon after, I returned to my office and Taji came to say goodbye to me. Taji was a small and rather frail interpreter for the Japanese. There was something in his appearance that was not at all Japanese but he was by far the best interpreter of Japanese I have ever met. He acted on the staff of the senior command and always when he interpreted I felt there was, somewhere in his spirit, something that was on our side and not the side of the military in Japan. He told me for the first time that morning that his mother had been English, and a Christian. At once I understood that it was she in him and in his memory who had pleaded so often and so subtly for us. I was so moved by the thought of the spirit of this dead woman still adding to the meaning of life and, in a sense, presiding over all her son did in the midst of those horrors, that I said: 'We have got a lot to thank your mother for, Taji.'

For a moment Taji, who was Japanese enough to have all their self-control, looked as if he would not be able to speak. He just murmured: 'Thank you. My mother had a very difficult life.'

I was sorry to see him go, and tried to help him in a career which, I believe, went on to prosper. But before he went he said to me: 'You know the thing you said to the Japanese General?'

I did not know what he meant and asked: 'What thing, Taji? I have said so many things by now.'

'You remember saying to the General that there is a way of losing which becomes a way of winning? Well, I carry that in my heart. And I want you to know how the General was thunderstruck to see you sitting beside the Admiral on the day of the surrender. He felt you must hate them for not seeing that you were a General yourself, and that you were entitled to special treatment and should have been sent to join the other Generals in Manchuria.'

'Taji, tell the General that I was just a soldier and no more. God bless you.'

Within days, Christie came to us, as commander of the Allied Forces in the Netherlands East Indies (AFNEI). He arrived in a Mitchell bomber, almost unannounced. I call him Christie because all those who served under him in Burma and Indonesia called him that among themselves, and continued to think of him as that in their hearts and minds to the end of his and their days. He was by birth a baronet, his full name and title General Sir Philip Christison. He had already distinguished himself as a young senior officer in the First World War, and did even more in the Second World War in the hard battle for Burma. He had inherited his baronetcy from his father, who had earned it as an eminent doctor in Edinburgh. Christie himself had taken a medical degree and had started service in the 1914–18 war as a doctor, but he soon discovered a gift for military service.

To understand the significant role Christie played in Indonesia (despite the abuse, the spurious judgements and even the deviousness of the Dutch), some background history is necessary.

When the war broke out in 1939 the professional British army had many officers, some in senior positions or who were to move into senior positions during the war, who had served in the First World War. Not one of them had ever forgotten the slaughterhouse that Europe had become in those years. That war had left Britain and her dominions with more than a million dead, and with a million of their women condemned, as a result, to live to the end of their days the sorrowing lives of unfulfilled widows. I myself, when I came to Europe in the bitter winter of 1928–9 with the world already in the rapidly tightening grip of a depression, found this aspect alone a terrible expression of the horror of the war in which perhaps Britain's most gifted and promising generation of young men were lost. I was so appalled by it all that I wrote a letter to *The Times*, saying that we should establish for those who wished it a legal form of bigamy, and even if necessary polygamy, while this sad vacuum in the life and spirit of the land existed. *The Times* returned the letter to me with disdain, unaccompanied even by the usual polite slip: 'The Editor regrets . . .'.

What added to the effects of the First World War on the spirit of Britain – and also that of France where the number of dead was even greater – was the fact that it was the last time war was seen by men as a romantic form of fulfilment of their manhood, not only because of the killing but also because of the terrible experience of witnessing and being part of such senseless destruction. One statistic alone expresses the horror of it: the average life of a subaltern after the moment of his arrival on the Western Front was four days. The anguish of the 1914–18 war was indeed so profound as to make tragic music in the hearts and minds of many gifted poets whose work was never to be equalled either in abundance or in quality by that that emerged from the Second World War.

For the professional soldiers who had been lucky enough to survive the First World War, it remained unforgettable. And its impact was all the more profound because, unlike in France and other countries, the British war effort for some two years or more was sustained entirely by volunteers (conscription came later under Lloyd George). Thus the British army fought its greatest war in history for some years entirely with men who had volunteered for action, with a small professional army. It was not surprising therefore that when the Second World War broke out, which as far as we in Britain were concerned was not a romantic war at all but rather a sort of world police action, it was reluctantly entered into and endured in the hope that some good would survive the onslaught of terrible evil.

Thus it was that the officers of the British army were to conduct the Second World War with the utmost concern for the lives of their men. As a result Britain's casualties in that war were less than half what they had been in the First World War, despite the fact that it lasted for some six years as opposed to four.

There was, too, something else in the British army which guided its conduct, a tradition which, I believe, goes back to King Arthur and his Knights. I was once asked, what is the myth of the British people? It is a question to which there is no quick answer, except that one can say it is the myth of the search for the Holy Grail, of Merlin, of Arthur and his Round Table, and its concept of recognizing for the first time the importance of the neglected feminine virtues of life, which made every knight serve a physical lady as a mirror of the feminine spirit which inspired him from within. It was present to such an extent in the spirit of Britain that the Knight, and all that went with the concept of the Knight, was never a class concept which only the aristocracy (and, increasingly, the gentry and middle classes) possessed; it was there, as Dickens so amply showed, deep in the heart of the working classes. The stories of

Dickens are full of working-class gentlemen. What else, for instance, could one call Mark Tapley of *Martin Chuzzlewit* but a gentle and parfit knight?

It was this spirit which so often characterized the officers of the British army. Take, for example, Wolfe of Quebec. It was he who in Canada one dark night crossed the St Lawrence River to scale the heights leading to the Plains of Abraham where, in the morning, he defeated the brave Montcalm and died, going to his death quoting perhaps the greatest elegy ever written in the English language:

> The boast of heraldry, the pomp of pow'r,
> And all that beauty, all that wealth e'er gave,
> Awaits alike th'inevitable hour,
> The paths of glory lead but to the grave.

And then, of course, most moving of all was the Duke of Wellington. It is strange that he should have earned the nickname of 'The Iron Duke' because he was one of the most caring and feeling of men. How could anyone doubt that, after what he wrote among the carnage after the Battle of Waterloo: 'Nothing except a battle lost can be half so melancholy as a battle won?'

But for me there is one story about Wellington that cannot be told often enough to convey the meaning of what I have been trying to say. After his recall from retirement to help out Britain at a time of social and political crisis, Wellington became Prime Minister, only at the end of it all to have Apsley House, his home overlooking Hyde Park, Green Park and the roofs of Charles I's Whitehall, surrounded by an angry mob jeering and howling their disapproval and threatening to stone the building.

He had lived with that atmosphere for some years when a deputation from the War Office called on him. They had come, they said, because at last they were making a much-needed effort to regularize the pay of the British private soldier. One of the things they were doing was to issue each man with a paybook in which his own personal dues could be recorded. They had brought a sample of the paybook to show him, and thought that to be more effective there should be a name inserted in the appropriate space on the front. They wondered if Wellington could suggest a typical soldier's name for them to use.

Wellington took the paybook and walked away, deep in thought, to the window overlooking the park. He stood there for a long time,

and when he turned to rejoin the War Office group they realized
he had been standing there to recover his composure, because
something had happened to bring tears to his eyes. He apologized
and explained that their request had recalled to him one of his
most critical battles against Napoleon's marshals. At one moment
in the battle, Wellington said, he noticed that one flank of his army
was in danger of being overwhelmed by an assault of cavalry. He
rushed forward with his ADC to see what action they should take.
When he came near he saw that a collection of British infantry,
apparently with all their officers dead, had been rallied by a wounded
private who was holding their position against a determined
onslaught of the French. They held it long enough for Wellington to
reinforce them and so prevent what could have been a fatal pene-
tration of his defences. The name of that private, Wellington told
them, was Tommy Atkins. Would they please put that on their
paybook.

The result was that from then until the Second World War, all over
the British Empire and wherever the British army was forced to fight,
British soldiers were known by friend and foe as 'Tommies', as
Kipling wrote:

> O it's Tommy this, an' Tommy that, an' 'Tommy, go away';
> But it's 'Thank you, Mister Atkins,' when the band begins to play –
> . . .
> Then it's Tommy this, an' Tommy that, an' 'Tommy, 'ow's yer soul?'
> But it's 'Thin red line of 'eroes' when the drums begin to roll –
> . . .

And what was true of the British army was also true of the
English-speaking world of America. I think, for instance, of the
American general sailing with his forces to slaughter and death on
the beaches of Omaha in Normandy, reciting the St Crispin's speech
from *Henry V* to his officers and men: they were all fortified in spirit
because it made them aware of a pattern in their life that was already
there, and that had been passed on so securely from the remote
history of Great Britain and the English-speaking peoples that
nothing could shift it.

So, in the opening years of the war, the disasters inflicted on the
French and British armies were not caused by their incompetence.
They were caused by the failure of their political masters and the
inadequate and reprehensible way in which they had conducted

what they euphemistically called peace. Had the Archangel Michael been in command of our armies at the outbreak of the war, starved as our soldiers were by our politicians and the indifference of our public, he would have done no better than our generals did.

Indeed, Britain had never begun a war without her soldiers lacking the numbers, the tools and the training they should have had to do their duty, and they had for years complained of their condition. As I now again became part of that army, coming out of nearly seven years of war, I was over and over again impressed with the quality I have tried to describe, not just among the officers, but also among the regular soldiers who had graduated in the terrible university of war.

And all that was good in the soldiers of Great Britain was made manifest in General Philip Christison, who now appeared in our midst. He was one of the finest generals of the Fourteenth Army. Well over six feet tall and broad-shouldered, his bearing matched his height. His face was always expressive and his eyes could often be described only by that terrible word, 'twinkling'. Spiritually, he matched his physique. When I saw him for the first time in *Cumberland*, sitting there calmly with young Telfer-Smollet, his ADC, on one side and the Admiral on the other, he seemed totally at ease – an ease which, I was to learn, had always become greater, the fiercer and more critical the battle in Burma. There he had had what was regarded as the most difficult of all commands, in a long campaign in the infested jungles, marshes and forests of the Arakan.

I stress this because it relates so clearly to the born soldier that he was, that made him leave the obvious humanities of medicine for a service to humanity much harder to understand. The pattern of the soldier in the spirit of man is a defence which mankind and its spirit need for their survival and well-being. However vital the caring values of the feminine aspect of human beings, the feminine will always need male armour to defend it against threats to real life. The pattern of the soldier is there because life demands it, and in the end life always knows best.

I have known an exceptional doctor, Michael Wood, a good friend and a natural healer who created the flying doctor service in Kenya. The legendary plastic surgeon Archibald McIndoe (whose services to the burnt and sadly maimed airmen and soldiers of the last war are forever remembered) was to say that Michael was the most inspired young surgeon he had ever met, because at the most critical, decisive moments in the most desperate operations, Michael confessed to an immense feeling of resolution and calm rising in his spirit, of a kind that McIndoe had never heard of in anyone else.

So what was the distance between the sense of resolution which accounted for Christie's ease in battle, and the spirit of the real doctor in him? Like all real soldiers (and I refer to the pattern of the soldier in all three services) he had another interest which he pursued as much as his career allowed. He loved birds. He studied and observed them and, before the war, had written some of the best books available on them. He was also by nature – not surprisingly with his sense of healing – a truly religious person.

His Corps, the 15 Indian Army Corps, was affectionately known to everybody as 'the fighting hockey sticks'. The nickname was derived from the fact that there were three Roman Vs on the flashes that the soldiers and officers wore on their jungle-green uniforms, arranged in such a manner that they crossed and looked like hockey-sticks rampant. No Corps in my experience had earned itself a better or more balanced reputation.

It was not surprising, therefore, that the warm humanity in the man that confronted me, like that of the Admiral, was immediately apparent and drew me to him. He had already told the Admiral, and now told me, that he could make no sense of the situation in Java from the confused and hurried information available at Lord Mountbatten's headquarters; so much so that after his meeting with Mountbatten, when he was abruptly told for the first time of his new command, he felt that he must come to Indonesia to see the Admiral and get to know the problem as the Admiral and his staff saw it.

He felt it to be all the more essential because Mountbatten had said to him: 'I am giving you this command with a warning that if you get yourself in trouble I shall not be able to help you. You will be out on your own, facing a problem and a scene that at the moment I cannot size up properly myself. If you make mistakes they will be your mistakes. You will have to be a soldier-statesman. But, I repeat, if you get into a mess you will have to carry the can.'

Repeating that phrase the General smiled at the recollection and said that he had replied: 'But, Supremo, that is not unusual. What have soldiers always been there for in history but to carry the can?'

From there he began a conference that was to last late into the night and was to be continued early the following morning. I have

only to add that before we got down to the real business of the day I
handed Christie a military appreciation of the situation and of how
I thought it should be handled. At the top of it I had written Foch's
maxim, which he had ordered all under his command to ask of
themselves and their actions: *'De quoi s'agit-'il?'* – 'What exactly do we
want to achieve?'

My report was written out in the form prescribed during the
month I had spent at staff college, and it ended with the conclusion
that we would need at least three military divisions to do what I imagined we would be called upon to do in Indonesia. Christie read it
through and then looked up at me with that slightly ironical expression I was to come to know well.

'Three divisions?' he asked. 'Is that all? Are you sure?'

'Yes, sir.'

He smiled. 'It is a strange coincidence, but that is all we're going
to get. That, and no more.'

I do not like referring to the problems I still had with my physical
condition and the effects of years in prison. I had a great deal to do
but nevertheless took only too eagerly to my bed. When the
Admiral's steward called me with a very large pot of tea and some
toast at dawn the next day I had some difficulty in getting dressed in
time for our breakfast meeting.

The Admiral said he and the General had continued talking after
I had left them the night before. The conference had confirmed the
conclusion they had already formed that the situation was not only
terribly confused, but would inevitably get more confused unless the
problems were tackled immediately. They had both agreed that I was
the only person who could clarify matters in the mind of the
Supremo. I was to leave immediately to meet him at his headquarters in Kandy after which, they were certain, he would insist on my
going on to see the War Cabinet in London, and possibly even The
Hague to address the obstinacy with which the Dutch were continuing to inflict pre-war values and considerations on Indonesia. For
unless our superiors in London and The Hague saw the problem
steadily and in the round, we would never get it right here in
Indonesia.

The General and the Admiral, between whom there had quickly
developed a rare understanding, each wrote on a piece of paper an
explanation of the purpose of my mission and gave me due authority, and these two pieces of paper became my only passport on the
journey ahead. I then hastened ashore to brief my growing staff and

to await the coming of the naval officer who was to take over in my absence.

I had made provisional arrangements to meet Sjahrir and Amir Sjarifoeddin, because I had become increasingly convinced that we must somehow keep in touch and get to know and understand what was valid and had to be recognized in this manifest and increasing phenomenon of Indonesian nationalism. I could not see us performing the intermediary role which had been so quickly and arbitrarily imposed on us unless we came to terms with the day-to-day and objective application of what the mission demanded. Now, however, I had no time to meet them and so I got in touch with a young Indonesian to whom I had had a fleeting introduction. He was Ali Boediardjo, a person of intellect and quality of spirit, from a deeply rooted and esteemed Indonesian family. I asked him to explain to Sjahrir how I had particularly wanted to call on him, not officially but in a personal capacity as a soldier with a special function. I was sorry, therefore, to have to inform him that I was leaving that day on an important mission to our Supreme Commander that could take me to London and even to The Hague, but that I would not forget our first meeting. Wherever I went I would try to do what I could to make our presence in Java as creative an element as possible, and I hoped that he and all the people he knew would do the same.

My packing took a matter of minutes. Looking back I have often thought that I was at that moment rather like the Bushmen I was to know in the vast deserts of Africa, who had little of material possessions. One day I had said to them: 'If I asked you at this moment to accompany me on a long journey, how long would it take you to get ready?'

They looked at me and with a smile said: 'Would you like us to show you?' They were very fond of make-believe. I said I would be pleased if they would show me. I timed them on my watch and they were ready for the journey within three minutes.

I did not time my own packing, but everything went into one haversack. I was still wearing the best of my two uniforms, which was of course the khaki one I had worn with the Eighth Army in the Western Desert. In addition I had only my second-best, my rather crumpled khaki hat, and something the Admiral had given me before I left – an army greatcoat, which someone had left behind in the ship. He said they could not possibly let their one and only Pongo – the naval slang for a soldier – face the cold of England after so many years in the tropics without the required wrapping. I had never heard an army greatcoat, or any other kind of coat, described as 'wrapping', but it sounded infinitely more impressive than any other description could have done.

So at three that afternoon I boarded a Mitchell bomber provided by the Dutch. It was fast but small, with room for only one passenger and its crew of three. The Dutch Lieutenant-Colonel Asjes, who flew the aircraft to Singapore, landed us all there with impressive precision and ease, but during the whole flight we had only a brief, shouted exchange of essential information. It could have been that the noise of the engines made conversation impossible, but strangely I had a feeling that that was not the whole reason and that it was already perhaps one of those trivial things that forecast the shadow to come.

I had not seen Singapore since 1926. From the air the development and spread of the settlement on the island was almost overwhelming. It was a grey evening, not clouded but truly grey in almost a European way, and the place looked lifeless and unwelcoming. The traffic to the airport, such as it was, had already ceased, and as soon as we landed I made for the transport officer's station, which Lieutenant-Colonel Asjes pointed out to me.

I arrived there as the airport commander, a young RAF officer, was closing up for the night. I showed him my two written authorities with their emphasis that, whatever the circumstances and demands on transport, I was to have the utmost priority. He looked at them again and again, scratched his head and then, rather ruefully but pleasantly, said to me: 'You really have brought me a problem. I will have to get you out in the first aircraft tomorrow, at first light. But,' and he thought about the problem, 'have any arrangements been made for you to stay somewhere tonight? I've had no instructions. Singapore is full to bursting. I would take you to my own mess but it's already over-full. What the devil are we to do?'

I asked him if there was a cloakroom in his office, and a washbasin where I could shave in the morning. There was, of course, but he apologized that there were no facilities even to make a cup of tea, and only his own jug of drinking water. I told him he need not worry; if he agreed, I would bed down in his office for the night and be ready to leave first thing in the morning. I did not bother to tell him how his office, after my years in prison, seemed almost like a little bit of heaven to me, and that going without food, not just for hours but for more than a day, would be no problem after my prison training.

I had a good night, and early in the morning he was back and put me on an aircraft full of senior officers on their way to Ceylon. We landed in the evening, after a long, long flight over the Bay of Bengal. This time the transport office had received warning of my coming. I was asked to go to the Colombo NAAFI for refreshments. From there I would be taken to a 'plane that would fly me to the Supreme Commander's headquarters in Kandy, which I had also last seen in 1926 as a picturesque and most becoming hill-station for well-to-do tea planters and colonial officials.

I was almost overcome by what the NAAFI had to offer, dazed by its abundance and by the smart ATS in crisp tropical uniforms serving all ranks of the services. There were the most seductive smells of food cooking; of bacon, of coffee, of all the things that had been denied to us and we had dreamed about for so long in prison. I immediately ordered what I have always loved, a plate of bacon and eggs, loads of toast and marmalade, and a pot of coffee and hot milk. I was really hungry and have never enjoyed anything more.

Then, as the time for me to go drew near, I got up with my haversack and was on the point of leaving when an ATS stopped me. 'I am sorry to trouble you, sir. Here is your bill.'

I looked at her in amazement, and exclaimed: 'My God, do you still use money?'

In all our years in prison what money there was was shared by all, and we never thought of it as anything important, just as something that came and went, in and out of a common pool. The whole concept of a world in which people were still individually paid, and had the right to demand payment, had died in me, so that when I exclaimed as I did, it was not only because I was taken by surprise but because I was also filled with a sense of horror that what money represented was still around.

I did not know what to do, until I saw next to my table a group of officers having something like a Devonshire afternoon tea. I had been aware of them, on and off, watching me. I went over to them and explained: 'Forgive me, I've just come from Java and have no money to pay my bill. I wonder if one of you would be good enough to pay it for me? I promise you that in return, if you give me your address, when I finally get back to London I'll take you to dinner at Claridges.'

One of the officers immediately exclaimed: 'Delighted, old boy, delighted!'

As a result, nearly three years later, I took him to Claridges and we dined in splendour together.

With that heart-warming introduction to the world of the services in Ceylon I flew to Kandy, found a car waiting for me at the airport and was driven straight to see Lord Mountbatten.

CHAPTER FOUR

Mountbatten

THE AIR OF the early evening in Kandy was a singular joy to senses like mine, after years of being weighed upon by the heavy equatorial atmosphere of Java. One often thinks of air that is good in terms of wine, which is such a profound symbol in nature and in terms of human sensations, and it held good for this evening. The air was like a light and subtle cool white wine, not lucid as it tends to be in hilly places, but of the transparency of fine smoked glass which, since it was already dewfall, held a distinct fragrance of plants and grasses and other delights of a rich and abundant nature. And over all, there was an immense calm.

When one pictures how that part of the world looks on maps, one has an impression of the vast land mass of India from the Himalayas leading southwards to the Equator, and narrowing to a point which looks almost as if geologically India wants to penetrate the heart of Ceylon. Yet there was nothing at all of the Hindu in that calm; there was nothing of the charged atmosphere of Java, in which I had now lived for more than four years. The calm was the calm of Buddha and not of pagan gods, and one understood just from the atmosphere that evening why Ceylon was still a country of Buddha, whereas the India that gave him birth had already lost that calm more than a thousand years before.

I was taken to walk through the surroundings of Lord Mountbatten's headquarters, and as I walked the calm was also within me. Only a few weeks before one might have thought of Kipling's lines:

Never the lotus closes,
Never the wild fowl awake
But a soul goes out on the night wind,
That died for England's sake.

The dying was, of course, not the dying in bed but on active service, and for the moment, thank God, that kind of dying had come to an end. Instead there was this moment, not of lotus closing and wild fowl awakening, but of the lotuses drawing through their mysterious roots the essences which would make them open with a sigh at midnight. Not only the fowl but all the birds had abandoned their bright song and were settling down for their rest; the water birds were standing each on one leg in the quicksilver unrippled reflections around them and going to sleep, and the singing of the birds diminished to a musical gurgle as they pressed deeper and deeper into their nests.

And then there was Mountbatten. I had not met him but of course knew a great deal about him. I knew not only of his remarkable record of courage and ability in war, of the powers of command which enabled him to direct the British forces and their impressive Indian support on land, sea and air, and in the calm of victory we now enjoyed, but also of him from civilian intimates, in particular the admiration which Paul Robeson and his wife Essie had for him and Lady Mountbatten. The Robesons' relationship with the Mountbattens, indeed, had become at one time a matter of scandalous and irresponsible talk, and exercised to the full the always-active gossip-mongers who were to be found at El Vino's and other bars in Fleet Street, and who tended to make what had been once regarded as 'the street of adventure' a street of diminishing journalistic worth. In the end, when the gossip was riding high, wide and ugly, Queen Mary in her indomitable way decided to put a stop to it and let it be known that she had invited the Mountbattens to lunch with her and the King. Here I had some connection, in the sense that Paul Robeson and Essie were in the circle of friends I had made in London: the memory of the warmth with which Paul had spoken of Mountbatten was with me as I made my way towards his office.

Mountbatten, at that moment when I was to see him face to face for the first time, was perhaps at the height of his many-sided spirit. Physically he was, of course, incredibly handsome, handsome in a way which was illuminated by the feeling that came from him of boundless vitality and energies demanding instant expression and, as so often in great men, a keen sense of theatre. In his presence, even when nothing was said, as one looked at him one thought of the most contemporary of images; of a car with the engine already tuned and humming, quietly ready to take him swiftly off into another dimension of action. With it all I knew already that he had a special feeling for the underdogs and the rejected in life. I think part of the attraction of the Robesons for him was in their blackness and in the sense that they were ambassadors of the rejected black masses of the world. All his intuitions tended to make him radical and look to the left rather than to the right in politics, and made what I had to say somewhat easier.

I entered his room and immediately, as we did in the army, stood to attention; but already he was out of his seat and, with his hand outstretched, he came to meet me. Outwardly everything about him was immaculate. There was no need for the housewives of the spirit with their critical and moralistic brooms to go behind his footsteps and mop where his spirit had trod. Whether right or wrong, his spirit was polished, swift and clean. And as we talked I became increasingly aware that he had the same sort of understanding of the basic cultural and political differences between the Dutch and the Indonesians as the Admiral had inherited from all that was Irish in his ancestry. It was not altogether surprising because I knew that even before the war Mountbatten had been politically interested in all matters concerning India, and possessed a touch of the radicalism that already made him suspect to Conservatives, some even accusing him of being at heart pro-Labour in his politics.

Any account in detail of what I had to tell him would be repetitive. What was most important was the conclusion to which it led. He was aware of the importance of the national spirit that was increasingly awake and up and doing among the Indonesians. He grasped fully the importance of the point that the Dutch approach would be doomed if they did not recognize the validity of such a natural phenomenon. He understood how that natural spirit must have been encouraged by the fact that the Dutch had failed in their elementary duty of protecting the country from the Japanese invasion. The Indonesians had not witnessed the gallant contribution made by the Dutch at sea and in the air; they only saw how the armies that had been gathered, presumably in their defence, had surrendered with barely more than a perfunctory skirmish within a week of the Japanese landings. The Dutch Commander-in-Chief had already been captured before the surrender by some Japanese soldiers on bicycles, who had found their way into his headquarters. Almost overnight the whole of European Java abandoned their uniforms and rifles and, under the Japanese, resumed their previous occupations.

I said to Mountbatten that I, for one, had never held it against the Dutch that they had surrendered in this manner. They had their women and children with them, and if they had really gone into battle in any determined and protracted way, with Indonesia already reduced to a mere sideshow in the rapidly expanding theatre of operations against the Japanese, they would not only have done nothing of real value to the war effort but they would have ensured, I believe, the massacre of the civilian population. I say that because the Japanese army, in those early, heady days after the attack on Pearl Harbor, was dominated by the spirit of the men who had not only perpetrated that infamy but had also condoned the infamous massacre of the Chinese civilian population at Nanking.

The point, however, was that the Indonesians, who knew none of these things, simply saw in their masters' surrender a shameful and degrading spectacle. All this made what was happening in Indonesia finally irresistible, and the sooner it was recognized the better.

When I told Mountbatten all this and of my own experience of the Japanese pattern even before the war, he said that it made complete sense to him. I begged him to urge the British government to be aware of our problem in communications, and not to accept the Dutch version of anything happening in Java until they had heard our own account of it. In addition to the restricted way in which we had to communicate, the Dutch were in any case always ahead of us thanks to their new Philips radio.

In time, he said, that would be put right, but obviously we could have no idea of the pressure not only on his systems of communication but also on those of the rest of the world, which were hard put in any case to serve the military as it needed to be served, and to deal with the sudden call from the democracies for immediate demobilization, to bring back to their homes millions of Americans and hundreds of thousands of Britons after nearly seven years of war.

'However,' he said as he got up from his chair with one of his rare smiles, 'no amount of signalling could possibly have been a substitute for these hours we have talked together. I have a lot to re-think tonight, and we shall meet again in the morning to talk further. But it is quite clear to me that there is some very hard and clear thinking to be done in London, and above all in The Hague, otherwise we shall never get your problem straight. It is urgent. Do not hesitate to talk to them in London as you have talked to me. Take your time. I am certain we will get a good hearing in London. The problem will be what London can do about The Hague.'

I went to an early rest in a most comfortable bed, reassured to a degree that I had not been before.

The meeting the next morning was short, practical and fitted to all the weight of responsibility that Mountbatten had to discharge in the course of a single day. He had already given instructions to his staff to get me to London as soon as possible. He wanted me to report to the War Cabinet, and particularly to the Prime Minister, for whom he appeared to have a high regard. Yet he qualified this with a request which was something of a pointer to the future. He wanted me, before I saw anybody else, to go and see Stafford Cripps, who was at the Board of Trade – an office apparently remote from what were our most pressing affairs – and be guided by him.

Stafford Cripps had already, before the war, been one of the foremost members of the socialist movement urging the British government to grant complete independence to India. He was a Quaker in spirit, as everybody knew, and was regarded as a person of the highest integrity. Knowledge of this made me even more certain that our Indonesian problem would not be seen in a slanted way.

Mountbatten also told me that his Director of Military Intelligence, General Penney, had already preceded me to London and should by now have seen Stafford Cripps. He would see to it that the War Cabinet put me immediately in contact with General Penney. I then left Mountbatten and went to spend some hours with General Slim.

Behind the Fourteenth Army, shining like a polar star, lay Slim's spirit which had turned the Battle of Kohima into one of the bravest and most sustained battles ever fought. An outstanding commander, his person in every way matched his reputation. He was one of the most impressive of all the soldiers I met in the course of the war. For Slim had qualities of background and spirit which, great as other war leaders were, he shared only with Wavell.

Often at night I see a roll-call in my spirit and a parade of chivalry, in command of which is Archie Wavell. He and Auchinleck are two of the outstanding soldiers who never wrote their own biographies.

Theirs were written by others who admired them, but none of them, I feel, did justice to the inner quality they possessed and on which their impact on historic events ultimately depended.

Wavell, even earlier than Slim, had demonstrated his own love of writing and of literature with his book on Allenby and with an anthology of verse, *Other Men's Flowers*, which to this day remains a favourite. From the beginning he had had to take the onslaught on all fronts in Africa and in Greece of the Axis forces launched against the British who, good as they were, were outnumbered and unprepared, and almost entirely without the aircraft that were to play so vital a role in the war. At the same time he had to show statesman-like qualities and, although he may have been completely inexperienced in that role, he acquitted himself as well as he did as a soldier.

Auchinleck, who came after him ('The Auk', as he was called), was in many ways the most knightly of them all. There is no room in the sweep of the story I am telling to describe in detail all that I felt about him. I would just like to mention one tiny incident which illustrates the striking quality of the man within the soldier. In *A Passage to India*, written in the 1920s, E.M. Forster remarks somewhere that, of all the people he had met in India, he was particularly impressed by a young officer on the Viceroy's staff, a certain Major Auchinleck.

And then there were all the others leading on to Christie: Mountbatten; the young David Stirling (a close friend who was to create the SAS, and became my ally in the battle against racialism in Africa); and that ill-fated and strange genius Orde Wingate, whom I knew well in Abyssinia. They are an impressive parade in memory; and always they stand there, vivid and alive, with the refrain of Guillaume Apollinaire, the poet who himself died in the course of the 1914–18 war, echoing in my mind:

> Où s'ont-ils ces beaux militaires,
> Soldats passés? Où sont les guerres,
> Où les guerres d'autrefois?

But to return to Bill Slim. As all who served with him and under him will remember, he had a measure of greatness which proved itself in his staff, a staff always totally loyal and never subject to the politicking and the jealousies that would break out, Iago-like, in the midst of the horrors of war at the highest levels of command. He was free of it all, as Wavell was; and he was, like Wavell, one of the best-read men I have known. His reading, particularly of history, and the history of the Commonwealth, was profound. Like Wavell too, he was himself an accomplished writer, and his book on his 'Forgotten Army' is one of the classics of war and inspiring reading to this day. He started out as a schoolmaster and then discovered his own gift for war. He understood the social and spiritual implications of what justified war, and also what would be demanded of soldiers in times of peace. As a result he was deeply concerned about the future of the British Commonwealth.

He was of course intensely human. He was also the one general who broke the precept of high command in war that commanders-in-chief are too precious to risk being killed in battle themselves. The Fourteenth Army was full of stories of how often he had disregarded it and of how, even in the closing days of the campaign in Burma, he had led a company of Gurkhas in a bayonet charge against the Japanese. It was no wonder that the Gurkhas not only admired him but had something almost religious in their judgement of him.

I left him with my own sense of history immensely enriched and also with an increasing realization that I was not merely engaged in passing on intelligence that in a military and political sense was indispensable, but that this intelligence could not be properly evaluated unless its roots in history were known, and that therefore I would continue to be engaged in re-educating the men in power I was to meet, not least the Dutch. And thereby, I knew, hung a difficulty, because the Dutch themselves were inclined to be blind to the history of their own making and had, in regard to Indonesia, eyes that would not see and ears that would not hear.

I spent the rest of the day in getting four proper jungle-green uniforms, proper shoes, a new hat and also a battledress against the cold expected in England – in fact a decent travelling wardrobe. Most important of all, I acquired an identity card as an officer of the Indian Army (to which I was now transferred and in which I was immediately given a regular commission) complete with photograph. This latter was not like passport versions but was something far more disturbing, for the face on it seemed to me the face almost of a stranger, still only its partially redeemed prison self.

So I left that evening for England, and had several days of flying and nights at places like Bahrain, Alexandria and somewhere in the Bouches du Rhône in France, on the way to my destination at Lyneham, in Wiltshire. Those days in the air were very precious to me. Because the roar of the engines of the unpressurized bomber was too loud for conversation with the other passengers, I could just sit back and let all the events that were essential to me come at me of their own accord. I had a tremendous feeling of certainty that I could do whatever I had to do successfully, although at the same time I did not know what that would be. I felt very much like the British soldiers who sang: 'We don't know where we're going, but we're on our way . . .'.

There was a moment during this journey when I felt that if only I could be in total command of what was to come it would be more effective than having to pass on all that I knew and foresaw to others who did not have my background and knowledge. Mercifully I soon recognized this fantasy for what it was. I had not been bad at small, independent commands, but I lacked all the special qualities of administration, and attention to everyday detail, and so many other things which would be essential for the proper exercise of such an exalted function. I was lucky enough always to be contained in a framework of soldiering where I could get on and live according to my given nature.

With that sort of sense I landed at Lyneham one early afternoon in late September, the month in which, way back in 1939, the war had begun for me. It was an afternoon not quite as bright as that first September day of war, but as calm, and as resolved. There was a car waiting for me, and I drove up to London through what Blake called 'England's green and pleasant land'. I was in a War Cabinet office in time for tea and toast, and thought it one of the most wonderful rituals ever invented.

I just had a moment to call the mother of Ingaret Giffard, whom I one day hoped to marry. She nearly fainted with shock at hearing my voice confirm that I was not dead as reported but alive and well. I asked her to arrange for Ingaret, who was somewhere in the country, to meet me at her home at 13 Cadogan Street, in Chelsea, sometime that evening.

And so to the Board of Trade.

CHAPTER FIVE

London

No ONE I KNEW ever questioned Stafford Cripps's integrity; but there was an implication that many, even intimate acquaintances of his, thought him somewhat aloof and cold and perhaps slightly inhuman. On the whole I had an unconditioned preconception of him. I had different views about the Commonwealth, and I think even different assumptions about certain basic values of life, but in so far as I had a tendency it was one of respect. Yet when I met him I felt none of these simplified things. Rather I felt him to be of the breed, though by no means the sweep, of South Africa's beloved 'Oom Jannie', Jan Smuts, who even in our own country was thought of as rather cold – people did not know of the fierce and incorruptible love of which, in all he did, he was almost a victim.

Like Smuts, Stafford Cripps's great gift was the power of reason and of the mind. But all those who thought he could be left there on some Everest of the human spirit I knew to be wrong, because I was immediately impressed with the kind of paradox which Dante resolves at the end of his *Divine Comedy* in the abiding statement that, with intellect and feeling joined, he found 'the love that moves the sun and the other stars'. As in Smuts, this love was something not worn on the sleeve but expressed in the thought, and above all the forethought, which he hastened to give to men and their urgent causes in life.

Of course I liked Cripps immediately, and I was very moved by the hearing he gave me on all that concerned Indonesia, because he asked questions that prompted me to say more than I had been able to tell most of the people I had met before. At the end he said it was obvious that I had to see the Prime Minister as soon as possible, and that he would arrange for the secretariat of the War Cabinet to make an appointment for me. Would I please hold myself ready for that and nothing else, because it would be at short notice.

I was not to see him again for some two years but I should say, on the question of his integrity, that when as Chancellor of the Exchequer he had to say on a Friday, in answer to the press, that the pound would not be devalued even though he knew he would have to announce devaluation on the Monday, it explained fully to me the illness which overtook him soon afterwards and caused him to die, I believe, before his time.

The call from the Prime Minister came early the next afternoon. I had been occupied seeing various people I had to meet, indeed more now than anticipated because, some two days before I arrived, General Penney had been taken off to the Royal Masonic Hospital with acute hepatitis. I had to take over his immediate duties as well, and had chosen to do so at the Cabinet offices in order to be ready for the Prime Minister's call. While I waited for him in his private office at Westminster, in the Houses of Parliament, his Parliamentary Private Secretary was almost on fire with enthusiasm. The Labour Party's sweeping election victory over the Conservatives under Churchill had inspired him and his colleagues with optimism, and he talked of all the reforms they were going to bring about, not just in Britain and the Commonwealth but throughout the world, and in all of life. This was all most informative and agreeable to me, because in my own way I too was full of new hope for the future.

Clement Attlee was small in stature and slight in frame. Nothing about him, neither his dress nor his outward appearance, would have made one turn and look at him as he walked in the streets of London. The truth, I was to find, was different, as I came to realize what a truly impressive spirit he was. There was in him a certain decisiveness, a feeling of authority that seemed military and showed how near, always, was the Major Attlee he had been. After the briefest forms of welcome he sat down in a comfortable office armchair and, although I can hardly believe my memory, it was as if in the process he drew up his knees and curled up in his chair, rather like a young person about to be told a stirring tale. Then there came a crisp, almost whispered: 'Well, Colonel. Tell me.'

I had been warned that he had very little time, but he listened to the end without any interruption and without the slightest lessening of his attention, conveying an increasing feeling of renewed interest and something of urgent importance for him to decide. I was to discover more and more that he had a gift almost amounting to genius for listening with all of himself to those who had something to say.

At the end he said to me: 'Thank you very much. I find what you have told me of great importance, and I think it of even greater importance that you should go to The Hague and tell all this to the Dutch. Take whatever time you need to tell them all you feel they should know.'

He turned to his Parliamentary Private Secretary and said: 'Will you make arrangements for this officer to go to The Hague at once? Inform our Ambassador of the importance I attach to his mission. Indeed, I will give you a personal note for this officer to take with him.'

He then turned back to me: 'Will you please come and report to me at once on your return? Thank you again.'

With that he uncurled himself, as it were, and nimbly left the room through a door, back, I assumed, to the House of Commons.

So the next day I found myself once more at the civilian airport of London, teeming with human beings, mostly in uniform, and in a state of 'organized chaos'. Again, with what was little more than another slip of paper, I got through the security screens on to an aircraft and very soon was in The Hague, being met by the British Chargé d'Affaires. From there I was taken off to the Embassy, and straight into the drawing-room where the Ambassador and his wife, Nevile and Portia Bland, were waiting for me. Without these two exceptionally kind people I would not have had the strength to carry on doing all that I still had to do, for I was far from recovered from the consequences of imprisonment under the Japanese. Somewhere else, one day, I will say more about Nevile and Portia and all they did for me in a personal way, but they saw to it that I had a quiet lunch and an afternoon of rest, and in the evening escorted me to the hotel restaurant Les Vieux Doelens.

I think the whole of the Dutch Cabinet, headed by the Prime Minister, Professor Schermerhorn, sat down with me at a large oval table for dinner that night at Les Vieux Doelens. I knew only one of the people there – Jonkherr van Kleffens, who was I believe the one and only aristocrat amongst them. I had met him very briefly in December 1939 when I went on a short mission to the Netherlands on behalf of our Foreign Office, and was welcomed by the Dutch High Command. He was still there, in his capacity as Secretary of

State for Foreign Affairs. I had liked him then and liked him now, though I was never to know him well because he was, in a way, a personality apart: he had a knowledge of the wide world and its history, and an extensive and uncommon experience of international affairs (which all the others lacked), for which the only word is 'sophistication'.

All the others were men of the people, in the best sense; men who had behaved with dignity and who had been the keepers of what was best in the Dutch spirit during the monstrous years of the Nazi occupation. First among them was the Prime Minister. I did not know what the verdict of his countrymen was going to be regarding him in the years that followed, I only knew that he seemed to me a remarkable and quietly impressive human being. I remember, too, Professor Logemann, who had the affairs of the empire, particularly Indonesia, in his keeping. He and I had a common idiom, for he had spent a year or two in the university town of Stellenbosch, near Cape Town, and had liked it enormously.

As I sat with them there, a kind of sadness came over me that they, and what they represented of Holland, had never been experienced by their colonies. The Indonesians, including the Dutch-born Indonesians, had known only that side of the Dutch character that the chartered company had chosen to show, and that, as I have indicated, was not only inadequate but at times utterly reprehensible.

That evening also gave me an illustration of what Dr van Mook, the Governor-General designate of Indonesia, whose name had just appeared in urgent telegrams from Mountbatten in Java, was to suffer from, among other problems. He had no roots in the Holland that these men represented, and so never had in The Hague anyone who gave him a chance, because there was always in these men a certain imperviousness which was not really to the credit of the Holland they represented. Their tendency was to dismiss van Mook, particularly because of the role he had played as a young man in the affair of the '*Stuw*' (the 'Thrust'), the progressive and rather militant Indonesian-born European movement for greater participation in their government.

But however important all this became to an understanding of our problems later on, it was held in abeyance that evening. After a moving Grace said by the Prime Minister, there started an extremely active dialogue between him and me. For my part I had barely finished the first course when to my horror, at the moment when I most needed the part of me which spoke fluent High Dutch, I felt that something that had already happened to me before (hitherto, thank God, in private) was now in danger of happening in public – my stomach, after so many years of malnourishment, was about to begin a bout of hiccups. My body, long after it had ceased to be the ghost represented on my identity card, would often rebel at being taken for granted as if those three and a half years in prison had never been. On this occasion the spasm refused to be just a spasm, and it lasted into the early hours of the morning when we finished, and sent me exhausted to my bed in the Embassy.

It could not have happened at a more difficult moment because, however fluent I was in Dutch, I had never yet in my life had to speak it for so long and never on what was truly an historic occasion. I explained and apologized to the Prime Minister, and it was a measure of his humanity and quality that I was listened to, and allowed to explain myself, with a show of concern, patience and forbearance. I cannot, even in retrospect, recall a single sign of irritability; it was simply not there, and everyone helped me to say what I had to say.

As I spoke it became clear that they had been subjected to the influence of their advance reconnaissance party in Java under Mr van der Plas. This was, of course, fundamentally a reflection of their innocence and, in a sense, their ignorance of history. They had a picture in their minds of a scorched-earth Java, of a land – after gallant resistance and protracted guerrilla activities – ravished and laid waste, bridges blown, power stations and factories destroyed, and all the plantations, to which the prosperity of Holland owed so much, neglected and run to seed. They listened to me with astonishment when I told them that not a bridge had been blown, not a power station or factory destroyed. No plantation had gone to seed and even the railways were running comparatively well.

To spare their feelings I did not emphasize the fact that there had never been any real fighting on land, and that even the gallant battle fought to let well-organized Dutch forces on the coast withdraw from the Japanese and move into the fortress of Bandoeng had been fought by an Australian brigade under the command of Brigadier Blackburn. I had no desire to emphasize this and, as I have already said, I in any case believed it was a mercy that Dutch resistance had not been greater because, if it had been, the Dutch population of Java would probably have been utterly destroyed.

As the evening went on, the prospect of an almost immediate resumption of the economy in Indonesia was obvious on all their faces. But what was alarming was that already, after weeks in Indonesia, the increasing Dutch presence in Java had not resulted in any warning of the growing rebellion. In so far as they knew about it, it was still thought to be something artificially inseminated by the Japanese. They believed that once the Japanese had gone everything could be picked up where the war had left it and that, perhaps after some show of force, all would be well and continue as before.

At one moment I was so taken aback by the absence of a really up-to-date report of the situation in Java that, in the midst of my stomach's loudest eruption, I was forced to exclaim: 'But have you not read Colonel Abdul Kadir Widjojoatmodjo's report?'

They had not only not read it but wanted to know who this ''Dul' was, and I was very nearly reduced to despair at the vacuum which I, in a quick visit, had somehow to try to fill.

Indonesian nationalism, and my plea that it should be recognized, was discussed at length, but I felt that they were obstinately predisposed to reject it. They all referred to Queen Wilhelmina's famous broadcast of 1942, which had figured so much in wartime propaganda, particularly after the Japanese surrender. Without going into the detail of this broadcast, it had suggested some improvement in the very strict hold that the Dutch had kept on truly contemporary reforms of the structure of local government. Compared to what had gone before, it had some substance, but to me it seemed, however welcome, so far from what was needed as to be almost purely cosmetic. Of course it was not something to be disregarded but, as I said over and over again, the concessions it made to Indonesian aspirations of self-government were cosmetic rather than real, and I did not think they would be adequate for the current situation, particularly in the context of a world where even Great Britain was going to launch a process of independence for one and all in their empire; a winding-up of what had been the largest, the greatest and, I still believe, the best-organized and most civilized empire in the history of the world.

In all senses the evening was of real importance, above all because it was to start a continuing dialogue among them about the future. What struck me then, however, and was to strike me increasingly as evidence unfolded in the course of ridding Indonesia of the Japanese, was how exaggerated had been the view which held the Dutch empire up as the finest model of empire. There is no doubt that the Dutch empire, by the outbreak of the Second World War, had achieved many things for Indonesia which it could not have achieved on its own, but at the same time it had denied the rights of the peoples of Indonesia in a way which the outside world never suspected.

Looking back on that evening, I think it was one of the most important occasions in that process of re-education which alone could succeed in preventing an outbreak of civil war and finally the destruction of the Dutch empire. I was still full of hope that this could be done. I had no idea at that moment of the speed with which the nationalist movement was being orchestrated, militarily and violently, in Indonesia. I believe I left a sense of hope, and even my own measure of optimism, in the minds of the Dutch Cabinet, and also a sense of how my optimism was utterly dependent on their responding with speed and grace in recognizing what was valid in Indonesia.

The next day I had a long session alone with Professor Logemann, and indeed, in the week I spent in The Hague, saw more and more of him. On one occasion he showed me a summary of a conversation he had had – for the first time by radio – with Dr van Mook. It consisted of a list of grievances against Admiral Patterson and General Christison, and was a rehearsal of Mr van der Plas's observations. Suddenly all my doubts were reinforced.

I protested immediately and asked why Dr van Mook had not sorted out these grievances direct with General Christison, who had the power to address them then and there in Batavia, without spreading them all around The Hague, and from there to London. I spoke strongly about the duty of everyone in Java to do all they could to deal with events on the spot; only if they could not should they call in Lord Mountbatten; and only if he was incapable of dealing with the problem should they appeal to the government in London. The British had every right, in this role which had been thrust upon them so abruptly, to expect something similar from the representatives of The Hague in Indonesia. Professor Logemann saw the point and took it with grace.

There followed meetings of all kinds and, as the days went on, there arose a general feeling in the Dutch government and among everybody I had seen that I, as a staff officer of Mountbatten's fresh from the field, should deliver a radio broadcast to the Dutch people. Without entering into the political implications, I should give them a picture of a Java unscorched and even more ready than the Netherlands to resume its role in the economy of the world.

One evening I spoke to a packed meeting at a kind of glorified chamber of commerce, crowded with men representing all the vested interests the Dutch had in Java. The meeting was in one way more informed than the government, and already much more critical and suspicious of the British presence in Java. I had to answer what I thought were almost offensive judgements in that regard. But on the whole the meeting passed very well and, after hours of discussion between us, the chairman of the occasion, thanking me, also thanked the British, though he suggested that the affairs of Java could no longer be left in the hands of amateurs (which I took to mean the British) but should be restored to professionals like themselves.

In due course I did make a broadcast in Dutch to the Dutch people. I have no record of it, but I do know that not only did my Ambassador and Ted Lambert, his Chargé d'Affaires, think it 'tremendous' but that even the most vested interests in the country seemed to give it a cheer. However, while making the broadcast I noticed something that revealed the bitter deprivation to which Holland had been subjected under Nazi rule. The equipment in the studio was outworn, and the recording which was played back to me squeaked like a ship caught in a storm – this in one of the most radio-conscious countries in the world. It showed how far Europe still had to go on the road to recovery, and made me thank God every night when I went to bed for General Marshall, who I believe to this day was one of the most enlightened statesmen Europe has ever seen. His plan (generally known as Marshall Aid) to help put even the defeated countries of Europe on the road to full economic rehabilitation, was, as Churchill said, 'the greatest single act of magnanimity in the history of statesmanship'.

I also had a meeting with a group of Dutch resistance men, the majority of them in their early thirties, and a most moving discussion about how they hoped their country would develop after the horrors of war. Unlike the meetings I had where most people seemed already well on their way to recovering their round physical selves, these men were spare in feature, their faces finely drawn, and with a look in their eyes of suffering nobly endured which I have never forgotten.

There was also evidence of how the shadow of war still lay over Europe. Holland was full of Canadian soldiers. I remember one evening of tremendous pleasure when I went with the British Ambassador and his staff to an ice hockey tournament and how the Ambassador, when he was recognized as the Ambassador of Britain, was given a prolonged cheer.

But my mission was taking too long, far longer than I had

expected, and I felt that I must get back to Christie and my Admiral as soon as possible because the sense of escalation in the problems in Indonesia frightened me. I had already spent more than a week in Holland alone. It had, however, been necessary, in that there was a kind of historic imperviousness in the Netherlands which was going to get in the way of a solution to the situation. To sum it up simply, the people of the establishment in Holland, members of the government and of the powerful commercial establishments, had never really seen the Indonesians for the remarkable people they were. On one occasion, discussing the phenomenon of nationalism with Professor Logemann, he confessed he simply could not believe the phenomenon was real, considering all the wonderful things that the Dutch had done for the Indonesians since they first occupied Java at the beginning of the seventeenth century.

I said to him, speaking as one who had been born in a British colony and in the context of empire, that I believed there came a moment when colonial subjects, no matter how beneficial their subjection, found that colonialism was not good enough for them. It could seem unfair, it could seem all sorts of other things, but there was an imponderable longing for their own identity which was unrecognized in the assumptions and hypotheses on which colonialism was based. The time it took to show itself was not important. I had friends who, on the first night of their marriage, knew that the marriage was wrong and yet only divorced each other thirty years later.

And then there was the sort of thing which Idenburg said. One of van Mook's intimate advisers, he was the son of the great Idenburg whose name, in recognition of his services, was bestowed on one of the highest mountain ranges in New Guinea, the Idenburg Range. He argued that the mistake we British always made, and that I was making in regard to Java, was to weigh the Dutch and the Oriental in the same scale, and that that was unfair and unequal. I told him there was no such thing as an Oriental mind. It was an abstraction and did not apply to living cultures at all. You could perhaps speak of a 'Western spirit', but if you looked at Asia from Mont Blanc there was no common 'Oriental spirit'. There were the Arabian countries and their diaspora in North Africa; there was the Iranian civilization; there was India, whose people were, like ourselves, a Sanskrit people, although implanted in an Asian context (even China had no influence on India); there was the very great civilization of China itself; there was Japan, and so on. They all had their own states of mind. Idenburg's argument seemed a frightening indication of the Dutch lack of awareness towards not only the indigenous peoples of Indonesia but all the diverse cultures of Asia, and it showed how, in four hundred years or more of continuous and on the whole decent rule, the Dutch did not have the right look in their eye when they spoke to the Indonesians. That could now be their undoing.

When I finally arrived back in London the omens hardly seemed auspicious. First of all I was subjected to a tremendous security check. The moment I stepped out of the aircraft two warrant officers who were examining the list of passengers looked at one another, came over and asked me to follow them because the transport officer had particularly instructed them to bring me to him. I found the transport officer not in battledress but in formal officer's uniform, his Sam Browne so polished that one could see one's face in it. He looked the exaggerated kind of army officer one still sees, alas, on television, and from the word go he was suspicious and intolerably rude.

He looked me up and down and said: 'Can I look at your travelling papers?'

All I had to give him was my identity card.

'Hmm,' he said, 'is that all you've got?'

I said yes, it was all I had carried on me ever since I left Lord Mountbatten's headquarters in Ceylon.

'So is that what you purport to be, the emissary of Lord Mountbatten?' There was a note of scorn in his voice.

'I am on this occasion. I have been on a mission to The Hague on behalf of the Prime Minister.'

At that he threw his pencil down and looked at me as if I was guilty of *folie de grandeur*.

I was compelled to say: 'I know it may look odd to you, but, first of all, in talking to me I would like you to be aware of the fact that I am a senior officer and entitled to the respect demanded by my rank.'

He seemed to get angry at that and said: 'You must, if you have no papers, give me a name and address to which I can telephone.'

'Very well. Would you please telephone the Secretariat at Number 10?'

At that he seemed to think me more provoking than ever, but in the end he telephoned. The look of amazement and disbelief on his face when he heard my story confirmed by Downing Street was gratifying enough to wipe out any trace of unpleasantness in my memory of the event.

'They are sending a car for you,' he stuttered. 'You can go.'

I hasten to add that this, in some nine years of war, was the only time that I met an officer who behaved in such a fashion, and I mention it only because it seemed at the time not a good omen.

I arrived at Downing Street just as news came through from Java of the murder of a Brigadier Mallaby and other members of his party at Sourabaya. In my mind alarm bells rang. What on earth were they doing in Sourabaya? It was the last place to go to without proper preparation. Eastern and central Java were the areas in which the nationalists and the spreading army of Soedirman were best organized and at their most fanatic and, for us, were of little immediate interest because the internment and prisoner-of-war camps there were the smallest and least important in the islands.

Fortunately the explanations and more detailed reports that followed suggested that the Admiral and Christie had, as one might have expected, not allowed this setback to get out of proportion. They handled it with calm and dispatch, and did not allow it to have any influence on our overall policy in Java.

There followed many days when I still had to see people with influence in all dimensions in Indonesia. I went to see General Penney in his hospital: 'Penney from heaven' as the soldiers on the beaches at Anzio called him. He was very unwell, and upset that he had been unable to fulfil his mission, but the report I gave him reassured him. I also gave him a piece of information that was of great value to him: among the papers captured at the Japanese High Command after their surrender, there had been clear evidence that the Japanese had been prepared to withdraw to the centre of Java and had fully intended to fight to the death and, if not killed in battle, to commit *hara-kiri*. And, before they did that, they would massacre all the prisoners-of-war they had in their hands.

Another brief and very warm meeting with the Prime Minister helped me to realize more and more that his apparent anonymity was meaningful because it was an indication of the extent to which he was perhaps the least egotistical statesman I have ever known. Attlee not only thanked me but honoured me in asking whether I was prepared to make a broadcast on the BBC to the nation. I said I would do so if I could do it anonymously, just as an officer on the staff of Mountbatten. I duly did it, and it was felt to have been of great service and provoked immense interest all over the country. The spirit in which I spoke is perhaps expressed in the conclusion, which I had forgotten until my research assistant unearthed the BBC recording of it from their archives. This is how I ended:

> Do remember, once more, that these people have had no real news for three and a half years of what has been happening in the world. All they have had in that time is Japanese propaganda of the vilest type and, all this time, their youngest and most impressionable boys have had held up to them as heroes the most brutal type of soldiery, who showed continually a complete and almost joyous disregard of human life. Killing and being killed are drilled into them by routine example as a great, exciting and romantic thing. Everywhere in my experience of crowds and riots in the island, I have been struck by the fact that the sort of 'storm-troopers' of these demonstrations were young boys of from 8 to 14 years of age. That is not political, it is a tragic and abnormal psychology, created by a collective callow passion in an atmosphere of organized lying and intimidation.
>
> And, finally, you can have no idea really how exhausted, tired and profoundly distressed all classes of the community in Java are. There is not a family in Java which has not suffered brutal bereavement, which is not partly broken up and, to some extent, wrenched out of its normal social pattern. No one in Java today is normal, and many of the people in the island who have had families and associations in other parts of the world do become upset when they get there and learn with a first rude shock what has happened in the past three and a half years.
>
> I am a soldier and know little of political things, and therefore probably underrate them; but this aspect of the trouble in Java is by far the most important. It is essentially a human problem, and it requires all that we have of human understanding and imagination and sympathy for all classes of people, even for the nationalists, if we are to solve it with dignity and success. We want a very light, a deft, firm and sensitive touch to manage the startled and the wounded steed.
>
> Already I feel that Java, in spite of Sourabaya, is on the first steps to becoming more normal. If we continue to approach it in a human, understanding way, I am convinced that in a few months you will have good tidings of this great Java sorrow.

On my last day in London the Foreign Secretary, Ernest Bevin, sent for me. It was supposed to be a rather short and formal meeting but it lasted for more than an hour. His was a very warm and immediate personality, and he made me feel more than adequately rewarded for all that I might have done. But what I did not expect was his knowledge and interest in history, which I became aware of when he said he had noticed that I was a South African. Did I know anything of a people he had always admired very much, the Boers? He pronounced the name as 'Boors'.

I said yes, in fact I was one myself, coming from an old pioneering family. And then he told me how Tom Shaw, a founder of the Labour Party and a man of vision of a kind produced on a considerable scale in its early days, had influenced him enormously. One day Tom Shaw sent for him to tell him about a meeting he had just had with the Prime Minister of the day, Campbell-Bannerman. Bevin spoke with warmth of how Parliament had functioned in those days when, regardless of what happened within the House of Commons, opponents treated one another with consideration and respect. Campbell-Bannerman was meticulous in the way in which he kept the Opposition informed, and he told Tom Shaw that a Boer delegation from the defeated republics in South Africa had just been to see him to ask if they could not now be allowed to return to a form of self-government. (I might add that as a child I knew almost everyone on that delegation, so short are the slides and spans of history.) Campbell-Bannerman told Shaw he had looked at them and said: 'Gentlemen, I am extremely disappointed in you.'

The Boer delegation were astonished and thought that somehow they had failed badly, and asked him anxiously: 'But why?'

'Gentlemen, I am disappointed that you ask me for so little, because I want to give you so much more.'

'More, sir?' they asked him, still bewildered.

'Yes, more,' he replied. 'I would like to give you the Union of South Africa.' I mention this here because it expresses a vital difference in the approach of the rulers of empire to the colonies and dominions they ruled, and was of relevance to all that we faced in Java.

The meeting with Bevin was important to my own historical perspective as well, because it marked the increasing division between what I call the original Labour Party and the new ideological socialism that I think was to overtake it and ruin it. I have always had – and still have – a feeling of identity with the original Labour Party. I myself marched with the unemployed in Hyde Park in the Great Depression, and Ernest Bevin, Tom Shaw, Keir Hardie and George Lansbury were all people I respected enormously.

Later in the day I went to the War Office to see Archie Nye. He was the Assistant Director of Military Intelligence. The DMI was away, I think on a grand-piano-buying session; he played the piano very well. Archie Nye was to be one of the best high commissioners Britain had ever sent to Canada, and he and his DMI, who was also a distinguished soldier, are two more illustrations of the range and quality of the British officers in the army at the end of the war.

Archie Nye cross-examined me at length, of course, and at the end of it asked: 'Do you really think all this is still possible, and that it is not too late?'

I said that if we acted quickly, now that our troops had landed and were in position, I thought it was.

He looked at me rather sadly and said: 'Well, young fellow, I am not at all certain. My reading of history has taught me how men always give too little and too late. Men of power, and even men in their private lives, somehow always seem too late. They start by giving too little and end up by giving far more than they were originally asked for, and even that "far more" will by that time not be enough. However, do not let me depress you. Go, and you all have a bloody good try.'

And so at last I had come to the end of my mission. I would like here to refer to a personal aspect of my own time during the mission, to one night only, simply because I think it is necessary to evoke the atmosphere in which these events were unfolding – the living humanity which most historians ignore, writing their histories as if they were not part of humanity and its fumbling search for greater reality.

On my last night in London, Ingaret and I had two intimate friends to dinner. An incident had occurred that afternoon which caused a lot of laughter when it was retold. There had been a postman's knock at the door. I had gone to answer it and was handed a cable. I read the cable aloud: 'You need have no more anxiety about the fate of Colonel van der Post. He is now safe in Allied hands.'

Everybody's immediate reaction was to complain how typical that was of War Office inefficiency, but I said no. Really it moved me to tears because it illustrated how, in the midst of those terrible hurricanes of communication that had stormed through the world and of which Mountbatten had told me in detail, the British War Office still had the imagination to think of what went on in the home of each individual soldier. It was the same approach which prescribed that every soldier who fell in the war was not part of a faceless collective horde but was there as an individual sacrifice, a warm and living human entity, uniquely himself even in death.

That evening Ingaret's housekeeper, Mrs Pearce, cooked for us, as far as the wartime system of rationing permitted. She was there with her small daughter Dorothy, as she had been throughout the war. A Cockney, born within the sound of Bow Bells, she remembered that when on Sundays the bells tolled for the morning service she and her three sisters were taught to stop whatever they were doing and sit in the nearest chair, fold their hands in their laps, and listen respectfully to the bells. She was typical of that world for which, at that very moment, plans were being made in the socialist office-of-works to bulldoze what they regarded as slums and put monstrous high-rise buildings in their place, claiming to improve standards of living but in fact destroying the last representatives of the vanished Kingdom of Cockaigne, the 'Cockneys' who still every year saluted their Pearly King and Queen and were such an enrichment of the English char-acter, all spirits without a trace of a slum in their minds. When urged to let Dorothy be evacuated from the bombing in London, Mrs Pearce had resolutely refused: 'I am not going to let that Hitler separ-ate me from my daughter.'

As a result Dorothy, who was so busy helping her in the kitchen, was growing up full of a sense of self-respect at having been hon-oured by her mother, who knew from the beginning that she would have hated not to share in the risks her mother ran in the bombing of London. Her example was another confirmation to me of the spirit in which the British nation had come through the war, united in all castes and classes of society, from children in their kindergar-tens to old men nearing the end of their days, and which ultimately had led to the defeat of fascism in the world.

Every morning throughout the war Mrs Pearce had accompanied Ingaret to a little factory in Chelsea where they both made fuses for the bombs of the RAF; and every evening Ingaret put on a tin hat and went with our chimney-sweep to do fire duty in the bombed streets of London – a chimney-sweep who was awarded a George Cross for gallantry.

Ingaret herself was a gold medallist from RADA, the writer of a best-selling novel, *Sigh No More, Ladies*, and the author of *Because We Must*, the play produced at Wyndham's some three years before the war that gave Vivien Leigh her first West End part. She had aban-doned all that to do her service throughout the war. Our guests were two dear friends, Athene Seyler and Nicholas 'Beau' Hannen.

Athene was a brilliant comedy actress and a woman of intellect. A friend of George Bernard Shaw and a personality much loved on the London stage, she had as far as I knew been a confirmed atheist. But a book Ingaret gave her during the war, out of an intuition and without having even read it herself, yet feeling it was meant for Athene, completely converted her and she was baptized and received into the Anglican Church at Westminster. Ingaret and Sybil Thorndyke were there as her godmothers.

Beau, as he was known to one and all because he was as beau within as he was beau without, was a great and generous human being and a very fine actor.

I sat there with them, knowing that I would be gone the next day and somewhat troubled that I was not regretting my fate more because of this conviction I had that I must get back to Java because I was urgently needed there. Beau was wearing, as always, something very distinctive, a mushroom-coloured velvet suit. I recognized it instantly. It was the suit he had worn when he played the part of the Prime Minister in George Bernard Shaw's *The Apple Cart*. I had been at the play, standing in for Francis Birrell, the drama critic for the *Athenaeum and Nation*, which I did from time to time. Watching Beau throughout the performance I thought, 'One day, when I have the money, I would love a suit just like that.'

In the course of dinner I told Beau the story. To my amazement he stood up, pushed his food aside as he left the table and started to take off his clothes. Mrs Pearce was just coming into the dining-room and shut the door again with a face of alarm. Beau took no notice and finished undressing until he stood there in the most impeccable, uncreased and dazzling underwear I had ever seen. Then he handed me the suit and said: 'Dear boy, it's yours!'

He would not listen to my protests and the evening ended with me taking him home wrapped in my greatcoat and depositing him and Athene at their house in Chelsea.

The evening was a tiny mirror in a vast hall of mirrors of world events, but this little gathering somehow conveyed for me the essence of that wider world, and warmed my heart as I hastened to Lyneham the next morning and headed for the East.

CHAPTER SIX

'Merdeka!'

THE JOURNEY BACK to Kandy took no longer than the outward
journey to London, but by this time my unease was so great that it
felt as if it were taking weeks instead of days. However, I arrived at
Kandy just in time to report to Mountbatten, who was on the point
of leaving for a conference of all the officers in the High Command
in the South-east Asia and Pacific area. My meeting him did not
really matter all that much on this occasion because he had been singularly well informed about all that had happened in London. It was
important, however, in a personal sense because the occasion
somehow confirmed the rapport which I felt we had established on
our first meeting. He also encouraged me by saying that he had
received a message of thanks from the Prime Minister for sending
me, and a special appreciation of the work I had done. The message
noted that Attlee hoped he would send others like me to report to
them all from time to time, because it served as no cables could to
keep us in their minds.

Before leaving he referred me to his Chief of Staff, General
Browning. Around the General had arisen the legend of the gallant,
though failed, operation at Arnhem which was to be filmed as *A
Bridge too Far*. Browning was always referred to in the army as 'Boy
Browning', partly because he always looked rather young and fresh
and was exceedingly good-looking. He was very much a 'persona'
soldier, caring immensely about appearances. Though no doubt a
very gallant and courageous soldier, I never felt he had the depth of
character and the real inner vision which the exceptional soldiers I

have mentioned all possessed. He had not long since arrived and his outlook had not yet detached itself from war as experienced in Europe; and in so far as it was detached he was thinking of war in the future. I felt he was not really interested in what I had to tell him and that he saw what was happening in Indonesia in purely military terms – which was, of course, the least of our priorities.

Something else that was of special meaning to me occurred in Kandy. I met General Slim again. He was just recovering from a severe attack of hepatitis, and I found him in a hammock in the garden of his house wearing pyjamas. It was a really hot Kandy day. Lady Slim was with him and, as she always did on the rare occasions when he was at home, was taking remarkable and imaginative care of him. He could not have been more interested in my report, and again we talked not only about what was happening in South-east Asia but also about what was going to become of the empires. The news had only just come through that Dorman-Smith, the newly appointed Governor-General of Burma, was being replaced by a Labour politician whose name I do not remember but who had endeared himself to me when, in his first meeting with the press, he answered a question by remarking: 'I know nothing of hunting and shooting, but I know everything about shunting and tooting.' The news of his appointment was followed by the announcement that Burma would be granted almost immediate independence. And, of course, it was already known that independence for India would not be far behind.

I left Kandy as soon as I could for Singapore and Batavia. There was no need to linger in Singapore because a special Allied Land Forces command for South-east Asia (ALFSEA) was being formed. That it had taken nearly two and a half months to get this far was a sign to me of how hard-pressed Mountbatten's forces had been. So I hurried to Batavia to get back to Christie and the Admiral, which I did at noon on a warm and thunderous October day. I hardly recognized the airport at Batavia, so overcharged had it become with airborne traffic. Aircraft were arriving and leaving almost every minute. The British army was already deployed and in position, but the necessary auxiliary build-up, as well as the increased demands of the Dutch, were almost more than a single little airport, good as it was, could manage.

From that moment onwards I was to be even more deeply involved with Indonesia than I had been before, and to give some idea of my involvement I think it is appropriate to reproduce here a personal note which the Director of Military Intelligence, who had followed

General Penney in that post, wrote to me at the end of his term on Mountbatten's staff:

HEADQUARTERS
AIR COMMAND
FAR EAST

10th January 1947

My dear Lawrie,

I'm leaving for UK on the 24th Jan. so this is to bid you adieu in the East and to express the hope that we will meet soon again in the West.

May I say something which, of course, you are fully aware of. Since December '45, to my knowledge, it has been your view of the situation which has pulled the big bells when peals were rung. Nick, Spud, Boy and I depended entirely on your interpretations. They were never wrong! You have done more in your quiet way to influence policy than anyone else. And with few exceptions I believe our policies have been right.

My regret is that we had to abandon the ship before the crew and the engines were working smoothly. The working-up period will be long but she'll find herself eventually. You did much of her construction from the laying of her keel upwards.

I have always been sorry that we could not work more directly together. I find your Service a wee bit jealous of its information and its sources. I had always to avoid giving offence.

But you taught me all I ever knew about NEI [the Netherlands East Indies] and I am very grateful. It will stand me in good stead in my new job of Head of RAF Intelligence at the Air Ministry and as a member of the TIC [an abbreviation for the Supreme Intelligence Command]. Whenever you are in Town I do hope you will get in touch with me in King Charles St.

I'm sure you are looking forward to visiting your properties in England and the Union and I hope you find them well.

Best wishes and luck!

Yours ever,

(Air Marshal) Lawrie Pendred
DMI, SACSEA under Supremo Mountbatten

An intimation of what, in a military sense alone, the task in Indonesia involved was revealed in the vast headquarters which had been established to enable 15 Army Corps to function properly as a self-

contained army group. It was my first intimate contact with a headquarters of this kind since my brief experience of Wavell's establishment at Lembang before the Japanese invasion. My own experience
of war had mostly been of small, independent commands, but I had
already been dismayed by what I had seen of the headquarters of the
Eighth Army in Egypt and then of the military forces deployed in
South-east Asia.

The organization of the Eighth Army's headquarters in Cairo had
presented me with a paradox which it took me some time to understand. In Wavell's classic biography of Allenby, he praises Allenby for
the way in which he abolished the headquarters of his predecessor,
General Murray, in a grand hotel in Cairo and took his own headquarters closer to his front against the Turks in Palestine, in order to
have a more immediate grasp of the evolution of his brilliant and
successful campaign. It seemed to me, therefore, a contradiction that
one of the first things Wavell appeared to do was to establish himself
in another grand hotel in Cairo to exercise his command. Prepared
as I had been by my training at staff college to know all there was to
know about military establishments and the movement of armies in
a modern war, I was not prepared for what I saw in Cairo, and later
in the King David Hotel in Jerusalem. I was to discover, however, that
as the war had become more sophisticated and technological, it took
at least twenty men in the rear to keep one soldier in the firing line
in the Western Desert. And then, when I was summoned to serve
under Wavell in Indonesia, the increase in staff work, even stream-
lined as it was for the Fourteenth Army, was greater than anything I
had known.

The sight of those huge buildings in which General Christison had
to establish himself in Batavia after the Japanese surrender seemed
like a form of military hubris to me. I was even more dismayed when
I discovered that the British army, in their anxiety to show their goodwill towards the Dutch, had taken in a large number of Dutch officers and their staff to work side by side with them. They did this to
try and remove all the in-built Dutch prejudices and suspicions that
were immediately activated by the successful conclusion of the war
against the Japanese, and to show that the British had no secret
agenda and were not trying to retard the establishment of the Dutch
in Indonesia in order to promote their own commercial interests in
Malaya, as Mr van der Plas and his staff were already on occasions
saying openly to their press.

That, even more than the size of the operation, seemed wrong to me. I had read three books before the war on the problems that arose between allies making common cause against an enemy, as Britain and France had done in the 1914–18 war. Two of the books were by André Maurois, who was a liaison officer with the British army at a very high level during that war. His was an essay in these things by intimation rather than professional military exhortation. The books were, of course, *Les Silences du Colonel Bramble* and *Les Discourses de Dr O'Grady*.

The third book was General Spears's autobiography in which, professionally and thoroughly, he goes into the problems and proper handling of liaison duties in wartime. A good friend of mine, the son of a famous French general, told me: 'General Spears spoke French so well that the French High Command were quite suspicious of him and thought that he must be some sort of Frenchman disguised as an Englishman, and not altogether to be trusted.' Spears's conclusion, with emphasis, was that liaison was not a matter for amateurs, however gifted. It was something that demanded the highest professional qualities as well as sensitivities and imagination that come only with a gift for liaison, for understanding rather than judgement; and that, above all, it required the closest possible affection and trust in the ally with whom the liaison had to be kept up.

But here at AFNEI (Allied Forces in the Netherlands East Indies), a number of offices had been allotted to Dutch officers and civil affairs experts who were to be available in uniform to advise on civilian matters, and who were to move into positions which had already been earmarked for them while they were away from the firing line in their offices in Delhi and Perth. Not only were these offices now occupied by people who seemed stuffed with all sorts of historical prejudices and preconditioning inherited from Dutch East India Company rule, but in addition almost all the British officers who needed secretaries had been provided with young Dutch women, among whom there were many capable secretaries and potential secretaries, all anxious for meaningful employment of some kind. The result was that, in a situation which demanded that absolute confidentiality should be the rule for given periods of time, not only was there no room for British discretion or privacy in the establishment but, ultimately, there was no provision for secrecy.

All business tended sooner or later to become a matter of office gossip and politics, the politics that one finds in all large groups but with a new dimension of intrigue, rumour-mongering and emotion that was utterly foreign to the British and certainly did not help to provide the proper atmosphere for some of our most profound and complex military demands. All this presented General Christison and his staff with an in-built and continuing problem that should not have been inflicted on them. Proper and adequate briefing of the British forces in Java had never been more necessary and often depended on up-to-date intelligence which could not be shared with the Dutch, who more and more used all information to feed their prejudices. Yet there were no conditions for confidential and even secret exchange in matters of purely British concern, and in moments of crisis.

As for the British, who had had this task imposed on them so suddenly and unexpectedly within a few days of the Japanese capitulation after years of fighting, the failure of the Dutch to understand and appreciate the generosity of spirit which made them undertake such a task on behalf of an ally seemed to me unpardonable, and with hindsight comes very near to being unforgivable.

Writing now, fifty years after the event, there are still Dutch people who think of Arnhem not in terms of an heroic attempt to rid Holland of the Nazi occupation but as a serious disaster inflicted on them by the British (Prince Bernhard of Holland himself is amply reported to have condemned this heroic failure). And in Batavia Admiral Helfrich – who became one of the most influential members of the Dutch delegation and was presented to the world as a kind of Dutch Churchill instead of a staff officer who had never heard a shot fired in battle – accused the British not only of inefficiency but of treachery and cowardice.

Far from being tardy in dispatching British forces to Indonesia, Lord Mountbatten had set about the task with such willingness and determination that they arrived a week before the planned date. What is more, the senior battalion of the Seaforths, who were the first British troops to land in Batavia, did not come in troopships as originally planned. Britain had very few ships left after so many years of war, and the demand on shipping continued to be colossal. Instead they made the six-day journey from Port Swettenham packed into infantry landing craft, without proper facilities and with hardly enough air to breathe. The landing craft stopped just long enough to take on water and then turned about to fetch more British troops, while the men on their way to their barracks in the city were amazed not to be welcomed as forces had been elsewhere in areas liberated from the Japanese. Instead, odd groups of tattered Indonesians on the route would stop and turn to the convoy and hold their clenched fists up to heaven and shout *'Merdeka!'* The sound was as strange in those calm tropical surroundings as the meaning was hidden. It meant 'Liberty! Independence!'

Even my beloved and loyal friend 'Dul got these things wrong and believed that this must have been the mood in the whole of Java when the Japanese capitulated. I cannot sufficiently stress that it was not so, as he would have known if he had stood with me in the streets of Bandoeng on the night of that full moon, watching the stumbling columns of half-starved and horrendously enfeebled Britons, and seeing how the crowds wept and broke through the Japanese cordons to embrace and thank them. In that mood I encountered no hostility from Indonesians but only a universal atmosphere of thanksgiving intertwined, as I have written, with calm and steady nationalist propaganda and preparation. That was always there.

I have often thought of such moments in history as 'moments of innocence' when it is as if, after great suffering inflicted not only on the collective formations of life but on individuals, there comes a moment when the past is wiped from the mind; and there is no definite vision of the future but only a signal from life that what has happened must never be allowed to happen again, and all are free of impediments of spirit and mind that would prevent a new beginning and a renewal of life on earth. This is collectively experienced, particularly at the end of great wars. I was not in London for the Victory in Europe celebrations, I have only heard about them, but what I have heard makes me certain of what I am saying, and moves me deeply.

At moments like these my fears for the future were always accompanied by the recollection of the great moment of innocence at the end of the 1914–18 war, when hundreds of thousands of French people flocked to Paris to greet Woodrow Wilson and to take into their hearts his great conception of the future embodied in his Fourteen Points – which his country then rejected.

The way in which that moment of innocence had been allowed to run to waste by the politicians terrified me, and I feared lest the same might happen in Java in the days ahead. I thought nothing must be allowed to waste this moment. There must be no Dutch equivalent of Lloyd George and Clemenceau who had destroyed that earlier innocence, Lloyd George with his determination to 'squeeze the Germans till the pips squeak' or Clemenceau with his spirit of revenge which was so deeply ingrained in the Treaty of Versailles. I felt that everything I did in the days to come must serve this imperative.

Unfortunately, for us in Indonesia the moment of innocence was retreating. I had hoped that what I had done would not only preserve such a moment of innocence but also, what was an immediate danger, prevent us from going to war at the behest of a totally outmoded urge on the part of the Dutch.

Yet I had not lost all hope of recovering something of that moment. Whenever I was inclined to be overcome by all the negations I encountered on my return to Batavia, I kept in mind the faces of the nationalist leaders I had met at that first meeting and the way I spoke to them. I had by now heard that all the people who were at that meeting had taken it very seriously and had responded to it within and among themselves and their confidants. They did not feel (as people in the interior did) that their self-determination was something that inevitably demanded a war to establish itself but hoped that sufficient goodwill could perhaps still be found in the Netherlands to come to some sort of peaceful arrangement.

I had taken with me to Holland the names of all those who had participated with me in that meeting, and when I went through it in detail with Professor Logemann he had remarked: 'I do not know them all, but I know some of them personally and most by reputation, and I think they are all good and decent men.'

I was encouraged by this because it manifested the essential liberal spirit of the Schermerhorn government, and balanced the instant dismissal of Indonesian claims by Mr van der Plas and his men. For the first time it seemed that between the Logemann and Sjahrir elements there could be a productive two-way traffic. In spite of the frantic reactions of the Dutch in Java at the slightest hint of communicating with the Indonesians, and claims that it constituted a recognition of a 'rebel minority' in the islands, that is what the Admiral and, above all, General Christison decided to explore as soon as possible.

There seemed to me, in all the resistance we were encountering, not one, but a parcel of paradoxes, all of different psychologies and nuances of spirit. There were two streams at least in Holland. One I would briefly label as that of the liberal Logemann and Schermerhorn. The second – which I feared could prove a majority – was the approach of vested interests and popular legend, embodying not just criticism and mistrust of the British but a renewal of economic and commercial greed. And then there was a third element too, which though small was important – the psychology of the Dutch who were born and bred in Java, men such as Dr van Mook. They, like the Europeans born in South Africa under the Dutch East India Company's rule, had their own quarrel with their mother country and sought increased political influence in the affairs of Indonesia.

Among the Indonesians themselves there was a common emotion and determination to achieve self-government, but it was in no sense yet fully integrated. It was there most actively and obviously in the areas where the Japanese had methodically trained young Indonesians as soldiers and taught them the most brutal methods of war. They had had no other model except the Japanese for nearly four years and, although psychologically totally different sorts of people, they thought that they would have to fight, and that it was only by fighting that they would get their way.

Potentially more formidable, there was a profound Muslim content throughout all the Indonesian diversities of character. For instance in Atjeh, in the northernmost province of Sumatra, the Muslims had been fighting on and off for centuries against foreign (particularly Dutch) occupation. In Java itself there was a fanatical Muslim element, and the militancy which I have mentioned was naturally present in the young men of the islands: it was they who were organized under a radical Muslim leader and became known as the 'Pemoeda'.

Islam has always seemed to me on the whole to be a religion which inflames rather than illuminates the human spirit. I know there are profound minority manifestations of Islam in the world of Sufi, but as far as Java and Sumatra were concerned the inflammatory rather than the illuminatory seemed to have the greater attraction. In Bantam, in Java itself, this was particularly true, and the rebellions and the violence that had flared up there throughout recent history were notorious. It was astonishing to me that even Dr van Mook – who was, after all, born among the Indonesians – should have thought that they had no real fight in them, and that when it came to confrontation they would be a push-over. He should have known how, collectively as well as individually, the Javanese had again and again throughout the history of the Dutch occupation proved their courage in battle and, at times, demonstrated the eruptive passion and violence which they themselves described as 'mata gelap' – the 'darkening of the eye' – in the individual.

But, thank God, there were also the people that I had already met, and there were thousands of others like 'Dul, unidentified and unknown, particularly among the middle classes and *petite noblesse*.

From the moment of my return from London I felt that we had no time to lose in rediscovering and encouraging what was still valid and constructive in the world of Java. I often, in the quiet of the night, thought how I would like to have approached the problem myself. I thought what an immense opportunity the Dutch had missed when, on 15 August, the Japanese had capitulated so dramatically. If only their broadcast then, prompted by decent intelligence (the lack of which was a criminal failure of duty), had started with a declaration of joy at the ending of the war, followed by a modest statement of how the Dutch were coming back to support the setting right of all that had been done during the brutal Japanese occupation; that they were coming back, not to repeat the pattern which had been the rule for the islands before the war, but to improve in every way the life of all the citizens of Indonesia. I would not have talked in political terms at all but as rulers who felt deeply how circumstances had forced them to fail in their duty to protect the islands, and who were now coming to do better in every way than they had done before. I would have made no mention of judgement and justice, or of retribution to be meted out to collaborators.

The Dutch should have been aware, when they heard that there had been no resistance, that, in a sense, everybody who had stayed at their posts keeping the trains running, the power stations working, the factories vibrating and the plantations in order, could have been accused of collaboration. When Mr van der Plas arrived, the Japanese ostensibly were the masters, but the running of the complex economy of the islands had been entirely under Indonesian control and, considering how terribly isolated and starved their world had been under the Japanese, they had done their work extremely well in a way that was a credit to the Dutch, who had trained them in these matters over the years, as well as a tribute to their capacity for self-management and self-rule.

Some statement expressing goodwill, and an acknowledgement of the inadequacies of the past and a desire to create a better new world in the future, would have worked wonders; and then I think the welcome for the Dutch would have been totally different, and the militant spirits, from General Soedirman down to the *heiho* (as I had now discovered the Japanese-trained Javanese officers were known), would have been quickly brought under control and into harmony with the liberal values of Sjahrir and his kind.

This was all the more urgent because the example of Sourabaya and the violent experience there had inspired the militant Javanese, and the fighting spread to such an extent that soon even Bandoeng was a beleaguered city. For many months, when the road and railway to Bandoeng were cut by fierce fighting, the remarkable 13 Squadron of the RAF delivered supplies and kept Bandoeng alive.

I am not sure, as the situation turned out, that there was any need to occupy Bandoeng. All that we had to do and could do, seeing that the whole of Java for all practical purposes was already in Indonesian hands, was to create in Batavia an impregnable bridgehead from which we could proceed to prepare the country as a whole for its future.

The result was that our first approaches to bring the Indonesians into contact with the British forces, and also to introduce them to decent consideration by the growing Dutch contingent, took place towards the end of November, in the first instance through me. These promised so well that early in December we had a meeting at General Christison's headquarters between military representatives of the Javanese and representatives of the General and his Chief of Staff Brigadier Wingrove, the Brigadier known as 'Pooh' in the army and responsible to the General for all military operations in Java.

He and I spent a whole day with two Javanese colonels, but the meeting, which was never meant to be more than exploratory, was in a sense a failure. Neither the Indonesian colonels nor Pooh Wingrove were really, by training or outlook, the best emissaries in a role that demanded great flexibility and a sense of history. Pooh Wingrove behaved impeccably, almost too much so and in such an English way that as a person he made no real sense to the Indonesians, and nor did they to him. He felt that they were quite unrealistic and hopeless. They felt rejected and despised. All of which shows how psychologically unprepared everyone was in every way for the kind of dialogue that had any hope of succeeding between Indonesians, British and Dutch.

A good and committed soldier and in every way a decent and sensitive person, Pooh Wingrove had never really had to play that sort of role before. Indeed, his mind was already elsewhere in the future. Like so many professional British soldiers he was ready to accept demotion from his wartime rank, in anticipation of the contraction of the British army which would soon follow, and a return to the shelter of his own regiment, from where he could get on to the right ladder of regular promotion which was the rule in times of peace.

As for the Indonesian officers, preconditioned already to what Dutch senior officers in the past had been accustomed to inflict on them, they took it all as a personal insult, for when they turned away I heard one say to another: 'It is no good talking to this man. You can see that he is only being polite, but really at heart he despises us.'

I turned to him immediately and in my broken Malay said: 'Forgive me, but you are wrong. How could we, who have read Raffles and learned to know about this part of the world from him, ever despise a people whom he loved and admired so much?'

The effect was quite startling. It was the first time I experienced the magic that still surrounded Raffles's name among the educated people of Java. After that I was to use it frequently, almost as my personal visiting card, when meeting the Indonesians who knew nothing about us and the British of the day. I was to discover that, even now, they spoke of him with affection, and I met Indonesians who said his period in Indonesia was the best thing that had ever happened to them.

Within two weeks my contacts with the Indonesians had borne such fruit that we were able to have a meeting between the Dutch at the highest level and Sjahrir and his colleagues, in the house into which I had just been moved from my office at the Konigsplain.

The house was situated on the wealthier fringes of Batavia and was ideally placed for the purposes for which it was to be used. On my return from London I found that 'Dul and his wife, two Dutch women secretaries and a young captain had already been installed as the nucleus of the staff I would need. Alan Greenhalgh and van Till had been there briefly but had already left Java when I returned. The house belonged to the Royal Dutch Shell Company and had a garden all round it and access to a tennis court. On the other side of the tennis court stood a large, imposing white house which was used by the director of Shell's operation in Indonesia. Opposite, across the street, was a much larger house and grounds which were to become almost immediately the home of the British Minister, and the Embassy of the future.

I was to thank my luck over and over again that 'Dul had decided to live with me, and that his wife Sri was to run the household for us both. Sri was a woman of strong character, like so many Javanese women who, from the outside, were regarded as almost over-submissive and deferential to their men, kneeling and bowing low to their husbands and their friends as they entered the precincts of their home. She would dutifully sleep at the foot of his bed, but inside herself there was a dimension in which she could erupt, as the earth on which she lived and had her being exploded with the lava in its veins. Sri appeared the most feminine of naturally feminine women, an appearance belied by this volcanic spirit which enabled Javanese women to influence the conduct of their men perhaps even more than women in so-called emancipated European cultures. I always thought it expressed itself symbolically when the Javanese *petite noblesse* wore their national dress and with it the curved crescent-moon shaped dagger called a *kris*. By tradition no one except the man could withdraw the dagger from its sheath, but only the woman could replace it in the sheath when it had served its purpose.

I had arrived back in Java, therefore, to find myself installed in a well-ordered and viable establishment. The staff officer, who had entered the army towards the end of the war, was a young man called Kenneth Pope. He was very English in manner and in spirit, sensitive, steady and loyal, and I cannot speak more highly of the way in which he served with me almost until the end of the British occupation. I was later to have a succession of seconds-in-command but, because of the mobile character of the post-war army, none of them stayed very long and, though they rendered us all good service, it was always rather perfunctory, with another future in mind; if they have survived they would not, I believe, expect any special mention here.

What was also very important in the house, and which contributed enormously to the well-being of my spirit in the exacting months that followed, was a grand piano. Piled high upon it were what we used to call 'albums', anthologies that the teachers of music at schools and colleges used for instruction. There, for the first time in ten years, in my rare moments of leisure in the evenings, I was able to try to play the piano again. To do so properly, I realized at once, I would have to spend days doing scales for which I had neither time nor, for that matter, any taste. I contented myself by playing what I could play and found, as always, that in playing, however badly, the music did more for me than when I listened to the best of pianists on the best of gramophone records.

The first piece, I remember, was an arrangement for piano of *Finlandia*, which I found comparatively easy because it consisted almost entirely of wonderful chords rather than the runs which are

so often the essential part of the Chopin I love. Chopin was almost
out of the question: I began with some of the simple minuets and bits
of nocturnes that were easy but – oh dear! – when the runs began I
had to decide, not only for my own sake but for the sake of Sri and
her servants who in any case did not care very much for Western
music, to desist. Occasionally there was an outbreak of shooting in
the area. In the silences I would hear the bee-droning sound of
bullets, fired perhaps a mile or two away, coming to the end of their
lethal flight. Somehow, once at the piano I was away and living in a
world where men were free and held on course by something greater
than themselves. I often thought of Haydn who, when Napoleon's
forces came storming into his city, sat down at his piano and fiercely
played his music as a protest against the chaos and destruction that
Napoleon and his armies were bringing into the heart of the world
from which the miracle of Western music sprang. For me Sibelius's
chords will always be like some ponderable imponderable on which
I built and rebuilt my own post-war mind in Batavia.

So in this house the first meeting took place one night between
Sjarifoeddin and five other Indonesians who, with Sjahrir, had
formed what they called their government and had stayed on in
Batavia to conduct, as they claimed, the affairs of the nation in all
their negotiations with the British and the Dutch. Soekarno and
Hatta still remained in the safety of central Java and, at about this
time, and for the first time in many years, Soekarno went to see his
mother again. Sixty thousand Indonesians followed him of their
own accord to witness the meeting, and that meeting became, as it
were, a meeting between the whole of Indonesian man and the
natural spirit which had made him what he was at his best. The long-
felt wish of the deepest collective unconscious of Indonesia found
fulfilment in that moment, and even in Batavia – so far removed, so
increasingly caught up in the turmoil of the running feud between
Ambonese and Indonesians and the nationalists of Java – even there
I went to a house where people were in tears because of the report
of the meeting which had just reached them.

I have dwelt on this to explain why Soekarno and Hatta, the two
great leaders, as they were still regarded in spite of their so-called
collaboration with the Japanese, were not at this meeting. Indeed
they were not to be there for a considerable time, but it is necessary
to emphasize that their absence in a way confirmed their role and
validity in the popular imagination of the day.

The Dutch delegation was led by Dr van Mook, with Mr van der

Plas and some of his old officials. No one else was present. I had deliberately organized this first meeting between Dutch and Indonesians in such a way that they could be on their own. I knew that I would hear all that was necessary from 'Dul later. I did not expect that it would immediately produce great things, but it was a beginning, and from then until the end of the British occupation of Java, more and more of these meetings took place on an ascending scale of importance. But, despite these meetings, the accusations from Dr van Mook's headquarters in The Hague and from newspapers in Holland that the British had failed in their duty to bring the Dutch into proper contact with the Indonesians, continued unabated. We were always in the wrong because, just as often, we were being assailed for doing too much with the Indonesians and giving them a recognition they did not merit.

As these meetings and their preliminaries became more significant, and therefore more complicated to organize, the need to extend our own contact between Batavia and the interior became more pressing. What made it even more so was the urgency of our immediate task of freeing the Dutch internees and prisoners-of-war, who were still confined to their prison camps. It was quite clear by now that this task was never going to be completed without the active participation of the Indonesians, who held nearly 70,000 (mostly Dutch) internees and prisoners in their power. It was a cruel fate to befall people who had suffered so much under the Japanese, but on the whole the Indonesians performed the task with humanity.

Yet it was impossible to get the Dutch to understand that the Indonesians should be turned to for help in getting these people out of the interior, and out of Java to somewhere like Australia, as soon as possible. They were insistent that nothing that might give a glimmer of recognition to 'the rebels' (as they insisted on calling the Indonesians) could be promoted. I had a feeling at moments that they cared little about what was happening to the Dutch women and children and others so unfairly imprisoned and interned. And I have to record that, knowing what imprisonment under the Japanese had been like, I found the feelings evoked in me personally almost more than I could cope with when I realized that these Dutch in command, who had fled from Java and had never gone short of food or suffered in any physical way, could make such expedient political philosophy of the fate of their re-interned and re-imprisoned countrymen. It was almost more than I could stomach at the time, and I am inclined to stomach it even less when I recall it now.

Fortunately Pooh Wingrove was succeeded as staff officer to Christie by Ian Lauder, a born man of action who had distinguished himself in Burma, and he immediately made the release and recovery of the internees almost his personal cause. So when, with the help of Sjahrir and Sjarifoeddin (who was by now his 'Minister of the Interior'), I had a chance to go to the Indonesian military headquarters at Solo, Ian Lauder was the first to support me actively.

In due course I found myself in a sleeper, comfortable but nearly stifled because the air-conditioning had long since broken down, on my way to the interior. Conditions were uncertain in this new Indonesian world even for Indonesians, and somewhere along the way the train was held up, and scattered shooting broke out all around us. A young Indonesian officer came rushing into my compartment, pulled down the blinds and explained there was some trouble outside and that I must on no account show myself, because the sight of a white officer in foreign uniform could have dire consequences. He had obviously been trained as a *heiho* by the Japanese. His hair was black and shone like silk, and he wore it down to his waist; and he had a sword almost too big for him, a samurai sword, dangling from his middle. Though perfectly correct in his approach to me, he was clearly keeping his emotions under control with difficulty.

At one moment when the firing was at its most intense, I myself was not unalarmed by what was going on and came near to diving for cover, but thought better of it when a couple of bullets came up through the floor. When the tumult of the shooting and shouting voices outside became more remote, I composed myself by taking out my dispatch book and looking at a translation I had begun in my house some days before of Rilke's beautiful sonnet 'Autumn Day', and I proceeded to work on that again. This sonnet has always been for me a prelude to Rilke's other poems, like 'The Annunciation' for example, which expressed his fundamental spirit of reverence for all forms of life and creation. I began writing it out:

> Lord it is time. Heavy was your summer yield.
> Cast your shadow over the sunny hour
> And let the cold winds break over the tired field.
> Make the last fruit rich with your power divine
> Give them one more southern day.
> Accomplish them and in your swift way
> Press the goodness that remains into good, red wine.

Those who have no home, now shall build no more.
They who are lonely have long to wait
To read and write letters – for it is too late
And like leaves whirled before your breath
To drift in streets made grey with fate.

I had just got to the last stanza when the officer reappeared, obviously relieved to see me sitting there quiet and apparently unalarmed, and asked what I was writing. I instantly responded to this change of mood and told him I was translating a poem of Rilke's from the German. That at once aroused his interest.

'A poem!' he exclaimed, and spontaneously he came to sit next to me and look at my book. 'A poem! That is very strange. I myself am a poet!'

As a result of the conversation that followed I wrote out for him the original in German, my whole translation in English, and a Dutch version in prose. That done, the young officer vanished, a long whistle blast broke the silence that had descended on the scene without, and our train was on its way once more. I never saw the officer again but some three months later I received from him a Javanese literary quarterly in which the Rilke poem from my material had been rendered in Malay, which had become the official language of Java.

Though the rest of the journey to Solo went smoothly, our arrival was not untroubled. I was made to wait at the station in my compartment with the blind drawn until some senior officers arrived and took me off by car to a hotel where I was given a small suite, the doors were quickly shut and locked, and I was told not to stir. In these conditions I spent an uncomfortable time, disturbed by sounds of a commotion outside. My arrival had coincided with the arrival of a lot of wounded and resentful Indonesian officers and men from the front that had been formed around Semarang and Amberawa, and they were in no mood to endure European faces, particularly now that the Europeans had turned the Japanese as well as the British forces on them.

However, on one of the days that followed I had a meeting with some Indonesian senior staff officers which, as the day progressed, went better and better. It impressed me greatly because it showed that fundamentally these were responsible people and that, if these contacts could become more frequent and a process of real consultation could be started, they would be oddly proud as well as happy to evacuate the women and children as soon as possible. We there and then arranged that a meeting with Brigadier Lauder would follow as soon as we could organize it.

From then on, whatever the Dutch might say, and indeed did say vociferously, contacts in the military area grew more frequent and were widened. In due course I brought two British senior officers with me back to the interior. Again the circumstances were anxious, if not downright dangerous. Veterans of such fighting as there had been, who were trusted as a kind of royal guard to the Indonesian leaders, guarded our rooms and our hotel all the time we were there. But the talks happily prospered. From then on, the full evacuation of the women and other internees was planned and after some months took place, without any of the trouble and consequences which the Dutch had warned us would follow any attempt to involve the Indonesians in our affairs. The fact that these negotiations went so well, I believe, did much to lessen suspicion of the British in the interior, and were greatly to Ian Lauder's credit.

CHAPTER SEVEN

Carrying the Can

URGENT AS OUR task of recovering and evacuating the internees and prisoners-of-war was, it was only a small part of the work I had to do. The military side of my appointment officially was that of Military-Political Officer, first to Lord Mountbatten, then the Admiral, then General Christison, and in due course also to Gilbert MacKereth, who came as special Minister from the Foreign Office to take charge of the political aspects of the work I had done almost exclusively up to that moment.

But, long before his arrival, my staff had grown and I was given a colonel who was known to one and all on the staff as 'Ham', an endearment from his surname which was Hamilton. Like me he dealt exclusively with the intelligence essential for immediate military operations and affairs. He had a gift, almost a genius, for just being what he was and getting people to like him. Profoundly religious, though he never wore it on his sleeve, he was a first-class officer and a man of immense sensitivities. Having him on my staff made me feel once again how very lucky I was with all those who worked with me.

One of the best pieces of luck had been the secretary who, in my absence, had been drawn for me out of a pool of young Dutch women ready to serve on General Christison's staff. She was a young Jewish woman called Sybil Bauer. She had been named Sybil because her mother was a Sassoon and came of that famous far-flung clan which traced its origins back to the exile in Baghdad mentioned in the Old Testament: ever since then, apparently, there has been no clan without a Sybil in it. (For instance, I had already known in London a Sybil Sassoon in the person of Lady Cholmondeley.)

Sybil had come through internment under the Japanese with a very special record. She had worked like a young man rather than a young woman, doing all sorts of hard labour for which the other women were not strong enough. She had never lost her balance, and had come out of the experience unembittered and smiling. She was as efficient and loyal as she was good to look at, with fine-drawn features and eyes of an almost antique darkness, and an abiding expression of serenity which is almost impossible to define. In addition she spoke Javanese, Medoerese, Malay, English and of course Dutch, all fluently and all indispensable for the work she had to do. Although she was not housed in my mess but lived with friends in a pavilion nearby, from the first day of her appointment to the last day of mine, she served me and what I had to do in a way that could not have been bettered.

Thus I was able to do work, which at times was dangerous work, night and day. I never really knew how I managed to do it all. I am certain it could have been done better, but I am also certain that what I did was the best that I could do. And I would not have been able to do it in those exacting early days if it had not been for my Admiral and *Cumberland*, Kenneth Pope, 'Dul and his Sri, and Sybil.

I now no longer worked directly for my Admiral but under General Christison. Fortunately they had the best possible understanding between them, and it was fully understood that every Saturday I could – unless there was an emergency – spend the afternoon and night in *Cumberland*. It was the equivalent in war of what a weekend in the country is to people escaping from the turmoil of London. It was indeed a superior sort of country house, maintained in a ship. I was treated in deed and in spirit by everyone, from the Admiral down to the able seamen, as a kind of mascot to the ship, and was described by them all as 'our one and only Pongo'.

Very often on Saturday evenings we would dine in a special wardroom with officers like Flags and Charles Hart, and they were always very happy and relaxed occasions. The Admiral developed a ritual for the end of dinner. Always, of course, there was port available but he preferred to offer Constantia, one of the oldest and most famous of South African wines from the first vineyard in the Cape, which, among other wines, the Navy introduced to Great Britain. (Jane Austen, whose brothers were in the Navy, knew all about it, and when, in *Persuasion*, a young lady jumped from the Cobb in Lyme

Regis and fainted, Jane Austen tells us she was revived with Constantia. It was also known by the poet Baudelaire, who actually stayed in Constantia with a famous Cape family distantly related to my mother. He was on the voyage which produced his great poem 'The Albatross', and stopped off at the Cape and there wrote the poem which has the lines in it: '*O, ma Constance, ma soeur!*')

The Admiral also had something even more special, a unique liqueur made at the Cape since its earliest days, called van der Hum. When the moment came for toasting the King and serving coffee to his guests, the Admiral would pass round the van der Hum and announce, in that inimitable voice that came to him when he was teasing people he liked: 'Gentlemen, please take some "van der Post", because in this ship he makes things "Hum"!'

When I thought of that ship still not being released to go home, as it had been on the point of doing when the troubles in Indonesia and French Indochina were flung into Lord Mountbatten's lap, I was deeply moved by the grace with which the crew continued to maintain their ship and contain their longing to be home after a long war, as well as preserving intact and enhancing that wonderful England-in-miniature in this chaotic extension of another sort of war.

As for General Christison, I have never admired a general more, because from the very beginning he had taken up what Mountbatten had described as 'the can' and had carried it in a way I believe no one could have bettered. Unfamiliar and unpredictable and complicated as were the demands made on him, his broad shoulders took on this heavy and enigmatic burden. He – and we all – obviously made mistakes, but the mistakes were not due to any lack of care. An instinctive feeling for what was right and fair, which is so profound a value of the British, had to be his compass, rather than the totally inadequate and unreal briefing he had been given for what he had to do.

His burden was made all the more difficult because the Dutch had no clear view themselves, no agreed and common vision of how to handle the problems crowding in on their outdated, imperialistic sensibilities. And to complicate matters further, there was the press. I have already described how an advance party of special correspondents had arrived on the day of my first meeting with the Indonesian leaders, but soon the world's press began trickling in and finally there came a fully organized visitation of authorized war correspondents. I had no precise warning of when they would arrive, and my first inkling was the sight of a whole group of men in uniform bearing the green flashes that all war correspondents wore.

They were, I regret to say, a sight that shocked me with feelings of shame and indignation because most of them looked like walking Christmas trees: there was hardly a person who was not sporting a pair of German field-glasses, opera-glasses, a camera, a wrist-watch, and heaven knows what else. One of the first things they had done, apparently, was to find out where the Japanese had housed the loot they had accumulated all over Java and had intended taking back to Japan, and help themselves.

I was astonished, too, to see among them a South African whom I had known well in London and who had become a distinguished sports commentator. He seemed to have more booty on him than anybody else. He gave a whoop of joy at seeing me, calling out 'Good God, old Lawrie, we all thought you were dead!' I am afraid I did not respond as kindly as I should have done but told the group, who ranged themselves in a circle around me, how distasteful I found their appearance in the streets of a city still so impoverished. I was particularly incensed because, before I found my tongue, I had heard several of the correspondents saying: 'Perhaps he could tell us where we could get some Japanese swords?'

I turned my back on the scene as quickly as possible and on reaching my office telephoned Hugo Charteris, who was Press Officer for the British Forces in Burma and for a time in South-east Asia. He was as shocked as I was. Before we put our telephones down he repeated his first reaction in a voice full of dismay: 'I do hope you will not think that we are all like that!'

I said of course not, because I remembered so well how in the Western Desert the best of the war correspondents, armed only with cameras and notebooks, had served with a courage and commitment as great as those of any soldier. And then, as someone who had started a writer's life on a newspaper at the age of seventeen under a remarkable editor, I have always had an immense respect for the profession. Although I was not in it for long, as I grew older I realized increasingly how one cannot have a decent democracy without a free, truthful and independent press. Some of the men in the Western Desert were personal friends, like Desmond Young, Alan Moorehead and Uys Krige (the South African poet and writer of a classic book of escape, *The Way Out*, as well as an incomparable piece of the quality of a Greek tragedy called *The Death of a Zulu*). There were many others like them, but I feel compelled to refer to this example because it illustrates the horror that the press were to become for us in Java, engaged as we were in a war-that-was-not-a-war.

We suffered a great deal from an increasingly slanted and bigoted press – more and more of them Dutch – and it became important to me to remind myself that there were honourable exceptions among them.

That evening I had a most pleasant visit from *The Times* war correspondent in the Far East, Ian Morrison, whom I had met before and grew to know very well. The son of a distinguished correspondent of *The Times*, and every bit as good as his father, he was spirited and courageous and, before he was killed in Korea, became the subject of Han Suyin's book, *A Many Splendoured Thing*. He was also, I thought, one of the few men I have seen of whom I could say that he had a truly beautiful face, particularly eyes that were of a very special blue. At times I used to think that they were almost purple. He had an immense attraction for women, and in himself an abiding need of women in his life. I remember once in Fleet Street, in the spring of 1938 on a particularly beautiful Sunday when we had met for a drink, that as we parted he looked around and said: 'What a lovely day. It's the sort of day on which one must find a beautiful woman to take out to tea.'

He was to stay with me in my mess for some days and in due course, when a distinguished and attractive American war correspondent, Martha Gellhorn, appeared on the scene, they quickly became friends. One evening I lent them my jeep, but asked them not to go outside a certain area because it had been a day of desultory shooting between Ambonese and Javanese. They had not been away long when they returned, both with surface wounds on their hands. He had been driving and had a wound on his left hand, she one on her right – clearly already they had been holding hands.

But to return to the Dutch press: even in its most respectable form it went on reporting affairs in Java with singular prejudice and a distinctly anti-British slant. However difficult our tasks were, working and serving under wartime conditions, on top of it all we were subjected to them breathing down our necks. At the beginning I had to sit beside General Christison at all his press conferences, and I was always impressed with the patience, dignity, self-control and, on the whole, wisdom with which he answered their questions. But that was never conveyed to The Hague. Within three months people at the Foreign Office were remarking sarcastically that General Christison seemed to have a genius for getting himself misquoted. This was as untrue as it was unfair, but it was typical of the increasingly snide manner in which a whispering campaign – started by the Dutch in

Java, transplanted to The Hague, and spread from there to London – undermined both the General and all of us serving in Java.

I had also accompanied Christie to earlier meetings in Singapore when General Sir Miles Dempsey had arrived to assume command of ALFSEA. General Dempsey was one of several officers who had before the war been attached to military missions summoned by Smuts to advise his staff at Roberts Heights, outside Pretoria. Although I had very little to do with him directly, his experiences had created in him a readiness to hear and to believe. One of his first actions in Singapore had been to send his Chief of Intelligence, Brigadier Murphy (inevitably known as 'Spud'), to see me. As a result of the meeting General Dempsey asked me to send him, every day if possible, a dispatch summing up the intelligence and interpretations of the situation. This was a chore which I could not delegate to Kenneth Pope and, except in my absence, I was to continue it until the day of the final evacuation, using a secret signals channel which the Foreign Office arranged for us in Java.

I have two fat files of the originals of these signals. Even to me, who sent most of them, today they convey a feeling of the inability to see the forest for the daily growth of trees, underbrush and shrubbery. All those names of so many individuals, and the accounts of their many little good, bad and indifferent deeds, have really lost all meaning in the sieve which distance and time make of events so large and significant in their own unforgiving day.

None of the generals and their executive officers stayed in position long. They were always changing and always I had this role that I have described not only of gathering intelligence and bringing them up to date, but also of their inevitable re-education. The special position I acquired caused me to be accused of always knowing better, and being dogmatic and domineering in my ways and in the advice I gave. As far as I was concerned, this was not in the least due to any hidden, egotistical agenda in my spirit. It would have been a scandal if I had not known better, simply because of my history and origin, and the fact that a knowledge of Japan through direct experience had given me a special insight into the life of the Japanese and the nations of the Far East.

My nightly signals to General Dempsey provided him with a very detailed account of what was happening in Indonesia, and enabled him to pass on what was relevant and important first thing in the morning to Lord Mountbatten. Thus when the Supremo got his daily battering from The Hague, via the Foreign Office, he already had our own version of what I believed had truly happened, and what it portended.

During my absence in Europe, Dr van Mook as designate Governor-General had loomed increasingly large on the scene. I had already sensed in The Hague a whiff of how our relations with the Dutch and the Indonesians would develop, and I have related how Professor Logemann, the relevant Dutch Minister, had described the Indonesians I myself had brought to his notice as honest and decent people with whom The Hague could well talk. It was increasingly obvious that we could not fulfil our mission successfully in Java unless we kept the contacts I had made with Logemann's 'decent' Javanese, as well as working as closely as possible with Dr van Mook.

One of the difficulties in preparing for wider and more authoritative meetings than those that had already been held was, as I saw it, that none of us, perhaps not even Sjahrir himself, could accurately judge the extent to which the Indonesians in Java possessed the power to speak for the whole of Indonesia. I had come back to find what I had feared most: we ourselves, notably aided and abetted by the Japanese, had already become involved in the struggle to prevent the violence in the Indonesian movement which had characterized it in the interior from the moment Soedirman surrounded the Japanese division at Wonosobo and forced it to surrender.

Since the murder of Brigadier Mallaby and the battle for Sourabaya that followed, the Indonesians had lost 6,000 people in the fighting. They had also sustained many other casualties in the battles for Amberawa and Semarang and in the organized skirmishes that cut off Bandoeng from Batavia. These battles may in a sense have been fortunate. The young Indonesian armed forces, consisting of the Javanese equivalent of young cavaliers, were passionately committed by instinct and by their experience of the Japanese to independence, come what may. In this kind of desultory war, they not only spent some of their passion but also forfeited confidence in themselves. Thus it was easier to promote the work of people like Sjahrir in creating an increasing belief that a modern state could not be achieved by violence but as far as possible had to come about through an orderly and steady democratic evolution.

All along I had been concerned about Sumatra. Many of the Indonesian leaders, like Sjahrir, Soekarno and Sjarifoeddin, came from Sumatra. I felt certain that what was happening in Java was also happening in Sumatra, but we had no real knowledge of what was going on there. This was not surprising because Sumatra, for all its geographical listing as an island, is really vast enough to be recognized as a minor continent. Before the war the connections with Java had been of the closest and most intimate kind. Under the Japanese they had been greatly diminished. Now, what contact there was came to us from Medan in the north-west of Sumatra where one of our three divisions was establishing its headquarters, and from one outpost of a brigade deployed at Padang on the west coast. For the moment, what was happening elsewhere was almost totally unknown. It seemed to me, therefore, of the utmost importance that whoever we had to deal with in Java should also be able to speak for their countrymen in Sumatra (if the Sumatrans wanted that), and that it would greatly simplify the negotiations which I hoped we could begin on an increasing scale between the Dutch and the rest of Indonesia.

I therefore thought it imperative to organize, with 'Dul's assistance, a truly representative meeting between the Indonesians in Java and those in Sumatra, where they could start the dialogue necessary between themselves without outside influences or active participation on the part of the British or the Dutch. And so I proposed that we should take a small representative Indonesian mission to the interior of Sumatra and meet some of the leaders there to see to what extent they and their aspirations harmonized with those of the Indonesians in Java.

This idea, of course, encountered the most severe objections from the Dutch and the eternal complaint that we were once again giving the rebels a recognition that they did not warrant, and harming the just cause of the Dutch. But it was abundantly clear to us all that it was in the interests not only of Java but of the Dutch themselves, if they were ever to get back into Java without violence, that they should talk to as representative a body of Indonesians as possible.

As soon as I could after my return from London, I took a mission from Java, under the leadership of Sjarifoeddin, to Sumatra. It was for me an unforgettable journey, in a way that had nothing to do with the mission, because of what we saw of Sumatra from the air. We flew first of all to Padang, crossing, for a thousand miles or more, dense and seemingly interminable forest and jungle and a whole unknown world of abundant plant life that I knew of first (and as if I had always known it) from reading Conrad's *Lord Jim*, and had then myself experienced in the westernmost jungles and forests of Java. I remembered, in what was a foretaste of what I now saw from the air, how I had walked in forests where on one occasion I fell up to my neck in the moss between the trees. It was a world given over to vegetation and silence. I would lie at night on my blanket on the damp earth as the last of the sunlight was flushing the tips of the trees with a Van Gogh yellow. Though I could see the apes calling to one another, their mouths wide open, their mournful sound did not penetrate the silence where I lay, so thick were the leaves, the moss, the grass and, above all, the giant ferns between the trunks.

All these things that were happening are not only strangely fresh in my memory fifty years after I experienced them, they are also preserved in a letter I was to write to my mother after a late-night session at Padang, in the early morning of 13 December 1945. Despite the urgent intelligence which Brigadier Hutchinson, the Brigadier in command at Padang, conveyed to us, which had kept Amir Sjarifoeddin, his companions and myself talking until late in the night, I woke up after only a few hours' sleep with just one imperative thought: I must write to Mother. I quickly washed, shaved and dressed, and opened my dispatch book at my dressing-table. Then I read the date – which I would have overlooked because dates, in the world where I was occupied, had ceased to matter – and saw that it was my thirty-ninth birthday. I realized that although I had bombarded my mother with cables, I had not written her a letter since I had been released. So, in the midst of all the urgent preoccupations stimulated by the new intelligence we had accumulated the night before, I wrote to her. I had forgotten this letter and its contents, but I was shown a copy of it again very recently by a sister who had been so moved by it that she had copied it out for herself. I give it here because it expresses many things which I had since forgotten, and adds nuances to my description of the state of mind with which I went from prison back to active service, and how this dramatic world and its ancient setting were always interwoven with my own movement of spirit.

15 Corps HQ, Java
13 December 1945

From Lt. Col. van der Post
British Army in India.

My Dearest Mother,
I am writing this to you from Padang in Sumatra and the address marked off at the top is merely put in to give you my permanent address. I came here by plane on a special mission yesterday and tomorrow I am going to Medan, after that back to Batavia.

This is the first letter I have written to you since my release. I have often wanted to but my work did not give me the time or freedom of mind to write you the letter I wanted to write. But today is my birthday and I can't think of a better day for thanking you for all you have been to me and the unselfish love you have given all of us. I think you are the greatest person I have ever known and though my fate and character keep my life far from you, you are always very close to me. I never regretted my life in prison, thanks to your example of facing adversity and sorrow without ever flinching. I have not in the war done anything you need be ashamed of and in prison I worked hard to help others. Life there was cruel and very grim but it uplifted rather than depressed me. I did feel we would not get out of it alive, death was always near us, but the only thing that worried me was the thought that I might not get the chance to say thank you to you. I have learnt to see a new meaning in life, in essence the one you have always had and I know that nothing is wasted and forgotten, that all that is true and faithful to the real goodness of life can never perish.

Of course, when I came out I longed to come home as I do every day, but I felt my duty was here. I am one of the few, perhaps the only one, who can help. I am so much part of the misery, the very great and tragic misery that has been inflicted on these millions of people, that I have to stay and see it through. How long it will take I do not know, but it may take another year.

I am on the staff of General Sir Philip Christison. He is a great man and has been a good leader and friend to me. And my work is mostly to keep the nationalists and extremists as calm and as reasonable as possible. I know many of them and see a lot of them, often under rather exciting circumstances. The other day I got a personal letter from Lord Louis Mountbatten which thanked and praised me for what I had done and he sent me a message he had received from Mr Bevin who said: 'Both the Prime Minister and I wish to thank you for lending Colonel van der Post to us. His contribution to the solution of this very difficult problem has been a very noteworthy one.' Please keep all this news in the family.

The curious thing is my Afrikaans has turned completely into Dutch: that is why I am writing this letter in English. This empire of the Dutch is enormous. Here in Sumatra I have just flown over 1,200 miles of gigantic mountain peaks covered with jungle, uninhabited and wild, and a sort of Voortrekker's instinct awoke in me and I felt a real desire to go and trek through it all again. I did a lot of trekking behind the Japanese lines in Java and lived in endless rain, wet and hungry, on great mountain-tops too.

I flew yesterday over some of them; one of them Djaja Sempoer – the Mountain of the Arrow – on which I had my last headquarters and also over the lovely valley of Lebaksembada – which again in the Sundanese's lovely language means the valley that was well made – where we had many exciting moments with the Japanese.

It has been a strange war but only people who have seen what the Japanese are really like as conquerors can appreciate what the world has been saved from and what a good war it has been.

My love to you Dearest Mother and all the family. The blessings of Xmas to you.

Always,
Laurens.

Looking back on events in Indonesia during that urgent and enigmatic December, I now realize how much I had already achieved in my own way since my return from London. And my letter to my mother confirms, I believe, that there was no egoism in my decision to stay on after the capitulation of the Japanese. It also serves to stress what time may have diminished: how much I relied – and knew I could rely – on the recognition that I received from Attlee and his government and, above all, from Lord Mountbatten, and did not have to depend solely on this strange feeling of a mission I personally had to fulfil.

I had hardly finished writing the letter when there was a loud knock on my door and a summons to join Brigadier Hutchinson. He had had a sleepless night. Like all the brigadiers in 15 Army Corps, he had proved himself over and over again in Burma. But unlike the others he was through and through a soldier and nothing but a soldier, and tended to behave more like a seasoned warrant officer than the commander of a brigade, to such an extent that the bully beef of his own small ration of adjectives consisted chiefly of the infamous four-letter word which characterized the language of professional sergeant-majors and corporals. Not surprisingly, his nickname was just that one four-letter word.

One of his patrols had just come back with disturbing evidence of how the extreme side of nationalism was showing itself, even in an area under his efficient and uncompromising direction. The patrol had been sent out to search for one of his officers. He had gone out with a nurse in the early afternoon the day before, planning to have an evening supper at a lovely cove not far from Padang, and had not come back. At dawn the patrol had found both the nurse and the officer with their throats cut, on the road to the cove. This, the first manifestation of the nationalists in the area going to such extremes, was so obvious that it needed no further explanation, and we left almost immediately to board our old Dakota.

The Dakota was an American aircraft for which we all had a special affection. It was slow compared to other aircraft, but by heaven it was steady and reliable. Dakotas landed all over Europe and in all sorts of places in the Far East on impossible airstrips, at night and by day, and gave all those who had experience of airborne soldiery a confidence in what we were doing which none of us would have liked to do without.

We landed at a small airstrip where cars were waiting to take us to Fort de Kock, a famous Dutch hill-station where the leader of the Sumatran Indonesians, Abdul Ghani, had made his headquarters. As we drove up the winding road into the jungle-covered hills, and passed little country towns and villages, we saw, in the playing fields outside the schools, not only boys but also young girls in uniform drilling with wooden rifles for the war they felt had to come in order to assert their right to be themselves. I realized how well I had read the signs in Java, because there was no doubt that the pattern which was being enacted here among the indigenous people of Sumatra was exactly like that in Java, as I had surmised from the beginning, almost as if both had been organized by the same cosmic power. It was clear that the Dutch were up against an expression of an irrevocable and ultimately irresistible manifestation of a law of life: that everything, from the least and humblest to the greatest and most powerful of living things, has a character, deep-rooted in life, demanding to be recognized and allowed to live to the end of its inbuilt ration of time. There is ultimately only one law, and that is the law of life, a law that can never be wrong, and the sooner it is recognized the better for humanity.

And so came the meeting at Fort de Kock. Amir Sjarifoeddin and his delegation received a great welcome from Abdul Ghani. I left them to talk alone, and then afterwards had an hour with Abdul Ghani myself. He was, even by Indonesian standards, physically small, but what he lacked in inches he made up for in energy and intelligence. Even the Indonesians felt that there were moments when he was almost too clever for his own – and their people's – good. But he was a real asset to the diversity needed to express this extraordinary, spontaneous unanimity that had suddenly presented itself out of the instincts and intuition of the peoples of Indonesia.

He also had what quite a number of the Indonesian leaders lacked because of the weight of the vision pressing down on their spirits –

a wonderful sense of fun and mischief and wit. On one occasion the somewhat infamous Dutch commander, Westerling, who in years to come staged his disastrous coup and threw events out of their valid and inescapable course, burst into Abdul Ghani's office and shouted:

'I am Westerling!'

And Abdul Ghani calmly looked up and replied: 'I am Abdul Ghani, Easterling!'

The pun of course lay in his use of the Dutch word 'Oosterling'; and in Dutch 'Westerling' can also mean 'Westerner'.

All in all I think that meeting at Fort de Kock was of immense importance to what followed, and to the confidence with which men like Sjahrir and Sjarifoeddin and Hatta could proceed to organize a representative Indonesian government in the interior of Java, keeping Soekarno confined to the role which had restricted him for years when, in the interests of his people, he had had to collaborate so openly and apparently ardently with the Japanese.

We returned to Batavia. Within a very short time a more representative Indonesian group, with Sjahrir in command, met Dr van Mook and his staff again in my house. General Christison once more was insistent that this should be purely an occasion between the Dutch and the Indonesians, who after all had to understand one another if the situation in Indonesia was not to be resolved in violence. I cleared out my mess for the occasion and Sri remained to serve them all dinner. 'Dul acted as host, and they talked for hours on end. We never knew or asked for more about the meeting than Sjahrir and Dr van Mook chose to tell us.

All these meetings had not led to an immediate understanding – or even a hint of acceptance – of the reality of nationalism by the Dutch, nor had any of us believed that they could; but they had been of importance because the two groups were no longer merely abstractions, based only on rumours, reputation and gossip. We were thus encouraged to work harder than ever for more meetings between them.

Sjahrir and his 'Cabinet' were confident enough by now to settle themselves in Batavia where they could be in regular touch with the British and, whenever possible, with the Dutch, while Soekarno and Hatta made their homes in the ancient sultanates of Djokja and Solo in the interior where, not without reason, they felt they were safe in a way they could never be in Batavia.

This fear for the safety of Hatta and Soekarno was constantly in my mind as well. As the Dutch presence in Java increased, the

Ambonese who were already in Batavia (having been released from captivity in well-organized bodies by the Japanese) were settling all sorts of issues and grievances with Javanese soldiery who had had contact with them before the war. These confrontations had become so violent and extensive that reluctantly, and perhaps ill-advisedly, we increased the military area in Batavia wherein British edicts would apply. The extension to our perimeter came as a complete surprise to the Indonesians (because, for military reasons, we could not disclose our intentions in advance) but that it was accomplished without any bloodshed on our part was very largely due to the use we made of the Unit of Psychological Warfare of the Indian Army, which had established itself in Batavia.

This unit was commanded with great tact and to positive ends by an ex-schoolmaster called Peterson who, in this area of military public relations, had to deal with complicated issues such as liberty of the press and of broadcasting which under the Japanese had been completely staffed by Indonesians. The fact that he did it so constructively greatly aided our efforts to promote peace and a sense of emerging order in Indonesia.

However, this extension of the military area under British edict in Batavia shows how sensitive General Christison and his staff had become to the outbursts of the Ambonese and other impromptu incursions of violence in the capital. Although at times they thought I was making too much of the matter, the General had already had constant complaints from Dutch officers, who were often senior in rank to me, that I had ordered them about in a manner which was intolerable. But as I was in direct contact with the situation in a way in which no one else was, I was often rung up at night by Indonesians saying that the Ambonese were running amok in their district. I then had to call the Dutch officer on duty and order him to put a stop to it.

'You have no right to talk to me like that!' the Dutch officer would say angrily. 'You are my junior in rank and have no right to give me orders!'

'I am not giving you an order. I am repeating to you the instructions from my General which you are not observing at the moment, and in reality the order is from General Christison and not from me.'

I was grateful, therefore, that one afternoon the General himself witnessed the kind of difficulties with which I had to cope, and saw how suddenly trouble could erupt in the city without warning. Late one afternoon I had already begun my evening report for General

Dempsey in Singapore when Paul Vogt came on the telephone and told me that all his intelligence pointed to a major Ambonese incident occurring somewhere in the centre of Batavia, and that they were deeply perturbed about the extent of it and its consequences. I immediately stopped what I was doing, took my jeep, and went as fast as I could to staff headquarters. As I got out of the jeep an alarming and prolonged outburst of rifle and machine-gun fire broke out at the back of the headquarters, and apparently also in the area beyond it because, amidst the whistle and whine of bullets fired nearby, there was occasionally also the drone of bullets fired from further away.

The immediate reaction in the area around me was, if looked at purely visually, rather comic. As I braked to a halt, I looked across to the officers' mess next to our headquarters where, with the sun already touching the palm trees and announcing what pioneers in Africa called sundown, soldiers were relaxing with their evening pints of beer after a long day. As the firing broke out, all these men, veterans of years of fighting against the Japanese, by common reflex dropped their beer, threw themselves backwards over their chairs, landed on the floor of the ample veranda and quickly rolled on to their stomachs before peering cautiously around them.

I too lost no time in getting inside the headquarters, not only because of the bullets flying around but also because the shooting emphasized that I must do what I had come to do. As I bounded up the wide staircase and came out on the passage on the first floor I was amazed to see my General calmly walking down the corridor towards me. He already had a look on his face which born soldiers have when the shooting begins, a look almost of destiny, as if saying to themselves: 'This is the end to which I was born, and where I have to take over.'

However, his face came out of its concentration when he saw me, and he said: 'So, you are working late as well? What on earth is this row about?'

I told him that I had just come to find out and asked if he would mind coming with me to my office and I would get all the information I could. Within two minutes I had the Dutch officer on the line, told him of the gunfire, and said: 'I am certain you must know all about this.'

'It is no concern of yours. I am in charge here today!' he replied.

'It is every concern of my General's. In fact he is standing right beside me at the moment and I will not hesitate to hand you over to him if you do not change your tone.'

The last thing I wanted to do, of course, was to get my General embroiled with such a voice. Within seconds the officer told me he would look into the matter and stop the fighting as soon as possible, and minutes later the sound of shooting died away. But meanwhile a number of innocent and impoverished citizens of Batavia had been killed in the pursuit of heaven only knew what sort of grievances, imagined or real.

Fortunately the extension of our perimeter improved the situation but it did not stop the inevitable vacuums and loopholes that exist in every system, no matter how good. The most alarming instance of all was when I sent Kenneth Pope one day on an urgent mission to see Sjahrir. He was just in time to find Sjahrir put up against the wall of his house by an illicit Ambonese patrol who were about to shoot him. After this my General took all these incidents very seriously and we had Sjahrir and several other members of the Indonesian Cabinet under indirect observation all the time, because any assassination on that level at that stage would have ended for good any prospect of a peaceful settlement between the Dutch and the Indonesians.

We had then some weeks in which we could develop more and more meetings, official and unofficial, between both sides. Thanks to the situation of my mess on the outskirts of the city, 'Dul and I, every day and often far into the night, saw and received Javanese nationalists of influence and talked to them, and also organized secret meetings for them with any people on the Dutch side that 'Dul thought they should see.

It was interesting in those months how gradually 'Dul and I changed roles. 'Dul, who was supposed to be my liaison with Dr van Mook and the Dutch, more and more depended on me for his contacts with the Indonesians. It was sad to see how this noble and great-hearted Indonesian, with his own vision of a raceless and classless Indonesia, gradually became so suspect to his own countrymen that they ceased seeing him of their own accord and instead made me the intermediary. Simultaneously, all the many Dutch friends I had acquired during captivity – for I had made a very special point of seeing that the Dutch and the British in prison had a good relationship – swiftly dropped away from me.

Trying to develop this relationship in prison had not been easy, indeed was rather disheartening, because our ordinary soldiers and airmen did not get on easily with their Dutch fellow prisoners. There was somehow a deep national temperamental difference which tended to set them apart. However, we did have the good fortune to have a most wonderful self-contained and well-equipped Dutch medical unit with us. We could not have had better and more dedicated people put in charge of our health. They were commanded by a Colonel Wilkins who, prompted perhaps by his English-sounding name, seemed more interested in Shakespeare than in medicine; so interested, in fact, that he was affectionately known by our troops as 'Shakespeare' Wilkins. He took a major part in our impromptu dramatic productions in the camp and ran his unit extraordinarily well.

There had also been in our camp other Dutch officers of outstanding quality, in particular an officer who had fought one of the few military actions against the Japanese at Balikpapan (an oil production centre in Borneo) and had been brought by the Japanese to Java. He was called Sim de Waal and he became a good friend of mine in prison until the Japanese decided to send him to Manchuria to join the most senior Allied officers held in captivity there. There were also Dutch schoolmasters and interesting Dutch civil servants like Idenburg, and an ex-Governor of western Java, Mr Hoogewind, who all endeared themselves to us, but on the whole our men seemed to prefer making friends with the Chinese, the Ambonese and the Medanoese. They were instantly at their ease with them, particularly with the Chinese, not least because they found the Chinese laughed at the same things as they did.

But it is the memory of the medical unit in particular that stays with me, because I was now to find in Indonesia that, after centuries of Dutch rule in Java, it was of Dutch doctors and Dutch schoolmasters that the Javanese spoke with the most genuine gratitude and affection. It is amazing how, without fail, in the midst of the turmoil and dissension of those days, that contribution from the life of Holland was invariably spoken of with warmth.

It was inevitable, of course, with all that I had to do in this new world of turmoil, that I should lose contact with the Dutch I had known in prison, but even such contacts as remained, and new ones that I had made among the Dutch people, quickly began to fade and diminish. As fast as I made friends among the Indonesians of all persuasions, I seemed to lose them among the Dutch. People with whom I had endured captivity for three and a half years became visibly formal in their manner and ultimately avoided me. It was something which progressed slowly and remorselessly and continued until the end of my mission in Java. Fortunately for the purposes of my mission, I think that in this changing of roles both 'Dul and I gained

a balance and a sense of the totality in which we were involved which
we could not possibly have done if just confined to our national roles.

Soon we were able to envisage and explore with the Foreign Office
the possibility of a large formal meeting between the Dutch under
Dr van Mook and the Indonesians under Sjahrir on a higher level.
Our greatest difficulty was to arrange such a meeting with the Dutch,
but in the end it became possible and the Foreign Office intimated
that they would designate one of the most senior ambassadors in the
diplomatic service, Sir Archibald Clark Kerr, then Ambassador in
Moscow, to preside over such a meeting.

This would not have been possible if it had not been for the
appearance, fairly early on in the year, of Gilbert MacKereth whom
the Foreign Office had decided to send to establish a presence in
Batavia. He was an experienced Foreign Office servant, not from the
highest and more spectacular reaches of the official ambassadorial
world but one who had steadily come up from the consular service,
and had been picked out as singularly suitable for this role. Having
him there was one of the best and most truly good things that happened to me in the whole period of my official work in Java. And
there could hardly have been a better choice to represent Great
Britain in the complexities and turmoil of Indonesia and South-east
Asia.

In all the years of experience I was to have in working with the
Foreign Office both officially and unofficially, I have always thought
that the decision to abolish the consular service as a separate department was detrimental. Because consuls spent a considerable time in
just one area or country, they were able to acquire an unrivalled
knowledge of its working and of the potential within its relationship
with Great Britain. Nor were they subject to the terrible afflictions of
careerism. The addition of the consular service to the ranks of the
Foreign Office has not enriched the diplomatic service but rather has
gradually reduced it to carrying out, I think inadequately and not
half as well, what the consuls did so well on their own. Increasingly
the work that the great ambassadors of Britain performed so
uniquely has been diminished in importance, and the secretaries of
state, with political appointees as heads of the Foreign Office, have
taken over, reducing embassies abroad to serving the commercial and
materialistic aims of their country, instead of being a real influence
in the eventualities of our time.

As for Gilbert MacKereth, he had in full and overflowing measure
all the qualities which the consular service predisposed its officers to

cultivate. He had even served for years in Ethiopia, which created a bond between us because of my own experience there. He had actually been stationed for years at Harar, one of the first cities we helped to liberate from the Italians. There he had, like me, gone into the bazaars and souks to see if among its oldest inhabitants he could trace any memory of the poet Rimbaud who, towards the end of the nineteenth century, was held by legend to have been an arms dealer if not a gun runner in the city. It had been as sad to him as it had been to me to find that someone so young, so good-looking and so remarkable as Rimbaud should have left no trace of memory behind.

What was more, MacKereth had distinguished himself as a soldier in France in the First World War. Towards the end, in the most bloody of the final phases on the Western Front, he had become one of the youngest brigade commanders. Ordered by the Staff to participate in a general assault on entrenched German lines, he did not take for granted their planning of the manner in which he would have to conduct the coming battle but instead, three nights before, went with his batman to explore the narrow no-man's land between his and the German forces. He came to the conclusion that the Staff's plan for the assault would be a disaster, that it would gain nothing and would lead to the probable elimination of his brigade.

He reported to his General in those terms. His General, however, was totally unsympathetic and summed up his response by saying: 'I have heard you, MacKereth, but my orders stand, and I am sure you will see that they are properly carried out.'

To which MacKereth replied: 'I am sorry, sir, but I have to tell you here and now that I cannot possibly obey such a disastrous order.'

When he told me of the incident I found I had a curious link with him. There was a passage in our manual of King's Regulations which he had absorbed and digested as thoroughly as I myself had done. Indeed I had frequently used it to justify occasions when I was completely out of touch with my base and had to do things that were in apparent conflict with my original orders and briefing. The passage declares that if an officer does not carry out an order, knowing that by carrying it out he will defeat the original purpose for which the order was given, he shall not be found guilty of disobeying the order. I cannot express how much this provision in the King's Regulations, which to this day I still think is a singularly enlightened public document, brought me help and comfort in Indonesia. But MacKereth had quoted it to his General in vain. I remember saying to him that perhaps it was because he did not have the advantage that I had possessed of being out of touch with the officer who, months before, had given me the order. However, his refusal was taken very seriously. He could easily have been court-martialled and shot for disobeying an order, but the horror of the bloodshed in France had so entered into the new sort of officers who were replacing the old that he was merely removed from his command. A new brigadier was appointed who gallantly carried out the order and lost nearly the whole of his brigade in the process.

Out of that war Gilbert MacKereth had emerged with a strange affliction – he had to wear dark glasses almost night and day. It was almost as if his eyes could no longer endure the light of what they had seen for so long in the trenches. This lasted until he met Crichton-Miller, the pioneer of modern psychology-in-depth, who rendered such distinguished service to the nerve-racked and shell-shocked soldiers who were cast adrift at the end of the war and who failed to make their peace with life, as if inwardly they were still at war (as indeed they were). Crichton-Miller calmly said to him: 'You know, the trouble is that you are blaming on the glare of the day the horror which is not there but singularly in yourself. The light you are shading your eyes from is not in the sun, but within.'

From then on the glare became a light within, and with the light came understanding. The darkness in which he had been sheltering had been his own rejection of the light that would heal him. In a flash he was on the way to finding his peace, and emerged to become one of the most complete and whole people I have ever known.

This brief sketch of Gilbert MacKereth would be even more incomplete if I did not talk about his wife, Muriel. It has always been for me a source of confidence and joy in the workings of life that two people like Gilbert and Muriel should have come together as man and woman as well, and achieved a greater wholeness than they had possessed as individuals. They so complemented each other that one never had the feeling one often has with couples, that one would prefer to enjoy them separately. One enjoyed them even more as individuals when they were together.

Muriel had gone happily with Gilbert MacKereth wherever his eventful consular life had taken him, and while he was dealing with the complexities of his own office she would create a lovelier garden to leave for her successors. She was proud of the flower- and partic-ularly the rose-gardens she had made in widely differing parts of the world. She was beautiful, not in a *Picture Post* way but in a truly straightforward feminine way: she was tallish, slim, elegant, moved beautifully, expressed herself with extraordinary sensitivity and lucidity, and had an immense sense of fun.

She and Gilbert came into my life at a moment when I already had eight years of war behind me. I had therefore been moving entirely in a male world, much of it brutalized, and had been deprived of the kind of values which women bring to human relationships. This made the impact of Muriel's profoundly feminine self on my imagination all the greater because she gave me a kind of care and affection that I had been denied for so long. She showed this in so many ways throughout that period in Java that without her I do not think that I could have taken the increasing rejection, and ultimately hatred, that was hurled at me by the Dutch.

Typical of her singular, selfless femininity was the kindness that she showed to Sybil on my staff, who had found herself, during her most sensitive adolescent years, a captive of the Japanese. Muriel was aware of this, aware of the potential which only a woman could bring alive in Sybil's mind and spirit, and established a very special relationship with her. When she came to leave Java with her husband, Muriel gave Sybil a beautiful necklace of moonstones which had been for generations in her own family. I think being given that gift was one of the most important things that had ever happened to that young woman.

Finally, with happy synchronicity, the MacKereths' charming residence in Batavia was just across the wide street and immediately opposite my own mess. We were neighbours not only in spirit but also in location. That too, in its way, made a significant contribution to the kind of communication necessary to achieve what we did.

This synchronicity had within it another bonus, which made one almost fearful that such unaccustomed bounty from Providence might conceal a price to pay in the future. There happened to be an all-weather tennis court which in peacetime the two houses had shared between them, and I found that Gilbert loved tennis as much as I did. He had got his tennis Blue at Cambridge. I had only played for my school in Africa but I was born into a house in the interior which had one of the very few private tennis courts to be found north of the Orange River. Tennis had been a game in my life ever since I could remember, and now in our hard-pressed days Gilbert and I would snatch a couple of hours and have four or five sets of singles. It was for both of us psychologically, and for my physical rehabilitation, of tremendous importance, and it did not matter that Gilbert usually beat me. However, there were days when, in some curious way, a kind of reflex-self which I did not know existed came to my aid and I would beat him, and it caused a great deal of banter and celebration.

The phase that preceded the coming of Sir Archibald Clark Kerr from Moscow was further enriched by General Christison. I have already referred to the way in which the Dutch, not only in Indonesia but also in The Hague, were increasingly to turn against me. For the time being, I had the good fortune to be protected in this regard by both the General and Mountbatten who saw the future exactly as I, and now MacKereth, did. Even Mountbatten had not, as yet, inherited more than a mite of the hatred ultimately conceived towards him by those who increasingly replaced the likes of the liberal Schermerhorn and Logemann. Instead it was General Christison who became for a time almost the sole focus of Dutch criticism, and this finally led to a malicious persecution which I found very hard to endure on his behalf. But he went on as if, once he had left his office for some peace in the residence put at his disposal, he had no cares in the world. He remained his calm, composed, balanced, generous and, above all, affectionate self. This last may seem a strange adjective to use for a General but I had come to the conclusion that all the truly outstanding generals had this quality of feeling and affection, and were not merely extensions of a reasoned and coldly classical, Caesar-like military command.

One of the greatest examples in British military history was Wellington, of course, and then there was Sir John Moore, also the product of decades of war in America, India and the Peninsula, who was buried at Corunna. He never failed to inspire a positive tide of feeling among the men of the forlorn armies he had to lead, as British generals so often did at the beginning of great endeavours. The moving ballad on his burial, in a grave dug by the bayonets of his soldiers, is just one expression of the emotion that went through all who had served with him when they heard of his death.

And, of course, drawing on the history of Greece, as I so often do, there is the timeless example of Xenophon and his lost and apparently doomed ten thousand, and their march to the sea, where their cry '*Thalassa! Thalassa!*' ('The sea! The sea!') at last could be uttered with a final sense of home-coming, and which will echo for ever in the history of the spirit of soldiers raised to a great height by a commander of genius and compassion.

General Christison never commanded the largest of armies but he fought in crucial positions in many critical campaigns and shared this quality to the full. I have many memories of incidents that illustrate what I have in mind, but there is one unfailing memory which comes to me often. It conveys a great era of history and should speak for itself.

Like the headquarters staff of all armies, that of the 15 Army Corps tried as much as possible to keep to regular hours. With calls being made upon them night and day, they were forced to do so, not only for the sake of their own sanity and well-being but for the sake of the overall purpose they were serving. Calls made upon them out of hours were, on the whole, adequately dealt with by a small but efficient duty staff. My own work, however, was singularly alien to any such concept. Most things I had to do were rooted in totally unconventional and unpredictable circumstances, and I was forced very often to call on the General out of hours, both for his information and to make certain that he approved of my response to the challenges new intelligence demanded of us.

I saw a lot of him, therefore, in his so-called off-duty life in Batavia, and the occasion I have in mind happened not once but several times. I would go to him, most frequently in the early evening, when something had arisen which he should know of before I signalled it to General Dempsey in Singapore and through him to Lord Mountbatten. On these occasions I was often to find him at ease in the ample garden of his own mess. The comfortable Madeira chairs would be set out, the table laid beautifully for tea and refreshment, and the General would be surrounded by the Indian warrant officers of the 15 Indian Army Corps. There was no need that he should ever see all his officers, but he felt, as all good commanding officers in the Indian Army did, the need to be there, in a more intimate manner, for these members of the great and diverse Indian contribution to his forces. He himself would be serving them with tea, and it is amazing how he gained in stature by it and enlarged that sense of all belonging to the authentic pattern of the soldier that was always there, in spite of differences of creed, race and religion, in the nature of the Indian Army.

I somehow could not imagine this happening in other colonial armies. I may be wrong, but in all that I have read of the history of empire this seemed to me to be something unique in the Indian Army, and it told one an enormous amount ultimately about Britain's centuries-long association with India.

I often wondered if it ever occurred to the Dutch what an extra-ordinary phenomenon it was that the 15 Indian Army Corps was here at all – after some six years of war, with every soldier anxious to have done with war and go home – and entrusted with the mission that the British had undertaken in Indonesia. It was all the more extraordinary if one remembers that, from the moment the Japanese entered the war, they made an immense effort to seduce the Indian Army and tried through people like Subhas Chandra Bose to create an Indian rebel army, as it were, against the British. In this the Japanese had failed miserably. And now here, within months of the British giving independence to India, they could yet trust an essentially Indian army with a mission of holding the fort on behalf of an ally bitterly resented at that particular moment by the native population of Indonesia, with whom, obviously, the native ingredient dominant in the 15 Indian Army Corps could not help but have an historic feeling of sympathy.

There was a moment when it was felt that, as we had an essentially Indian force in Java, it would be a good thing if we could extract a message to Soekarno from Nehru himself (who was already designated within a few months to take over an independent India from Britain) that would help us in the difficult task we had to perform. This was achieved principally by Mr Panjabi, a civil servant from India, who had appeared in our midst largely to take care of commercial interests in India, but who also had a brief to observe and report back to Nehru on what was going on. He enabled me to get a verbal message for Soekarno to the effect that Nehru wanted Soekarno to know that no one could have pressed harder for the British to leave India than he had. He had succeeded, but he sometimes wondered if he had not pressed just a little too hard, and whether the British should perhaps have stayed a while longer. However, the British were leaving him with three elements of government that were indispensable for a viable modern democracy: a non-political and incorruptible civil service; a non-political and incorruptible judicial system; and, above all, a non-political and incorruptible army. Soekarno, from his observation, had as yet got none of these things and in the circumstances he thought Soekarno should pipe down.

All the points that Nehru made in general were vividly illustrated by the three Indian Army divisions we had in Java, particularly the 5th Division which I had already encountered in Abyssinia and the Western Desert and which had fought so brilliantly in the battle for

Sourabaya. For instance, there was a moment in Ethiopia a few days after the battle of Keren when I went into Keren myself. There I noticed the men of the 5th Division, who had fought the battle together, walking about with their little fingers linked. It was such an extraordinary and heart-warming sight that I mentioned it to General Platt, who said there was a particular reason for it.

He told me how he had taken his Brigade and had trained it for the battle of Keren to come. He had thought that, under those conditions, the one British battalion (a battalion of the Camerons) would probably not do as well as the Indians who were born to the heat and physical conditions in which the battle had to be fought. During the battle he had to commit every force at his disposal before he could win, and the Indian battalion seemed to have got to the top of Brigadier's Peak first. But when the Indian soldiers themselves got to the top they found seven dead Camerons mixed with the dead Italians: the Camerons had got there first. After this the Camerons and their two sister battalions had become inseparable.

In those early days of 1946, when the political outcome of what we were trying to bring about was so often disappointing, General Christison began a Sunday ritual that gave me and all who worked for him a singular joy and encouragement. Each Sunday morning I would come back from my night in *Cumberland* as fast as I could, because so much of importance would accumulate at my little headquarters overnight that I had to be there early for the start of the day. And each Sunday, in the tradition of Indonesia as well as of the British world, 'Dul's wife Sri would make the midday meal a very special occasion.

Sri was not only a wonderful cook and housekeeper in the best Indonesian sense but, with her natural taste, had acquired much of what was good in Western cooking in the course of her husband's service abroad, and had earned us the reputation of having the best table in Java. I am certain that, as far as the British army was concerned, this was more than true and I appreciated how extraordinarily lucky we were to have Sri to look after us.

One Sunday General Christison joined us at this meal, and from then on he made it a habit always to have his Sunday meal with us. From the start it had its own ritual, because he brought with him Alistair McLean, one of his Staff brigadiers, who I think was almost as good a piper as Alan Breck in Stevenson's *Kidnapped* had been. He would be there ready to pipe in the dinner for the General once he was seated with his ADC at our table. The sound of the pipes on those very still afternoons, which yet trembled with the strain of containing all the earthquake energy and electricity that charged the atmosphere of those days, and those tunes of ancient Scotland, home of the Camerons, would dominate the tense silence. The sound would also somehow arouse the curiosity of this fringe neighbourhood of Batavia, and young children and spectators would accumulate in the streets outside the low walls that surrounded our garden, trying very hard – with their innate sense of courtesy – to look as if they just happened to be there, listening wide-eyed and with straining ears to the antique sound. Then, when Alistair McLean had completed his march round and round the table, he would go outside and march around the whole house as if he were bringing it too into all that there was of hospitality and blessing in the rousing music. Back in the room he would stand to attention beside the General's chair and, although it was Java and it was a tropical afternoon and not, as these occasions were in the Highlands of Scotland, the beginning of the darkness of night, he would accept a glass of neat whisky from the General. As custom decreed, he would drink it down in one long gulp and then with a flourish of chivalry, would put down the glass, turn smartly about and withdraw to his own quarters, his pipes like a living thing under his arm.

Somehow, from the very first Sunday dinner, this ritual of the pipes and their evocative sound in that remote equatorial world of islands did not seem out of place at all; on the contrary, it all looked and sounded singularly appropriate. And then in the middle of the third or fourth Sunday dinner I suddenly knew why. As a child in the African bush my schoolteacher had taught me a ballad called 'The Relief of Lucknow'. I cannot recall the ballad in detail but I remember that the indication that at last relief was coming reached a beleaguered Lucknow with the sound of those pipes:

> Faint and far beyond the Gumty
> Rose and fell the pipers' blast . . .

What made the recollection so singularly appropriate was that the half-starved and besieged British in Lucknow heard it also in the same tropical atmosphere in which I was listening in such comfort now. Such moments were essential for us who were so hard pressed at the time.

*

The meetings with the Dutch and the Indonesians went on and were arranged and rearranged, and their progress can be followed on a day-to-day basis in my official report which follows (p. 208) and which to me reads today rather like the chart of a severely ill patient in hospital with its outline of the up-and-down temperature between one crisis and another.

At the second meeting in my house between the Dutch and the Indonesians, the Dutch were free to present their own interpretation, unchallenged, of the meaning of the British presence in Java to the Indonesians. Sjahrir in particular emerged not only depressed but with a suspicion of the British that was totally uncharacteristic and, as he shared it with me, rather alarming. I think it was a tribute to the trust we had established that I was able to guide him out of it. Now, steadily, the Indonesians' confidence in themselves was increasing and their self-esteem gained as international awareness of their existence and their problem grew, so much so that we were truly ready for the coming of Sir Archibald Clark Kerr.

Looking back, I think the moment was well chosen. I knew very little about the Ambassador's record except that he was said to have been one of the few ambassadors to whom Stalin really listened, and in recognition of his services he became Lord Inverchapel while he was with us.

Although we were fully prepared, his actual arrival was unexpected. I was at Semarang where I had gone to settle some problems with the Indonesians over the evacuation of the Dutch internees in their power. It was an extremely sensitive area where severe fighting had taken place between ourselves (with the Japanese) and the young Javanese militants. The battle had been so intense and the Japanese had fought so well that in thanking them afterwards we told their young colonel he had really earned a DSO. Every year for a long time afterwards in his Christmas cards to me he wrote, with a huge exclamation mark, a plaintive: 'Any news of my DSO?!' I had hardly arrived at Semarang when I was given a message that I was to fly back immediately to Batavia because the Ambassador was expected the following day.

My own personal contribution, apart from all the work I was doing, was to give him a quiet evening in my mess, where some of the more distinguished and non-political Indonesians I had got to know came to meet him. I was assisted by Paul Vogt, who had links with the surprisingly sophisticated cultural life of Batavia. At heart Vogt was an artist, and he had got to know Batavia in a way which the

Dutch themselves did not. He had assembled for me a superb little chamber group consisting of a cellist, a violinist and a guitarist. In addition I had a young Indonesian of the Sastro Mulyono family, who went under his childhood name of Bambang and was really a kind of Indonesian Mozart. From the time he could finger a piano, and without teaching of any kind, he played superbly. His rendering of the *Appassionata*, entirely by ear and from coaching by the more experienced musicians around him, was wonderful. It all gave a distinct Batavian flavour to Sir Archibald's welcome.

Paul Vogt had been physically badly shaken by his experience in Sourabaya, where he had been with the murdered Brigadier Mallaby. Indeed he had only escaped with his life when he managed to swim down a drain. This had increased his tendency to deafness, and I now lost no time in organizing his return to Switzerland, just praying that he would not be prosecuted under Swiss law for having disobeyed it by serving actively in the military forces of an alien country. Happily, with the help of the Foreign Office, I managed to prevent his prosecution and in time the commission of Captain which I had conferred on him in the jungles of Bantam was recognized by the War Office in London. He was given a Captain's pension and was able to settle down on the shores of Lake Maggiore, where he lives to this day, to follow his instinctive gift for sculpture to which I had been first introduced in the house he had built for himself in the valley of Lebaksembada. In the midst of a perfectly organized geophysical museum, there stood a bust he had done, in the heart of the jungle, of Winston Churchill, based on a portrait from the *Illustrated London News*. It was later sent to Batavia to be auctioned for an Allied war fund.

I saw, of course, a great deal of the Ambassador, but I did not really get to know him as a person. We were too busy and too deeply focused on the work we had to do to have time to register each other as individuals. I liked him enormously for having the courage to defy local Dutch opinion (and even an appeal by Dr van Mook to The Hague), for his delicacy in paying an informal courtesy call on Sjahrir, and for all the preparatory work that he did to enable me to keep in touch with the Indonesians.

And then he had a natural eccentricity that tended to endear him to me. He insisted on writing all his dispatches himself, rather than dictate them to secretaries. Moreover, he refused to write them with any contemporary pen and had instead an assortment of quills, which he cut and sharpened himself and with which he wrote in a most elegant, eighteenth-century hand. The dispatches were always extremely well written and had, I think, an unusual refinement, even in a Foreign Office where, at the time, the standard of writing was singularly high. In all his time in Java he worked away calmly and steadily, and brought his relationships with the Indonesians to such a point that he could recognize and speak to Soekarno himself.

For our first official meeting in *Cumberland* I think I rather startled everyone by bringing the whole of my small staff, including three young Dutch women, to help me through the discussions. As all three women had been born in Indonesia and had a youthful view of the country and its future, I thought that they could convey the extraordinary atmosphere, which in the background so dominated all negotiations, as nothing else could. Indeed, the questions put to them by Sir Archibald were so perceptive that they drew perceptive answers. We also had an addition from the DMI's staff in Singapore, a very fine, fastidious and attractive young woman called Elizabeth Ebberly, who was an assistant to Jimmy Alms, a new and permanent Intelligence brigadier.

All through March Sir Archibald, with Gilbert MacKereth by his side and now with his own house and staff, worked so tactfully and so well that a final meeting at the highest levels yet achieved was able to take place between the Indonesians, for the first time firmly under Sjahrir, and Dr van Mook and his new staff. All the old guard, Dr van der Plas and the others, had been ditched, and new people like Idenburg brought in. The heads of the so-called Dutch military intelligence were also involved, and General Spoor, a young soldier, was appointed as Commander-in-Chief of the Dutch forces to come and assist Dr van Mook and to replace the unbelievable Admiral Helfrich.

It was high time that Admiral Helfrich was sacked. I had been at a conference with him once, before the Japanese invasion, discussing the possibilities of a combined operation between Admiral Palliser (Wavell's naval adviser) and myself. He had seemed to me even then a most vain and presumptuous boaster and natural bully, and possibly a coward at heart. Ever since his arrival with Mr van der Plas he had been a source of mischief-making and yet, armed with the power of this strange illusion that the Dutch had about him, they did not see through him, despite his making such remarks as: 'The only thing the Indonesians understand are whiffs of grapeshot.' These remarks presupposed an experience he never had, because nobody could recollect when he had ever been involved even in a skirmish let alone a battle. It was a relief to find him at last out of the way. Yet his was one of the voices still listened to, to the end of our time, by people in high places in Java and Holland.

These meetings under Sir Archibald Clark Kerr went so well that at the end an agreement was reached and duly sent off to The Hague for ratification. The agreement seemed to us to be a valid if not generous resolution of the differences between the Dutch and the Indonesians. Both Sjahrir and Dr van Mook emerged satisfied. I say both, but I was never quite certain of van Mook. Sjahrir, I knew, felt that they had done better than anyone could have foretold only a few weeks before. Dr van Mook, rationally and intellectually, was also satisfied, but I always felt that within him was the beat of the historic Dutch unconscious which denied what reason dictated; and that, in the end, this unsleeping Dutch East India Company pattern, however disguised, could have its way and wreck all that we appeared to have achieved.

Sir Archibald went home to deserved acclaim because the essence of the agreement that he achieved in Indonesia substantially remained, however new the words and new the people who later negotiated the final settlement during the British occupation. Yet the agreement itself, although officially ready and waiting for signature, was never ratified, and the consequences of this for Sjahrir, who had gained immensely in prestige by it, were severe.

In the months that followed 'Dul and I had constant hard and unremitting work to keep the Indonesians from veering off towards militant nationalism. 'Dul had much more success with the Dutch at first, and it often looked as if I and the Sjahrir element would fail. But I knew somehow that, just like the Dutch, the Indonesians also had an historic heart of their own, and that it would not fail them.

The Malay culture to which the Indonesian people belong, despite the Hindu, Buddhist and Muslim layers imposed on them, has a fundamental quality which is in their word '*malu*', the element from which their name for themselves originated and which means 'gentleness'. They are in every way a people who prize gentleness, politeness and consideration for one another in their social behaviour, but at the same time there is another element which is almost a sense of rebellion against what they instinctively seem to feel is a hubris of gentleness. It produces a phenomenon which in Malaya is called '*amok*' and in Indonesia '*mata gelap*', and which, as we have seen, means 'the dark eye'. Both in Indonesia and in Malaya, at around the age of forty, a male may suddenly seem to rebel against all this goodness and gentleness and considerate behaviour that he has displayed all his life, and run amok with his dagger, murdering anyone in his way.

It was truly frightening in Malaya to see the horror which seized remote communities when the cry of '*Amok!*' went up; and it was as great a horror when '*Mata gelap!*' was heard and the realization seized a Javanese community that an eye had suddenly darkened in their midst.

Both these concepts describe to me, of course, how we too in the West know this phenomenon collectively. Our wars have not really been due to the reasons we have had for justifying them: at heart we all have inadequacies and an unconscious hubris that can lead to a collective darkening of the eye – such a darkening as seized the whole of the German race under Hitler and led to one of the most terrible events in history, the Holocaust.

There had also been collective occurrences of '*mata gelap*' in Indonesia, to which I have not yet referred. It was constantly at work among the people of Atjeh in the north of Sumatra, and in the history of western Java, the part of Java known as the Bantam of Sundawa. The Bantamese would often break out and inflict violence on the structures of law and order of their day. It is not for nothing that from their poultry came the Bantam cock which the Europeans imported as the best fighters for the cock-fighting that was for so many centuries a European sport.

I was always aware that somehow we had to conduct things in such a way that this earthquake aspect of the Javanese people would not take over. Therefore, in those often discouraging months that followed Sir Archibald Clark Kerr's mission, and amidst general disappointment over the failure of The Hague to ratify what everybody had regarded as a successful agreement, I concentrated entirely on working with Sjahrir, because I feared the reappearance of the military tendency, particularly among the young, in a natural reaction against the agreement on which Sjahrir had staked his reputation.

One of the major events of that period was the reappearance of a Javanese called Tan Malakka after some twenty-five years of exile, during which he had taken refuge in Tashkent in Stalinist Russia. Tashkent was reported to have had for a generation a Russian school of revolution, to support potential communist outbreaks elsewhere in the world. Tan Malakka was the most famous of contemporary nationalist personalities because, as his exile continued, he gained in the mythological stature which was inevitably conferred on him by the increasing national awareness of the Indonesian people. His coming was feared by the Dutch as much as it was looked forward to by the Indonesians. Although he was cheered by thousands when he arrived in Solo, and in time some irregular soldiery grouped themselves around his image, his reappearance had no serious repercussions. That this was so was, in a sense, a measure of the way in which Sjahrir had managed to increase the stature of the present nationalist leadership.

Also there was always among the Indonesian people this tendency I have mentioned towards Muslim fundamentalism. Dr Moewardi, for instance, who was present at my first meeting with the Indonesian nationalists, was a recognized leader of the potentially powerful Muslim fundamentalist element among the young. It was a factor we always had to take into account. There was a moment while Sjahrir was regrouping his men in Solo when these irregular forces abolished the Sultanate of Solo, the oldest and most prestigious of the hereditary structures of Indonesia. Sjahrir became embroiled in the coup and he too was captured. Maria Ulfah Santoso, who happened to be on her way to see Soekarno, instantly mobilized her bodyguard to go to the rescue of Sjahrir. The supporters of the coup vanished overnight. Nonetheless, it was a warning signal of the negative aspects of the long delay in ratifying the Clark Kerr agreement.

Something occurred in sorting out the coup and its consequences which I did not sufficiently appreciate at the time, although it was to become part of my and 'Dul's considerations. The aftermath of the coup served to bring Soekarno out of the purely constitutional role of President which had been conferred on him by the Indonesian nationalists. He, whom Dr van Mook and others had dismissed as simply an inspired windbag and potentially a coward who would never fight, had acted with impressive resolution and initiative. His own countrymen, however, did not fail to recognize this and immediately he was absolved of whatever censure there might have been in the label of 'collaborator with the Japanese' which they too had thrust on him. From that moment he started on his way to becoming an alternative (in the far-off future) to Sjahrir, Hatta and Sjarifoeddin, who were then gaining in power and prestige.

I, for my part, knew that the Indonesians had actually benefited from the past period of apparent ineffectualness. They and their cause, unknown or even unsuspected before the war, had come – through us – to be acknowledged by the world. There was something at work which was indifferent to what we as individuals were doing, and which was creating a climate that in the end would be more decisive than anything we could achieve, though we would serve the immediate demands of the situation with the same commitment as we worked for the wider vision.

But before that moment came, sadly for me and indeed us all, General Christison was recalled. He left, as was his nature, carrying his can and those of several other of the exalted actors on the scene, and dropped them all in the first waste disposal unit of time to vanish without a rattle or a ripple.

But the providence which disposes the fall of a sparrow saw to it that chance at its nicest ordered things so that 'Christie' served his last appointment in the British Army by Arthur's Seat in the Castle overlooking Edinburgh, and ended his service as Colonel-in-Chief of his regiment – which perhaps mattered to him most of all.

And it was at Inverness, the depot of his regiment, the Camerons, that many years later he and I had our last meeting of all. He and the Burma Star Association arranged it so that the city conferred its treasured Freedom upon me for the occasion, and my General and I were driven together through street after street of the city in the long, level light of an abundant summer's evening.

CHAPTER EIGHT

Strange Interlude

FOR ME PERSONALLY the most important change was the going of General Christison, but many other 'important' personalities also returned to Europe at the same time, ostensibly to ratify what Sir Archibald Clark Kerr had achieved, and left the stage for a moment empty. And yet the theatre itself had never been more crowded or more anxious for a feeling of resolution and a better future. It was most noticeable in the sense in which the military establishments in South-east Asia now lost much of their wartime importance and almost rendered themselves – to use one of the sinister euphemisms of our time – redundant.

It is true that Singapore continued, not only until the end of our occupation in Java but beyond, to have a life and a certain importance of its own, but it was a diminishing one. As long as Lord Mountbatten remained in command the island was for us an important intermediary point between him and the other duties he had in South-east Asia, and we continued until the end to go there regularly for conferences. But in itself it was increasingly a shade of what it had been.

In Java, too, it seemed to me that with the going of General Christison the role of what the Foreign Office, when I was there in London, had called the soldier-statesman in Indonesia was becoming more and more that of an outright military commander. He was there as impressive evidence that if the overall policy in Java failed to such an extent that the violence which had characterized the beginning of our occupation recurred on an increasing scale, he could act in a decisive manner and reimpose an ordered evolution of events immediately.

Fortunately, the political aspect of the military appointment which General Christison had had to carry in the beginning was now served and contained by Gilbert MacKereth, who made the military task infinitely simpler. And the soldier who came to take General Christison's place was an expression of this new simplification of military duties. His name was General Sir Montague ('Monty') Stopford and, by this strange synchronicity which haunted events, he was a direct descendant of the Admiral Stopford who had commanded the fleet that came with Stamford Raffles to remove the French revolutionary sympathizers among the Dutch from the islands. He was in every way a fine soldier and a gentleman.

How little taste, therefore, he had for his appointment to the command of 15 Army Corps in those circumstances, emerged very clearly in the talk we had when I first met him at the airport and took him to his headquarters in Batavia. All that he had read of the record of our occupation, and the briefing he had had, made him feel that he was in for a dimension of deceitfulness and intrigue totally unbecoming to an officer and a gentleman. In fact, some time early on in Batavia, he said to me: 'I cannot imagine circumstances more lethal for a simple soldier than this mess of pottage you have in Indonesia.'

He did not stay long, therefore, and his place was almost immediately taken by the comparatively young General Mansergh, who had distinguished himself as a brigadier not only in Burma but also in the fighting in Java. He had been given the command of the 5th Division and promoted General, and from there had been promoted to the command of the whole of 15 Army Corps. His appointment could not have marked more strikingly for me the new era that was going to take over in the fate of Indonesia. He was to stay in command until the evacuation of the British forces, and the role he played in that period is fully and objectively described in the report that I shall present in due course.

What could not figure in that report were the difficulties that his appointment caused for me and, to a minor degree, Gilbert MacKereth. In this regard, among so many other reasons, I could not have welcomed more the presence of Gilbert MacKereth, who had arrived as Consul-General among us but had now become the British Minister in Batavia. In a very short space of time, he had worked himself into a mastery of the role which no other adviser or consultant had had before, and I knew that, whatever the difficulties

with General Mansergh, the vision, in so far as vision could be introduced into our mission in Java, was as safe as it could ever be. He was
the one person who escaped censure and gained the respect of
Indonesians and Dutch alike. This I think was due mainly to the fact
that he was unusually gifted and was doing his work not in pursuit of
a career but out of a sense of vocation. There were no corners or
angles to his personality to which prejudices could attach themselves,
and as far as our policy went his decisions were final. But as he gained
in reputation, I continued to gain in notoriety among the Dutch as a
kind of villain, and all that was wrong was blamed on what people
regarded as my most undesirable influence on him and on the people
who made our policy.

As for General Mansergh himself, I had met him just after the
battle for Sourabaya – which he conducted superbly – and after he
had been in command of the 5th Division for some weeks. We had
thought it would be a good thing if Sir Archibald Clark Kerr also
went to Sourabaya to see General Mansergh and perhaps have an
evening with all the soldiers in his command, so that he could talk to
them and explain what the British occupation of Java was really all
about.

General Mansergh presided over this crowded meeting of soldiers
and managed it as well as he had done his battle. I remember I
thought he did it so well because he seemed to have a lot of theatre
in him, and to be everything that Lord Slim depicted him to be in his
great book about the 'Forgotten Army'. There he tells of a visit to
General Mansergh's brigade in Burma and how he found the
General, in the midst of a front-line battlefield, dressed, as always, as
if he were going to 'a fashionable duck shoot' in England.

It was obvious, even to me, that he was a person who attached an
enormous importance to appearances. He reminded me very much
in that regard of 'Boy' Browning and the *bella figura* persona I have
described on the occasion of my visit to Mountbatten's headquarters.
Yet this was not a shallow form of vanity, as it is with most people; it
was rather that the world's approval of himself and his conduct was
important to him. And this world, I was to find, included the 'society'
that had emerged amongst the growing Dutch presence in Batavia.
Something similar, though to a less alarming degree, was certainly
palpable among the officers of his staff, who had more of a taste and
a sympathy for this Dutch aspect of Indonesia than they had for the
Indonesians and their cause. In fact this was most understandable
because the professional soldiers of the Indian Army whose life and

love had been the army and India felt, like many people in Britain, that the coming independence threatened all that, and they resented it, regarding it as an unnecessary outcome of history uniquely fostered by left-wing politicians.

Nonetheless, in this the officers could not have been further removed from their men. This visit to Sourabaya showed that there were, even within the European battalion in our Indian divisions, young wartime soldiers who really belonged already to the radicalism which had brought the Labour government to power in Great Britain, and who had an inbuilt predisposition to sympathize with the Indonesians. Gilbert MacKereth, in his own report to the Secretary of State at the end of his mission, was to remark how the brutal behaviour of the Dutch and their soldiery towards the Indonesians had shocked the ordinary British soldiers.

General Mansergh, who was much more drawn to the social life around the Dutch Governor-General's Palace than any of his predecessors, had picked up this hostility of the Dutch from the beginning and was, I believe, influenced by it from start to finish as far as I was concerned as well. I could not understand it at first, but came to see that it was a problem all of us have experienced one way or another in life. How does one deal reasonably with the unreasonable? It was an irrational element and I had to accept that there was nothing I would ever be able to do about it. I had to live with it and concentrate more than ever on the role I had to play. But it was partially explained to me by Victor Campbell, who had come almost at the same time as Gilbert MacKereth, as one of the principal brigadiers. He was always a constructive and helpful person to have on the staff, and we felt not only respect but also friendship for one another. Towards the end of the British occupation in Indonesia he was to say to me:

'You must not worry too much about General Mansergh. He is a fine soldier, but in your regard he really could not help it. I have seen a lot of it. You will be surprised in the army; the higher you go the more envy and jealousy play a role. It may surprise you, but I believe the General was impossibly jealous of you. Your role gave you something that the army could not deal with in terms of rank. Certain powers are confined within the system of ranking, and you had a something that had nothing whatsoever to do with rank; his feelings about you, therefore, were something that the General could not control. He just could not accept that people could rate you more highly than himself.'

This was the one and only occasion in Java on which Victor and I ever discussed the General. We were to do so again thirty years later when he was happily installed as Lord Sheriff of Devonshire, but at the time neither he nor I would have discussed our General if we were not all about to separate for good.

This situation created moments of great practical difficulty. For instance, there were the conferences we had in Batavia where I always accompanied the General as his political-military adviser. I was dismayed when, in his briefing to the conferences, he would depart in so many carefully nuanced ways from what I thought was an accurate and complete interpretation of the Indonesian scene. This did not matter too much because the contact I had with MacKereth, particularly the nightly briefing, was conveyed to the new brigadier in command of Intelligence in Singapore (the Jimmy Alms I have mentioned) and put to good use. Jimmy Alms was not only a most helpful, civilized, sensitive and intelligent soldier, he also had a real understanding of the difficulties confronting those responsible for British policy all over South-east Asia.

But it did matter when Mountbatten himself attended the conferences in Singapore. I would sit and listen to the General's contribution which, in effect, was often somewhat subversive and focused unnecessarily on the official Dutch view of things in Batavia. I would, of course, already have discussed things fully with the General and could not speak unless I was asked to. In the circumstances I feared being called upon to speak, because I would not know how to handle the differences between my view and that of the General. But Mountbatten, who was extremely intuitive, always picked up such unease.

In this regard it is perhaps important to stress this quality in Mountbatten. Modern psychologists-in-depth have come to recognize (from a hypothesis developed by C.G. Jung and which all people who are truly modern need to understand) that differences arise in human relationships for no apparent external reason. These difficulties they now refer to as being caused by 'type', because of the fact, now I think empirically established, that each human being is born one of a number of different human types.

I have no need to explain in detail, except to say that all men dominated by their intuitive faculties to the extent that Mountbatten was are compelled from birth, consciously or unconsciously, to take very seriously all their intuitive intimations of reality. The psychological speciality in command of Mountbatten's character was the non-rational, the intuitive. It explained why people who served under him found it so difficult to understand him and to contain what he imposed upon them. The intuitive, of course, is a facility much more highly developed in women than in men, and the difference explains why men and women have difficulties with each other; because while the man resorts to reason and logic, the woman intuitively arrives at the right conclusion, to the man's dismay, long before his reason and logic take him there.

Moreover, Mountbatten had the courage of his intuitions in no mean degree. The result of this at these conferences was that, from the very first conference to the last, he would end by saying: 'Gentlemen, I would like to hear from Colonel van der Post what he thinks of what we have been saying to one another.'

Then, of course, not only was the cat out of the bag but the tiger was out of its cage. However diplomatically and delicately I tried to do it, the General, as I could tell from his face which wore an expression I grew to know well, inwardly seethed with rage. Such occasions certainly did nothing to endear me to him and might perhaps support Victor Campbell's explanation of an attack of jealousy. I am certain that, whatever it was, it was largely unconscious, and it seemed to me that for days afterwards the General's behaviour was not rational but that of a woman scorned.

The General was almost painfully correct towards me in public, but this did not prevent the people who really knew him and had become my friends from feeling his hostility. Perhaps nobody felt it more than Muriel MacKereth. Yet the way in which she showed her regard for me did not, in the end, endear me to the General any more than had Mountbatten's interventions.

The MacKereths had a dinner party for the General, some of his senior officers and some distinguished guests, to which I was also invited; and after dinner and the toast to the King, Gilbert MacKereth suddenly walked up to the grand piano, rapped on it very smartly so that the conversation ceased, and said: 'General Mansergh and guests! I have something of rather a difficult nature to convey to the General, and hope you will forgive my doing so because it is something that should be dealt with at once. It is simply this, General. There is one of your officers present who is not correctly dressed.'

There was a look of astonishment on all faces, also on mine, which turned to a feeling of alarm when Gilbert added: 'Colonel van der Post, will you please come here and I will ask my wife Muriel to correct your inadequacy of uniform.'

Of course I could not do anything but walk forward. In her hands Muriel had all the ribbons that went with my campaign medals and other awards to pin on to my uniform. She kissed me on both cheeks and said: 'Now, see that you are properly dressed in future.'

Though it had never occurred to me that in my work there was any need to dress beyond my ordinary uniform, it was clear that the General found the attention drawn to me on this occasion unforgivable.

Perhaps what illustrated my problem best of all was what happened at the final conference with Mountbatten at Singapore, before he left to take up his appointment as the last Viceroy in India. At this meeting a rather alarmist view of impeding unrest and violence in Sumatra was presented by General Mansergh. It sounded truly as if he had got it straight from the vast Dutch intelligence organization called NEFIS. Whatever NEFIS's intention, in the end it became an organized system of gossip and rumour-mongering, even working off old scores and providing people who had collaborated with the Japanese with secret roles in a 'resistance' that had never existed in Indonesia.

Knowing that the conference was to be chiefly concerned with Sumatra, General Mansergh had got General Headley, who was in charge of the division deployed in Sumatra, to accompany him. Since communications in Sumatra were primitive, I had always taken great care to check the intelligence that came from there with my own officers. If I had seen in advance the kind of intelligence General Mansergh was going to offer to the conference I would have done everything within my means to see that it was not presented at all.

Fortunately, as it was Mountbatten's last conference, Gilbert MacKereth was also there. When, after General Mansergh's rather alarmist report, Mountbatten turned to me and asked me what I had to say about it, for once I could reply: 'Sir, as Mr MacKereth is here and he has the latest and total intelligence picture in his possession, may I ask that you ask him to talk to us about it?'

Gilbert MacKereth did it superbly, but of course turned upside down the strangely biased slant General Mansergh had given to the account, and the conference dissolved, I thought, in perfect order and harmony. But I was hardly back at my quarters in Singapore when a summons came from Mountbatten for Gilbert MacKereth and myself to return to him immediately. Short as the time had been since we left the conference, Mountbatten's intuitive self had been unusually alerted and to some extent alarmed. I believe he sensed something false in the meeting, and in the talk he had with his own intelligence people on the way back to headquarters they must have put it to him that the General's report about conditions in Sumatra was alarmist and NEFIS-inspired. As General Headley's intelligence officers were my subordinates, he had also been summoned and was waiting when we arrived, awed and apprehensive, without Mansergh.

It was not difficult for me to answer Mountbatten's questions but General Headley, who was also the officer in charge of all my officers in Sumatra, received the full wrath of the Supreme Commander. It was so elemental an explosion, a kind of volcanic eruption, that I watched it in amazement. Mountbatten was not the tool of his anger; it was a form of vision which seemed to make him more clear-sighted. I have always envied this quality because when I get angry I tend to get more confused.

I had heard from others, from admirals and generals, about this aspect of Mountbatten's character, but this was the first time that I had witnessed it myself. I must add that there was something to me singularly pure and innocent about it, because it was an anger that heightened human perceptions and added something to an apprecia-tion of events and their seriousness which nothing else could have done. The Greeks, as always, had the best word for it: a catharsis of spirit. But when we came outside, General Headley, a very fine soldier and a gallant Gurkha officer whose men were truly devoted to him, looked so shaken that MacKereth took him by the arm and said: 'General, do not mind being upset. I want to tell you that, all the way through the meeting, I drew comfort from the fact that as a young boy at school I was part of a group who repeatedly ducked Mountbatten because we thought he was getting a bit too big for his boots!'

Although General Mansergh was not present on this occasion, as far as I was concerned he reacted as if he himself had been person-ally upbraided, and I was grateful that I never again had to see him so near a total, non-rational loss of self-control as he then demon-strated.

I risk this comment, of course, in hindsight and could not have made it at the time. Years later, when the General retired, he came to call on me at my home in Chelsea and greeted me as if we had always been the best of friends: he obviously had no recollection of what had passed between us in the army.

Something even worse happened between Brigadier Ian Lauder and myself. I liked Ian Lauder and admired his record and the way in which he had handled the extremely difficult task of getting the re-interned men, women and children out of the Indonesian camps in the interior and safely aboard 'planes to Australia, with the full help and co-operation of the Indonesian authorities and soldiers. This co-operation had been brought about despite enormous and unnecessary difficulties made by the Dutch authorities at the highest level. I was even told at one point that Holland regarded any co-operation with the nationalists as constituting a recognition of their validity, with such consequences for the Dutch that they would rather – however tragically and regretfully – leave the internees to the mercy of the rebels. In my report I stressed how the meeting I had organized in the interior between Ian Lauder and the Indonesian military, particularly their air officers, at great risk to him and myself, had been decisive. Ian Lauder had impressed them all with his sincerity and straightforward soldierly approach to the problem, and from that day onwards his relationship gained in such strength that it withstood the wear and tear of the trouble that MacKereth and I had with Dr van Mook and his advisers, until they were forced to yield and Lauder's plan went into full operation. So, thanks to Ian Lauder and his staff, as well as to the influence of Sjahrir and myself, and the innate decency of the Indonesians in general, it should have been a cause for gratitude on the part of the Dutch instead of an additional incentive for disliking us more.

The consequence of it all, however, was that something which had occupied almost the whole of Ian Lauder's imagination on the staff had now come to an end, and he was free, as he was entitled to be, to interest himself in the whole area in which I myself was working. And slowly I became aware that the general atmosphere of hostility towards me was affecting him too. It showed itself particularly at a moment when Mountbatten decided to visit us in Batavia, just for a day. He was to arrive early in the morning and to leave in the evening, and the day before his arrival Ian Lauder sent for me and said, peremptorily: 'I do not want to see you at headquarters tomorrow. For once you are to keep out of the way. We don't want you to add to the clutter of the Supreme Commander's visit.'

So with that I was, as it were, confined to my mess. But I knew that, just as you could not keep Mountbatten's intuition out of the most exalted conferences, so he would know that there was something missing in his reception at headquarters as organized by General

Mansergh and Ian Lauder. I therefore went to see Sjahrir, told him about the impending visit the next day and said that, knowing Mountbatten as I did, I could not see him coming through Batavia without insisting on visiting him. Sjahrir therefore arranged to keep his own day clear and said that, whatever the time and place, should Mountbatten wish to see him he would be happy to meet him.

I therefore had a day at my mess to do a lot of minor but important things that had been neglected. Nevertheless, occupied though I was, I could not help being aware of the fact that something unusual was happening in Batavia. Mountbatten had arrived even earlier than expected, and his arrival had caused immense excitement in the city among all sections of the population. In nearly four centuries, it was the nearest thing that Java had experienced to a royal visit. The Dutch East India Company was so utterly obsessed with trading and profits, it never seemed to have occurred to them that their relationship with the mother country needed to be expressed in the symbolism of royalty. I could not help contrasting this with the coronation of King George and Queen Mary in 1911. Their coronation was not only consecrated in Westminster Abbey, as British coronations always are, but the new King and Queen went and had it re-done, as it were, in the great Durbar in India.

Mountbatten for a moment, therefore, moved into the place that the sense of royalty has in the instinctive nature of all men, no matter what the rational ideologies of our day pretend to the contrary. And the kind of focus that only the Crown and its associations can give was proved by the impact of Mountbatten's visit, largely because he was kin to our Royal family.

So there was Mountbatten in Batavia, looking, as he always did, his very best in his uniform. A uniform, particularly a naval uniform, was his natural dress and he wore it with distinction and I believe had never looked more handsome. I could judge the effect he had by the reaction of the three young Dutch women on my staff: they all fell hopelessly in love with him, and remained so for weeks. It was impossible not to be aware of the change his visit made to the feel of Batavia. It was there in the vibration of the light and the sounds that went on all day long, which I knew were not the sounds that belonged to normal days.

And then, suddenly, at half past three in the afternoon, three jeeps drove at speed into the forecourt of my mess. I heard them coming and instantly went out on to the veranda: there was Mountbatten, driving his own jeep, with Ian Lauder. Mountbatten demanded to know where I had been hiding all day, and why I had not been at headquarters to see him. He was really quite angry with me.

I forget what lame excuse I made. It was difficult because I did not want to get Ian Lauder into trouble. He stood aside, his face expressing a powerful look of anger at having been as it were caught out -- angry with me, angry with everything around him except himself.

As the afternoon wore on, it became clear that Mountbatten had been offended by what he thought was gross inefficiency in the exclusion from his conference of somebody who was, after all, his own appointment in the beginning, who had represented him so often and kept him informed, and who should have been there to add to the intelligence he needed. I knew from what was said later that neither General Mansergh nor Ian Lauder gained in his confidence by so silly an indulgence of personal feelings. Yet this episode, far from decreasing their strange feelings about me, made them even stronger and more obvious.

I jumped into the jeep beside Mountbatten and took him straight to Sjahrir's house, where they had what was almost an over-long meeting. Mountbatten then had to rush to get to his 'plane before it was too dark to take off, on a quick flight to Singapore. There is no doubt that this meeting, pregnant as it was with significance, in the end did much to foster the Indonesians' trust in the British.

During the strange interlude which followed Clark Kerr's departure, the Admiral continued to be a great source of help and comfort. *Cumberland* was still there, but I knew the time for a recall must be approaching. One day, when the Admiral had dropped in for a snack at my mess (as he often did when he had business ashore) and told me that he would soon be leaving, he talked to me very seriously and said he wanted me to ask myself whether my mission in Java, which he understood better than anybody else, had come to an end, and whether I should not now pack up and go, because, he concluded: 'I see nothing but grief and trouble for you, which may not end in the way that you have tried to make it end. Go now, while you have done well, and go without any reproach to yourself.'

I knew that in this there was also great concern for my health. I myself had not realized the physical strain that went with the enormous amount of work I had to do. The work in itself was so urgent and important that it blinded me to everything else. There were many evenings when I was so utterly exhausted that I thought I could not go on, and I began to do something which I had never done before, except for pleasure; I would have a large whisky to see me through. This went on for some weeks, until one evening when I was thinking, 'I can't get through this evening. I must have another whisky,' and got up to get myself one. Suddenly a voice within me said: 'Do you realize, you have already had five glasses? And five glasses of whisky now cannot do for you what one glass did in the beginning – and it is not helping you at all, but making you worse.'

Such a feeling of horror went through me that from that moment on, I have avoided spirits like the plague except when medically necessary – as, for instance, during bouts of recurring malaria that I was still getting at the time. Then I found that a series of double brandies was the only cure for that terrible Antarctic cold which enters one's blood and makes one shiver all over like a ship breaking up with the cold, before one bursts out in a heavenly perspiration and the fever breaks.

I was, however, very tired and the Admiral asked if I would like to take a few days off and sail around Java and Bali, and back through the Sunda Strait in one of his cruisers, *Kent*. I jumped at the offer. It was a short voyage but one of the loveliest I have had among many lovely and memorable voyages. It was wonderful just to sit in comfort in the cool of the quarterdeck and watch the island of Java from the sea. The days went by and I sat there like someone in a dream, and slept a dreamless sleep at night, and when we returned to Batavia I felt that I had made – even in those few days – a recovery of physical strength which somehow I would be able to maintain. I perhaps never fully recovered in all the time that I still had to serve in Java, but I was now strong enough to endure to the end. It was one of many things I owed to the sensitivity and care of Admiral Patterson.

During this period too, while the main actors were away in Europe and before other actors with new parts came on to the scene, 'Dul and I worked away and quietly consolidated the ground we had gained. In between, there were strange distractions; as, for instance, from some people who purported to be gathering evidence for a major trial of Japanese war criminals.

Before Group Captain Nichols, my fellow prisoner commander, took our 2,000-odd British prisoners-of-war by sea to England, he and I had drawn up a list, not a long list it is true, of Japanese – and Japanese warrant officers in particular – who had treated us with comparative decency. Beyond that we had agreed that we would not take part in any of these war trials, which we both deplored and saw as a part of the past with no place in the future. It was a matter of pride to us both that of all our men who went home so few felt sour and bitter or resentful. It therefore seemed to me strange that these people gathering evidence of war crimes, who certainly had not shared the experience of imprisonment under the Japanese, were far more bothered about what they had heard of our ordeal than we who had actually experienced it. To me one of the unexpected lessons of imprisonment was that, much as we had suffered, we had endured the suffering in such a way that it had become a form of enrichment.

But there were two people who came on this war crimes mission whom I knew and whom I could understand because they had both really suffered terribly and their survival had been miraculous. Squadron Leader Pitts had been in command of a detachment of RAF prisoners who were taken to the infamous island of Haruko, which the Japanese were bent on turning into some sort of island 'aircraft-carrier', and among them was one of his senior officers, Squadron Leader Blackwood (whose family published that institution of the British empire, *Blackwood's* magazine).

In Haruko under the Japanese they had suffered cruelly. Much of the suffering, I am certain, was not inflicted on them out of sheer brutality but had been a result of the hopeless inefficiency and inadequacy of Japanese logistics in the region. They suffered appallingly from lack of food and from the Japanese guards who claimed that their weakness was not due to starvation but to an 'improper state of mind'. The men were cruelly driven, and beaten, and died; and, finally, when the Japanese realized that all their vainglorious dreams would never come to pass, they were all crammed into one small vessel and sent on their way back to Java. On the journey, Blackwood told me, they died at such a rate that there was a day on which they threw nineteen dead overboard, and never a day in which the number of dead to be dumped into the sea was less than ten.

They arrived back in Java in a state to which Nichols and I and all the people with us were able to bear witness. We had heard that the Haruko people were coming to us and that they were in a deplorable condition, and we drew heavily on our small reserves to give them the best welcome we could and feed them in a way we could not feed ourselves. I remember helping to carry in many of them, so truly 'as light as a feather' that two of us could carry a man on the palms of our outstretched hands. Even to us, the suffering they had endured was unimaginable and produced in us a rage which I deplored in the civilians who had not shared our suffering. But, thanks to the way in which we husbanded our meagre supplies, we were able to nurse them so that a handful survived, including Blackwood and Squadron Leader Pitts who, understandably, found the experience unforgivable. The ordeal had taken over the whole of Pitts's imagination and he was plainly out for revenge on the Japanese – any Japanese. I did all I could to help what I thought was valid in his search, and thereafter wanted him to return to England; but somehow he haunted Indonesia and Malaya for months, as if he were bound by a strange kind of umbilical cord to the scene which had mothered this spirit of revenge within him.

Blackwood, because I knew him, I took into my own mess and kept for a while. Unlike Pitts he was not looking for revenge but said he was gathering material for a book he wanted to write. Then one evening, as I was writing my special report for Singapore, suddenly overhead there was the sound of a pistol shot and immediately afterwards a flurry of footsteps. Blackwood came flying down the stairs, his eyes those of a man in the grip of sheer horror, and came to a stop at the desk where I had been typing. He stood to attention, and said: 'Sir, I have come to report to you that I have just shot myself.'

On questioning he told me that he had gone to wash himself, had looked up into the mirror over the basin and simply could not endure his own face; and he felt he hated it so much he wanted to have done with it, and the only thing was to shoot the reflection in the mirror. As a result I got him on an aircraft the next day for England and I never saw or heard from him again.

In this period, too, I suddenly found that I had an ally and friend in the heart of Dr van Mook's camp. He was the youngest son of the Sultan of Pontianak, one of the richest of Dutch possessions on Borneo. In the course of the Japanese occupation something went wrong between the Japanese and the Sultan, and the Sultan and all his family were executed. But, unbeknown to the Japanese, there was this youngest son who had been sent to become a professional officer in the Dutch army and who had been imprisoned with us under the name of Max Al Kahdri.

I have mentioned Max Al Kahdri in my book, *The Night of the New Moon*, and anyone interested to know more of him will find in it an account of him and of the very brave and dangerous role he played in maintaining a secret radio throughout our imprisonment. The relationship I developed with him in prison helped us in acquiring intelligence, but I also cultivated our friendship for its own sake.

Max Al Kahdri suddenly appeared in my office just as I was getting ready to do my summing-up of the day for Singapore. I was quite startled to hear a voice in remarkably good English say: 'So there you are, the villain himself! Villain or not, I am glad to see you!' There was Max in a truly splendid uniform, much improved in looks by the good food he had enjoyed since his release from the Japanese but essentially the same unashamed, unrepentant, dashing and rather reckless person, with a flair of his own and a love of life and the good things in it. As the only surviving member of his family he had become Sultan himself, and now had many temptations to indulge.

He told me that he had just been to The Hague as one of van Mook's officers. There, among other things, he had heard all sorts of derogatory talk about me which, knowing me as well as he did, he had not taken too seriously. He thought that that was one of the troubles we had to face; that we took talk in Holland, and particularly talk between van Mook and the Indonesians in Java and Sumatra, too seriously. They simply could not help it, he said, they would go on talking and talking for years and heaven knows how the talking would end. But as far as he was concerned, he wanted them to concentrate more and more on building their fortunes on the outer islands ruled over by people like himself who were friendly to them and where unlimited economic opportunities still awaited them. Indeed he took this aspect of the future very seriously. He was going back with van Mook on a more prestigious mission, and he hoped to put this aspect of the future to The Hague with more authority and with all his conviction.

'But,' he added, 'they are a snooty lot in The Hague and heaven knows how far I will get with them.'

I thought at the time that he was making too little of what the Dutch had already done in regard to the outer islands, but it was good for me to hear what he had to say about Holland. All that had been best in the wartime spirit of Holland, and that had been expressed by the liberal men I had met in their Cabinet, seemed almost spent, and there were various groupings emerging: there was the Holland which regarded itself as the inheritor of empire; there was the Holland of the powerful, vested interests who had made such a rich living out of their colonies; and there was a third Holland that was new and wanted to break with the past, but had no outstanding leaders and somehow did not yet know how to set about it. Max thought a great deal of squabbling would go on among the three groupings and that the vested interests could still prevail. The importance of what he said went home all the more because I recognized the experience and history of my own people who had suffered so much exactly in that regard.

At the risk of repeating myself perhaps overmuch, all this is to emphasize what an error I made in not taking more seriously Max Al Kahdri's reference to the snobbishness of The Hague. At the end of the day that snobbishness strengthened the opposition to van Mook in Holland and undermined his self-confidence, because he was only too well aware that those Dutch born in Java, like himself, were rejected by the upper circles of colonial society. In Holland he was given the derogatory epithet of '*Indische Jongen*' – 'Boy from the Indies'. The word 'Boy' was all the more derogatory because it was commonly used by the Dutch, as it was by the British in places like Malaya, for summoning native waiters and servants, whatever their age. How I remember in restaurants and hotels the sound of an unfeeling 'Boy!' being called out, loud and peremptory, and how it made me squirm. But for the fact that van Mook was an extremely able public servant, particularly in commercial matters, and the Dutch really had no one of equal quality during and immediately after the war to replace him, he would have been rejected long since.

There now came a moment which I had dreaded, when I had to say goodbye to the Admiral and *Cumberland*. The night before she sailed away for good we had a last dinner party in the Admiral's cuddy. Flags and Charles Hart and a small number of the senior officers were there and we had a lovely supper and a lot of good talk and laughter. When our supper was finished the Admiral gave Charles Hart and me a signal to send off as usual, remarking that it was the last time he would ask our little partnership to do that in *Cumberland*; and then he wanted us to join him and the other officers in the wardroom. Charles Hart and I duly went off to send the signal, the shortest signal we had ever sent and which I shall quote verbatim at the end of my account of the evening, of which it was really an anticipation.

In the wardroom we had perhaps the most cheerful of our many meetings there. Someone produced a violin and played many of the tunes that we had all come to associate with war, some of which were also part of the world into which I had been born. It was remarkable how often these songs were about a woman. For instance in the Boer

War there was a song that was constantly sung by British soldiers from all over the Commonwealth, 'Goodbye, Dolly Grey'. And to my surprise the violinist played one about a woman who had been celebrated in song by the Boer commandos and which was sung with a particularly valedictory and nostalgic flavour by the thousands of Boer prisoners-of-war conveyed by the navy to St Helena, Ceylon and even India, a woman called Sarie Marais. I am of course biased, but it is one of the best tunes about a woman who, under various names and guises, comes up constantly in the imagination of fighting men in times of war. And, perhaps symbolically, there was a tune which both the Germans in the Western Desert and we who fought against them shared, perhaps an unconscious expression of the fact that the caring and feminine values of life would one day be served in common by all men, and that the fighting would stop for good. It was, of course, the tune of 'Lili Marlene'.

Then there were also some of the tunes of the First World War. Perhaps because it was one of the most horrible wars ever fought, there was no room in anybody's imagination then for what woman meant to man. The tunes were instead all about places – 'It's a Long Way to Tipperary' and, one which American soldiers brought to France and used as a sentimental and characteristic idiom essential to the Americas, 'There's a Long, Long Trail A-Winding'.

The evening was brought to an end by the Admiral and Flags once again turning themselves into a human ball and rolling from one end of the wardroom to the wall opposite, and back again.

There was a final toast, and with the toast the Admiral spoke some words which moved me deeply. I cannot repeat them because they are words that only had their full meaning in that particular context, at that time and in that place; but in a sense they amounted to a good goodbye, not only to me, to whom the Admiral with a smile said he was handing over the safekeeping of his baby, but to an era which every man there knew was vanishing for ever behind them. They were going back as they had wished to do, and deserved to, with a longing for home which only those who have served in armies and navies and the great merchant marines for years abroad can understand. They longed to be back, to walk their inconspicuous quiet lanes to some pub they had in mind, or just to be back in some familiar street in London, Glasgow or Liverpool which, from that remote distance, had come to look like a heaven on earth.

It was all very moving but beautifully contained. And then it was over. The Admiral and the officers came on to the quarterdeck with me. All the watch had been assembled, and they stood by the railing as I said goodbye and saluted the Admiral and his quarterdeck for the last time and went down the gangway into the boat waiting to take me ashore. It was only a matter of months since I had first used that gangway in my tattered prison clothes, but in my mind already it was almost a lifetime. In the half-light, with the ship already bedded down for the night, and conscious of all those special and dear faces lining the rails above me, the journey to the quay passed very quickly, or so it seemed. I looked at the lights of *Cumberland* for as long as I could until they were reduced to just the riding lights, indicating to all who might approach in the dark that there was a ship anchored in that great roadstead.

It was a very wet season in Java: there had been the usual evening of thunder and rain; a storm had swept down on us on wings of lightning which presented itself in the darkness as wide flashes of purple light; and the rain had fallen in big round drops and had extinguished all the electricity in the day, and all impurity in the air. The night could not have been clearer or better for such a goodbye.

I went quickly ashore and found my Indian driver. It was very late, both for him and for me who, for months now, had together worked what today are called 'unsocial' hours. I had to wake him, asleep over the wheel of the car. I did it as gently as I could, but he woke up as if he had been guilty in falling asleep, and I quickly reassured him. At the end of my reassurances he must have noticed something that was not normal in my voice because he looked at me and said with anxiety: '*Tighai*, Colonel Sahib?'

It was, of course, his Hindustani way of asking me if all was well. I hastened to reassure him, with deep feeling: '*Tighai*, Driver Sahib.'

And with that we drove away from the harbour, content with all that the Admiral had said on behalf of the ship and the sailors serving with him in that last signal that Charles Hart and I had sent: 'ALL DONE AND HASTENING HOME.'

CHAPTER NINE

The Reckoning

FOR MANY DAYS afterwards when I woke in the morning and looked at the day, I found myself instinctively turning towards Tandjongh Priok. It was almost as if I expected some indication there in the sky, a black hole perhaps, to mark the place which *Cumberland* had left empty. It was a strange kind of reaction, something utterly primordial which had developed in the war and especially in prison, that in the moments when one became particularly aware of the horror and the pity of it all, one would find oneself looking at the sky, listening to those odd moments of silence for a sign that the universe had taken it all in and was prepared to mark the day at the very least with a sign of its own disapproval, even if it could not interfere in all the terrible things that were taking place. Perhaps it was enough that one heard on occasions in the silence a bird release the most tender note of song, as though in the heart beating in its sensitive little breast there was a reproof of what had been happening in the perils of the day.

I think particularly of some of the executions I was made to witness, at least two of which I had been told were also to be my own. I had to watch people being killed in a variety of ritualistic ways. At their climax I would look away for relief to the universe, very often to a universe singularly beautiful and resolved, presided over by two great peaks, the Raja and Goenoeng Gedeh. The beauty, the majesty of that view, the sky filling with the sails of the fleets of clouds setting out for the unhorizoned deep of the day, remained undiminished. It seemed to set an example to one's spirit from Creation itself, rebuking the presumption and excesses perpetrated below.

I found myself doing this instinctively for days, looking towards the scene over the harbour. It did not really matter that the sky was empty. The overall view of those mornings, ushering in the vast days full of nothing but the drama of the sky, turned the moment into one of sacred communion.

However, very soon there came a summons from Singapore which marked another step forward in the great changes that were coming over the scene. It was a signal marked 'Most Immediate' from Jimmy Alms. He wanted me to come to Singapore immediately. I knew it must be very important because my monthly meeting with him in Singapore was only a week or so away. I organized things accordingly so that by the next morning at breakfast time I was in Singapore and went straight to his office at the headquarters of ALFSEA.

Alms was already there and was relieved to see me. He explained that there had been a summons from MacArthur's Allied Head-quarters in Japan for all the senior intelligence officers to meet at Hong Kong in a few days' time, and his General had delegated him and his colleague Malcolm to go to the conference. He was certain it portended a reappraisal of military and other policies not only in South-east Asia but also thoughout the whole of the Pacific command, and he needed me to give him a full briefing on the current situation in Indonesia.

Malcolm was, in a way, both Jimmy Alms's equal and also his second-in-command. For reasons that will become obvious I prefer not to use his surname, only the Christian name by which I always referred to him and warmly remember him. He had already served with distinction in the Indian Civil Service (ICS) and had now been appointed directly by the Government of India to his new post. Like so many of his colleagues in the ICS, he identified utterly with India, its reality, its history and its future, and put all that he had of the best of Englishness in him at its service. But, unlike Jimmy, he had a very deep religious, almost mystical streak, and I was not surprised to dis-cover that he had a profound knowledge of all the sacred books and wonderful myths and legends of India, and that his great love was Urdu poetry which he wrote extremely well himself. When I was with him I found that all I had learned as a boy through my friends in the Indian community in Port Natal in Africa suddenly came alive, and I could share and discuss things with him which I had not discussed with anybody for many years.

Malcolm did not join us until the end of the day. Jimmy and I exchanged news of what was happening in Indonesia, of all that the war had meant in South-east Asia, and what its impact was likely to be in the future. We had an immensely absorbing and, to me, enriching day and then; in the late afternoon, we decided to go to Jimmy's house, which he and Malcolm shared.

On the way he said to me: 'I am really perturbed about Malcolm. He is oddly preoccupied at the moment. It is extraordinary but he is firmly convinced that he and I will not come back alive from Hong Kong. He can't explain, it is a matter of conviction – and you know his convictions go very deep. I took him so seriously I tried to persuade the General to excuse him from going, but he thinks Malcolm is too important to be left behind for so superstitious a reason.'

The next day I accompanied them to the airport. For some reason their 'plane was not ready and while the RAF engineers worked away on it with the thoroughness which had characterized their work throughout the war, we teased Malcolm and Jimmy about the delay in what now seems the most insensitive way. Finally the 'plane took off into the blue of morning, before the build-up of thunder and cloud could impede it on its way to its first stop at Saigon, in Indochina. I then went back to headquarters to spend the morning working with the Chief of Staff. At 12.30 p.m. there came a signal marked 'Most Immediate' which he quickly read and then handed to me. The RAF at Saigon had lost contact with the aircraft carrying Jimmy Alms and Malcolm. It should have been in Saigon long since. They would like to send out reconnaissance 'planes into the Gulf of Siam.

The Chief of Staff immediately concurred and ordered the RAF at Singapore to conduct a thorough sweep through their end of the Gulf of Siam. We knew, of course, that aircraft had met with disaster in the early days of flying when trying to go straight through those masses of cloud that I have so often described. Even a flight of Hurricanes, stout as they were, had tried it once and only two out of five had come through. But Jimmy and Malcolm's aircraft had left too early to have encountered a real build-up of cloud.

The search from both the Singapore and the Saigon ends carried on until dark, and was continued from dawn until late the following day, but nothing was found. They had vanished for good with nothing to indicate why except for this strange, disturbing apprehension of Malcolm's – the only door, perhaps, to something beyond creation as we know it which had opened and swiftly shut on them.

Now, as well as looking in the direction of Tandjongh Priok, I would often look to the sky and all that it indicated of those dramatic heavens over the whole of South-east Asia and beyond. I often looked, too, in the direction of Singapore. The great forces of nature no longer appeared as indifferent as one had taken them to be, for it seemed as if the changes that were on our doorstep might be of such urgency and importance that they had chosen this tragic way of drawing our attention to elements of life and time that our rational selves were inclined to ignore.

One consequence of this tragic event was that we had no representative at the Hong Kong conference. The briefing I had given Jimmy Alms was never delivered, and we in Indonesia heard no more about it.

In the months that followed I was aware of other changes – in the world which dominated the dimensions in which I had to work, and in my own observations of what was happening around me in Indonesia. I have described those months of sheer hard work when MacKereth and I had to keep the Dutch and the Indonesians continually in contact. There was nothing that happened that we did not treat as being of great significance. All the ups and downs of what we went through are recorded in detail in my report, but what is not recorded is a growing fear I had of what time itself could be doing to shape the events with which we were concerned. It seemed to me more and more that time was not just a measure but had a character and a dominant contract of its own in shaping life. There was no living thing that did not possess an inbuilt portion of the inexorable character of the law of time, a law which demanded fulfilment of this character. If it were not done fully and fairly, it would be done foully through some back door of the spirit, or perhaps – because of human fallibility – it would become an uneasy mixture of both fair and foul. For the moment I feared that, as far as the British were concerned, we might not only be running out of our own time but also be losing touch with the character of the time which enclosed us in Java, and that there were pressures working on us that came from this dimension that we also had to observe.

Of course I had always had some fears: the first, at the beginning, of what the Japanese could still do before they acknowledged defeat; and then, even after defeat was acknowledged, the fear of what they might do before the Allies arrived to take over from them. That fear had vanished when the Japanese General had raised his glass to me and said: 'We Japanese have switched, and when we Japanese switch, we switch sincerely.'

With my knowledge of the history of Japan, I knew that this image of 'switching', stark as it was, could not have been more accurate and symbolic. Electricity was still a miracle to the Japanese at that time, as we had discovered in prison. The Japanese commander, when the light bulbs in his office needed changing, insisted on having one of our most qualified RAF engineers to do it for him. Unexpected light came from electricity, and it was as if this was one of those imperative images from the unsleeping Shinto spirit of the Japanese, directing them to illumination of a new and more contemporary way ahead. They had 'switched' symbolically, in the way the Japanese General put it to me, and had turned on the light of Western civilization almost overnight when Commodore Perry and his ships sailed for the second time into Japanese waters, in 1854, and compelled the Japanese to open themselves impartially to the West. I had no doubt that from that moment of surrender in Java they had turned on a new light.

However, in its place there came another fear. When I knew that the British were taking over the task of occupying Java, and when the broadcasts of revenge from the Dutch stations in Australia continued, I became afraid that the British might be stampeded into fighting a war on behalf of the Dutch that they were not prepared to fight within their own empire.

That fear began to diminish the moment I talked at length with Admiral Patterson, and it vanished totally with my visit to England and The Hague. In spite of what I had seen before I left for England of the manifestations of militant nationalism in Java, I had still retained a hope that if only we could do it fast enough we could peacefully occupy Java and Sumatra and hold them, as it were, in a suspended state of trust for some six months or more to enable all those in Indonesia and even in Holland to recover a sense of how the world had moved on, and to find a balance to what had come so acutely alive under the Japanese. I refer to the Japanese again because I was to find that in my rather perilous visits to central Java, the young Javanese who had fought and suffered heavily in these battles held it against us that we had used the hated Japanese against them.

We had already come a long way from that brief and sharp explosion of violence and fighting that we ourselves had had with the Indonesians. And this hope to which I have referred had revived over the months that followed. The possibility of a democratic alternative emerged more and more strongly with the extension of the hold that Soetan Sjahrir, the new Soekarno, Hatta and the men I have described secured among the population. The fear I had in those days was that the Indonesians might become involved in that most dreadful form of war, a civil war, and that violence might take root in a way that would make an ordered solution impossible. How justified that fear was had only just been confirmed by the repercussions of the arrival of Tan Malakka and armed followers of Soedirman, and the inflamed fundamentalism in the interior.

But Sjahrir had emerged to become a valid and indeed dominant representative of the Indonesian people. I am certain that, despite the failure so far of the contacts between the Indonesians and the Dutch which had undoubtedly damaged his prestige, there was something else which did not fail to penetrate the Indonesian national awareness. Gradually they realized that, through Sjahrir, through the British and the dialogue they promoted between the Indonesians and London and The Hague, their existence and their long suppressed desire for independence had been brought to the notice of the awakening world, and of the budding new United Nations, and that it was part of the reckoning that the nations of the world were having with their past and the future.

In that sense time had served the Indonesian cause well, and in saying all I have done about the Indonesians I want to stress that I was never in danger of being, as the Dutch claimed, an instrument of Indonesian nationalism. All my experience of nationalism in my native country, particularly ethnic nationalism, had led to a total rejection in my spirit of what I felt was such an outdated approach to life. But I did believe in a concept of nation, a nation in the way in which a truly American people had been created around a small Western – and initially totally British – nucleus of immigrants. That small British element had, however, since been subjected to an influx of people from nations which ethnically and in their cultural variations could not have been more diverse and some of which had been living in states of enmity with one another for centuries. They all came in their millions to take refuge in America and, in the process, in spite of an incredible nostalgia for their places of origin, became Americans.

MacKereth and I differed in one nuance about what was happening. He never committed himself quite to trusting Sjahrir as I did. He did not mistrust him, but he treated him always on the merits of the day and did not make the kind of long-term investment in Sjahrir's influence on the scene that I did. I knew precisely what his difficulty was in understanding Sjahrir. Like all English people, though to a markedly lesser degree, he did not realize what it meant to have been a conquered race. I myself came from people who, in their commitment first of all to Africa, had found themselves in a state of rebellion against remote control by the Dutch. In the process I had not become a nationalist, as most of the Afrikaner people ultimately tended to be until the collapse of apartheid, but I had developed, as fellow countrymen on the world stage like Botha and Smuts had done, something in my spirit which I called and still can only call 'British'.

The British empire, of course, has ceased to exist, and has become what is generally regarded as a ghost of its former self in the shape of the Commonwealth. I accept the simile of the ghost, but only in its deeper meaning, the ghost being the most profound indication of something to come, and which is not yet. This ghost comes, perhaps, as the emerging spirit in the countries the British once ruled as colonies, to serve a state of spirit of a future 'Commonwealth of the mind' that I call British.

This 'British' state of spirit is a strange compound, something that goes back perhaps to Magna Carta and the rule of law which led to an increasing emphasis on the individual rights of men. It became all the more rooted because it was promoted and enriched by artists and by some of the greatest literature the world has ever known. It was supported by the increasingly rich inventiveness of Britain, not only in the growth of its democracies but in the invention of the widest assortment of games in the world since the Greeks. This 'Britishness' encouraged man's sense of curiosity about the world, promoted exploration, discovery and trade and, in a strangely random and haphazard way, grew spontaneously and inspirationally into a state of empire, without any kind of political ideology. And at every advance in its power to trade and influence world affairs, it was always subjected to the most critical scrutiny by a brave and enlightened element of the British people.

Unlike other empires, particularly the empires of the charter companies, the British empire had never been an empire purely of power and trade. From the start it was not just a question of power but a question of the spirit. Nancy Astor told me of a discussion she had had with Stalin when she, her husband and son, and Bernard Shaw had visited Russia. Stalin, genuinely puzzled, had asked: 'How could so small an island as Britain have acquired so large an empire?' to which Nancy Astor replied: 'Because the British were the first country in the world to have the Bible translated into its native language.' She described Stalin's face after he'd heard her answer – not only had she failed to illuminate him, but her extreme simplification had confirmed his low opinion of women in general.

All these things tended to contribute to the sense of 'Britishness' which is still there wherever the English language is spoken. It is not confined to Britain. In many ways it is expressed with an equal dignity and authority in the Americas, in Canada, in Australia, in New Zealand, even in India – much as the Indians appear to reject their British past – and everywhere where the British have been in Africa.

Here now, in Indonesia, I felt I recognized something similar. It was obviously not what one would call 'Britishness', but it was a state of spirit that was greater than its Indonesian and Dutch components; and I felt that in a way Sjahrir (and many others with him) were motivated by this transforming spirit which I tried to serve within myself. It was, I think, a great bond between us, and it was through this bond that I felt there was hope that we could still, before we left Java, enable him and the Dutch to come into a state of partnership that would serve their better selves.

I felt all this so deeply and in a sense found it such a source of strength that all the unpleasant things I had to go through externally were of no account. MacKereth and I did our work with a new sense of urgency that grew day by day, and it was work so well done that both The Hague and the Foreign Office thought that at last the time had come for a meeting between the Dutch and the Indonesians under British auspices – a meeting as important as that with Clark Kerr had been.

So in the middle of October Lord Killearn (as Miles Lampson had now become) was sent to Batavia to preside over such a meeting. I have little more to add to what I say in the report about Lord Killearn and his mission. I knew him well by reputation, of course, because no one could have been involved with what had happened in the Sudan and Egypt and also in the Far East without knowing about him. As he rose in rank and seniority he was increasingly one of the most talked-about men in the Foreign Service. The talk was always ambivalent, and I have neither the knowledge nor the personal experience of the man to entitle me to make any meaningful contribution to it. Nor did I see enough of him as a man in action in Batavia to justify any indulgence in judgement, or even opinion, beyond what I felt about what he did in Batavia and the consequences. Both he and his wife struck me as people with great and always hungry egos. That, of course, was one of the many charges that informed gossip held against him – and gossip in public service is not necessarily reliable.

Lord Killearn had hardly arrived among us when Max Al Kahdri reappeared in my life for the second and last time, saying in effect: 'You see what I told you before? Here we go again. More and more talk and you can go on with the talk, but I do not believe that there will ever be more than talk in it. I just wish that they would concentrate more on the outer islands.'

That, of course, was something he had said all along. And in saying so this time he was as dismissive of the snobs at The Hague but showed much more respect for the vested interests that were increasingly focusing their designs on the former Dutch colonies.

The atmosphere in which Lord Killearn was called upon to preside over the meeting of the Dutch and the Javanese – on a scale and with an authority that neither side had possessed when first they met under Clark Kerr – had greatly changed. General Spoor, head of the Dutch armed forces in Java, had already remarked to General Mansergh that he must not be surprised if he undertook military initiatives here and there without referring to him. In addition, Admiral Pinke, who had succeeded the charlatan Admiral Helfrich and who was hardly an improvement – the Dutch themselves thought him blunt and outspoken – had a plan of his own already for military action against the Javanese. Indeed he had, just before Lord Killearn's arrival, shown his hand by ordering his bombers to bombard a port on the east coast of Java where the Indonesians were collecting rice which they had promised to the Government of India, so hard pressed to feed its vast and expanding population. There had been an outcry from Dutch officialdom over this commercial transaction which they said the Indian government had concluded over their heads directly with Sjahrir's government. The Dutch bombers, with suspicious accuracy, hit only the stores in which the rice for India was being accumulated.

All these things were signs that the contribution of the British occupation to the situation in Indonesia was nearly exhausted, and the sooner the governments in London and The Hague took over the better, not only for ourselves but also for the Dutch and the Indonesians. We had truly kept them in touch. We had given them time to recover their full post-war selves. The Indonesians, judging by what I had seen increasingly on my short visits to the interior, were genuinely and peacefully in command of the greatest part of Indonesia, and the military options which some Indonesians had in mind were diminishing by the time Lord Killearn arrived.

So in bringing them together for the last time we were performing what was still a real and potentially memorable service. The Indonesians had come to trust the British in the same way that they had trusted them more than one hundred years before when the moment came for Raffles to go back to Singapore. The Dutch, on the other hand, were now at a fever-pitch of fury. I remember one leading newspaper article saying something to the effect that time was a great healer, and that the Dutch could only pray that God would in time remove from their minds and hearts the memory of the terrible things the British had done to them – the British who had left behind hundreds of their own dead in bringing the Dutch back to Indonesia!

Yet, in spite of the clamour, the moment for Lord Killearn was, as I have suggested, more auspicious than it had been for Clark Kerr. Clark Kerr had come to Indonesia at a time when there was not this sense of urgency that invested the scene now. The Indonesians knew it was their last chance to come to an agreement sponsored and supported by the British and, through the British, by the outside world. The best of the Dutch, in their heart of hearts, knew that there was ultimately no other way. But they were in the minority. Their military and those with vested interests were certain they had the capacity to replace the British. It was always interesting to MacKereth and myself how in all their signals and reports to The Hague, these representatives in Java spoke of their own supporters in terms of hundreds of thousands, but of the nationalists in hundreds. In fairness to Dr van Mook, however, I think he believed that the Dutch had a better chance for a more enlightened solution to their problems while the British were still there to promote it.

Van Mook's impatient outbursts may have hidden his reservations. I had had to endure one such outburst not long before when 'Dul begged me to come and talk to van Mook because he was so outraged by the news that a French division had just sailed through the Straits of Singapore, heading for Saigon to reinforce the French military presence in Indochina. The impact of this news on Dr van Mook was all the sharper because reports in the world press suggested that the division consisted largely of German ex-prisoners-of-war whom the de Gaulle government had released on condition that they served a full term in the swelling French Foreign Legion. He told me that it was monstrous that we should be there in Indonesia restraining the Dutch from exercising the same freedom that the French felt they had in Indochina. I told him that it was a matter that

he should get his government to take up with the British government, and the Americans, and that it was no concern of ours. I
stressed that the two states were not comparable, and in any case I
felt certain that the time would come when the French government
would regret that they did not have somebody like the British beside
them to restrain them from reimposing an outdated pre-war pattern
on Indochina.

I think that somewhere that rang a bell with him, and the incident
confirmed my feeling that the Dutch could do no better than Dr van
Mook. They particularly could not do better now, because the team
that he was going to head in the discussions under Lord Killearn
included the most conspicuous representation of post-war government at The Hague that there had been so far.

As far as the Indonesians were concerned, I remember Sjahrir and
Amir Sjarifoeddin coming to have a quiet supper with me and talking
about the impending negotiations, and my telling them something
that I had learned since my release from captivity and that I felt to
be of importance – the recognition that reality is always between two,
the thing and its reflection: between the event and what that event
symbolizes, between the aware and the unaware, between the conscious and the unconscious, between oneself and one's reflection as
an individual, and between oneself and what comes to one as an
opposite. Always one has to deal with this paradox, and to overcome
it with something greater.

As soon as one is aware of what the solution has to be, one must
not wait until it is dragged out of one, because its positive value is
then greatly diminished. Unforced, as a gift, it will have an enormous
impact far beyond what it would be if painfully extracted from
oneself. The party most conscious of the totality of the problem must
never forget the element of giving, which a valid opposition
demands.

This is a brief summary of what was a long and rewarding discussion for all three of us, and I knew that Sjahrir, in his own way, would
continue what we had started as a serious dialogue within himself,
and take that to the conference.

Within two days of our meeting in the middle of October, Lord
Killearn arrived to head this final conference between the two most
authoritative delegations of Indonesians and Dutch that Indonesia
had yet seen. The essence of the four weeks or so that Lord Killearn
spent in our midst, finally bringing Indonesians and Dutch together
at Linggadjati and culminating in the famous Linggadjati Agree-

ment, is summed up in my official report. There is nothing that I can add here except to stress that it achieved in substance nothing more, really, than had already been achieved by Sir Archibald Clark Kerr's mission. There appeared only two additions, on analysis not of great substance. I think they were really just a form of window-dressing to make the agreement appear more impressive to the world. One of these provided for a pledge from both the Dutch and the Indonesians that they would run down their armies. In this the Dutch were not sincere, for they continued to build up their forces as fast as they possibly could in Indonesia. The second consisted of a clause for arbitration, but in view of the many months we had already spent as a channel of mediation I do not think this had any further meaning whatsoever.

MacKereth and I should have rejoiced, as everybody around us appeared to do, at the outcome of the Linggadjati conference. It was, perhaps, again a significant historical synchronicity that the agreement was made at a place which still had in Indonesian memory, despite their Muslim convictions, associations with the Buddhist period of many centuries before. These associations with the calm of Buddha rather than the flame of Islam helped, I think, to sponsor the new agreement's acceptance in the watching world.

Of course we rejoiced in the fact that the agreement proved how well we had all done under Sir Archibald Clark Kerr, though we had a feeling that we could have done better had Lord Killearn, with the extra vision gained by standing as I thought so shamelessly on Gilbert MacKereth's broad shoulders, added something extra to the solution of our problems. But he was content to appropriate, as it were, all that had been achieved as something which he alone had done and nobody else could have done.

I myself was not surprised. I had first met him at a reception given for him by Gilbert and Muriel, at which all the people of note who could be of help and were legitimately committed to a proper solution were there to meet him. When Gilbert MacKereth took me over to be introduced, Lord Killearn was talking to one of the brigadiers on our staff in a casual and not very interested sort of way; and when MacKereth introduced me and pronounced my name, he gave a start. I thought he was going to spill his drink, because he immediately stopped talking and gave me a rather startled glance, which immediately seemed to suggest a deeply pre-conditioned attitude to me. I did not know, of course, how he had been briefed before he came, but it was quite clear to me that he had already decided that he would have nothing to do with me, and would clearly show the Dutch that this was his intention.

The look and the attention he gave me came and went very swiftly: he nodded quickly and formally over his glass in my direction without saying a word to me, and then took MacKereth by the arm and said: 'I have to have a word with you . . .', and walked away.

I did not see or speak to him again but I heard, of course, a great deal about him, especially indirectly through MacKereth, who never for a moment criticized him or said anything disparaging about him. It would have been utterly foreign to him to have diminished in any way any contribution his service could make, through Killearn, to our problems. But it was clear to everybody else that MacKereth did not really matter to Killearn at all. For Killearn it was entirely an affair between himself, Lady Killearn, the Dutch and the Indonesians. I think that in this he did himself and his mission no service, because no one was more respected by both Dutch and Indonesians than MacKereth, and in diminishing him and his work I believe Killearn diminished himself among the Dutch and the Indonesians.

I have only to say that all this was astonishing to me, after the experience of working with Sir Archibald Clark Kerr who, with all his eccentricities, was so much a great servant of a great service. The Foreign Office (and I was to know it well in the next forty years) is an exceptional institution, staffed on the whole by people of unusual quality who so very often serve inferior political masters with impressive skill and loyalty because, perhaps like Christison, they find their meaning by carrying out their duties, just as Christie carried his can.

The ink with which the final Linggadjati agreement had been drafted was not yet dry when, in mid-November, the Dutch delegation left for Holland, supposedly to get it ratified immediately. However, the relevant part of the delegation did not return until the new year had begun, and by then a completely new phase in the history of Indonesia was in the making.

Preparations had already been made at AFNEI, the headquarters of the Allied forces in the Netherlands East Indies, for the evacuation without delay of the British forces, and 15 Army Corps could at last send its men home. All was so efficiently organized that by 30 November 1946 this had been achieved.

The Dutch took even less trouble from then on to hide the flexing of their military and other muscles. One of the last acts of General Mansergh only days before he left the island (and which I think must have strained even his tendency to favour the Dutch cause) was to countermand a scandalous Dutch ultimatum to the Indonesians which would have done much to impede what everyone expected would be a ratification of Linggadjati. He had to cancel it in the most severe terms. The word 'scandalous' was used by MacKereth in his report of the incident to the Secretary of State, and he always chose his words well and with accuracy. The cancellation was so just and so obvious that the Dutch accepted it fully, however graceless the manner of their acceptance.

And then there were certain things outstanding which I felt to be of immense importance to us all. One at least, that should stand as a headstone of history, is the record of all that the British sacrificed and achieved in Indonesia. The campaign report and the other means of accounting for this piece of our history have been shamefully neglected, and the only account which deals with the whole of the story is the official report which in due course I was to write myself for the Secretary of State for Foreign Affairs, and which appears later in this book.

Also something else happened that chronologically may not be in the place which outer eventuality demands, but its meaning is timeless, and it stood out at the time as a warning to me. It was an occurrence of the '*mata gelap*', the 'darkening of the eye' that I have already described and it followed the classical pattern. Without any warning that it was going to happen, the people of Sunda suddenly ran amok and massacred a small Chinese community of some 1,500 men, women and children. It happened sufficiently near our perimeter for a Dutch detachment of gunners and infantry, who held one of the key exits to the area under our control, to be able to tell from smoke and other indications that something abnormal had occurred.

When the news came through, several days after the event, I went to visit the Dutch outpost. It was again one of those rare afternoons without cloud, as if it was apparently fully occupied with a meaning of its own, the companion of unusual events that I had known so often in those long years behind me. I had, for once, a good and very informative discussion with the Dutch officer in command who, significantly enough, had served with the Princess Irene Brigade in France and had quite a different outlook on the British from most of the Dutch.

When I left him the sun was already beginning to sink, and its long level rays were lengthening the shadows. The road at one point brought me to the banks of an urgent stream which also flowed past the place of the massacre, and there I saw one of the giant lizards for which Java is famous and which measure anything from twelve to fourteen feet. In the outer islands like Komodo I believe they are even larger and are spoken of in the West as the Dragons of Komodo. To me however this lizard was monster enough. It was the first I had ever seen, and it was sitting there obscenely confident and golden in the levelling sunlight, licking its lips beside a headless and rotting Chinese body. But, in between licking its lips and lowering its head to the corpse it was feeding on, there was a moment when it was absolutely still. It suddenly became diabolically heraldic, and seemed to represent all the powerful forces in the unconscious of mankind, always there waiting to emerge and overwhelm if they are not allowed their part in the conscious development of all that is still unfulfilled in man's nature.

Increasingly in modern psychology these forces are summed up by the incomparable term, the 'shadow', with its inverted power and diabolical chivalry, to which de Nerval's great poem about '*le Prince d'Aquitaine a la tour abolie*', and Andrew Lang's translation of it as 'the dark, dishonoured son of Aquitaine', intuitively refer. Milton, too, in his *Paradise Lost* had a clear sense of this reversed nobility and the chivalrous potential of Mephistopheles when he made him declare that it is 'better to reign in hell than serve in heaven'. I prayed that when our forces had withdrawn, the Dutch would do nothing to provoke this strange underground build-up of anger in the peoples of Indonesia, because all that I had seen that day emphasized what an indescribable horror it would become.

The lizard seemed a strangely symbolic warning, not only for me and all of us who had been engaged in the war, but, above all, for the Indonesians. These prehistoric forces will always be there. However unseen, however unsuspected, they will be there waiting for a moment when they can lick their lips and savour the rotting corpses of men who have died because their society refuses to acknowledge that that pattern of their nature is spent, and that they must renew themselves in a more meaningful way than has been achieved before. Because of its abiding and timeless reality, the memory of the lizard haunts me still.

And then there is the most rewarding memory of all of that last fortnight of the British occupation in Java. Sjahrir and his Cabinet had decided that they would like to throw a party for all the British staff, not so much for the officers, who of course would not be excluded, but for the warrant officers and men on the staff who had made their officers' work possible.

The Dutch when they heard of it apparently thought it most inappropriate and, behind the scenes, tried to stop it. But the party took place and was a lovely occasion, not only because it was so unexpected but because I do not know of any other occasion on which an army of British occupation has been so saluted and praised by people with whom their relationship started in battle, and who had been compelled by them in ways that they may not always have desired.

MacKereth, summing it all up, concluded that the Indonesians had more to complain of under the British occupation than the Dutch felt they had. I have no scales in which to measure these things. I can only say that the evening warmed all of us in every way. Soetan Sjahrir stood at the door to welcome everybody, and shook everybody by the hand. He had dressed for the occasion as Dutch high officials had dressed for their formal dinner parties. He wore a well-cut and becoming white smoking jacket, black waistcoat, black trousers and a black tie, and outwardly expressed all the grace which he possessed within.

The Dutch afterwards said he did this to spite them. Nothing could be more untrue because, whatever his human failings, spite was not one of them. As well as his natural Indonesian self with its own culture and sense of decency, Sjahrir had in full the alchemy of the Holland of Erasmus, Rembrandt, van Gogh and William the Silent (for whom, when the news of his death broke, even the little children wept in the streets).

The evening ended with him speaking to the crowded assembly. It was a most moving address and I am sad that I did not have what everyone has today, a tape recorder, to give not only the full text of a speech delivered without notes in remarkably good English, but also the sound of his voice. In spite of its repetition in the official report, its importance and its place in history demand that this much of what he had to say to the departing British be quoted here:

Even in unfriendly contact or in conflict with us, we learned to appreciate and admire you. You introduced to our country by your personal
qualities some traits of Western culture our people have rarely seen
before from white people they know. I mean your politeness, your kindness, your dignified self-restraint. Long after you have left, when the

wounds caused by war and revolution of the last year will have been healed, I think this final impression of your army will be the lasting memory for our people of your stay in our country.

That sums up the spirit of an occasion that drove Dr van Mook to a characteristic outburst of protest. Sjahrir replied to Dr van Mook with a smile and said: 'When you decide to withdraw from Indonesia, Dr van Mook, I shall throw a far bigger party for you than I threw for the British.'

No one who heard him could have doubted the sincerity of his words and the emotion which accompanied them. And I am certain that he would not have been able to say them had not the memory of Raffles's years of reform of the Dutch system in Indonesia always been so present in his mind and the minds of the Indonesian leaders. I still rejoice at this recognition of what we had done, and it seems to me far more important than the clamour against us which went on in what was really a pathological memory of the Dutch, not only in Java but in parliament in Holland.

So the last remaining British were ready to withdraw, now really more concerned with the future of the great Indian Army Corps than with Java. Victor Campbell, who was one of the staff whom General Mansergh consulted, told me they would be fully occupied in doing what had been a custom in all British armies after the end of a campaign: seeing that officers who had served it well had proper military awards.

I had a strange feeling that my work was far from over, and it was an added source of assurance that MacKereth, 'Dul and all the Indonesians of note begged me to stay on, so stay I did. All along I had been self-employed, and that sense of self-employment did much, I think, to enrich my commitment.

By the last day of November 1946, only Ian Lauder and a fellow Brigadier McDonald of the headquarters staff remained behind to close the door on our military past in Indonesia. They spent their last night in my mess. Sri, as always, with the innate sense of hospitality of an aristocratic Javanese lady, had produced a superb dinner for them, but they, who normally relished their food, seemed to have no appetite. There was something at work in them which compelled them to drink whisky in alarming quantities and to talk endlessly to and fro about what had happened to them in Burma and other places, and now and then about what had happened in Indonesia, and what awaited them. I left them, knowing how early my days began, to go to bed, and although I got up earlier than usual I found them dressed and ready, waiting in our dining-room for their breakfast with another bottle of whisky in front of them.

They hardly said good morning and ignored me at breakfast, and I think I understood and had no subjective reaction to their rude indifference. I was just concerned with getting them decently on to their aeroplane.

When we ultimately arrived at the airport there was a large delegation of senior Dutch officers under Admiral Pinke waiting to see them off. The two Brigadiers immediately got out of my car and went over to greet and talk with animation to Admiral Pinke and his companions while their baggage was loaded into the aircraft. When the moment came for them to board, Ian Lauder shook each of them warmly by the hand and exchanged unusually emotional words with them. Then they all saluted one another. He then turned to me, as I stood waiting for him near the gangway. He looked at me steadily with strange, unknowing eyes while I came to attention and saluted him. He went on looking at me until I realized that what I thought was going to be a belated salute remained that unfeeling stare and no salute at all. He then turned ostentatiously about and, with his back to me, looked towards Admiral Pinke and his company, waved a hand in farewell to them, and boarded the aircraft, followed by McDonald.

I found myself wondering if it had ever happened before in the history of the British army that an officer had done that to a fellow officer.

I waited there until the aircraft had safely launched itself into the sky and vanished in the direction of Singapore, then went to do one of the last things Ian Lauder had asked of me, to send his final signal to headquarters in Singapore saying that he had brought the evacuation of AFNEI to a satisfactory end. I have forgotten the exact wording but I remember how it ended. It said simply: '*Adios.*' I do now know why, but it seemed to me to have an extra significance, as if in using a foreign word Ian Lauder was expressing an inrush of emotion such as he had not experienced before and which was indeed so foreign to him that he needed a foreign language to express it fully.

The whole incident left me feeling very sad for him and his fellow Brigadier. I was almost glad that they had sat through their last night drinking and talking about old times because they knew already that somewhere, knocking loudly at the door, was a future in which they would be lucky if they found appointments in the battalions they loved. More likely was employment in a much more junior capacity. Indeed the way things were going in India, they might not even find an army to employ them at all. All their instincts, which dedicated soldiers normally have as their ultimate retirement approaches, dreaded the world of the civilian as a selfish, cruel, ruthless and competitive world, compared with which the army at its best possesses all the qualities of a privileged monastic order.

The sadness was still there when some hours later I had a signal from Colin McLaren, whom I should perhaps have mentioned before because of the work he carried on in the Unit of Psychological Warfare. A great wit, he brightened my last months in Java. I had asked him to meet the two Brigadiers in Singapore, and now there came a typical McLaren signal: 'Your two Brigadiers duly poured out of their aircraft and safely delivered to their quarters. Back tomorrow. Colin.'

The British occupation was at an end. However, my strange commitment had not yet done with me. I had no idea how, when or where it would end. All I believed was that when it came I would recognize it and obey, as I had obeyed its beginning.

CHAPTER TEN

The Account Rendered

AND SO I SOLDIERED on in my new capacity as the British Minister's attaché all through what remained of November and December. I had taken it for granted that, as soon as his responsibilities in India allowed it, Mountbatten would do what all other Supreme Commanders in the war did at the end of every campaign, and write a campaign report on Indonesia for the British government. That was not enough for Gilbert MacKereth. No sooner were the Christmas festivities over than he came to me and said he wanted me to write an official report about the British occupation of Indonesia for the Secretary of State for Foreign Affairs.

I protested and said that I thought that until Mountbatten himself had written his campaign report I should not in any way pre-empt it, unless it was his express wish. But MacKereth was insistent. He said it was quite proper that as military attaché to the representative of the British government in Java I should write a report. He would make absolutely certain that Mountbatten understood, although in a sense it was unnecessary because he was sure that Mountbatten himself would welcome such an interim report, particularly from me. Besides, in MacKereth's own report to the Foreign Office he would make it clear that he had asked me to write the report, because he thought that with my experience of Java in war, in prison, in so-called liberation and right through the British occupation, there was no one better placed to do it.

In addition I had some reservations about the timing because he wanted it immediately. I had already undertaken to go on a very privileged tour of Java with Sjahrir, a tour that at one stage would include Soekarno and Hatta as well, and both MacKereth and I had agreed it was a unique opportunity and highly desirable that I should go. Moreover, I knew that I could not write such a report in the formal manner of a Foreign Office dispatch. What I could offer would be to write something which would make sense to people even if they had not heard of Java before, and the report would therefore have to be long.

I told all this to MacKereth and he teased me and said: 'I know you have got another book or two in you. Perhaps this is your opportunity – write me a book about it. I do not mind how long it is provided it is relevant.'

I started immediately. I woke at three o'clock every morning and sat down at my desk to the typewriter on which, throughout the British occupation, I had drafted all my 'Most Immediate' and 'Top Secret' signals for the Commander-in-Chief in Singapore and the Supremo at Kandy, so that I would be free by breakfast-time to get on with my other duties, which continued to be many and urgent.

I finished the report some three weeks later, on the day before I left with Sjahrir for the interior. I gave it to Gilbert MacKereth in the morning, and when I saw him the next day to say goodbye he looked up from his desk as I entered and said: 'Well done! Well done! It *is* long, as you warned me, but there is not a word that I would take away from it or add to it. I know it was difficult and I cannot thank you enough for doing it.'

This, then, is the report.

SECRET: FOR THE MINISTER ONLY

The British Occupation of Indonesia,
from September 19, 1945 to November 30, 1946

I BACKGROUND

1. When most of the Netherlands East Indies – by far the biggest portion of the third largest empire in the world – was suddenly transferred from General MacArthur's command to South East Asia Command on 15th of August 1945, neither his nor Lord Louis Mountbatten's expert advisers seem to have had an inkling of the sort of problems the new commander and his forces had

to expect. Allied intelligence, elsewhere so good, had failed lamentably in this remote and cloistered theatre of operations. In fact British and Dutch prisoners of war have left it on record that as they huddled round their newly installed radios in their camps in Java and Sumatra in the third week of August, they felt like the inhabitants of some backwater of Mars, so darkly did they appear to know and to be known. As the days went by, they failed obstinately to be comforted, and some even were ungrateful enough to be filled with increasing uneasiness by the leisurely reassurances of Ceylon and the sound and fury of the Dutch Government station in Australia. For all they heard, Allied intentions in those parts may well have been inspired by information extracted from some pre-war Baedeker and enlivened by the more enthusiastic recollections of Mr van der Plas, the ex-Governor of East Java, who at that very moment was speeding towards Kandy in the company of the Lt. Governor-General-designate for consultation with the Supreme Commander.

2. It is true that needs like malnutrition medicines and clothing, common to territories freed from the enemy, had been foreseen and as well as possible provided for. But the problem was much more difficult and complicated than that. The Japanese were leaving behind them a tremendous legacy of nationalism – a legacy so formidable that towards the end they themselves had been frightened by it. Yet, if the Dutch Radio in Australia, the station presumably most interested and therefore likeliest to be best informed, were to be believed, the Government, whose precipitate flight from Java in March 1942 had engendered so much bitterness in the aching and emaciated hearts of thousands of Dutch subjects, were coming back fully expecting that once they had hanged Soekarno and Hatta and mopped up a few Japanese collaborators, they could with reference to a document, called the Queen's Broadcast of 1942 (so vaguely known as to be popularly regarded as a royal sop to the Atlantic Charter), take up exactly where they had left off. It all sounded very strange to the men and women around whose bent heads evidence was accumulating daily of the tremendous changes the Japanese occupation had brought about in the traditional pattern of life around them and who on the whole were taking the Japanese warnings of the dangerous mood of the native population so seriously that many camps in essentially Indonesian areas flew no flags on the Queen's birthday on the 31st of August, 1945, lest thereby the

smouldering mass of nationalism should be blown into flame. One says 'on the whole' advisedly, because not everyone took these warnings seriously enough and from all camps there were self-released men and women, but mostly men, who despite all warnings, despite the expressed wish of the Supreme Allied Commander and the reiterated orders of their own camp commanders, spread themselves in their tens and scores far and wide over Java (Sumatra for various reasons was not badly affected) – only to end up after many tragic vicissitudes in another form of concentration camp, where they constituted a fresh problem which prolonged by many months the fulfilment of the Supreme Commander's task, as defined for these occasions at Potsdam.

3. Colonel van der Post who drove from camp to camp in Western and Central Java by car on these occasions describes on the last of them how widespread and strident the evidence of militant nationalism was, and how quickly the native sense of relief at the death-knell of Japanese tyranny, which in its early rapture had expressed itself towards the European internees in demonstrations of sympathy, was quickly changing into a vigilant coolness towards Europeans in general, and open hostility towards the Dutch in particular. For instance, when the British prisoners of war marched out of Bandoeng on the night of August 21, 1945, under a full moon, the native people had thronged their route and repeatedly broken through armed Japanese cordons to embrace them. Now, on the 30th of the month, the camps were receiving daily warnings of impending Indonesian attacks. Round the women's camps in Amberawa Indonesians were more and more insulting in their behaviour, and armed bands were beginning to defy the Japanese sentries and to break into them at night. For hundreds of miles, this officer reported, all the towns, villages and hamlets were flying the nationalist red-white flag. Slogans freely lifted with many a startling improvisation from the American Declaration of Independence, Rousseau's *Social Contract* and the stormier orations of the French Revolution, were beginning to appear wherever there was space for lettering on tramcars, trains, walls, steeples and even cycle-taxis. The fields were full of boys, absurdly young, marching and drilling with bamboo spears and wooden rifles. Barricades covered by armed guards were being thrown up all along the roads. A strange and ominous excitement was gripping the

national sub-conscious of Indonesia. Crowds collected on the vaguest rumour – the country in its entirety was fantastically rumour-ridden – and yelled and shouted with a strange glitter in their eyes on the slightest provocation, altogether behaving very oddly for a people who had a reputation before the war for modesty, reserve and a deep-seated aversion to wearing its enigmatic heart on European-made sleeves.

An Ambonese, violently pro-Dutch, who was sent by Col. van der Post to attend a mass-meeting called by Mr Soekarno, said that as he stood in the crowd waiting, an extraordinary excitement took control of him and everyone else there. By the time Boeng (Comrade) Soekarno came, his heart was beating so violently that he nearly swooned. All Mr Soekarno did on this occasion was to ask the crowd to go home and it went still trembling with excitement, the Ambonese going with them to report later on that it was 'the most remarkable experience of his life'.

4. As the day of the Allied landing approached, the excitement became more tense and determined, and it was obvious that it would continue to do so, until this swarming sense of nationalism had found its proper home. By the time the cruiser *Cumberland*, the flagship of the Rear-Admiral commanding the fifth cruiser squadron, anchored off Tandjongh Priok on the 15th of September 1945, the whole of Java and most of Sumatra were for all practical purposes in the hands of the Indonesian people. The railways, power-stations, water-works, posts and telegraphs, in fact all important utilities, already manned by essentially Indonesian personnel, were quietly taken over, the Japanese controllers either given notice to quit or as happened more frequently, merely ignored.

The ex-Governor of East Java, and the head of Netherlands Indies Civil Affairs landed that first night from the cruiser *Cumberland* to find Batavia in full Nationalist dress with a rather desperate Fascist flush in its face. That very morning a self-released Dutch internee who marched into his old shop in the main street of Batavia and demanded it back was murdered by the Indonesian employees in the place, the Japanese manager trying in vain to protect him. He was the first of a tragic series of many.

5. One has dwelt at some length on the immediate background of this report, for unless it is clearly understood how abruptly the Supreme Commander was made to acquire a vast new

command, and how much the reality in Indonesia differed from the illusions naturally and unavoidably cherished by men like the Governor of East Java, whose worst enemy could not accuse him of not loving those islands, and which in the last analysis became the expert adviser's source for instructing Allied and particularly Dutch planning, the events that followed could either not be understood at all or understood so inadequately as to lead only to the kind of bitter incomprehension which afflicts the whole of the Dutch-speaking world today. Equally important is the period of transition and preparation that followed the arrival of the *Cumberland* up to 30th of September, 1945, the day on which the British troops made their official entry into Batavia. For some reason this period has hardly been mentioned in official reports, and yet it very largely set the tone of the future.

II   TRANSITION AND PREPARATION

6. The immediate tasks of CS5, Rear Admiral Patterson, were
   (a)   to accept the formal surrender of the Japanese forces,
   (b)   to land supplies and specialist personnel for the relief and evacuation of prisoners of war and internees so entitled,
   (c)   to prepare the Japanese for concentration and disarmament by the main forces which were to follow.

All these tasks were tackled with characteristic naval energy and thoroughness. Task (a) was accomplished at once on the day of arrival, (b) was begun so well that by September 30th all British and American Recovered Allied Prisoners of War and Internees were, with a few exceptions, out of Java and Sumatra.

The Dutch Recovered Allied Prisoners of War and Internees, however, were a tougher problem. There were more of them – nearly 69,000 in Java alone – and most of them had their homes either in Java or Sumatra. It was obvious now that they could not walk straight back into their pre-war homes and that they would have to continue to summon from somewhere the strength to contain their fragile souls in patience for a while longer in their terrible camps.

The Japanese claimed that they could protect Recovered Allied Prisoners of War and Internees only in concentration. As reports came in daily of the deterioration of public security in the islands, as the toll of lives in incidents between self-released Dutch and Indonesians continued to mount (on 21st of September five persons, three of them Dutch, were murdered in the main streets of Batavia between 9 a.m. and noon; almost the same day Sourabaya reported its first European murders, significantly caused by the hoisting of the Dutch flag over the principal hotel in the town), the substantial justice of the Japanese claim had to be admitted. There was no way out of it but to make the captor also protector.

Task (c), hardly begun, had to be largely abandoned. Indeed the Admiral found himself in the paradoxical position of having to order the Japanese to re-deploy to a certain extent the forces which they had, as they thought, so obligingly concentrated for incarceration although it had meant depriving the country of the main backing of its (Japanese) police-force at a time when it could least afford it. Similarly, all thought of disarming large numbers of the Japanese had to be dismissed, if the Japanese were to maintain law and order in the simmering world around them. The phrase 'law and order', henceforth, runs like a signature tune through the theme of all instructions issued to the Japanese. Many a Dutch internee in Bandoeng and Semarang lived to thank the Admiral later for not disarming the Japanese just then. Yet tragic as the situation of the Recovered Allied Prisoners of War and Internees was, the main interest soon shifted to other aspects of the turbulent scene.

7. The Indonesian Republic had been proclaimed on 17th of August, 1945, in the house of His Majesty's Consul-General in Batavia, then occupied by Vice-Admiral Maeda of the Imperial Japanese Navy – an able, tenacious, far-seeing officer whose role in the critical transition period has not been sufficiently studied. How and why the Republic was proclaimed at that time makes a fascinating story but it is not really relevant here. Capt. Nakamura, the fat Japanese Civil Affairs officer, a student of criminal pathology and an amateur psycho-analyst, who regarded his own people as a race of schizophrenics and was a cool enough customer to take advantage of post-surrender confusion to the extent of hiding 10 million guilders of gold for his own use, acted as interpreter at the time and according to him the Japanese Chief of Staff did all he could to dissuade the Indonesians from proclaiming the Republic. No Dutchman will ever believe that but in a sense who the father and who the midwife were, is quite unimportant. What matters is the baby that was born. And no illegitimate child ever created more resentment in the family and more stir among the neighbours.

An enormous clamour immediately went up in the Dutch-speaking world for the Supreme Commander to order the immediate arrest of the Republican leaders and a ruthless stamping out of their movement by the Japanese.

It is important to note that the first Dutch reaction was repressive and as well to contrast it with our own reaction in roughly similar conditions in Burma, where we had tried to make friends not enemies of persons like Aung San. This contrast was fundamental. It coloured all events that followed and helps to explain why this clamour did not meet with its desired response.

8. In Batavia too the ex-Governor of East Java, as chief representative of his government, did his best to persuade the Admiral to take anti-nationalist measures. The Admiral, quietly, tactfully and steadfastly refused to do anything so crude. When asked to order the Japanese to haul down all red and white flags of Nationalist Indonesia, and to prohibit their display in future, he replied that people could fly any flag they liked as far as he was concerned but that he would not tolerate one section of the community forcing another to fly a flag they did not want. It may all seem trivial at this distance, but the Dutch are passionately devoted to the dangerous sport of flag-flying. It is probably from them that the Indonesians learnt a taste for it too. The two teams made a desperate business of it and an astonishing number of lives were lost putting their own flags up and pulling the other fellows' down.

9. The greatest controversy of all at the time raged round the leaders of the Republican movement. Mr van der Plas had prepared a black-list of 'dangerous' and 'criminal' Indonesians headed by Soekarno and Hatta, to be arrested immediately. When the Admiral refused to order the Japanese to do it, Mr van der Plas accepted the decision gracefully but returned to the charge with the argument that it would then have to be done just before British troops landed, otherwise he assured the Admiral, there would be widespread bloodshed.

With the parallel of Greece and the world criticism British action there evoked vivid in everyone's mind, it was an argument that had to be carefully considered. Mr van der Plas and General van Straaten urged it so persistently that the Military Adviser to the Admiral was ordered at one stage to prepare a scheme for arresting seventeen of the Indonesian leaders, including Soekarno and Hatta, on the night of the British landing. In case there should even then be fighting, arrangements were made to fly in 1,200 Dutch troops from Borneo to do the shooting. To all British sailors and soldiers who had been through a long war against intolerance and oppression the whole idea of arresting people because someone else did not approve of their politics was instinctively so abhorrent that it is not surprising that Mr van der Plas lost the argument. Unfortunately he and many of his countrymen found it hard to forgive us, and he himself on the night the Admiral's decision was made known to him, told a Dutch officer: 'The British are back at their old game, spreading confusion in the Far East. Look at the harm they are doing in Indo-China, and it is going to be the same here, so that they and Malaya can fish with profit in our troubled waters.'

10. It would be a mistake to think that the British attitude to the problems facing Dutch and Indonesians was just a barren negative. The Admiral was daily urging Mr van der Plas who responded willingly to make the more constructive and creative elements in Dutch policy known with all speed possible to the population which had been deprived of all contact with the world press and world thought for so long. He and his officers drew the attention of the Dutch authorities to their radio station in Australia, which even at that moment did little more than radiate fire and brimstone against Japanese collaborationists, and suggested for instance that the Queen's Broadcast of 1942 might be re-broadcast and made known again. It was characteristic of the fashion in which the Netherlands East Indies had been taken for granted that not a single copy of this very important document of state could be found in the baggage of any of the Dutch officers and officials who were pouring into the island. Eventually Australia was cabled for a copy. It arrived two days after the British troops landed.

11. Finally the Admiral did what he could to remedy another miscalculation in the Allied reckoning. It has always been a routine British military principle to take over territory occupied by the enemy with a proper Civil Affairs organisation. This principle had not been forgotten in the Allied plan for the Netherlands East Indies. In fact, the Dutch who were obviously charged with this part of the Allied task had been preparing for it for more than a year. Enormous numbers of ex-civil servants in Holland and Australia were formed into a Unit, Netherlands Indies Civil Affairs, and were standing by, fretting their hearts out for the day

of their return. Unfortunately it was becoming increasingly clear that Netherlands Indies Civil Affairs for some time to come would not only be unable to exercise any immediately useful function in the Netherlands East Indies, but would easily be a source of the most dangerous friction with the local population.

The Dutch disappointment was tremendous and their reaction was frankly incredulous. Here and there they backed up their unbelief by sending special parties into the interior. Few of them ever returned. Mr van der Plas's own secretary disappeared for ever on a mission to Bantam for his unbelieving master. Urgently the Admiral signalled Kandy to make all possible haste with the occupation and to send a mission of senior staff officers with a strong Civil Affairs section to examine a situation which was turning out to be something utterly different from anything it was ever thought to be. Signals alone could no longer bridge the gap between anticipation and reality. In the course of time one British Civil affairs officer equipped with out-of-date proclamations and pamphlets came from Ceylon, only to disappear into a vast building on some vague and ill-defined liaison with the unemployable Netherlands Indies Civil Affairs in Batavia.

12. Thus it happened that General Sir Philip Christison, whose 15 Indian Corps was being sent to the Netherlands East Indies on Britain's Potsdam mission, arrived in Batavia without a British Civil Affairs staff and without a political adviser for the first critical days. No British commander could ever have needed one more.

III OCCUPATION: *The First Phase – 'The Unwilling British'*

13. The landing of the first British troops took place on the morning of September 30 – some days ahead of the schedule originally drawn up for them. In response to the Admiral's signals and the pleas of the Dutch, the Supreme Commander was doing everything possible to speed up, with the extremely limited shipping available, the arrival of his forces. These first British troops, the senior Battalion of the Seaforth Highlanders, belonged to a regiment which more than 130 years before had distinguished itself in operations against the French and French Dutch supporters in Java. They had done the long journey from Port Swettenham crammed in Landing Craft Infantry and arrived tired, seasick and dishevelled. As fast as they disembarked, the Landing Craft

Infantry turned back towards Malaya for more troops.

One lingers over these small details because all the time in Holland, and in certain sections of the American press, we were already being criticised for half-heartedness and inexcusable tardiness in coming to the assistance of a gallant ally.

14. Despite the forebodings of the apostles of repression and arrest for the Republican leaders, the occupation of Batavia passed off without serious incidents. The few sailors who for 14 long and anxious days had been helping to guard the women's camps in Batavia could at last be reinforced. On the surface the city looked calmer than it had for some weeks. Yet all was far from well. A distinguished Indonesian who loyally fought with the Allies throughout the war, watched the entry of our troops into Batavia and was moved to write, in a stark and sober report of warning to his unseeing government: 'I have been here since the middle of September and I do not recognise my own countrymen. While the Allied troops everywhere in the Pacific were welcomed, here in Batavia the reception was cool. No British, no Chinese or Soviet flag was hung out. Their opposition is directed not only towards the Dutch but also to the Indonesians who took part in the fighting. The population clearly gives the impression of having been kept behind walls, although it has not been interned. A great social upheaval has been accomplished – the old aristocracy has gone – the landowner does not mean anything any more. The feeling of nationalism is developed in all layers of society. The people feel united in future grief and joy.'

The British, probably because it was easier for them to be objective, saw the problem thus almost from the start. A working majority of the Dutch government after fourteen long months has only just come to a similar view. This difference in appreciation of the situation, added to the profound difference in the political instincts of the two peoples, made the British Commander's task uncommonly difficult.

15. Now this task could be briefly defined as:
    (a) to disarm and evacuate the Japanese.
    (b) to recover the Allied Prisoners of War and Internees (APWI) in the islands and evacuate those so entitled.
    (c) the maintenance of law and order within the key areas necessary for the performance of (a) and (b), and the establishment of a civil administration.
    (d) the introduction of food and other non-warlike supplies.

(a), (b) and (d) require no comment but (c) from the beginning was the cause of the first serious tussle with the Dutch. General Christison on the day of his arrival was warmly cross-examined by the press on the qualification of 'within the key areas' added to the duty of 'maintaining law and order'. During the transition period it had been assumed, and the assumption coloured all public announcements, that the occupation forces would accept the responsibility of maintaining law and order everywhere. In fact the one lone Civil Affairs officer sent out from Kandy to survey the stormy Indonesian waters, like a dove from the Supreme Commander's ark, had in his possession a printed document in which the occupation forces were made responsible for law and order without any qualification whatsoever. But while he was on his way to Batavia, a whiff of reality had already reached the Supreme Commander's staff, and at a conference in Singapore with Mr Lawson, the Secretary of State for War, General Christison's task had been redefined and his responsibilities limited. He himself tried to make it clear to the press in Batavia that should he be called upon to sally out from his key areas to save human life or on any errand of mercy he would not hesitate to do so. Perhaps he did not make his meaning plain. He had already been grossly misrepresented in the press in Singapore and there might conceivably have been justice in a frustrated American journalist's bitter remark: 'The General has a singular aptitude for being misquoted in the press,' but whatever the reason, the General himself was blamed for this limitation of a vital responsibility. The Dutch press in particular resented his off-the-record references to the fact that we had just come through a war fought for political and religious tolerance, for the right of people to work life out in their own way provided they did so without peril or threat to their neighbours – surely a sentiment that needed no apology in the mouth of a General who had just brought his troops out of the grim Arakan and was committing them to another indeterminate exile in a foreign country. The word went round to the Palace, still with traces of sandalwood scent left in it by the Japanese commander-in-chief, it was repeated in the Dutch services, and re-echoed in The Hague: 'The General is anti-Dutch.'

This cry was to be repeated a thousand times and became the standard pattern for damnation of any British General or officer who did not do exactly what the Dutch wanted. That two persons, or for that matter two peoples, could hold different views without necessarily doing so dishonestly or with Machiavellian malice aforethought, so implicit an assumption in the life of the British people, was not a belief encouraged in Batavia in those days, even if the abnormal post-internee psychology of the place allowed it to exist at all.

16. While the British troops were speeding towards Java and Sumatra, and the Seaforths and sailors of the *Cumberland* were nightly dispersing with the greatest forbearance and good humour the yelling mobs that generated themselves spontaneously around the internees' camps, the General and the Admiral did their utmost to get from the Dutch an authoritative statement of future policy. They pointed out that one of the principal causes of unrest was the prevailing uncertainty over the intentions of the Dutch in these islands. The voice of revenge of Dutch Radio Australia had hardly been silenced, and references to the Queen's Broadcast of 1942 reiterated to the point of hysterical monotony were worse than useless. Few people knew what that broadcast contained and were merely irritated by oblique references to it. What appeared to be wanted was a statement of policy on the highest political level, giving practical expression to the principles outlined in that broadcast.

Our own history from the American War of Independence up to the Boer War and onwards had taught us to give early and to give well, if only not to be forced by inexorable events to give too much too late. In the absence of the complete text of the Queen's broadcast, Mr van der Plas addressed to the people of Indonesia a liberal, admirable and what appeared to be at the time [an] impeccable outline of Dutch policy. Without waiting for a report from Batavia, without even asking Mr van der Plas for an explanation, with only a newspaper report of his speech in front of them, the Dutch Government promptly disowned Mr van der Plas. The anti-Soekarno, anti-republican roar in their press reached a new height. The Hague has a bad record in the tenacious memories of both Indonesians and native-born Dutch for invariably spoiling the good intentions of its men on the spot. It would in the circumstances have been better if Mr van der Plas's statement had not been made, because the first public utterance it had drawn from The Hague was this misunderstanding and impulsively negative one.

17. By this time all the war-time leaders of the Netherlands East

Indies Government and its armed forces who had escaped
internment by their flight to Australia were assembling in
Batavia. Not all of them were prophets who possessed honour
with their incarcerated countrymen. For instance, the one who
knew Indonesia best and perhaps loved it most, Mr van der Plas,
had managed with ironic success to unite Dutch and
Indonesians in common mistrust and hatred of him. Again,
General van Oyen, the handsome ripened air-force officer, so
fond of his wine, his food and his women, was universally disliked by his countrymen, particularly by the ladies who rightly or
wrongly believed that he flew out of Bandoeng in March 1942
with his mistress, leaving his wife behind. He was about to take
over command of the Dutch forces in the Netherlands East
Indies.

Then there was the Commander-in-Chief himself, Admiral
Helfrich, who did have the respect of the older generation as a
fighter but who had never been known to voice a political
opinion more subtle or progressive than: 'Shoot the lot.' He
played such an important role in the events of the time that his
character is worth a slightly more detailed study. Both his
Christian name, Conrad, and surname suggest the German
origin which the back of his unrounded head proclaims. Self-
indulgent and vain, he imagined himself to be the most popular
Dutch leader of the war. Attempts had been made, indeed, to
turn him into a sort of Dutch Churchill, and his reputation as a
fighter was terrific, but he had hardly ever been under even indirect fire. During the battle of the Java Sea, for which he had collected so much of the honour [that] the gallant Admiral Karel
Doorman and his men had paid for with their lives, he had made
his contribution to the Dutch, British and American bravery of
the day quite properly from his office in Bandoeng with one of
our rear-admirals at his side. Accustomed to command and to
almost servile obedience, he did not take orders from others,
least of all civilians, with good grace, if he took them at all,
knowing full well that the regard in which he was once held by
the Queen and the people at home gave him a degree of immunity few servants of their country normally possess. His tone was
truculent, quarrelsome and anti-British from the start on
account of grievances conceived against our imagined 'cowardice and incompetence in Malaya'.

18. Finally, as leader of this team, there was Dr van Mook, the pre-

war Director of Economic Services in the Netherlands East
Indies, whose experience of high-level politics was confined to
that gained under abnormal war-time conditions. His reputation had been least touched by the flight to Australia and he was
the one man at the time to whom the Indonesians, Dutch and
British turned with some degree of hope. In a secret directive to
his own staff in June 1945, he had tried to weigh up probabilities
of future policy in the Netherlands East Indies and had come to
the conclusion that of all foreign powers Britain would be the
'least dangerous' for the Dutch to co-operate with. Moreover, he
had been born in the Netherlands East Indies, and his vision of
it did not travel instinctively, as most other Dutch people's did,
via The Hague on a Netherlands passport. The Hague knew this
and at times even resented it and called him an '*Indische Jongen*',
a boy from the Indies, who was not quite a gentleman. But he
had proved himself an able, uncompromising bargainer with the
Japanese before the war, and as such was not without respect.
His was ever an enigmatic personality. One would go to see him
in the Palace early in the morning and find him in the depths of
despair, blear-eyed, red-nosed, chain-smoking endless American
cigarettes that his trembling hands could hardly light, saying
passionately: 'I can't go on, I am going to resign,' only to meet
him later in the day, rubbing a pair of steadied hands, his eyes
cleared and with a smile on his face, asserting gleefully that
things had never gone better.

Looking back, reading through the signals of fourteen
months, does not make the puzzle of his personality any clearer,
probably because he himself has not yet decided which of the
several van Mooks he is going to be. At no time did one strike
what seemed to be any clear faith or even one central conviction
in him to integrate these various selves. If there had been, he
would surely have kept his word and resigned many times. In
those days, any one man of authority on the Dutch side with
some robust faith could have mastered the run-away circumstances that were scattering every coherent thought and feeling
left and right. It was their tragedy that they had no such man,
and that the Indonesians could produce several leaders with the
sort of faith tested in loneliness and in exile, and one at least with
a very deep faith and an exceptionally clear mind. Here anyway
is one deficiency which history will never be able to blame on us.
No British spiritual quarter-master-general could put it right. If

they want these things, nations must carry them in their own stores.

It is possible to continue the tale of the idiosyncrasies of the various personalities who crowded round the Governor-General but it is sufficient to record that they were a strangely assorted and uneasy team. As they were confronted with this unexpected scene, and there burst in on their privileged senses the full naked and uncensored story of the horror their countrymen had endured (who had suffered terribly, had suffered long and suffered much), the feeling of the urgency of putting things right became so compelling that they blindly attempted from time to time their own pet quack remedies, and so added to the general confusion. Had they shown more discipline and more loyalty to one another, acted more as a team with a single voice of authority, it is doubtful if their personal relationships with the British Command would have become so bad. But it was to Dr van Mook alone [that] the British felt they could turn with any hope of success. As a best bet of an uninspired bunch, they backed him as well as they could.

19. The general outline of Dutch policy towards the British Command in those days, apart from the enigmatic variations given to it from time to time by individuals like their admiral, was to try to convince General Christison and his staff that Indonesian nationalism was confined to a very small section of intellectuals, principally in Batavia; that nationalism was essentially a product of Fascist propaganda and that provided the British Commander acted with vigour against the Republican leaders the problem would disappear overnight with little bloodshed. They went further and claimed that we owed it to them, on account of the losses they had endured in the Allied cause, to give them the country back precisely as the Japanese had found it in March 1942. If it had not been for the help they gave us in December 1941, they claimed, somewhat unrealistically, they could have preserved their country from the ravages of war. In any case they refused to recognise the Nationalist movement as a National phenomenon. So little respect had they for the signs of the times, indeed, that in the last days of September and the first weeks of October, against the advice and pleas of British Recovered Allied Prisoners of War and Internees officers, they had begun to move several thousands of Dutch Allied Prisoners of War and Internees into unoccupied Sourabaya where there

had been no internee problem and where there was no allied protection. Throughout October and early November, particularly at the time of the Mallaby murder, the Dutch continued to press the British Commander officially and unofficially for action and more action against Indonesian extremists.

20. The British Commander replied that he would not hesitate to take action against anyone who tried to interfere with the accomplishment of his ordained task. But he had already formed the opinion that this was not a problem which could, even if it should, be solved militarily. He had done what he could to bring home to Kandy (he had sent a senior staff officer to report in person to the Supreme Commander, and South East Asia Command had done its bit by the Chiefs of Staff in sending a Major-General to London) the seriousness of the situation. He felt that the sooner the Dutch met the Indonesian leaders to talk things over the better and he had sounded [out] Dr van Mook who had proved not at all unwilling, although somewhat frightened by the reception of Mr van der Plas's one venture on the air and by the fire and brimstone of Admiral Helfrich's threats.

The great obstacle towards a meeting in the Dutch view was the personality of Dr Soekarno, the president of the Republic, regarded and labelled by the Dutch Government and people as the arch and criminal Japanese collaborator of the war, for whom a death sentence was the least that was expected. The merest hint that Dr van Mook and Soekarno should meet sent the Cabinet in The Hague into a frenzy.

'The day will come, Dr van Mook, when you and the Admiral,' the Indonesian adviser to the Palace exclaimed at a meeting early in November, 'if you are not careful, will beg heaven to give you back Soekarno.'

Back in The Hague H.M. Ambassador, with Colonel van der Post from Allied Forces Netherlands East Indies Headquarters (A.F.N.E.I.) to assist him with first-hand information, was doing his utmost to persuade the Dutch Government to trust their man on the spot and to back him up, should he decide it was necessary to meet the Indonesian leaders, even Soekarno. They were, after all, not asking the Dutch to do anything more than Britain had done over and over again in her history and was even then doing in Burma.

One meeting with Professor Schermerhorn, Professor Logemann and Mr van Kleffens alone lasted four hours. It began with a long survey of Dutch-British relationships from the time of our occupation of the Cape and Stamford Raffles in Java, to the Boer War, past the Fall of Singapore and so into the present. Then only did Professor Schermerhorn promise full support for Dr van Mook and agree that he could see Soekarno provided he did not send for him, and saw him then only as a nationalist leader and not as President of a Republic. It is significant comment on the spirit of the times that while Colonel van der Post was closeted with the Minister of Overseas Territories, Professor Logemann, in his office one afternoon soliciting on behalf of his General and the Supreme Commander [an] understanding of Dr van Mook's troubles and full support for his person and policy, he was shown a number of personal signals from Dr van Mook to the minister, complaining bitterly that General Christison was seeing the Indonesians behind his back and that he and his officers were fraternising with the Japanese and were indifferent to the troubles and sorrows of the Dutch. None of those complaints, as the Colonel immediately pointed out, had been brought to the General's notice. No attempt had been made to have them redressed or explained on the spot. The Minister saw the justice of his remarks and promised to forbid similar procedure in the future. It continued on an ascending scale to the end.

21. Meanwhile concern over the slowness with which Batavia appeared to be facing the political realities of the situation had brought the Foreign Office's principal adviser on the staff of the Supreme Commander, Mr Maberley Dening, to Batavia. He arrived in the last week of October and within twenty-four hours of his arrival met Wing-Commander Pitt Hardacre who had just completed an extended tour of the interior of Java. He was the last British officer to do so for many months. The remotest parts of the country now too were in the first fine raptures of the nationalist fever. No European was safe any longer outside the protected areas, frequently not even within them. The report of this officer (who had only narrowly escaped with his own life) gave Mr Dening an ominous picture of a native state in full preparation for war, flushed with confidence and eager for the fray. It carried conviction of what Allied Forces Netherlands East Indies had urged from the start, that no time must be lost in breaking down the political barriers between Dutch and Indonesians. And if any further proof were needed, there came

the fighting in Sourabaya on 28th October 1945, the murder of Brigadier Mallaby a few days later and the massacre of several score of Allied Prisoners of War and Internees.

The detail of what happened at Sourabaya is not really relevant to this review but it is interesting that the very latest evidence suggests that the Mallaby murder, far from being premeditated or a deliberate breach of faith, was caused more by the indescribable confusion and nervous excitement of everyone in the town. Had General Hawthorn, the General Officer Commanding Java at that time, had proper Civil Affairs and political officers on his staff to draft his unfortunate proclamations for him and to keep [in] continuous and informed contact with the population, the story of Sourabaya may well have been different. But the important lessons of Sourabaya were not these so much as the extent to which they proved that Indonesian nationalism was not a shallow, effeminate, intellectual cult but a people-wide, tough and urgent affair. It was all very well for Mr van der Plas to tell the Commander at Allied Forces Netherlands East Indies: 'The Indonesians are too nice a people to fight really hard.'

Sourabaya gave him and the Helfrich school who clamoured: 'A couple of whiffs of grapeshot and all will be over', the direct lie. From the 28th of October to the end of November when we finished our mopping-up operations in Sourabaya, using sea, air and land forces, we had 400 casualties. The Indonesians lost approximately 6,000 killed. And the heart is not out of them yet. Patrol encounters, minor attacks and artillery action are routine occurrences to this day.

22. Throughout those tragic days in November the British Headquarters worked ceaselessly to bring the Dutch and Indonesian leaders together. Dr van Mook and his advisers were still arguing among themselves over how the Indonesian leaders should be approached and once approached what should be said to them. A way out of their difficulties was that the Commander in Chief Allied Forces Netherlands East Indies should invite both Dutch and Indonesian leaders to meet under his chairmanship at his headquarters. All British energies were directed towards this end. It was a difficult and at times apparently hopeless task. So much of the problem was psychological and the least word out of its tiny place was apt to cancel anything like an approach from one side to the other.

On top of it all individual outbreaks of shooting increased daily. A desperate and unofficial war between Dutch and Dutch supporters and Indonesians started in Batavia. Scores of Dutch and Eurasians were kidnapped and disappeared from their homes, never to be seen again. Scores of Indonesians were spirited away and their kampongs and houses burnt down by Dutch soldiers and armed civilians acting on their own initiative. The hours between six in the evening and ten at night became really dangerous hours when the civilian out of doors never knew when and from where someone was going to shoot at him. It was not an atmosphere to breed confidence and goodwill. Yet at this critical moment something happened inside the Indonesian government which changed the whole outlook.

23. Sourabaya, although the allies did not appreciate it at the time, had been a far greater shock to the Indonesian leaders than to anyone else. Apart from the slur the Mallaby murder and the massacre of women and children had cast on their reputation, they saw more clearly than ever the danger they ran in leaving their Japanese-trained youth leaders too free a hand. Soekarno, Hatta and Amir Sjarifoeddin had seen Sourabaya for themselves when they flew down with General Hawthorn to help to stop the fighting and at times – they all three showed no lack of physical courage – had been right in the thick of the trouble. Throughout the ten days that followed Sourabaya, urgent discussions between Indonesian leaders went on in Batavia. Then suddenly it was announced that the Republic Government had resigned and a new cabinet been formed under the premiership of one Soetan Sjahrir.

It was for the Indonesians a revolutionary announcement. How radical the change really was only became clear as the names and reputations of the new cabinet ministers were examined. With the exception of Soekarno and Hatta every member of the previous government had disappeared, and no one was put in their place whom the most ardent Indonesian hater could accuse of either collaboration with the Japanese or insensate foreigner hatred.

Mr Sjahrir himself, a companion once in political exile of Hatta for four years, had organised a resistance movement against the Japanese in Java and had resolutely refused to serve for or under them. As chairman of the National Executive Committee of the Republic he had great influence with the

younger people of his country and the warm affection and
support of Mohammed Hatta. Already in the first days of
November he had published a most remarkable and stirring
pamphlet, 'Our Struggle', which quickly became the best of
best-sellers in Indonesia. 'Our Struggle' was a devastating attack
on Japanese thought and influence in the Nationalist movement
of his country; a moving, and what someone remembering his
exile and seeing what was happening in Batavia at the time may
have thought undeserved defence of European values, and a
resounding call for democratic tolerance and method in the
political life of his country. Although it was contrary to the first
constitution of his country, Sjahrir went to Soekarno and Hatta
with a cabinet on the British, not [the] American, model, won
their support and called an immediate meeting of the National
Committee of Indonesia, the shadow and makeshift parliament
of his country.

24. 'They are all honourable men and we should like to negotiate
with them', Professor Logemann said when he saw the cabinet
list in Holland.

'They are good people,' Dr van Mook told the Commander
and Mr Dening, 'but I wonder what power they have really got
and if it is really worth while talking to them. But we can try.'
And try they did.

25. Of two not ready parties, the Indonesians were by far the least
ready for negotiations. They had a major political reorganisation on their hands and could not be sure even then that the
National Executive meeting would confirm them in their office.
As a gesture, however, to the British Commander, who they
thought was doing his best to be fair to them (or else why should
the Dutch be saying such nasty things about him?) and to identify themselves in principle with the rule of negotiation, they
agreed to meet the Dutch. The meeting took place on 17th
November 1945. It lasted nearly four hours and the following
morning Mr Dening reported that it had produced no result
whatsoever. The only people who looked pleased after the
meeting were the Dutch. Everybody was patting them on the
back and saying how well they had behaved and what cads these
little Indonesians were, hedging and refusing to give frank
answers and asking for more time. Both the General and Mr
Dening were very angry. 'If there was ever any doubt in my
mind as to the incapacity of the Indonesians to govern or to do

anything else but talk, it was removed last night,' Mr Dening said, speaking for himself and the General. Another meeting was arranged for 22 November. The Indonesians asked for a week but the General would give them only five days.

The Dutch seemed for the moment to have proved their point that these fellows were hardly worth talking to. Yet, in the circumstances the Indonesians' reluctance to commit themselves was not really so strange as the fact that they had agreed in their unprepared state to come to a formal meeting at all. That was the real moral to be drawn from the meeting: the Indonesians had formally established their adherence to the rule of negotiation with the Dutch. Moreover they had reorganised their government in such a way that it was no longer necessary for Dr van Mook to invite Dr Soekarno when he wanted authoritative talks in the future. Dr Soekarno was now formal head of the state and had a prime minister to act for him. The embarrassment they saved both Dr van Mook and Professor Logemann by making this possible alone should have earned them the gratitude of the Dutch.

26. The meeting called for 22 November never took place.

'Sjahrir signing himself Prime Minister of the Government of the Republic of Indonesia,' to quote from a signal of Mr Walsh [a consular officer], 'wrote to General Christison that in accordance with a decision reached at a cabinet meeting it is of little use to meet Dutch representatives before there is an official statement which will be able to appease Indonesian minds since Dutch actions of the last few days caused great anger among all Indonesians, including the cabinet. At any time we are willing to discuss matters with the British.'

This message was described by Mr Walsh as typically pleasant and 'evasive'. It really seemed rather to the point and unevasive, and one mentions it only because Mr Walsh, along with Mr Dening and the General, was already being accused of being anti-Dutch and pro-Indonesian. It is difficult anywhere in their signals to find a single instance of pro-Indonesian sentiment. There is lots of evidence of their desire to be fair to both sides and if anything the Indonesians had perhaps more grounds for complaint than the Dutch in the way the facts were being interpreted.

27. The 'Dutch actions of the last few days' to which Mr Sjahrir referred in his letter were a record recrudescence of Dutch ini-

tiative in the matter of teaching the Indonesians a lesson. In fairness to the Dutch it should be remembered that daily now survivors rescued from Sourabaya and Central Java were coming into Batavia haggard with what they had suffered and seen others suffer at the hands of Indonesians.

But the reprisals individual Dutch soldiers and Dutch native mercenaries were taking in Batavia passed all possible bounds of excuse. The General in fact had been so concerned over the very serious disorders provoked in the capital on the 18th and 19th of November by the employment of native troops against his orders, that he informed Dr van Mook he would have to relieve General van Oyen of his command. The evidence of disobedience and atrocity on this occasion was overwhelming. The General himself had witnessed from his own office window the day before the burning of native houses behind his headquarters by Ambonese troops. His aide-de-camp had seen an Ambonese shoot down an old Indonesian coming out of his burning house with his family and nothing more dangerous than two suitcases in his hands; when the old man lay on the ground the soldier gave him another burst from his tommy-gun. (This Ambonese was sentenced subsequently to 14 days 'Confined to Barracks' for 'unnecessary cruelty in action'.) On the morning of the 21st, moreover, two Ambonese soldiers shot down and dangerously wounded Dr Mohammed Roem, a religious youth leader of great standing, just as he was entering his house. This was the last straw on the Indonesian cabinet's back. They called the meeting off.

28. The day before, Dr van Mook had told the Commander that the extremists had gained such control over the whole country that discussions between the moderate Indonesians and the Dutch could no longer serve any practical purpose. Dr van Mook had reached one of his depths of periodic despair. He talked of resigning. General van Oyen's dismissal depressed him in particular, because he was by no means having an easy time with his own military commanders, and even some of his senior civil servants were letting him down. In Sumatra, for instance, General Christison discovered a few days later that Governor Spits had refused off his own bat, without even informing Batavia or The Hague, to communicate Dr van Mook's written statement of policy to the Indonesian leaders because he thought it too liberal.

In Batavia, Admiral Helfrich was furious and dashed between his house and the Palace, the Palace and Allied Forces Netherlands East Indies, with apoplectic temper in his face. He hardly made any pretence any more either of loyalty to the Governor-General or to the Commander. When General Christison ordered the withdrawal of Dutch native troops from the town, he begged Headquarters for time in which to do it tactfully but told two American newspaper correspondents on the same day that he would ensure that the withdrawal did not take place. The lies that he and the Palace told over this order would fill a separate sheet. The point is that the withdrawal never took place, and Dutch and Indonesian atrocities continued to feed and grow fat on one another.

29. Sjahrir, after several unnecessary molestations, was shot at by Dutch troops in the end and saved from probable death only by the interference of a passing British officer. Amir Sjarifoeddin's car was shot at, one bullet going through the windscreen; four Indonesian officials collecting petrol from a Republican pump were shot down in cold blood by a couple of Dutch marines.

'They are young,' their officer, an old friend of the Political Officer at Allied Forces Netherlands East Indies, told him, 'and unless it is politically very important we do not really want to punish them.'

With all this happening Indonesian fears for the safety of their leaders increased to such an extent that they insisted on Soekarno and Hatta moving to Djokja. They had tried to make the whole cabinet go but Sjahrir made it a question of confidence that the cabinet should stay in Batavia to negotiate or, failing that, maintain contact with the British and the Dutch. The presidential party left Batavia on the 16th of December and have not been back since.

IV OCCUPATION: *The Second Phase – 'The Great Fumble'*

30. The brief period which followed the abortive meeting at General Christison's Headquarters from the 17th of November up to the end of the year was probably the most depressing of our occupation. The last month of what elsewhere had been such a brave and glorious year, here in the Netherlands East Indies drew to a close against a sordid background of rising lawlessness and savagery. Everywhere from our narrow perimeters in these islands, we stared straight into the hostile and suspicious

faces of a population firmly convinced that we were here merely to subjugate and cow their legitimate longing for independence.

Had they thought that we were doing it for ourselves, they probably would have understood it more and disliked it less, but that we were doing it for the Dutch who had abandoned them in such a 'cowardly manner', as they thought, to the Japanese, seemed unpardonable. They had not, it must be remembered, seen the Dutch air-force and the Dutch navy in their gallant effort to hold off the enemy forces from these islands. They had no idea of the heavy losses suffered by these two arms of the Dutch services. But they had seen a numerically not inferior Dutch army yield ingloriously, after one week of war on Java, without a shot having been fired almost, except by a few thousand Australians, English and Americans. Almost the next day they had witnessed the strange spectacle of these very same Dutch soldiers who a week before were jeering bitterly at the British over Singapore and singing the popular ditty of the day: '*We zijn niet bang*' ('We Are Not Afraid'), clicking their heels to sabre-legged NCOs and bowing at dawn in the direction of the palace of the emperor in Tokyo.

How could the simple native mind understand the current explanation many Dutch and British officers even found difficult to believe; that the armies of the Dutch Commander-in-Chief, General Ter Poorten, had done what was asked of them by the Allied Command in getting the Japanese landed, deployed and committed in the N.E.I. Thereafter it had been agreed, in order to prevent the massacre of the European civil population which would inevitably follow, [that] the Dutch forces would be free to surrender. All the natives knew was that their Lord and Master for three hundred years had failed ignominiously in a Lord and Master's most elementary task.

31. One cannot stress this enough because it was a fundamental factor in the complicated and embittered psychology of the moment. There is a popular tendency to believe that only the Dutch suffered under the Japanese occupation. It is true that only the Dutch and people defined as pro-Dutch were interned in the N.E.I. but very many thousands more of Indonesians than Dutch are lying coffin-small today in the steaming and far-flung islands of the South-West Pacific; many more Indonesian than Dutch families had been brutally broken up, although the full horror of what they suffered had never been told; the same

humiliations and tortures had been theirs to such an extent, too, that their young men had from time to time broken out in futile and immature rebellion as in Kediri in March 1945.

Unhappily it was common to assume that these people did not suffer because their suffering was inarticulate and had not found a professional mourner to hawk it out before a jaded international heart. Yet, this bitter leaven of the immediate past, working in the unconscious mind of the islands, uttered itself consciously in passionate outbursts of resentment at the merest suggestion of the Dutch now coming back to subdue them by force.

'In my experience and the experience of General van Oyen,' Admiral Helfrich told the Supreme Commander, Sir Alan Brooke and Sir Miles Dempsey on 6th December 1945, 'the most profitable way when dealing with native rabble is to hit immediately and to hit hard.'

It would be interesting to know when Admiral Helfrich and General van Oyen ever had experience of dealing with native rabble; the experience is not yet recorded in their written histories. But the point is that their instinct, like the instinct of many others, was to hit once more well and truly the poor native head which had already been hit so hard by professional Japanese hitters for nearly four years.

'They are ready to fight and kill us when they were only too ready to run and save themselves from the Japanese, and the British have come to help them,' the native thought as he looked back towards our barricades.

'We are prepared to use force of arms to keep Java inside the Kingdom,' Professor Logemann allowed a BBC reporter to broadcast on his behalf, and the qualifications made at the time are not worth quoting because this is the only part of the interview that stuck in the popular mind.

32. As for the Dutch, far from being grateful and agreeing with the native interpretation of our presence in these parts, they were heaping an increasing flow of invective and recrimination on British heads, blocking their signals channels to The Hague with complaints against the British General and his staff. The enormous stream of energy and good intentions released towards these islands by the victory in the Pacific appeared to be unexpectedly and irretrievably dammed. The Dutch salt had lost its savour in these islands and wherewith could it be put back

again? By some tremendous act of faith, a great and imaginative gesture of trust and generosity, was the British instinct all along the complicated chain of command from A.F.N.E.I. to A.L.F.S.E.A., A.L.F.S.E.A. to S.A.C.S.E.A., S.A.C.S.E.A. to the Chiefs of Staff, the Chiefs of Staff to Whitehall; and the precedents connected with them all in the minds of the soldiers remembering Kitchener and the defeated South African generals at Vereeniging; the Foreign Office, Campbell-Bannerman and the Transvaal Premier.

Yet, they could get no single or authoritative voice in The Hague to lift its tone above a glorified police-commissioner's level with a dreary mumble about 'law and order' and the inevitable Queen's Broadcast of 1942. For every step they got Dr van Mook and his team in Batavia to move forward, there was someone in The Hague who tried to jerk them back two. Yet, obstinately the great fumble for a solution on A.F.N.E.I.'s small level went on.

33. The first councils, at this distance, seem to have been councils of despair. The conviction had settled even in most British minds that it was no good talking any more to the Indonesians just then. Although Mr Sjahrir had scored a tremendous victory at the meeting of the National Executive and had his cabinet and policy endorsed by an 85 per cent majority on the 27th of November, the Dutch resolutely refused to admit the obvious conclusion that he had some influence with his countrymen. They were so accustomed to reading between the lines of events, out-orientalling the Orient in peeping under the surface of things, that they no longer read the lines at all.

In a document produced at the Supreme Commander's Conference in Singapore on the 6th of December and therefore written at the latest on the 4th of December, i.e. barely a week after Sjahrir's confirmation in office, Dr van Mook said 'Soekarno has faded into the background . . . It has become obvious that the Republic cannot work,' adding verbally: 'The country is being ruined more quickly than under the Japanese. There is a certainty of famine within three months.'

To which Admiral Helfrich added his typical quota: 'I cannot see any difference between moderates and extremists. The moderates are talking with two faces. Behind our backs they support the actions and plans of the extremists. We must stop parleying.'

34. All sorts of strange counsellors were, in fact, beginning to knock at the doors of men's minds. With their principal intelligence organisation N.E.F.I.S. [Netherlands Forces Intelligence Service] (under the Command of Lt. Col. Spoor, the Army's future Commander-in-Chief), little more than organised rumour-and-sensation-mongering, the Dutch continued to expect, and many even to wish for the worst. Our own command was seriously thinking and talking of evacuating Sourabaya and Semarang, concentrating all our forces in the island in the west and building up a model state under Dutch administration, which it was hoped the rest could be induced or taught to follow. The Supreme Commander's conference had seriously examined this and other similar proposals in detail.

General Christison himself was probing on breath-taking and imaginative lines of his own. He and General Dempsey both had a great many South African friends. General Christison knew them at University and on the international rugger field. General Dempsey had been lent as a G2 before the War to the South African Staff Corps at Roberts Heights and spent much of his leave in the 'trekker' country of the Transvaal. Both knew the history of the country well and had, particularly the C. in C. A.F.N.E.I., been deeply impressed by the story of the Great Trek. In this great fumble for a decent solution, they began to think of a Great Trek in this part of the world. Tragic as it would be, would it not be better and more dignified for the Dutch to turn their backs on the parts where the natives of the land did not want them and where it now seemed they could not return without considerable bloodshed, and instead, in the outer islands where they appeared welcome, in the great, terrible and unexplored Eldorado of New Guinea, find a Great Trekker's compensations, as their South African kinsmen once had done? It was, they knew, easy to have courage and vision in the troubles of another. There was a Zulu proverb which said rightly: 'It is easier to put out the fire in a neighbour's hut than to cope with the smoke in your own.'

The idea was never very much more than an idea and apart from the fact that it illustrates how far the search for a solution ranged in people's minds, would not be worth mentioning, had not something of it come to life in the Dutch plan for New Guinea.

35. Dr van Mook too had a plan of his own. He had already told Mr

Dening on the 26th of November – his impulse to resign so strong on the 21st of the month had died its natural, routine death in the meantime – that he had been thinking of making a somewhat different approach to the question of negotiations with the Indonesians. He did not explain what it was but merely added that it would be necessary for him to go to Holland to secure the consent of his Government. For a brief moment he lifted the curtain, as he did more freely with Mr Dening than anybody else in Batavia at the time, over his own troubles in the Palace. 'Admiral Helfrich was quite hopeless'; 'Van Oyen ought to go but I have been embarrassed by the suddenness of the demand'; 'They (the Dutch military leaders) are apt to get excited and ignore the realities of the situation.'

Now at Singapore on the 6th of December he mentioned it again: 'The only further possible step towards a political solution would be a definite and detailed offer from our side, based on the present discussions, which might become acceptable to them (the Indonesians) as soon as they feel safe enough to proclaim its acceptance. In order to be certain of the validity of the offer it might be necessary for me to consult with the Netherlands Cabinet and to make a short trip to Holland for this purpose. I could, however, only do so if there was a reasonable certainty that no calamitous happening would take place during my absence.'

36. Before Dr van Mook left for Holland, he saw Mr Sjahrir again informally at the house of an A.F.N.E.I. officer in Batavia. Their first meeting arranged on A.F.N.E.I. initiative had taken place on the 3rd of December, just before the Singapore meeting. Although Sjahrir had been discouraged and greatly embarrassed with his own people by Professor Logemann's tactless statement of policy to the BBC reporter, he had been sufficiently heartened by Dr van Mook's attitude to agree to another and more representative meeting.

The Singapore Conference in the meantime had attracted the excited interest of all the excited minds in Java. The fact that the C.I.G.S. and the Supreme Commander were both attending the conference convinced 'everyone' that decisions of the utmost importance would be taken. The Dutch feared that we would decide to evacuate Sourabaya and Semarang, the Indonesians ironically dreaded a signal for the march on Djokja. When Mr Sjahrir asked Dr van Mook at their second meeting about

Singapore, Dr van Mook gave him some replies which convinced him that the British were going to support the Dutch in more vigorous action against the Indonesians. Dr van Mook had told Mr Walsh that he did not propose to enter into political discussions at this meeting as 'he evidently hopes Mr Sjahrir [will] gain confidence'.

Mr Sjahrir gained so little confidence that the third meeting planned never took place. How alarmed he was can be gathered in a statement he made to the press, appealing to the United Nations to solve the problem, strongly stating that if the British tried to keep 'law and order' by force or planned military action against the Indonesians they would resist to the best of their ability. Dr van Mook denied strenuously that he had said anything that could possibly have worried Mr Sjahrir. The fact remains that this second meeting left the Indonesian Premier for a time more suspicious of British intentions than he had ever been before or since.

Dr van Mook left Java for Holland on the 15th of December. Whatever he may have revealed to Mr Sjahrir, he said no more of his plan to the British. All that was known was that he was determined that when his own tiresome commanders went, General Christison would have to go too. A.F.N.E.I. pleaded that someone from its HQ should go to England at the same time to be on hand if wanted. The plea was refused.

37. Dr van Mook had hardly left for Holland when A.F.N.E.I. began preparations for giving him both the 'reasonable certainty that no calamitous happenings would take place during his absence' and the unintimidated area for potentially stable negotiations he had asked for at Singapore. The object, as the operational staff at A.F.N.E.I. put it, was to clean up Batavia, enlarge our perimeter to lines more in accordance with military requirements, reorganise the civil police and disarm civilians, mostly Dutch, in the town. There was hardly an intelligence officer at A.F.N.E.I. who liked either the scheme or its timing. They all knew that lawlessness was on the increase. In the course of their duties they were getting shot at more than most people. But at this moment, whatever they may have thought earlier on in the occupation, they were convinced that the main source of the trouble was the lack of discipline among the Dutch native troops and Eurasian officers, the pathological abhorrence of reason and moderation towards Indonesians of officers who should have set an example,

like Admiral Helfrich, General van Oyen and Major-General Uhl, as well as the state of hysteria of the Dutch civilian population. (A British Member of Parliament had already asked questions in the Commons about a frantic appeal from the Red Cross in Batavia for the evacuation of 200,000 persons in 'imminent danger of being massacred'.)

How far all this was spontaneous and how far deliberate design it is impossible to say. All one can do is to point out the extraordinary facility with which the reactionary colonial Dutch continually cancelled out in practice the much advertised good official intentions. The native troops were a case in point. The bulk of them were Ambonese and Medanoese, good fighting material, deeply and simply religious, but passionate and impulsive people, who would follow good officers anywhere. If there was a section of the population who had proved themselves willing to die for the Dutch flag, they had, and they were, in spite of their disillusionment after the 1942 surrender, fully prepared to do so again. Had their officers and leaders wanted to, they could easily have led them to any purpose essential. But with the sort of intelligence and uncontrolled and sensational special pleading Netherlands Forces Intelligence Service was daily broadcasting (its TOP SECRET distribution list must have been the largest of any Intelligence document in the world, starting with Prince Bernhard at the top, down to battalion commanders and secretaries in the Netherlands Indies Civil Affairs offices in Batavia), it was only too easy to persuade them they were fulfilling a noble task by their unlicensed killing and kidnapping of Indonesians. Their headquarters in the 10th Battalion, once commanded and spiritually prepared by a Dutch reserve officer, politically ambitious, Fascist in outlook and the founder of the reactionary Eenheids Group of which another Dutch officer who was about to become head of the Civil Police was also a prominent member, had become a sort of unofficial Gestapo headquarters and detention camp. Heaven alone knew what happened there. The British military police, nominally in charge in Batavia, kept away from it as much as possible. Several male Eurasian prisoners suspected of collaboration with the Japanese, the Political Officer at Allied Headquarters was proudly informed by one of the Dutch police-officers, were 'executed' there without trial. Many Indonesians suspected of atrocities were dragged to the 10th Battalion and, so their relatives said, not seen again.

Dutch soldiers and civilians, armed to the teeth, were nightly shooting their rifles off at somebody or something in the neighbourhood. There is no doubt that in the beginning the Dutch and Eurasians had suffered heavily at the hands of the Indonesians – five hundred were the kidnapping figures submitted by the Dutch for the two worst months in Batavia – but in the weeks of 18 November–31 December, the balance was being heavily and cruelly redressed. The cleaning-up, many officers thought, should have started with disciplinary action against the Dutch.

Yet so heavily did Dr van Mook's Singapore argument weigh with the Commander and so anxious was he to give the Dutch and Indonesians the chance for unintimidated negotiation in the capital that notwithstanding the approach of Christmas, he decided to go ahead with this limited operation.

38. Singapore and London, however, needed a lot of convincing of the necessity of the scheme and it was not put in operation until the 27th of December. By that time some original features had been added. Both the Psychological Warfare (P.W.) adviser and the Political Officer at Allied Forces Netherlands East Indies, in frequent contact with the new Indonesian leaders and military officers, had become convinced that they would go a long way in co-operating with us on purely non-political, humanitarian, and public welfare tasks. They had for instance just run a train loaded with food and stores through to the beleaguered city of Bandoeng. Dr van Mook and the Dutch had belittled this effort of the Indonesians and described it as a subtle attempt on the part of the extremists to throw dust in our eyes. That the Indonesians might conceivably want to prove their goodwill towards the Potsdam cause, was dismissed as utter nonsense. Yet, what other 'native' people would have run a train of food for thousands of foreigners encased well in the midst of their armed forces and regarded by the majority of the population as mortal enemies?

Fortunately there were officers in Allied Forces Netherlands East Indies who were still old-fashioned enough to believe in giving everyone a chance, and as a result the Commander ordered that the necessary Indonesian authorities could be taken into the planners' last-minute confidence. He decreed too that the operation would be carried out only by British troops and that the Dutch would not be informed of the plan until one hour before the Indonesians were. This last stipulation was added because it had been our experience that the Dutch Command was congenitally incapable of keeping any secrets to itself, and much of the success of the operation depended on its secrecy.

Finally the Psychological Warfare adviser and the Political Officer pressed successfully for P.W. representatives to be sent ahead of the armed troops to explain to the natives what was happening, to broadcast full information in Malay at regular intervals and to put up carefully prepared posters and proclamations in advance. These proclamations were by no means perfect and many sentences still creaked under the strain of holding a British balance between military advisers who prided themselves on being 'pro-Dutch', and junior officers, who would have to do the work and felt that the Indonesians were getting a raw deal. But they were an improvement on the literature that had been used at Sourabaya. In fact, although the parallel between the two cases should not be stretched too far, the method to be used was a reversal of Sourabaya.

39. At 10 o'clock on the morning of the 27th of December General Christison informed Dr Blom, Count van Bylandt and their Admiral; at 11 o'clock he told Sjahrir and Sjarifoeddin of the operation. Already P.W. officers were moving out into the villages and kampongs on the outskirts of Batavia described by the Dutch as extremists' and kidnappers' dens, well ahead of our troops and quite unescorted. The operation was a bloodless success.

When one looks back on the unscrupulous, ungrateful and scurrilous campaign conducted by the Dutch against that small unit of young and comparatively junior officers of the Unit of Psychological Warfare (afterwards F.E.P.D.) one wonders who remembers the service they rendered British, Dutch and Indonesians that day. They had shown throughout the planning of their operation a more balanced sense of the British function in the N.E.I. than officers old enough to be their fathers and when the time came took on that part of the task which carried the greatest risk. One has not seen their names in despatches, although one of the senior officers who wanted to do it all 'the Dutch way' shortly afterwards was awarded a C.B.E. In fact, Mr Peterson who did most of the P.W. planning was already recalled more or less in disgrace on Dutch instigation and Dutch complaints, and Major Morice, who managed the radio station and himself took an advanced P.W. party into the kampongs on the 27th of December, had long since been blacklisted and ear-marked for dismissal. It is difficult to write of the cavalier treatment imposed on these officers without some bitterness. But more of that later.

40. The operation in time became a model for similar British operations, soon to be launched in Buitenzorg and Bandoeng. It is true that General Schilling even at that late hour nearly spoilt things with an unauthorised and unilateral order of the day, placing the Indonesian Government troops – T.K.R. – in Batavia under command of the head of the Dutch police. General Christison promptly sat with the full weight of his six foot two authority on both the General and his announcement. It was true also that the disarmament of civilians was a one-sided affair because the Dutch resolutely refused to touch their civilians, and the head of their police confessed later to a British friend at Allied Forces Netherlands East Indies, that far from disarming his civilian countrymen at this time, he thought the peril to their safety so grave that he armed several hundreds of them: 'I was a bad soldier but did it for what I thought best.'

Unauthorised shooting by native troops moreover continued for many a day and in the new year reached a record pitch of violence. But all in all, Dr van Mook had got what he asked for at Singapore. An area free from tarnish of physical intimidation by Indonesian extremists was his for his 'new approach'.

41. And yet there was little gratitude shown to the General who had carried out this difficult operation with such skill against the advice of some of his officers and in the face of severe misgivings in Singapore and London. Instead, a loud prestige bleat went up from the lowest in Batavia to the highest in The Hague.

Dr van Mook was in England with the Dutch Prime Minister and Minister for Foreign Affairs at the time, 'creating an excellent impression', as one signal from London put it. He made adroit use of a golden occasion to complain of the 'constant dealings of British authorities with the Indonesians which was creating the impression in Batavia that the Dutch leaders were being treated as a minor third party in the picture until Sjahrir had reached an agreement with them'. 'He instanced the absence of any reference to the Dutch in the announcement by General Christison of the new military measures against the extremists', and also 'the failure of the Allied authorities to make use of Dutch Civil Affairs personnel and technicians', implying that we preferred running public utilities with 'British personnel and the help of Indonesian soldiers'. It all must have sounded very convincing for there was no one from the British Headquarters to pin down the half-truth convincingness of it. The complaint reached London on the day the operation began in Batavia: that part of it which referred to General Christison's operation announcement travelled so fast from Batavia to The Hague, The Hague to London, that it precluded any redress or explanation on the spot. The method was as characteristic as it was monotonous.

42. More was yet to come. Although General Christison had already been informed in confidence by Count van Bylandt on the 29th of December of the impending departure for good from those waters of Admiral Helfrich and his old gang, the behaviour of the Dutch native troops was becoming so scandalous that he had to order the removal of one unit from Batavia and confined all the rest to their barracks for some days. He reported to Singapore in the strongest terms on the behaviour of their officers. Had General Christison not acted severely at that moment, the British administration would have received the worst world press it had yet had – not that this consideration was specially prominent in the Commander's mind. The entire non-Dutch section of the large band of press-men in Batavia were filing daily more and more embittered reports about the slackness and one-sidedness of 'law and order' in the town. Mr Dening himself had appealed to the Foreign Office to press the Dutch for an official announcement disclaiming and condemning these outrages and for definite instructions putting an end to their indiscipline. The Dutch government refused categorically at first and saw it as a misguided pro-Indonesian move, and in its turn cried a long wail of woe against us.

On the 7th of January the Netherlands Ambassador informed the Foreign Office that 'Dr van Mook himself was now in some doubt in the light of the latest developments whether it was worth while for him to return to Batavia'. The ground had been cut from under Dr van Mook's feet, our Ambassador was told in The Hague. Once more Dr van Mook went to London alone for further clarifications. In Batavia nobody had any doubt whatsoever that he would return, for everyone knew that no one

could cry the wolf of his resignation better than Dr van Mook
himself.

V   OCCUPATION: *The Third Phase – 'The Dutch Plaintiff'*

43. The day on which Dr van Mook complained in England that the
Dutch were being treated as 'minor third parties' and their civil
affairs and technical personnel not used, A.F.N.E.I. had called a
conference of Dutch and Indonesians, including their influential Minister of Home Affairs, Amir Sjarifoeddin, to discuss precisely this problem – a fact which none of the henchmen at the
Palace apparently thought important enough to report to the Lt.
Governor-General when they cabled their complaints. The
situation was undoubtedly painful and depressing for the Dutch.
It was not their, or for that matter the maligned British
Commander's fault that all public services were in the hands of
the Indonesians. They had come back to the N.E.I. genuinely
eager to take up their old jobs only to find the way barred by ex-
native subordinates whom a British Commander now 'unfairly'
refused to kick out.

'The withdrawal of approximately 50,000 Hollanders from
all public services and industries', Colonel Abdul Kadir
Widjojoatmodjo, Dr van Mook's gifted special adviser on
Indonesian affairs, reported to Professor Logemann, 'gave the
Indonesians the opportunity to do and try everything for themselves. They have done this and perhaps even if things did not
go as well as before the war, still they do go on.'

The achievement, considering the Indonesians were running
a country which had been living on its technical capital for three
and a half years and had been looted of all its most valuable
technical possessions and reserves by the Japanese, was surely
very remarkable. In Batavia, for instance, the town had never
been without power and light or water. Both water-works and
power-stations were well inside what the Dutch called extremist-
controlled areas, and could have been cut off from the capital
without the allied commander being able to prevent or to
remedy it except by a major military operation.

It is perhaps not out of place to note here that in fourteen
months of allied occupation these supplies were never interfered
with – the first electrical breakdown came three weeks after the
British troops left. Stranger still, neither the allies nor the Dutch
had even been asked to pay for these vital services they were

receiving from the servants of the Republic. The situation obviously was odd but just as obviously it could not be changed by decree and certainly not by force. The Indonesians were quite capable at any moment, if their sense of the national fitness of things was hurt, [of walking] out on both Dr van Mook and the General, and neither the Dutch nor the British had the staffs to make up for wholesale technical desertion. It was difficult enough to get unskilled labour to unload the ships in the harbours.

The Commander wisely decided to make the changes [that] there had to be gradually, getting Dutch and Indonesians wherever possible to co-operate and to talk things over first. He made it a rule for the principal officers concerned on his staff not to dismiss any Indonesians and not to introduce any Dutch technicians except on the grounds of efficiency. In other words he refused to make an essentially technical problem political. Even with these self-imposed restrictions on his policy, he was able to refute Dr van Mook's charge with a quite impressive list of Dutch technicians and personnel introduced into the public utilities and services in the N.E.I.

44. In civil affairs the Dutch complaint was still more elaborate and more insistent. The Dutch claimed that the Civil Affairs Agreement concluded at Brisbane in December 1944 with the U.S.A. and in London in August 1945, was not being observed either in the letter or the spirit by the allied military commander. But this agreement had clearly foreseen a first phase during which the supreme allied commander would '*de facto* possess full authority to take all necessary measures'. 'As soon as and as fully as the military situation in their judgement would permit, they would notify the Lt. Governor-General of the extent to which responsibility for the civil administration would be resumed.'

The right of the allied commander to control the resumption of civil affairs responsibilities by the Dutch could therefore not be questioned, so criticism made the most of the rate at which he was allowing Dutch civil servants to resume their former functions.

Actually the General was going almost too fast in this respect for some of his advisers. He had already, acting under orders from S.A.C.S.E.A., completed his preparations for setting up Dutch civil and military courts in all the allied perimeters, making the Dutch the sole judges of offences against the administration [and] knowing that it would raise an outcry of anti-Indonesian pro-Dutch bias from all over the islands. Members of his own staff thought it fundamentally unsound that the *de facto* authority should not only deprive itself of its legal responsibilities but also place it in the hands of a recipient who would so often be called up to judge issues in which it was an emotional and material party to the dispute.

Both S.E.A.C. and General Christison were no doubt strongly influenced by the admirable anxiety to get the Indonesians, of whom seven hundred were already languishing in allied prisons, brought to justice as speedily as possible. As yet there were no courts and these unfortunate people arrested in the confusion and abnormality of the time could neither be heard nor tried. The Dutch used this fact as their main argument rather than the one that there could hardly be a more striking demonstration of their sovereign rights and powers in these islands than this assumption of legal and judicial office. Formally they gave assurances that their principal object was to get the unfortunate seven hundred heard and tried with the greatest speed. Dr van Mook himself told the Commander verbally that short of murder and kidnapping, these people would be deftly and generously dealt with. The sequence of this narrative might be usefully broken here to note that when the courts did start to function they were slow, ponderous, formalistically pre-war, and extraordinarily severe. One of the first cases heard was of an Indonesian found in the 'unauthorised possession of firearms'. He was condemned to ten years' penal servitude. Later on coolies and mandoers [headmen] were tried more quickly but the majority of the prisoners suspected of nationalist influence or prestige have continued in gaol. Allied headquarters, for instance, tried from March 1946 until its departure to speed up the trial of the son of an Indonesian 'Foreign Affairs' official, a sensitive and artistic boy in his teens charged with a similar offence, without success.

The Commander opened the courts as ordered by S.E.A.C. on the third day of the new year. At the same time A.L.F.S.E.A. was urged to allow the immediate entry of 584 Dutch civil servants and later by stages up to a total of 1,250 whom the Dutch civil affairs authorities said they needed. Branches of the Dutch civil affairs were already functioning in Bandoeng and Semarang and a start was to be made at Buitenzorg.

'Now that we are strong enough,' Mr Walsh reported to the

Foreign Office, 'we are doing everything possible to bring in Dutch technicians, and men qualified by experience for executive positions.'

In the same way the civil police in Batavia since the completion of Operation Pegasus [to expand the British perimeter around Batavia] at the end of the year had become essentially a Dutch organisation. The British Provost Marshal was still its nominal head but the reorganisation was placed in the hands of the Dutch police. They screened the old policemen and in one swoop drafted 200 Dutchmen into the reorganised force. The result was an illustration of the sort of probabilities which General Christison had to balance against every step he took: out of two hundred Indonesians in the force one hundred and seventy walked out almost overnight. 'It is due to intimidation by extremists,' the Dutch explained plaintively to Mr Walsh.

'It is a question of timing', Mr Walsh informed London when notified of Dr van Mook's stage-door complaint, 'and it will serve Dutch interests best in the long run if we go slow and avoid strikes.'

45. Louder still and really much easier to understand and sympathise with was the Dutch demand for permission to land more troops in Java and Sumatra. The anxiety of the government in Holland to help in the task of protecting their own people who, according to all press reports and the tendentious telegrams from the Palace in Batavia, were hardly protected at all, and as the Red Cross had expressed it, voicing the belief of the majority of the Dutch people, [were] 'in imminent danger of being massacred', was as great as it was natural. Every British staff officer who had to speak repeatedly for his department on this plea which was raised almost daily, felt this keenly. And at The Hague Colonel van der Post had been asked by an honourable and upright old General, 'What of the old Indonesians who are well disposed towards us and would like to see us back; what of my old soldiers and servants? Won't they think it strange that we do not come to help them? They will see your flag and they will see the nationalist flag and won't they wonder: Where is the flag of my master?'

There was practically no one in Holland who was not emotionally deeply concerned over the fate of their countrymen in the East. Some of them, like Dr Meyer Ranneft, may have been worried in terms of rubber and coffee but many, very many, like

the old General quoted, were concerned because they thought
the honour and face of their country were being irretrievably
lost by the failure to protect their own kind and well-wishers. The
opposition, His Majesty's Ambassador in The Hague reported
at the time, was coming not from people who had money interests in the N.E.I. They, Professor Schermerhorn had told him,
were almost solidly behind the liberal Government. It came
from people with no money but wandering in a pre-war daze.

It was of no avail telling them that the honour and face had
been lost, for what they were worth, on the 1st of March 1942,
and that the worst way of regaining them now was by being
more ruthless with their old native subjects than they had been
with the Japanese. It was no good explaining that the landing of
Dutch troops at that moment would undoubtedly make the
situation of the thousands of internees in the hands of the
Indonesians much more perilous, and aggravate any real military dangers there were; perhaps even make it impossible for
Dutch and Indonesians ever again to work peacefully side by
side.

'We have explained to them many times', Mr Walsh said on
the 2nd of January 1946, 'that the operation of landing forces
was a matter of timing not principle. They realised this but keep
on returning to the charge.'

A.F.N.E.I. just had to go on saying no and be misunderstood,
and though these things can never be proved, the British officers
with most experience of the problem believe to this day it would
have gone hard for all, had the decision been otherwise.

46. What rankled deeply too – though in a more confused way – was
allied headquarters' latest approach to the problem of the
internees. Whether we came to the rescue too late, and having
come, protected them adequately or not, the Dutch will probably, with the exception of the persons who actually saw our
Indian troops and their officers die in their defence against very
great odds like that heroic R.I.A.S.C. detachment at Sourabaya,
continue to debate until the end of time.

The fact remains that by the end of 1945, the recovery of prisoners of war and internees was well under way and would have
been complete had it not been for the many who disobeyed
orders and left their areas of concentration. When the Japanese
surrender came, there were only three concentration areas of
prisoners of war and internees in Java: Batavia, Bandoeng and

the Semarang-Amberawa complex in the centre of the island. Two more concentration areas were subsequently created, very much against our advice, on an order from Colonel Asjes, the competent Dutch officer for these affairs, and Mr van der Plas, in the Magelang-Salatiga area and in Sourabaya. Outside these areas there should not, if orders had been obeyed, have been one person who had undergone internment by the Japanese. It is of interest that the internees concentrated in the new areas were only rendered safe, as in Sourabaya, or extricated from situations of grave peril, as at Magelang, after severe fighting by our forces. Once more the reality had not conformed to the anticipated military pattern.

Allied headquarters started the new year gloomily with the new complication of the several thousands of self-released internees on its hands. Their exact number will probably never be known. The only indication is that out of a total of 25,484 persons evacuated from the interior in Java, only 4,440 proved to be persons previously interned by the Japanese. The Dutch estimated that there were still 25,000 internees left at the end of November 1946 – the Indonesians said 9,000 – but it is unlikely that any of these were also internees under the Japanese. To get this class of person alive out of the excited and suspicious interior by purely military measures was patently impossible. If it could be done at all, it was only with the full help of the Indonesians, particularly their military leaders who were notoriously less open to reason and persuasion than any other section of the population. Happily, both Mr Sjahrir and Dr Amir Sjarifoeddin, the civil head of the Indonesian military organisations, pledged their government without argument to all the help they could give. They went even further and offered to relieve us of our Potsdam obligation as far as evacuating the Japanese was concerned. The offer had its embarrassing side but was not altogether unwelcome, for 20,000 Japanese in East Java had already disarmed themselves and allowed the Indonesians to intern them in many places. They too had to be brought to the sea before the task of allied headquarters could be declared closed.

47. Discussions with the Indonesians began at allied headquarters early in the new year. It was the first time anyone on the staff except the intelligence officers had come in contact with senior officers of the new Indonesian armies. The Indonesians were represented by a Major-General, a Colonel and a Major; smart,

correct and passive in bright new uniforms. The Chief of Staff,
at allied headquarters, presided and it was clear from the start
that the Indonesians were under suspicion of dumb insolence
and that the meeting might not go well. The Dutch staff officer
present looked grim and plainly disgusted. The approach was
distinctly military and the tendency on our side was not to argue
but to order, though later when the Chief of Staff got to know
his men no one could have been better. He was, however,
annoyed by the Indonesians' not illogical demand that once they
had delivered all the internees and Japanese safely to us, we
should among other things agree to evacuate Sourabaya and
Semarang as our Potsdam mission would then be completed.

With such valuable hostages as the internees in their hands,
the temptation to bargain had been a little too much for some of
the military leaders in Djokja. This angered the Chief of Staff,
who used some abrupt and downright language, and it looked as
if the conference would break up.

'It is obvious', said the Colonel who was acting as spokesman,
with un-Indonesian tears in his eyes, 'that you do not respect and
trust us and we had perhaps better return to Djokja.'

But a way was found in the end to continue discussions and
the incident is recorded here only to illustrate how much more
psychological than political or military all sorts of issues always
turned out to be. All three Indonesian officers present that day
afterwards loyally co-operated with allied headquarters. The
evacuation started not very long after the conference, was interrupted for some months and only seriously resumed in May.

If it had not been for the understanding and confidence
gained on that day, the most important conference of all held in
Djokja in April, when the Indonesian high command finally
undertook almost unconditionally to evacuate both internees
and Japanese, would not have gone as well. The only two serious
conditions asked for then were: (a) arms for one battalion of
infantry to escort the internees and Japanese, (b) an undertaking
by the Dutch not to rearm any of the male internees for use
against the Indonesians. (a) was accepted by allied headquarters
after some Dutch objections had been overcome. (b) was rejected
because Dr van Mook refused categorically to give the guaran-
tee asked for. Both the Chief of Staff and his political officer had
thought (a) would be impossible for the Dutch to swallow but
that consent to (b) could be taken for granted and warned the

Indonesians accordingly. For the Dutch too the problem here was obviously psychological.

48. It is not the intention of this report to go into the accomplishments of the Recovered Allied Prisoners of War and Internees' organisation in detail but this much has been necessary in order to make clear how it fitted into the general pattern of the Dutch complaints against the British. They argued bitterly that allied headquarters in having discussions with the Indonesian generals, albeit in a purely Dutch interest, were recognising the republic of Indonesia and seriously prejudicing the Dutch position in the Netherlands East Indies. These too, no doubt, were the sort of discussions the Dutch described in London as negotiations behind Dr van Mook's back. They let it be known in various whispered ways, that of the two factors involved in this internee problem they regarded the humanitarian aspect as subordinate to the political; the saving of a few thousand Dutch lives would not be adequate compensation for the compromise on a vital political principle, which the method of deliverance chosen by allied headquarters entailed:

'It is a tragic thing,' Colonel Abdul Kadir Widjojoatmodjo told Colonel van der Post, 'but the political principles involved go so deep that the Dutch would in their desperation prefer losing their internees to getting them out by methods which amount to recognition of the republic, and a further loss of face for themselves. I know that is how Dr van Mook feels and after all he is right. We take individual misery too seriously. What are a few lives and a few years compared to the life of a nation?'

In view of Colonel Abdul Kadir's comment it was instructive to see how the official Dutch interest in their internees came alive only when it became political through the people who had relations in the interior, and professional humanitarian organisations. Yet, officially, it was to spare defenceless women and children that the armies surrendered so soon in 1942. What made it easier for the officials in the Palace to be philosophical about possible loss of life in 1946 is the fact perhaps that most of the internees now were Eurasians.

49. The final straw even on the Dutch back was the activity real and imagined of the Psychological Warfare division at headquarters. So fast had 15 Army Corps rushed out of the Arakan into the N.E.I. that it did not occur to anyone for several months that such a name was sticking somewhat oddly to a unit engaged on

the arduous task of psychological peace-making. Then it was quickly changed to the Far Eastern Publicity Detachment. This unit had been put in charge of the allied radio station in Batavia. It also published an evening newspaper and generally supervised and co-ordinated press and propaganda activities within the allied perimeters.

Differences of opinion with the Dutch officials duplicating similar duties had arisen in the very earliest days. These differences were inevitable, and fundamentally due to the differences in approach between Dutch and British policy, and never at any time should [they] have been laid at the door of the individuals who had some share in carrying it out. The Dutch attitude to start with briefly was that the British had a purely military function in these islands and anything beyond that was essentially a Dutch concern. In other words they had every right to call the political tune from The Hague to Batavia and we as loyal allies just had to do the military dance to it. That it could not be as simple as that caused them continuous and severe heartburning. They ignored the casualties' aspect entirely.

50. The story of Radio Batavia was a striking case in point. This station was taken over from its Japanese management and *de facto* Indonesian directorate early on the morning of 30th September by Colonel van der Post and Colonel Abdul Kadir Widjojoatmodjo. Within half an hour of the taking over the Indonesian staff (without whom the station could not work) threatened to walk out because they were ordered to broadcast an official proclamation in Dutch as well as in Malay and English. They were induced to work on but from the start the situation was difficult and uneasy.

The position deteriorated a few days later when Mr van der Plas asked General Christison for permission to broadcast in person. Three weeks of hard work by Admiral Patterson's advisers on Mr van der Plas had not yet convinced him that his name was distasteful and infuriating to the Indonesians. There was nothing Mr van der Plas could say in person to the Indonesians at that moment which would not have exactly the opposite of the desired effect. On this occasion he wanted to start an official announcement with the phrase: 'Mr van der Plas has persuaded the Allied Commander . . .' Colonel van der Post and Colonel Abdul Kadir thought this not merely an improper beginning to an official allied announcement but also knew that it was quite the wrong approach to the excited and suspicious native public.

'I see the General has chivalrously overruled you . . .', Mr van der Plas said as he came to do his broadcast after all.

51. Although Radio Batavia itself was a station equipped only with a low powered transmitter, it was linked by land-line with a network of stations to all parts of the island, including the high-powered transmitting station at Bandoeng. Up to this moment all the stations had been relaying Radio Batavia. No sooner did they hear Mr van der Plas's voice and announcement than angry crowds began to collect round the broadcasting studios all over the island. Radio Batavia was never to be relayed in the interior again. The young British major who had come to take charge of the station could not have had a more striking illustration of how difficult radio propaganda was going to be. Small wonder that he was doubly careful in his handling of all propaganda thereafter.

It was not that headquarters wanted to prevent the Dutch from broadcasting their propaganda. In fact one and all started off with the desire to help and it was not their fault that they were called upon to save the Dutch from themselves. The Dutch were only convinced of one thing: we were playing a deep British game and were hampering and delaying their propaganda because we wanted to delay their taking over in the N.E.I. There appeared to be no one on the Dutch side who would or could realise that the whole of the N.E.I. was tired and suspicious of the old colonial voices, however affectionate or however benevolent. Their only chance was someone fresh, speaking with the accent and voice of a new post-war world. Stories about how nice the Dutch government had been to Indonesian pilgrims to Mecca during the war and would be again in future, just sounded like a cheap bribe the way Mr van der Plas put it, and merely proved to them that the vision had not changed.

52. Criticism became still more severe after the formation of the Sjahrir government. 'These men are all honourable men,' Professor Logemann had said; 'we are prepared to negotiate with them at any time.' It did not, in the circumstances, seem a bad thing to make the voice of 'honourable' Indonesians heard in the interior. In fact, moderation and reason were likely to mean more to extremists from the lips of Indonesians themselves. So Mr Sjahrir's ministry of information were allowed the

full use of one of the Batavia station's wave lengths; the Dutch and the British shared the other equally between them. In addition the Dutch were promised the very powerful Bandoeng transmitter for their sole and uncontrolled use, once we could spare the troops to occupy and protect it – the station was some distance out of town. But so unfair were these arrangements considered to be by the Dutch that in time there was not an official of standing who was not drawn into the dispute. All sorts of strange and distinguished visitors travelling up and down the long and complicated line of allied communications to the N.E.I. dropped off at strategic points to knock at more and more exalted doors with their complaints.

Even the refined and fluent emissary of Prince Bernhard, Colonel Frowein, who was travelling backwards and forwards between Europe and the N.E.I. on a military liaison mission, took up the case because it had become such a serious source of anti-British feeling among the Dutch, and would talk it over with General Christison in Batavia, Mr Dening, Sir Miles Dempsey and the Supreme Commander in Singapore and so on and on back to Holland. Fortunately Colonel Frowein was one of the more constructive visitors.

Difficult as it was to foresee the shape of things to come, it was nearly impossible at times to follow the shape of things as they were, so rapidly did they tend to shift and change and [so often did] so many eccentric functionaries appear and reappear on the confused scene of the day.

53. Colonel Frowein had been a successful salesman in the north of France and Belgium before the war and had known Prince Bernhard when he had been forced as an impecunious minor prince to follow a similar occupation. He had a less hidebound and orthodox approach to life and talked of Professor Schermerhorn confidently as a friend. He had a healthy obsession with the idea of bringing the 'new Holland' and the 'new Indonesia' together, and tried to understand a little before he condemned. He was the first Dutch officer to call on Mr Sjahrir and was keen on bringing the Indonesian prime minister and Professor Schermerhorn together. He had put up the idea that the Dutch premier should come to Indonesia as early as December 1945 but was discouraged by the Palace in Batavia, who did not know what to make of him and did not altogether trust him.

He vanished from Batavia and his stopping places along our lines of communication early in 1946 and has only just reappeared in civilian clothes in Sumatra as the director of a large N.E.I. commercial concern. But while he was a 'military force' in being he tried to help and also to understand. He frankly admitted that Dutch propaganda had been bad and unhelpful and controlled by the wrong people, and recommended to his superiors that there should be a clean sweep of Dutch propagandists as well as the wholesale removal of service reactionaries like Admiral Helfrich. Nevertheless he sniped heavily at the Far Eastern Publicity Detachment with such effect that Mr Peterson, its adviser at allied headquarters, was recalled in December. His successor, Mr Titchener, new to the Netherlands East Indies but with much experience in many lands, had not been a week in Batavia when a similar campaign started against him. Major Morice had already been pilloried in print by Dutch officers of his staff on evidence they had collected in his mess where he had invited them to live for the sake of better mutual understanding and closer liaison. He too had to be posted elsewhere and it was touch and go whether Mr Titchener and his entire staff would not follow him. Happily they were allowed to continue doing an unpopular and thankless task honestly and fairly in the best British way.

54. The main sin of the Far Eastern Publicity Detachment in Dutch colonial eyes was their aversion to stamping on the means of expression of others because of disagreement with the views they expressed. They advised solidly against a policy of repression and defended the right of people to disagree publicly with one another. And they did not always win. They failed to prevent allied headquarters being pushed into the bombing of the Solo and Djokja radios.

Pressure from the Dutch to suppress and repress and ban something or other was long and incessant. There was not one Indonesian newspaper which at one time or another the Dutch did not ask allied headquarters to ban. At times they solicited even the arrest and detention of Indonesian staffs. The Indonesians in print could be maddening, provocative and inaccurate with the best. Yet had they been repressed they would have merely gone underground and left the country wide open to even more exaggerated and inaccurate rumour.

If there is a tendency in the Netherlands East Indies today for the extreme in politics to listen more and more and in places even to give way to reason, moderation and tolerance, it is in no small way due to the Far Eastern Publicity Detachment. Perhaps they did help to save the Dutch from themselves. Anyway since they closed down the Dutch have naturally changed the staff but they have not yet dared to alter the British policy.

55. One last glimpse at the Dutch complaints. The British, Dr van Mook told London, were seeing the Indonesian leaders more than they were seeing the Dutch. Allied headquarters here and in Singapore had large quotas of Dutch liaison officers on their staff. Mr van der Plas had an office next to General Christison and free access to him at all times; whilst Mr Walsh, his British political adviser, was tucked away in a back room neither to be seen nor heard. Allied headquarters had only one contact with the Indonesians: one lieutenant-colonel and his staff. So far, this officer had been used much more to bring Dutch and Indonesians together than Indonesians and British. He shared a house moreover with Colonel Abdul Kadir Widjojoatmodjo who was the Governor-General's principal adviser on Indonesian affairs.

Yet so anxious were we to be unbiased on the eve of Dr van Mook's return that Mr Dening addressed another warning to allied headquarters: 'We on our part must be especially careful not to create a situation whereby we can be held to have offered advantages to the Indonesians and to have excluded or failed to include the Dutch. We are supposed to be non-partisan in the matter, but by the military authority which we exercise we can easily fall into the error if we are not careful of affording opportunities to one side which are denied to the other . . . The Dutch are already expressing anxiety on this score and I should welcome any concrete evidence that their fears are groundless.'

A new phase in Dutch policy was to begin. The first phase in which they had fully expected the British to restore them in the Netherlands East Indies by military force was definitely at an end. The second phase in which they would try to keep us here for as long as possible while they built up a force for a policy 'of their own choosing' was inaugurated on the return of Dr van Mook.

VI   OCCUPATION: *The Fourth Phase – 'March 1946'*

56. When Dr van Mook left for Holland on the 15th of December 1945, he fully expected to be back by the end of the year. The

problem was now, he told us, quite clear to him, he knew what he wanted and had to do. Time was pressing desperately. The country, as he had informed Sir Alan Brooke, was being ruined more quickly than under the Japanese. He would work fast and in the new year direct his feet firmly towards the new approach he had recently been hinting at so much. The Indonesians, whose leaders had met him informally early in December, were already half-prepared and banked perhaps more heavily than anyone else on the early prospect of some large, new and generous gesture from Holland to break through the dreadful military and spiritual impasse of the day. But everyone had reckoned without the practised half-Nelson the politicians in The Hague could, when they wanted, put on to persons of authority who came from their colonies to explain and demand in Holland and invariably were made to stay and beg. By the end of the year there was no sign of the Governor-General's return.

A colourless official communiqué mentioned that he had accompanied the Prime Minister to England for important talks at Chequers. But what it was all about no one really knew. Even at the Palace in Batavia Dr Idenburg and Count van Bylandt who had been left in charge complained with some bitterness that Dr van Mook had given them no instructions and was telling them nothing of what was happening in Holland. By the end of the first week in the new year the whole country was back into the unrelieved and sullen confusion from which a flicker of new-year's eve hope had briefly lifted it. There seemed to be no horizon to the lack of authoritative and decisive leadership in these islands. And yet people had never been more ready and eager for leadership. They searched for it far and wide and the longing expressed itself in the pathetic eagerness with which they would group themselves round some shallow and picturesque local celebrity. It was a sad spectacle and yet potentially a situation full of good for Holland if she had the imagination to see it.

When at last the news did come that Dr van Mook had left Holland, the good effect it had in the N.E.I. was almost immediately cancelled by an official announcement from The Hague that the States General had decided to send forthwith a commission to investigate the policy of the Governor-General on the spot. No wonder Dr van Mook, when the news caught up with him in Cairo where he had broken his journey for three days, immediately caught severe influenza. A deadly paralysis of all belief in anything good or big ever coming out of The Hague crept over the hearts and minds of everyone. Some even contrasted it unfavourably with the Japanese who had left a taste for a more primitive leadership behind. The Japanese had always been careful to give the appearance of knowing what they wanted to do and doing it through men stage-dressed for the part, the glint of quite ordinary greed in their eyes outshone by the artificial light on their brows. People began to turn their thoughts to other places and other peoples for a solution.

57. In those first few weeks of the new year talk of an appeal for intervention or mediation of some kind to the United Nations reached a new intensity. Sjahrir, alarmed by the impression Dr van Mook gave him early in December that if the Indonesians were not careful the British and the Dutch would go straight ahead to restore law and order all over the N.E.I., had already appealed through the press for something of the kind.

Who thought of it first no one knew but as far back as November Mr MacMahon Ball, the Australian Government representative in Batavia, had discussed it and apparently even advised the Indonesian premier that the problem was one essentially for U.N.O. His immediate successors had favoured a similar course. Now fresh stimulus was given to the idea by the news that Russia had put 'Indonesia' down for discussion at the meeting of U.N.O. at the end of January. The idea never came to anything but so great was people's faith locally in U.N.O. and Russia at the time that for a moment it looked quite possible that U.N.O. one way or another would also appear on the crowded scene. London and The Hague prepared themselves accordingly.

58. We ourselves were thinking on lines of our own. We had for some time been examining the possibilities of third-party mediation in the dispute. Seen locally it appeared imperative that if there were to be mediation of any kind, it should in the first place be British, lest we be accused of trying to divest ourselves of our responsibilities in this part of the world. The names of Lord Hailey and Mr Noel Baker had already been mentioned tentatively in this regard by London to allied headquarters where the case for neutral British mediation had considerable support. The Indonesian leaders who were sounded on the allied commander's instructions, one and all warmly favoured

the idea and of the two names mentioned said they would welcome either but preferred Mr Noel Baker whose reputation as a champion of the oppressed was better known to their followers. Before the idea could be pursued much further, however, it was decided in London to send Sir Archibald Clark Kerr, His Majesty's Ambassador in Moscow 'forthwith on a special mission to Java'.

The news was known in the N.E.I. early on the 20th of January and caused considerable excitement. The Dutch were frankly puzzled but intensely curious and not without admiration for the adroit way in which Britain, as they saw it, had disarmed possible Russian criticism at U.N.O. by sending Stalin's favourite ambassador to the N.E.I. Their belief in the suppleness and profundity of British policy was colossal and they could not be convinced that a desire to speed up a solution of the dispute could be the only object of Sir Archibald Clark Kerr's mission. They knew that their government had approved and officially welcomed the mission but with it all they could not help being deeply suspicious. They had always quite naturally resented suggestions of third-party intervention in what they regarded as an essentially domestic dispute. They feared that we might bluff or dragoon them into concessions they were either not ready or thought it unwise to make. Above all they were determined that whatever independence the Indonesians would have to get, no one else should steal the honour of granting it from them.

'The dirtiest trick you can play on us', Dr Idenburg, the Governor's enlightened second-in-command, told a British officer at this time, 'is to deprive us of the opportunity and ability to give and give to the Indonesians.' It was a cardinal point in their policy that at the final meeting to seal agreement between Dutch and Indonesians no stranger should preside.

59. At the same time the Dutch thought we were exceedingly reckless in risking the reputation of our most senior ambassador on so doubtful a gamble. If he failed, the blow to our prestige they honestly thought would be irreparable and they warned us to that effect, for by long association with the East they had acquired all the oriental's paradoxical passion for keeping up appearances while having at heart no belief in them at all.

The Indonesians on the other hand were quite frankly pleased and reassured. In a flash the fears inspired by the Singapore Conference early in December were removed. Nothing dreadful could happen to them just yet, they thought, and with a new heart the Sjahrir government resumed the task of consolidating the revolution begun against their fascist-inspired politicians in the November before. They were not unflattered by this evidence that the outside world was taking their movement seriously, and their propaganda skilfully presented it in such a way that Sir Archibald Clark Kerr's coming did not look unlike a victory for their President and his Prime Minister – an interpretation which could not have been unwelcome to either, for as the constant comings and goings of important Indonesian personages between Batavia and Djokjakarta showed, the fight for political power in the interior was by no means over yet. This reaction the Dutch had foreseen and although it meant another weapon in the hands of Professor Logemann's 'honourable Indonesians', it was unwelcome to them, and in due course became part of a major grievance against us.

60. Dr van Mook returned the last week in January and heartened everyone with his healthy and confident appearance. Neither influenza in Cairo nor the commission to investigate his policy, hotfoot on his trail, seemed to have depressed him. And he had some substantial cause for confidence. He had safely in his pocket his first clear mandate from his superiors in The Hague to talk to the Indonesians. There was nothing ambiguous about it. It read more like a military order than a government directive with its: 'After your arrival in Batavia you will start immediate talks with the Sjahrir group within the framework of the fifteen points and the general line of action as communicated to the conference at Chequers.'

Moreover most things to give him a fresh start had been done in his absence. There was no Indonesian 'lawlessness' left in Batavia, his own 'tiresome' service commanders were either gone or busy packing and their places being taken by fresh and much younger officers. The new C. in C., General Spoor, of whom everyone expected great things was only forty and was already in Holland selecting a completely new staff. There had been a thorough spring-cleaning in his own civil services too. Men like the immovable and unimaginative Dr Blom who acted for him at times, the incorrigible and indestructible Mr van der Plas, and a whole series of old hands were finding themselves ditched overnight. The changes were not always to the good, for in some of the old bodies like the Governor of West Java, Mr

Hoogewind, there still beat fine young hearts which should have been spared, but the desire for new young blood refused to be denied.

On our side too there were changes that could not have been displeasing to him. General Christison – 'Twistison' was the Palace's bitter name for him – was getting a new command in England. His two principal staff officers, the D.G.S.(Q) and the B.G.S.(O), were posted to other units. The political adviser at allied headquarters, Mr Walsh, whose pre-war reputation for being anti-Dutch pursued him most unfairly in his new role on the staff, had been offered another post and his successor, Mr G. MacKereth, was not only senior to him but had experience in dealing with problems that arise out of the taking-over of allied territory previously occupied by the enemy and in particular of nationalist movements elsewhere. He had never been in the N.E.I. before and could not therefore have any bias one way or the other. While General Stopford, the new Commander-in-Chief of the allied forces, had a most distinguised record of service and the confidence of both the soldiers and politicians among his countrymen. He too had no experience or connections to make him pre-judge issues in the Netherlands East Indies, unless his rear-admiral ancestor whose ships helped to cover landings in the Netherlands East Indies in Raffles' day could be regarded as such.

Yet General Stopford was not without his misgivings, for as he surveyed the unfamiliar scene he remarked one day soon after his arrival to an officer on his staff: 'I have never seen a set of circumstances more neatly designed to get a general the sack.'

Dr van Mook appeared to have no such qualms as he stepped out of his Skymaster in Batavia.

61. Sir Archibald Clark Kerr arrived in Batavia a few days later at the beginning of February and the two months which followed were in many ways the most satisfactory of our occupation. No lasting agreement was to come out of this special mission in the end but our machinery of occupation never worked better. At last allied headquarters had a shape and tidiness which left no doubt as to where one responsibility ended and another began. The old political-military jumble which had been so unfair both to the Commander and his advisers was gone for good. Headquarters henceforth could speak with complete political and military authority.

This question of authority was most important: there had been a tendency from the very beginning for the Dutch to feel that the military commander and his political adviser were not really senior enough for their Governor-General to meet on his level. The Dutch have always been great sticklers for rank and seniority and they did instinctively at times try to bypass allied headquarters, preferring to deal with Singapore direct or, better still, with London. With Britain's most senior ambassador on hand in Java, however, there could be no excuse for avoiding reference to headquarters. Both Dutch and Indonesians were forced to stand face to face with their troubles on the spot. Political escapism was at an end for the time being. It was inspiring to see how this new sense of political authority bred confidence and decision all round. Our military task, so difficult and so far from complete, began to look easier because it was no longer allowed to be a vague, indeterminate mass. Dutch and Indonesians responded in a manner which threw into grim relief the groping, undirected and tragic months that had drifted so pointlessly by. Moreover, compliance was made easy for Dutch and Indonesians by the personality of His Majesty's Ambassador. He made it natural for them to have regular contact with him, and what they regarded as eccentricity in him but came to accept as a refreshing revolt against automatic and mass-prescribed behaviour, helped them to break out of the habits and prejudices that were hemming in the free flow of their minds. They recognised and respected his very deep and instinctive refusal to prejudge anyone or anything. The past, they felt, was not allowed to blur the immediate vision though it plainly had its meaning and place as evidenced by the Ambassador's strange preference for writing with a quill rather than a pen, in an attractive old-world hand.

Nor did he always send for people to see him; he frequently went to call on them. He was in this respect so unlike the Dutch who in authority tend to say: 'He ought to come and see me first,' or 'If he doesn't come to speak to me, I shall not speak to him.'

He was the first allied person of his standing and rank to call on Sjahrir in his home. Professor Schermerhorn was the first Dutchman, and that nine months later, and thirteen months after the allied landing. Nor did he speak to people as if they were N.C.O.s and he a sergeant-major. His judgement of their personalities was so shrewd and confident that he was not afraid to pull their legs, an approach to foreigners, particularly orientals, so dangerous that it has to be completely successful if it is to be justified.

62. The Ambassador's own special mission was not made any easier by its timing. Dr van Mook was ready to take the initiative immediately. He had after all spent six weeks preparing for it. But the Indonesians were still far from ready. Their political revolution of the year before was by no means yet consolidated and they needed time with the primitive means of communication at their disposal to get their persons and policy known to the people before they could dream of confronting the country with a formal decision to negotiate with the Dutch. Once they got their people to accept the fact of negotiation which everywhere had its embittered and impassioned opponents, the form and place of negotiation would still have to be decided.

Already Dr Soekarno was being pressed by the collaborationist old guard, by the older and more picturesque communists, by young leaders of callow youth movements, with Japanese swords and long hair which they had sworn not to cut until they were free, by a few fanatical hadjis, to do away with this young Sumatran upstart and his Christian following – four of Mr Sjahrir's ministers were Christians – and to break away from the Dutch and the English. The Indonesian capital in the interior, Djokjakarta, was full of strange, fanatical young men coming and going between the so-called fighting fronts, and of frenzied refugees from areas occupied by the allies.

To the casual visitor the country looked peaceful, industrious and prosperous in everything except medicine and clothes. Ruin and famine seemed figments of a biased European imagination in those busy and golden fields of rice. So, indeed they were in all except one thing: politically the native heart had seldom known greater agitation. The details of this prolonged Indonesian crisis with all the picturesque personalities worthy of a major revolution moving across its far-eastern half light are unfortunately not necessary for this record. What matters is that it took Mr Sjahrir nearly six weeks from the time of the Ambassador's arrival before he was ready and sure enough of the authority in his hand to talk. To all who know the inside story it was a most remarkable achievement. At one point Mr Sjahrir stayed away from the meetings of the Indonesian shadow parliament for two days while Dr Soekarno invited the opposition to form a new government. At the end they begged Mr Sjahrir to come back.

'I would have liked to stay away longer to teach them a lesson,' he told the Ambassador, 'but already I felt too ashamed for having kept you waiting so long.'

63. Throughout this crisis Dr Soekarno had stood loyally by Mr Sjahrir. He confounded the gloomy forebodings of Dr van Mook's expert advisers who were convinced that at the right moment he would turn on his Prime Minister and take devastating revenge on him for his November coup. His popularity with his own countrymen had never been higher: all parties from the Prime Minister's own circumspect socialist group to the fanatical followers of the K.R.I. – the nationalist movement from the Celebes – and the Hadji-inflamed Red and Black Buffaloes from West Bantam, found union in his person.

A party of newspaper correspondents who had just accompanied him on his first presidential tour of the interior were deeply impressed by the almost mystic attraction his personality had in the emotions and imaginations of his countrymen; the unfulfilled longing of three centuries for someone of their kind to walk at their head and direct them in the darkness of their own dim lives seemed miraculously fulfilled in this man who went high, wide and handsome through their midst. They turned out in thousands, stood for days on remote railway-sidings and along the dusty roads of East Java for a fleeting glimpse of him. At Malang sixty thousand people followed him as he went on foot to visit his aged Balinese mother for the first time in many years. According to the hard-boiled American pressmen who were present, this great toil-worn crowd went nearly frantic with devotion as he knelt at her feet and received a blessing from her hands on his handsome head. Not since the first coming of the Dutch had there been any figure which so satisfied the hungry symbolism of the national mind.

'They are forced to come, it is all stage-managed for foreign benefit,' the Dutch said, attributing as they often did designs and misdeeds to Indonesians which could only have been performed by a people with a genius for organisation and administration, while at the same time maintaining that they were not fit to govern themselves at all. Dr van Mook went further and said that this man Soekarno was a corrupt, vain and self-seeking creature who once before the war had sold out his companions in 'political crime' to the Dutch. How true that is, it is difficult to say but what is established is that this man too, however weak and despicable, had yet been imprisoned and exiled by the Dutch because they feared his opinions and the power he might become. Like so many of his ministers he too had been tested in banishment, and was now teaching the Dutch the bitter lesson that there is no school-tie link more powerful and more enduring than an Old Borstal tie.

No one was more aware of this great power he had over his people than Dr Soekarno. He loved and enjoyed it deeply but it is to his credit that in these critical days he used it all to bring his people with dignity and moderation to swell the rather thin intellectual ranks already drawn up around his Prime Minister.

64. His Majesty's Ambassador had been quick to appreciate the importance and place of Dr Soekarno in the Indonesian political scheme. The instinct which had made him pay a courtesy call on Mr Sjahrir – how the political Dutch hated him for it – urged him to go and see the Indonesian President too. But the merest hint of it sent Dr van Mook almost off his head with alarm and anxiety. His first argument against it, of course, was that it would be very bad for British prestige if our most senior ambassador went to visit the unrecognised collaborationist President of Indonesia in his native capital. It would be bad enough receiving him should he ask to see the Ambassador. When Sir Archibald said quietly that he thought our prestige could stand that, Dr van Mook produced the full series of arguments kept in stock for these occasions: it placed him in an impossible situation; he would be forced to resign; it weighed the scales unfairly against the Dutch; the Indonesians would make propaganda out of it; Soekarno would merely be flattered by it and become more difficult than ever before.

The depth of the Governor-General's feeling in matters of this sort can perhaps be best illustrated by this brief official account of what happened when the Ambassador five weeks later, at Mr Sjahrir's request, sent a mere British officer to Djokja to get the President's authority to negotiate. When he heard of the proposed visit Dr van Mook effected his most emotional scene to date. He repeated again that he was at the end of his tether and about to resign. He objected to a British officer going to Djokja on the grounds of the loss of face to the allies and 'pandering to Indonesians'.

In the end the Ambassador went to Semarang in the hope of meeting Dr Soekarno there: it was a compromise strongly advocated by his own British military advisers at headquarters who one and all thought the Dutch argument convincing. Unfortunately compromises have not the élan, the black-and-white simplicity revolutionary imagination seeks and thrives on: Dr Soekarno's people made it almost impossible for him to go and in the midst of it all both he and the Ambassador fell ill. Two illnesses have never been less 'diplomatic': a British officer who went with Mr Sjahrir to Djokja to accompany the Indonesian President to Semarang found him yellow and shivery with malaria. Moreover the internal political crisis was reaching a climax: it was more than he dared, for his premier's sake, to leave his capital for even a few hours. The Dutch were elated. They thought it was a setback which would humiliate and discipline in their way our methods of dealing with the Indonesians.

Yet the idea of such a meeting was never finally given up and it probably would have taken place had it not been made unnecessary by Dr Soekarno's gesture in giving Mr Sjahrir full powers to meet and negotiate an agreement with the Dutch about six weeks after the Ambassador's arrival. But before that Dr van Mook had called on the Ambassador. It was the 8th of March, the anniversary of the capitulation to the Japanese in 1942.

'Dr van Mook's hopes and fears', the Ambassador reported to London, 'tend to fluctuate widely. At the moment he is seeing nothing but confusion and darkness. His joy and relief at the reappointment of Mr Sjahrir as Prime Minister have now moved to something like despair about ever getting down to negotiations. In this he may be right but I confess that he does not yet carry me with him when he claims that the time has come to declare that the Indonesians have refused to negotiate and to set up a government under himself.' What had become of his famous 'new approach', so carefully considered in The Hague and in London? Was that to be so easily discouraged and cast to one side? 'Dr van Mook tends to glide over plans that have been agreed upon if they turn out not to suit his immediate book – a doubtful and ever changing volume,' the Ambassador stated. And yet he had started off by telling the Foreign Office in one of his first signals from Batavia: 'I like Dr van Mook too.'

65. The timing of events played an important role in the mental and political processes of the day. Throughout our occupation the

wrong thing would rush in to spoil the right moment, the right thing happen at the wrong time. So consistently bad and unco-ordinated was the timing that obviously the hypothesis on which we all based our conduct must have failed somewhere to take into account one or more of the fundamental factors of the situation. Whatever Dutch or Indonesians did, they invariably induced equal but opposite states of mind in one another and created a situation of lengthening parallels: and could we make parallels meet this side of infinity? No sooner had Dr van Mook dealt with interior Holland and returned to the political front-line in Java, than Mr Sjahrir would find it necessary to dash off to Djokjakarta to placate his hinterland. When Mr Sjahrir returned at last ready to talk, events in Holland would tend to have changed and made the Governor-General take up a posi-tion which once more rendered the situation fluid and inde-terminate for everyone. No one in the party most concerned seemed capable of holding up a firm head to circumstance with something of the spirit which is prepared to be lost in order to find itself.

The only person who really knew clearly what he wanted and with a quiet, courteous, inflexible determination set about getting it, was the Ambassador. And he got an ample share of timing that was bad thrust upon him. Almost one of the first things he had to do was to try and persuade H.M. Government in Australia that it had not chosen a good moment for sending s.s. *Manoora*, loaded with 700 Indonesians politically suspect with the Dutch, to Batavia. Allied headquarters itself did not mind very much, but Dr van Mook and his government had very deep feelings on the matter. Their relationship with Australia in spite of the generous asylum they had enjoyed there during the war and the hospitality it still extended to some thousands of Dutch evacuees was nearly as strained as it could be. This sense of strain went much deeper than mere irritation at the Australian waterside workers' unrepentant refusal to load the Dutch ships for Java, long overdue, in Australian waters. They believed quite seriously that it was Australia's policy first to bring them into dis-repute with the international world and then to supplant them in the N.E.I. In the last days of the war Dr Evatt [a prominent Australian Cabinet Minister], they said, had somewhere made a statement which left them in no doubt as to the dangerous desires of the Commonwealth. So vivid were these fears and so confusedly bitter their feelings in general about Australia that Dr van Mook and his officials found it too much at times to be civil to the representatives in Batavia of the Commonwealth. The coming of the *Manoora* now sent them once more wild with anger and anxiety.

66. Hardly had the Ambassador soothed the ruffled feelings in Batavia and got the timing readjusted when his own military authorities demanded a course of action which inevitably meant upsetting the Indonesians and bringing his own mission under serious suspicion. The Dutch were still clamouring for permission to bring their troops, held up for some months already in Malaya, ashore in the N.E.I. Their government at home, with an eye on the forthcoming elections, was getting more and more apprehensive of the effect the continued delay was having on the loyalty of its supporters. In India the Viceroy, who also had to discount in advance the certainty of a sweeping nationalist victory at the polls in the immediate future, was arguing with increased emphasis the necessity of beginning the withdrawal of the British Indian troops from the N.E.I. forthwith. In the circumstances the commanders of our forces both here and in Singapore demanded that the ban on the entry of Dutch troops should now be lifted. As if that were not enough we ourselves added to the fire of Indonesian suspicions by launching a large clearing operation round Bandoeng on the Batavia yule-tide model.

Finally to round off the series of ill-timed actions the Dutch chose this very moment to introduce their own currency. We ourselves had been heading off both Indonesians and Dutch for six months from just such a course of action. The economic consequences of unilateral financial action from whichever side it came had always appeared a highly dangerous and two-edged tool. Mr Doll [a financial expert on the scene] had warned Dutch and Indonesians against the perils of uncoordinated action in this regard. It was assumed that this was the kind of problem which would be raised very early on in the talks when the Ambassador did get the two parties to meet. But on the plea that they were running out of Japanese paper money (the currency at the time used by all and the only money in the possession of the 56,000,000-odd peasants and coolies in Java and Sumatra), the Dutch issued their politically controversial currency. The Dutch alone know how far the financial necessity they pleaded was used to disguise their political strategy. Already the Indonesians were lengthening the fatal opposite parallel until they too could issue the currency from which we had discouraged them for so long. The unfortunate millions of Java were to have not two but three paper currencies chafing one another in the same threadbare wallet. That, however, was still to come; the immediate point is that the issue of the currency just then made the Ambassador's task perhaps unfairly but in any case uncommonly more difficult.

This and the news of the landing of the first Dutch troops early in March coincided almost to a day, very nearly causing Dr Soekarno to revoke his decision to authorise Mr Sjahrir to negotiate an agreement. A British officer who arrived in Djokjakarta on the morning the Dutch troops landed to discuss the future talks with the Indonesian President had a ring-side view of the difficulties the Indonesian head of state had from his own countrymen on those occasions. The officer himself was heavily guarded and the sight of his British uniform seemed to fix the normally smiling Javanese faces in a sullen and smouldering look. The hotels were full of young men who had fought against us on the 'Bandoeng front' and the long-haired fanatics of the K.R.I. were besieging the entrances of the Palace with petitions for a declaration of open war.

'Is this', Dr Soekarno and Dr Hatta asked him as he walked into the Palace, 'the opening of economic and military hostilities against us?'

It speaks somewhat for the moral courage of both President and Vice-President and the confidence the Ambassador had, even at that distance, created in his mission in their minds, that on that day of all days they authorised Mr Sjahrir to go ahead.

67. The first formal meeting took place at Sir Archibald Clark Kerr's house on the 13th of March 1946. As far as humanly possible the ground had been prepared for success. Informal meetings between Dr van Mook and the Indonesian premier, and discussions between their various subordinates, had been organised for them frequently by the Ambassador's staff. The Indonesians had by now such confidence in the Ambassador that on the eve of the meeting they asked him to help them with the English draft of their counter-proposals; he had already advised Dr van Mook on the framing of the important preamble to the Dutch proposals before they were published nearly a

month before. The details of the agreement reached are now of interest only to the specialist in these matters. Moreover the problem, as Sjahrir told the Ambassador at their first meeting and as Colonel Abdul Kadir is still telling his superiors in The Hague to this day, is very largely psychological. It was never the substance which counted half as much as the manner. The 'how', not the 'what', was all-important.

By the 29th of March the Ambassador was able to report to London: 'Dr van Mook is in buoyant mood and confident that he will be able to persuade his government to accept a settlement on the lines of the Indonesian counterdraft.'

An agreement had been reached which came so near the fundamental requirements of the situation that its terms have relentlessly pursued everyone and every conference that has since tried a hand at solving the problem. It was not signed or initialled but early in April, Dutch, Indonesians and the Ambassador left for Holland all in good faith that a formal settlement was at hand. The Indonesian delegation consisted of two of their most trusted ministers and a secretary. Dr van Mook took with him Dr Idenburg, his adviser with most influence in royalist circles, the picturesque but feckless young Sultan of Pontianak, the Ambonese A.D.C. of the new Dutch Army Commander, and the harassed and persecution-haunted Eurasian Colonel, commander of his espionage service in the interior, hoping in this eclectic manner somehow to silence all conceivable arguments against the agreement.

The Ambassador left with his own personal staff. At the last moment a telegram had come from The Hague which indicated politely but clearly what the Dutch at heart thought of his mission and its apparent success. Many people, and most of all the Indonesians, had assumed that the Ambassador would be present at the discussions to be held in Holland. In fact the Indonesians had been strongly influenced by this assumption in agreeing to send a delegation to Holland. But the suggestion that the Ambassador might be in Holland for some days now caused the Dutch Government to suggest by cable that they would be grateful if Lord Inverchapel, as he had now formally become, would be their guest for one night in The Hague, after which they were sure he would be anxious to hasten to complete his preparations for the new duties which awaited him in Washington.

VII OCCUPATION: *The Fifth Phase – 'Keeping the Rule of Negotiation in Being'*

68. Lord Inverchapel, Dr van Mook and their party left Batavia in the early morning of the 4th of April. To the large mixed crowd pressing in on the aerodrome, they seemed to go in good faith, in good heart and with a sense of urgency. Their plane, vanishing rapidly over the palm trees towards the north-western seas, looked the sort of thing men in the days before they lost their feeling of wonder at machines would have called 'The Twentieth Century' or 'The Spirit of Progress'. Yet, in the early days of May the party which left with such a splash began to trickle back from Europe in twos and threes with something very near to a whimper.

One of the first stragglers to return was the Sultan of Pontianak. He was frank to the point of indiscretion about their reception in Holland – 'They are a snooty and unimaginative bunch over there', he told a British political officer, a friend from his less fortunate days. 'No one of any importance came to meet us or to see us. We were ignored most of the time.' They were strange words from the lips of a young lieutenant who had just jumped into a throne [and] a Colonelcy and been made an A.D.C. to the Queen. But stranger was still to come.

The Indonesian delegation had been whisked away to the remote and secluded Hoge Veluwe and what had happened there only very few of the highest ministers could tell. Dr van Mook himself, the Sultan said, had been ignored in a shameful and insulting manner. Out of twelve ministerial meetings with the Indonesians he had been present at only two. Angry groups had demonstrated outside his hotel in The Hague. One morning he had woken up to find a copy of Rembrandt's *Autopsy* pasted against the window of his room. The corpse was labelled 'Our Empire'; the leading surgeon, pointing at the body and saying, 'we are about to dismember it', had Dr van Mook's features. Another bitter humorist some days later made him wake up to a portrait of himself on the way to the gallows with a rope round his neck and a caption explaining that he was guilty of violating the Governor-General's oath. In the end he had a nervous breakdown and went to London to recover. It was noticeable how little his voice was heard there in the discussions between their ministers and ours on the future of Indonesia. But he found the solace and the moral support there which he always has in some strange way sought more from us than his own countrymen.

The Indonesian delegation too seem to have been bewildered by it all and were clear on only one thing: a bleak and wintry disillusion. No one seems to have thought even of keeping them in touch with their government. Of six urgent telegrams sent to Mr Sjahrir only the two least important reached him. Not without bitterness or reason did they say plainly on their return: 'The talks have achieved nothing.'

69. The Dutch ministers had slipped away from the Hooge Weluwe to England and once more discussed the problem on the highest level. It might have been a good gesture to have taken one of the Indonesian delegates with them. The possibilities of political agreement were discussed, but all through the Dutch ministers showed a significant preoccupation with the military aspects of the future. How long could Britain keep troops in the N.E.I.? And how many? What support could we give them in any unavoidable military action? They regretted it, but some form of military action would be necessary even after successful negotiations! Could we help them to build up a model state in West Java? At the end of it all they issued a communiqué to the press on their own initiative without prior reference to the Indonesian government as agreed before in Batavia. It was quite a long statement but the part that really mattered was this: 'The Government declaration of February 10th 1946 still forms a basis for succeeding discussions on the status of Indonesia.'

With that one sentence the Inverchapel draft agreement, not even mentioned by name, after only a perfunctory run was chased out of the political paddock, with a resounding slap on its flank. The Indonesians themselves found that they had been somewhat exalted in their interpretation of their mission and had been brought to Holland only for 'informal discussions'. 'The prospect of the coming elections', Sir Nevile Bland said, 'has given the Dutch Government cold feet.'

70. As the disillusioned emissaries reappeared in the corridors of official Batavia, everyone remarked how well they looked. The Dutch cooks, apparently, had lost none of their cunning. But while they had been putting on fat in Holland, the problem in the islands had been putting on muscle. The opposition to reason and moderation in the interior was by no means at an end. News of the failure of the mission did not take long to get around and people like the Japanese-trained commander-in-chief of the Indonesian armies, the vain, handsome, but

intensely patriotic General Soedirman; Dr Moewardi, the soft-spoken, gentle, but implacable leader of the Black Buffaloes; Dr Soebardjo, the scheming, cruel, pleasure-loving friend of the Japanese Admiral Maeda; the notorious Chinese-trained communist Tan Malakka; and Mr Soekirman, the slighted and hitherto unconsulted leader of the Masjoemi, the most religious and most powerful party in the two great islands, all seemed to vie with one another in exploiting this setback for the rule of agreement by negotiation. They had been defeated rather ignominiously by Mr Sjahrir in the prolonged crisis of February–March. They now worked frantically to reverse the tables. Dr Amir Sjarifoeddin, the able Minister of Defence, who had gone to Djokja months before to report to Soekarno, found the situation so obstinately convalescent that he had not yet returned to Batavia. Mr Sjahrir as usual took the situation very calmly but very seriously. He was quite philosophical about what had happened in Holland and even sympathised with Professor Schermerhorn's election difficulties. But he had to be practical. As long as there was a chance of the Dutch returning to negotiation on the March 1946 basis when their own election bogey was out of the way, he was prepared to fight this opposition once again.

'If the British can stabilise their perimeters and their line of communication to Bandoeng and keep an unofficial sort of truce going,' he said, 'I think I can tide over until after the elections. If they can't, well anything might happen.'

71. Meanwhile Dr van Mook too had returned. He too looked fatter and once more he was reported to be in a 'buoyant mood'. The report this time came from General Mansergh, who had led the British Indian troops so brilliantly in the battle for Sourabaya after the Mallaby murder, and had now taken over the command of the allied forces in the N.E.I.

'I have', he told the General, 'some modified proposals with me that might work.' What those proposals were he did not say, but he started to work on them at once. Judging by the advisers and constant stream of distinguished visitors who knocked at the Palace gates, the proposed course of action would not be confined to Java and Sumatra.

The Sultan of Pontianak had already hinted on his return that everyone was 'fed up' with Java and Sumatra. 'It will never go beyond talk with these two places,' he told his friends. 'There will never be an agreement. Much the best thing is to leave them alone and concentrate on the outer islands.' As he came himself from one of the most important of the outer islands, the sentiment was understandable. But there was more to it than that. Some of Dr van Mook's most trusted advisers, like Colonel Abdul Kadir, had urged him in the beginning to let Java and Sumatra have their political way and to concentrate all their resources and energies on the outer possessions which enclosed them, as the first nationalist novelist of Java had put it some decades before, in a girdle of emeralds. Java and Sumatra, particularly Java, once these rich islands were rehabilitated and prosperous, would come screaming to them and Holland for help.

Dr van Mook had indeed come back with something of this plan in his mind and while he waited for the results of the elections in Holland he announced his intention of calling a conference of representatives of the outer possessions.

This was to be the conference at Malino in the Celebes out of which grew the plan to create an autonomous Great Borneo and a State of East Indonesia which would include all the remaining islands in the East except New Guinea. The last part of the plan came to fulfilment at Den Pasar in December 1946, and the machinery of state with a Balinese President at its head, complete with a Prime Minister and cabinet, has been formally inaugurated in Batavia.

72. But this at the time was not all Dr van Mook had in mind. He could not cut his imagination suddenly free of 350 years of Dutch history in Java. He had after all been born in the country, had more right to call it his than many of the Sumatrans who were trying to run it. So he had a plan for Java too. In this he was at his most enigmatic. It is difficult to believe that his plan was embodied in the 'modified proposals' he had mentioned to General Mansergh. These proposals were the plan that had been dictated to him by the passing political necessities of the far-away Netherlands, and like the good civil servant he was by training, he worked on them; they were called 'a protocol'. Towards the end of May he handed them rather perfunctorily to the Indonesian Prime Minister. After what he had witnessed in March he could not seriously have believed in their chances of being accepted. Moreover, allied headquarters had made it possible for him to have informally with Mr Sjahrir some pre-

liminary discussions which made it quite clear what slender hopes of success the protocol had. It is significant that no one on the British side was taken into his confidence beforehand and the first glimpse allied headquarters, who was still paying the military piper for all political tunes, had of the protocol was when Mr Sjahrir lent his to a British officer.

Dr van Mook apologised profusely to His Majesty's Consul-General as he should have done, for Mr MacKereth had worked incessantly since March to keep alive the faith of the Indonesian Government in the uses of negotiation with the Dutch. He thought it had all been arranged and co-ordinated through London and The Hague and said he had reprimanded Count van Bylandt, the official responsible for the omission. But the apology would hardly wash. The real explanation was to be found in his own complete lack of faith in the protocol. He had never really believed in negotiating with independent Indonesians. However much he said he liked Mr Sjahrir and however much he respected his own subordinate Dr Amir Sjarifoeddin, he had no real desire to negotiate with them or any faith in their capacity for carrying out an agreement reached. There were, in this respect, two Dr van Mooks all the time: one was allowed to come to the surface when he spoke to our statesmen and diplomats; the other when he spoke to our soldiers. The first would pretend to have some faith in the rule of negotiation, the other none. This last was the real Dr van Mook, who was always more spontaneous and direct with our soldiers. He found it easier to impress our soldiers than our diplomats.

He loved above all his conferences at Singapore, and there once more at the beginning of August he let his unreal pet theory out of the bag. Java, he said, was rapidly going to economic ruin – had been threatened with famine eight months before – and within two months sheer economic decay would destroy the Indonesian Government. Mr Sjahrir and his cabinet would disappear and there would be no one representative to take their place. He was already prepared for the eventuality and would at the right moment appoint his own Indonesian Government. He spoke with more confidence because allied headquarters had helped him some weeks before to convince the Chiefs of Staff that the last British troops ought not to be withdrawn from the N.E.I. before the end of November. Meanwhile his own military forces were massing in the N.E.I. and his policy henceforth could be based on the certainty that, when we left, the Dutch forces would be no less than ours were at our maximum. He had lost the first objective of Dutch policy towards the British but the second, which was to keep us committed in the N.E.I. for as long as possible and which had seemed almost lost before March, had now been won handsomely without paying the price March had demanded. He could safely try out the pattern of his plan at Malino [and] perfect it at Den Pasar, and it is there today more ready than ever for the future should it be wanted.

73. But in the meanwhile, from May to August, the political adviser of the British Commander had a dogged, monotonous day-to-day struggle to keep alive the embers of a will to negotiate among Dutch and Indonesians. It says a great deal for the way in which we had managed the negotiations in March that no blame was attached to us for the ultimate failure. We were criticised only for having made them nearly successful. The Indonesians particularly had less and less heart in talks with the Dutch. The failure of the talks in Holland had been bad enough but the protocol, one of the vaguest documents produced in the history of our occupation, seemed to them much worse with its offer of further discussions at an Imperial Conference, date unspecified, with representatives of the whole Empire.

'It has been a great shock to us all,' Mr Sjahrir told headquarters. 'The situation in the interior has deteriorated very much and if bloodshed is to be avoided some way other than talking to the Dutch will have to be found.'

He was thinking seriously for the first time of moving the remnants of his government to the interior and from there launching an appeal to the United Nations before full-scale warfare broke over his country. Had it not been for the counsel of the political adviser to allied headquarters he would long since have appealed to U.N.O. over and over again.

Mr MacKereth had to urge him to give direct negotiations with the Dutch every fair and honest chance, and to stress that his proper reply to the perfunctory protocol, if he didn't like it, was to submit counter-proposals. He agreed but not without misgivings for on the 7th of June he wrote to Mr Brookes, the official Australian observer in Batavia who was about to return home, formally requesting him to ask his government whether it 'would be prepared to raise our question before U.N.O. on the terms of the draft agreement made under the chairmanship of Sir Archibald Clark Kerr'. He informed Mr Brookes at the same time that 'sporadic fighting continued', 'my own brother has recently been killed', 'the danger of violent fighting increases every day' [and that] 'irrespective of our counter-proposals the Dutch will drag on'.

On the 18th of June, Mr Sjahrir handed Mr MacKereth his counter-proposals and asked him if he would convey them to Dr van Mook. The Governor-General was most amiable but he would, he said, have to refer them to The Hague.

74. To this extent Mr Sjahrir had been right when he wrote to Mr Brookes early in June: 'We all think it unlikely that the Dutch will accept our proposals . . . they will once again drag on our question.' The weeks of June and July and August dragged wearily by without apparent point or profit. Hard work on Dutch and Indonesians had never before seemed to yield so small a return. Mr Sjahrir did make another attempt to be practical. He wrote to Dr van Mook and suggested that they should make a joint request to General Mansergh for a truce. The Governor-General took such a long time to reply and when he did, answered in such a manner that the proposal was impossible and in any case too late.

Mr Sjahrir was influenced in making the proposal by the alarming increase of tension in the interior. Dissatisfaction was so widespread and so confused that it even directed itself against the ancient aristocracies of the centre of the island. The Indonesian Government had already been forced to send its minister of home affairs, Mr Sjahrir's closest friend, to Solo, to deal with the followers of Tan Malakka and Dr Moewardi, who had deposed the Sultan from the oldest throne in the island. In Cheribon itself, where the Government's following was greatest, there had been a two-day battle between official forces and the Tan Malakkan irregulars. Now, towards the end of June, Mr Sjahrir in Solo, on his way to Djokja for a cabinet meeting with the President, was himself kidnapped with several members of his party, including a general of the official army, and taken at one o'clock in the morning to an isolated house in the hills. That nothing serious happened to them was due to a very spirited young lady, Maria Ulfah Santoso, the leading Indonesian feminist and the only woman member of the cabinet. The moment she heard the news she collected the remnants of the party, boarded the official train which was waiting in the station and hastened to Djokja to tell the President. He, the 'artist', 'the impractical, vague, vain dreamer', took energetic measures, declared a state of emergency, resumed full governmental authority and acted positively. Within a few days Mr Sjahrir was free and the deep-laid plot had not yet run its course. As the Indonesian premier walked into the Presidential palace to report some mornings later, he found that two of the guards had just been shot, the rest captured and the President and his staff were in the hands of the plotters. It was Mr Sjahrir's turn to set him free.

The story, picturesque as it is, would not have borne repeating were it not for the point it gave to Dr van Mook's argument that the Indonesian government were not worth talking to much, and [the way in which it] encouraged him and his countrymen to persist in their policy of postponement and delay, which was such an obvious contributory factor to the political instabilities of the day. And so it went on, all the familiar and characteristic factors repeating themselves week by week, pointing the same lessons, adorning the tale with the same moral, and no one profiting by them.

75. As the day of our departure approached our advice counted for less and less, suffering as it did from a law of galloping diminishing military returns. The loyalty of the Dutch commanders to the British General, whom they all said was the best and most understanding they ever had, became the thinnest of pretences. If Admiral Pinke, whose rudeness and salted heartiness had earned for him a reputation of great honesty, wanted to take independent action, he did and informed the British Commander afterwards or waited until the news leaked out before explaining. Thus he bombarded and machine-gunned the port of Banjoewangi from the air, his gunners hitting by accident with extreme accuracy only the sheds in which the Indonesians were collecting their rice for India – the Admiral had said privately he would not allow the rice through. The British Commander heard of it first from the press. It was a strange way of treating a headquarters which from the beginning had so strongly supported the Dutch argument that if there was rice to be spared in the interior, it should be spared for hungry Indonesians first.

General Spoor, the young liberal officer on whom great hopes had been placed, was quite frank about it.

'You must not be surprised', he told General Mansergh, 'if I do things here and there on my own in future. I know you can sack me but my troops are fed up and we have got to do something. Anyway you will soon be gone and then I shall come back.'

76. Jerked backwards and forwards between conflicting military loyalties, between the remote abstractionist in The Hague and the impassioned partisan in Batavia, with no centrally co-ordinated or authoritative plan, the political situation rocked like a runaway coach, careering down a perilous slope. Once more His Majesty's Special Commissioner for East Asia was sent from Singapore to Java on a mission very similar to that undertaken by Lord Inverchapel a year before. All the principal actors in Java, so well schooled in their parts, repeated perhaps more skilfully their performance of March 1946. The theme was essentially the same, although its orchestration now was fuller or, as Mr Sjahrir put it so concisely when he told the first meeting of the Dutch Indonesian Conference on the 7th of October that he trusted Lord Killearn's task would be easier to fulfil than Lord Inverchapel's because – and this is the really important point: 'The Dutch–Indonesian issue has further developed into maturity and become more distinct than at last time.'

Dr van Mook had been joined or rather had been grafted into the Dutch equivalent of a Royal Commission of three, headed by the ex-liberal Prime Minister of Holland, Professor Schermerhorn. Mr de Boer, the director of the great shipping combine, the KPM, which had once been one of the major powers in these waters, and Mr van Poll, who had been left sadder and wiser by duties on the other commission which in March had been here to investigate Dr van Mook's conduct, were the other two.

As he watched this exalted gathering meet for the first time in October in the house of His Majesty's Consul-General, the British soldier who had been here since the 15th of September 1945 could be pardoned for saying: 'I have seen this problem, easy in the beginning, going on to higher and higher levels, getting more and more difficult all the time. Soon it will reach such a height that the Almighty alone will be able to deal with it.'

77. The task of keeping the two parties together had now been taken over entirely by Lord Killearn from His Majesty's Consul-General, who through the long months of disillusionment that

followed the still-born March agreement had somehow managed to keep the flickering Indonesian faith in negotiation alive and had never allowed either Dutch or Indonesians to forget their obligations in giving negotiations with one another every honest and possible chance.

By the 12th of November, Lord Killearn was able to report to London that a draft agreement had been reached. It was substantially – even the time taken was nearly the same – the agreement of March in new clothing, but with two additional braces to the shoulder. Both these had been contained in the Indonesian counter-proposals handed by Mr MacKereth to the Governor-General in June:

(a)   a proposal for a mutual reduction of military forces.
(b)   an arbitration clause.

The ink of the initials of the delegations on the agreement was hardly dry when the Commission General flew to Holland to get it ratified. They would, they said, just as Dr van Mook had done very nearly a year before, when he went home to solicit approval for 'his new approach', be back in a fortnight. They did not return until the New Year.

Meanwhile on the 19th of February the last of the 91,799 British and British Indian troops that had once been in those islands had sailed for good from the Netherlands East Indies. One of their commander's last actions had been to countermand an illegal Dutch ultimatum to the Indonesian forces. Impatient of British restraint, the Dutch army commanders were straining at the bit. 'We pray that time, the soothing God,' the principal Dutch newspaper in Batavia wrote, 'will give us the heart and restraint to appreciate what the British have done for us' – the British who left 500 of their dead behind.

VIII   OCCUPATION: *The Last Phase – 'British Occupation at an End'*
78. The British occupation was at an end and there remains little more that can be usefully said about it. To those who served here and attempted to study the history of the episode it will always remain something of a mystery. How, for instance, did we come to accept such a last-minute imposition on our overburdened shoulders? Who is right after all: the Supreme Allied Commander who says the task was thrust on us, or America's Mr Wallace, so fondly quoted in the Dutch press to the effect that for the sake of our prestige we begged the United States for the job?

And once having acquired the burden, why were we so ill-informed about it? The story of the revolution in Bantam in 1926 after all was printed long before the war. Had no one in the Government and military departments concerned read *Max Havelaar*, the novel which is the nationalists' bible and which is ably translated in English and was once commended to popular attention by our own writers like D.H. Lawrence and Arnold Bennett? There was no reason except slackness why nationalism in the East Indies should have remained a mystery. And then having once come, why did our troops without exception prefer the Indonesians to the Dutch? They came without prejudice, and whose fault is it that they left with bias? The British Indian troops one can understand more easily but what made the Seaforths, the first troops to land and almost the last to leave, raise their clenched hands on the way to the docks and shout '*Merdeka*', the nationalist cry of liberty, at the incoming Dutch troops? And why was it the Dutch who called on God's help to prevent them from being bitter about us; and why was it the Indonesians (of whom we had killed six thousand in Sourabaya alone) who said to us through their Prime Minister: 'Even in unfriendly contact or in conflict with us, we learned to appreciate and admire you. You introduced to our country by your personal qualities some traits of Western culture our people have rarely seen before from white people they know. I mean your politeness, your kindness, your dignified self restraint. Long after you have left, when the wounds caused by war and revolution of the last year will have been healed, I think this final impression of your army will be the lasting memory for our people of your stay in our country'?

Only the enigmatic Dr van Mook raised an official voice on our behalf. At his conference with the racial minorities at Pangkalpinang in October when the Dutch delegates tended to speak of us as the runaway cowards from Malaya who became the looters and robbers of Java and Sumatra, he called them sharply to order and reprimanded them severely. What is more, in defending himself, he supported what had been three basic assumptions of our policy since November 1945, for he confessed that

(a) the Dutch had been wrong in regarding nationalism as the special product of the Japanese occupation – the roots went much deeper than that;

(b) it was obvious that there could be no military solution to the problem;

(c) they had been too ready to assume that the republic would soon collapse whereas it was clear that it had been consolidating itself all the time.

Nothing he could say, however, could remove the bitterness against Britain, and yet that at least need not remain too much of a mystery. We are by tradition feared and suspect in these islands. Holland in Europe has tended to woo us; Holland in the East has always regarded us, from the first massacre of Amboina in 1623 on, as dangerous commercial rivals. They have not forgiven us Stamford Raffles yet, and they cannot forgive us that Malaya appears prosperous and peaceful to them, and their own islands so unsettled. They are hurt because they are passionately convinced that they were the model colonists of the world and cannot see why the laws of life will not except them from the rule that colonisation, however good, sooner or later is not good enough from the point of view of the colonised. As a people they have tended in their colonies to be braver and more stubborn in defence of their consciences. Professor Toynbee has recorded in detail how they alone of all European nations were allowed to have commercial privileges in Japan and did not find the price of standing on their heads, tossing capers and spitting on the cross annually in the streets of Tokyo too expensive. One contrasts it with their predecessors, the despised Portuguese, who lost those privileges for displaying too much zeal for the same cross.

Generalisations are unfair but this much is necessary to explain the pull baker of old Holland in Europe, and the pull of the devil of the new in the Far East which made the situation so difficult to understand for those who know only one and not the other. By history and by training the Dutch in those islands have avoided risks and have made their way more with guile than by courage. They have not the imaginative courage which will give up everything in the belief that what life takes away with one hand is given back one day handsomely with the other. They know that we have tried to be fair but that is only a cause of greater bitterness because they expected and desired us to be more.

'You have dealt us the same measure,' Dr Idenburg says in his complicated way. 'You have tried to weigh us in the same balance and made the Indonesians equal to us. But the Oriental knows no equality and does not recognise it. What he gets at once is a minimum not a maximum. All you have done is to make us unequal.' Yet, it is an oriental Colonel Abdul Kadir Widjojoatmodjo who, standing by them honourably in their dire necessities, has advised them most consistently to throw their bread now on these stormy waters.

'Personally my experience shows that a friendly stranger is better than an antipathetic fellow-countryman; thus a friendly foreign nation will be better than a colony full of enmity or an antipathetic member of the same commonwealth . . . for the execution of all this, imagination and youthful force (which is not firmly rusted into pre-war conceptions) is necessary. The practical guidance of certain economic and financial affairs could be left in the hands of the Netherlands East Indies Government. I see no other solution. Armed force will only separate from us the Indonesians who are now for co-operation.'

Had it not been for the British forces and the older political instinct which never quite forsakes their leaders this armed force which would have separated Dutch and Indonesians would have been used. The results of such a war are difficult to contemplate but one thing is certain, few of the thousands of women and children the British forces came to rescue would have been saved and Holland may have well lost this part of her Empire even if she had won a bloody war. For the spirit of nationalism is everywhere. The whole century is on the march; its leaders for the moment are not the sources of its strength; its leaders are less necessary to it than the leaders of most other countries because they all feel the same; the difference between one leader and another, one part of the century and another, are not fundamental but differences only of degree. By holding this troubled fort so long we have given many of the Dutch and Indonesians coming out of their several mental and physical captivities a chance to survey the new post-war world and to come to values not unlike our own. With their help Britain has kept the rule of negotiation alive in the most threatening circumstances. It stands today some chance of survival and Holland has at last produced someone other than the lonely and enigmatic Dr van Mook to try his hand at a solution. Professor Schermerhorn is a liberal for liberalism's sake not merely for what he can get out of it. He has begun to read the history of his century and is not likely to repeat the mistakes of 1840. He may yet manage to lead his country to a peaceful solution, but it will be neither quick nor tidy.

As for ourselves the dogs of bitterness in the island villages will continue to bark at us but the caravan, as the Arabs have it, will move on. We need have only one regret and one cause of self-reproach: that it did not move on before.

CHAPTER ELEVEN

The Resolution

BY THE TIME I came back from nearly three weeks in the interior, Gilbert MacKereth had already sent the report to the Secretary of State for Foreign Affairs, accompanied by his own summing-up of the events of his period of service in Java, and an economic survey written by Tom Sharman, his Commercial Attaché, who had been a welcome appointment to our staff some months before. MacKereth had received a most appreciative cable of thanks from the Secretary of State, and in the days and months that followed he would from time to time relay messages from London and elsewhere which told him, and therefore me, how well my report had been received. Apparently it was in diplomatic circles what one would call a best-seller.

Some years later, when the war and its immediate aftermath were already forgotten in the popular mind and I myself no longer looked back, I suddenly received a cable from Gilbert and Muriel, who were on leave in France. It read: 'Congratulations. The news in *The Times* about your award has made us very happy and was not only deserved but scandalously delayed.'

I had not seen *The Times* that day. It was still rationed and I was not yet on the ration list. I rushed out to get a copy, and found that I had a headline and a paragraph all to myself, reporting that I had been appointed a Commander in the Order of the British Empire, followed by the citation, which said it was for 'conduct on active service in the field before 1942'. This was a strange wording after the heart-warming citation, and seemed as if whoever had drafted it at

source wanted to make it quite clear that it was not an award for
services in Java, as people have thought ever since, but rather for services before this period in Java was even thought of.

As for the investiture, it was so moving an occasion that I cannot
pass it by. The officers being invested were mostly of ranks senior to
mine, and I came at the end of a long line with a merchant marine
seaman who had performed acts of bravery and initiative on a scale
greater than any of us there could claim. Each officer, when it was
his turn, would take a step out of the line towards the King, come to
attention, bow, was invested in whatever manner was appropriate,
and then would step back and move on. The King obviously had no
time to speak to them all and, indeed, had not yet spoken to anyone
at any length that I could see.

It came to my turn. He invested me, and I then stepped back to
turn and walk away like the others. But his lips moved in that hesi-
tant way with which he controlled his stammer and I heard him say
quite firmly: 'Please don't go.' He then went on to tell me how much
he had enjoyed my dispatches from Java, and particularly my full
report of the British occupation. He discussed the whole of the
Indonesian situation with me in a remarkably informed and sensitive
way, and ended by asking me how I thought it would finish. I remember saying: 'I'm afraid, sir, it will end very badly.' 'I fear that you are
right,' he said, 'but if it does, please know it will not be your fault.
Thank you very much for what you've done.'

I then watched the merchant seaman in his turn standing to attention and bowing, and being invested by the King. The two of them,
sailors that they both were, found they had a lot to discuss. An
admiral had come over to congratulate me, saying in a way that only
seasoned admirals can: 'Young man, did you invent the atom bomb?
The King talked to you for so long!' At that moment we saw the
seaman coming towards us. The admiral lost all interest in me and
straightaway went to meet the seaman, joined by all the other naval
officers there who, it seemed to me, could not have been more
delighted that an ordinary seaman had done so well and that what
he had done had been so honourably acknowledged.

I had started the report with great reluctance, but it was quite extraordinary how writing it, and particularly having ended it to
MacKereth's unqualified approval, had been an act of emancipation
for me. It was with a tremendous sense of relief, almost of having

thrown a physical burden from my back, that I started on my journey to the interior.

I had never seen the interior of Java so peaceful as on this visit there with Sjahrir. I saw far less evidence of military preparedness than I had seen before the Japanese withdrawal. The calm, the order, touched perhaps with the increased confidence which the Indonesians were feeling in themselves and their destiny, seemed so authentic that it was more than a calm before the storm.

What was interesting, too, was that for the first time there were several occasions when I had the opportunity to talk at length both to Soekarno and to Hatta. They were lovely, civilized occasions of unusual quality, seeing and talking to these exceptional men, not about politics and war and military matters but about life in general, and especially about the culture and history of Indonesia. Hatta, in particular, impressed me now even more than he had already done before. He was a person of utter integrity, intelligence and balance, and such a good influence in Soekarno's life that I could well understand why he and Sjahrir were such close friends. For a moment or two I was allowed to glimpse behind his measured and always controlled manner, to the deep feelings that were there at the heart of the man, particularly when he talked about the two children he and Sjahrir had adopted and raised in their island exile before the war.

Soekarno was, as I had already realized, a person of immense and magnetic charm, and by any aesthetic standard an extremely good-looking and attractive person. He was also an extremely unusual and interesting person, possessing not only extraordinary qualities of rhetoric and power over the massed populace, but also great courage; he had suffered even more persecution than had Hatta and Sjahrir for his vision of an independent Indonesia. However, one had the feeling that his vision, intense as it was, remained singularly a collective vision, and that he saw its realization as something uniquely to be established through THE PEOPLE, in capital letters, and through the power of his own voice.

His belief in his power of speech was, I believe, something quite exceptional, and his awareness of it went far back into his childhood. He told me of the experience when, still short of his teens, he felt called to become an inspirational speaker. He woke up one night and found himself standing on his blankets on the boards which were used (just as we used them in prison) as beds, addressing his family. All the lights in the room were lit and the whole family (I had the impression from what he said that there were close on twenty of them) were gathered around him listening to him speaking, and he was told that he had already been addressing them in his sleep for many minutes. He said he knew then that he had been called upon by God himself to become the voice for his people.

His extraordinarily direct communication between a pattern of rhetoric of formidable energy in his unconscious, and his conscious self was, I believe, never broken, and he continued increasingly to be a man who spoke as much from his sleeping as from his waking senses. This was to give him so much power over people – and raised his dependence on the sense of power that speaking to multitudes gave him – that when he was ultimately parted from Sjahrir and Hatta he was corrupted, and had a great deal to answer for in what followed, plunging Java so cruelly into a desperate civil war during which, for instance, Amir Sjarifoeddin, who had done so much for the nationalist cause, was shot, despite Soekarno's orders to the contrary. (He died with an edition of Moffat's translation of the New Testament, which I had given him as a parting present, in his pocket.)

As a result I did not see in Soekarno the integrity of the truly individual vision that was present in Sjahrir, and in Hatta. Sjahrir's, for instance, was not only profoundly intuitive and instinctive, from the deepest natural levels of himself, but was also balanced with a conscious awareness of serving it with an exceptional intellect. It was no accident that a book of his about his vision of Java and life was published and republished in Malay, the official language of Indonesia, several times during our occupation of Indonesia.

To return to this memorable journey, one moment of immense personal meaning to me I owed to both Sjahrir and Soekarno. Sjahrir one evening, after a long talk about the history of Java, told Soekarno when I had left the room how much I longed to see the Boroboedoer, one of the greatest of sacred Buddhist monuments in the world.

The very next morning Soekarno himself got permission for a member of the Sultan of Solo's staff to take me on a side journey to the Boroboedoer, in the heart of Java. My guide was a man of about forty, of broad intelligence and an expert on the mythological legends and immensely long traditional, historical and spiritual inheritance of the Javanese. I had always wanted to go to the Boroboedoer but of course I had never had an opportunity before. I had read a great deal about it, however, and had seen books which illustrated it in detail, and I thought that, of all I had read about the story of Buddha and the diversities of Buddhism among the civilizations of South-east Asia, from India and Ceylon to China and Japan, there was nothing that had the same attraction for me as the Boroboedoer, not even the sacred city of Angkor Wat, which is held to be the most complete manifestation of Buddhism in the world.

There had always been, I felt, not only significance but a kind of poetic justice in Providence that this monument should have been rediscovered by Raffles. That he had the time to do this in his comparatively brief rule in Java, with all the work of restoring order and bringing extensive and profound reforms to the administration of Java in the midst of the Napoleonic Wars, is in itself most remarkable, and a testimony to the priorities of his spirit. When he came to write *The History of Java*, he began, typically, with the religion of the Javanese people, and within the first pages he was already drawing attention to the importance of the Boroboedoer.

Built as it was at the beginning of the ninth century under the Sailendra dynasty, which so enriched the culture and civilization of the Javanese, it would have been a good enough place to begin to describe the conscious religious manifestation of the Javanese spirit. Typically, however, Raffles went even further back to the very first whisper of the mythological axioms on which that culture was based. He began with the first of the Five Great Wars fought at the beginning of things, soon after the coming of 'the Word' to the Javanese. The first was fought over a woman, the daughter of a prince. Some 2,500 years of apparent peace followed and then there came another war, also over a woman, and also the daughter of a prince. Then a period of peace of some centuries was established. This in turn was followed by a third war, over another woman, which produced a period of another 2,500 years of peace and evolution, and so on to a final and fifth war, again over a woman, but this time a woman with a difference of immense importance for the human spirit. This woman was born not the daughter of a man but of some being of great spiritual meaning and power.

None of these wars appear to have been like wars in the history of other cultures – about territory, conquest and power in a worldly sense – but were all about women. In this there seemed to be a formidable correspondence with the way in which our own Hebraic-Greek-Roman story begins, for our own history too starts with the conscious awakening of Adam through a woman and continues in the war on the Plains of Troy and the Helen-Penelope complex of the Greek spirit that followed; and so on to the search for what is represented by the feminine in man which led to the appearance of the Mary whom Dante hails in his *Paradiso* as 'Virgin Mother, daughter of your Son'. And thus the European search has continued which the new historians, aware of the movement of the collective unconscious towards the wisdom of the feminine, have personified as the Sophia in man. For the Indonesians, and for us, the caring, feeling values of the human spirit are abidingly feminine.

It was the inheritance of all that such a cultural pattern implies in the spirit of Raffles that made him so aware of its existence in the Javanese people, and which throws into stark relief the astonishing unawareness and consequent neglect of its existence by their Dutch masters.

I think something of this sort was what I had so much in mind at the beginning, and to which I have tentatively referred, when Dr van Mook (and subsequently his colleagues) at the beginning of our occupation would recite a catalogue of all the good things the Dutch had brought to the Javanese. How could the Dutch accept, they asked, that the Javanese wished to get rid of them, as these 'rebels' said they did? What could possibly be wrong in their approach? And I had suggested to them all, improbable as it sounded, that it was because they had never had the right look in their eye when they spoke to the Javanese. I used, of course, the look in the eye as a symbol of seeing and recognizing these caring, feeling things.

For the Indonesians, in their indigenous heart of hearts, had values far more important than the materialistic Dutch catalogue of good and precious things. Far more important in the deeps of the Javanese soul was this search of the spirit, and values which were made manifest in the Boroboedoer already in the ninth century. The ordinary people of Java would mortgage everything they had to make a journey to Mecca, it is true. But they did so more out of a compulsive superstition and social fashion than from the underlying urges of their instinctive selves. Islam here and there inflamed the Indonesian spirit, as in Bantam and Atjeh, but it did not illuminate it, and their own highly illuminated culture and values remained relatively untouched. They took to Islam for much the same reasons that people bought indulgences for their salvation in the period of disintegration in the Middle Ages, as an insurance policy for life after death. They never had a real glimpse of the feminine in the Sufi interpretation of Islam, as Persia at its best did. Their abiding culture reserved itself for and through its natural self.

Another Dutch writer, Louis Couperus (whom I had recommended to Lady Mountbatten in the course of our long talk on the quarterdeck of the vanished *Cumberland*), also wrote about this clash

between the natural spirit of the Javanese and their rulers, orches-
trating it in his remarkable novel, *De Stille Kracht* (*The Hidden Force*).
There he describes at some length, yet quite explicitly, how the ordinary Javanese with 'a single penetrating glance' read the spirit of the
men who ruled over him, and saw immediately in the man he called
'*Tuan*', or 'Lord', what he regarded as the illusions of European
civilization. Though he gave his rulers the title of Lord and the
homage due to such masters, at heart he despised their values; he
would accept all demands with a smile, which his fellow Javanese
understood and which also made them smile. He never offended
against the forms of servility demanded of him and with salaams and
bows he acted as though he were the inferior, all the while 'silently
aware that he was the superior'. This was for Couperus the 'hidden
force' which, I must hasten to add, is only a partial rendering of the
full meaning of the Dutch '*stille*', which the English word 'still' means
in its reference to waters that run deep. And this precisely was the
kind of force which had now finally erupted in the Indonesians'
demand for self-determination. This is what those in command
among the British had recognized from the start, and this is why the
Dutch approach to the matter had been, and remained, so inadequate and ultimately so futile.

These and so many other similar thoughts, reinforced by all that I
had seen since I set out on this tour of Java, were in my mind as I
went towards the Boroboedoer. It was a lovely and special sort of day;
again, one of those rare days without cloud, almost as if it were
specifically designed to heighten my perceptions for the occasion.
Java, as earth so young and in the history of man already so old, had
never looked more beautiful, and deep in itself appeared to trans-
form the sense within me of being so privileged into one of being singularly blessed. And then, far from being an anti-climax – as
occasions for which one has been consciously prepared over the years
so often are – the Boroboedoer surpassed anything that I had imagined. I could see at once why it, and the inner temple of the sacred
city of Angkor Wat, were regarded as the finest and most complete
testaments of all that is best and most meaningful in the word and
the universe of Buddha.

I could write an essay on the detail not only of the bright, charged
Indonesian day but of the Boroboedoer. There was not just a world
but a whole universe fulfilled in that vision in stone of the temple, and
in the astonishing beauty, the abundance of detail and the diversity
of the carved and sculpted and sheer architectural art with which it

was expressed. One knew that this gigantic complex was not only a temple but also a tomb which contained the ashes of its architect, but ashes in a sense resurrected in all that was achieved and built upon his grave. All these details, illustrated, interpreted and expanded, are readily available to anybody interested. They were not, however, necessary for understanding that day, because perhaps the finest of the achievements of the Boroboedoer is that, massive and immense as it is in its structure, the proportions are so perfect and the spirit of it all so beautifully contained that, as it mounts stage by stage in its five terraces, up and up to the stone mandalas and the ultimate stupa on its summit, it is all gathered together and reaches to the heavens with an inevitability and a simplicity that moved me to tears.

It is from base to summit in stone the journey of the human spirit, as depicted by all the greatest artists. It encompasses all that is truly civilized in man and all that mediates so readily and so wonderfully if we would but look at it in art and cathedrals and churches and monuments that we have inherited, even in the stone cairns placed at fords and cross-roads of the human spirit by the ancient Hottentots of Southern Africa, filled with the spirit of their god-hero Heitse Eibib. It is there in the Pentateuch, the New Testament, Homer, Dante and all the other spirits that have joined in leading the search towards the still centre at the heart of the storm of being. And there it becomes a meeting between the human and the divine – a centre where something that is divine becomes human, and what is human achieves a small portion of the divine that is ultimately man's meaning and that makes him at last truly human on earth.

Indeed, the bottom terrace of the Boroboedoer is deeply rooted in this strangely symbolic earth of Java, and is an overwhelming witness to the fact that the vision of the architect is not some airy excitement of the senses, but surges up out of the area which Dante called *Inferno* and which the human being confronts in his own spirit with all the earthquake turmoil, the paradoxes and the inadequacies in the evolution of his greater awareness.

As the stupa rises from one level to the next, one's eyes circumnavigate the many beautiful carved images in stone of all the visions that lead one on and up. It is a parallel of all the imagery – however strange or foreign the cultural idiom – that confronted Dante as he emerged out of the *Inferno*, under the light of the Southern Cross, and started his journey up Mount Purgatory to *Paradiso*, which was to lead him to the discovery of the 'love that moves the sun and all the other stars'.

These emotions, evoked in me after all that I had experienced in Java, seemed, as the day went on, more and more to come together in the same way as these many diversities came together in the building, and to fill me with a strange kind of gratitude for what had happened to me in the past five years. It was a feeling without past record or future fears, and one I knew would never leave me again. This conclusion was the equivalent of what one wrote always at the end of one's solutions to the theorems of Euclid and Pythagoras with a schoolboy hand: QED. Something had not only been truly proved by what was demonstrated in the Boroboedoer but was also finally reiterated by the earth around me.

Raffles described it in his moment of rediscovery as overgrown earth wherever one walked and looked, rich with meaningful fragments of sacred Hindu ruins. It was as if to all inspired spirits, and particularly architects, the earth itself where the Boroboedoer stood was sacred and deeply still and calm at the centre of the volcanoes, earthquakes and lava that raged deep underneath its surface. It was, as Raffles's descriptions imply, so littered with these ruins of sacred Hindu imperatives that both the Hindu and the Buddhist in Javanese man had met there and were in harmony, at rest and at one, with none of the rivalry which elsewhere, even in India, set the Hindu and the Buddhist at one another's throats.

To complete this imagery of the earth as a centre between the opposites of life there was at one end of the plain the volcano of Merapi, the fire mountain. Outwardly no mountain could have been more beautiful and more symmetrical, and its sublime stature raised it over the plain. It looked as perfect as the incomparable Fuji-san of the Japanese, innocent and resolved as if in a dream of sleep. Alone and unique, even among the volcanoes of Java, it would erupt not with lava but with enormous balls of gas, heavier than air and aflame with temperatures not known on earth, and these balls of gas would go bouncing down those perfect slopes and roll for miles, destroying hamlets and villages and, of course, killing all in their way.

And then almost opposite it, on the more remote side above the clear young blue-pencil outline of the lower hills, the earth ascended to the mountain range of central Java, dominated by the peak called Ardjuno, the name the Javanese still use for the Hindu god who so often became man in Krishna.

This, even in hindsight, does not surprise me because the earth itself partakes profoundly of the symbolism which is at the heart and meaning of all life and matter. All the landscape painters, no matter whether of Europe, China or Japan, have extracted from the earth they want to paint the pattern in it that is symbolic and corresponds to a symbolic pattern they have within themselves, and through their conscious union they have achieved the immense impact they have had on the spirit of man. The historian Burckhardt, in his history of the Renaissance, stresses how the Latin spirit was quickened with the first stirrings of the Renaissance by its discovery of the landscape as a subject for painting and poetry. In Britain it was most evident in Turner, perhaps the greatest English painter of all, who started by imposing on the landscape the superbly drawn and formally painted classical compositions of things that were no longer to be discerned on land or sea, but then gradually reached, through his art, an incomparable marriage of the symbol without to that within.

There is so much more that I could say about that day, perhaps one of the most important days of all the years I had in Indonesia. At the end, with the sun going down into those hills and the shadows falling, I left the scene with a deep emotion of finality, as sad as it was grateful, because the experience was both a first and a last for me.

Strange, too, was that when we returned to the city we attended a gathering of some of the citizens of the interior of Java, Indonesian intellectuals and people of all sorts and conditions, not only of pure Javanese but also of mixed European blood. One of the first people I was introduced to turned out to be a member of the family which had produced the writer I have often quoted who wrote under the pen-name *Multatuli*, meaning 'I have suffered much', whose book about Java had so influenced me as a boy. The moment I discovered this, of course, we talked about literature and I also mentioned Couperus to him, at which he brightened and said that Couperus had this extraordinary insight into the Javanese character and culture because he himself had Javanese blood. This, if it were true, became all the more meaningful to me because Couperus also wrote what I think is one of the most important European novels, one of the very first truly illuminating psychological novels, not filled with conscious psychological insights but with a profound anticipation of what modern psychology is about, through the character of his compulsively neurotic, beautiful and privileged young heroine, a European woman called Eline Vere. I have never understood why so many of Couperus's books are translated into English when as far as I know *Eline Vere* is not, to our impoverishment; because the destructive neurosis of Eline Vere is at heart a symbol of the neurosis we in the West suffer from in our deepest soul, more sick by the day than we will admit. But, more pertinent to this moment in my life, it was proof of how the feminine in the Indonesian and the feminine in the European in symbols, and therefore in fact and meaning to come, were married in the mind and single person of the inspired European personality of Couperus.

There was proof too for me in my last evening, whose end concluded with a wonderful 36-hour performance of a gamelan orchestra and two sessions watching a *wayang* play, the popular Indonesian theatre that had not yet been overtaken by European cinema. To this day I remember those attentive faces, in the glow cast by lamps, concentrating on the movement of the shadows thrown by the puppet actors from behind the screen. My first reaction was an immediate association with the allegorical metaphor with which Plato confronted Socrates – human beings, shackled deep in their caves with their backs to their own fire, looking out at the mouth of the cave where a burning bright light of day casts the shadows of reality outside on to the walls of the cave. Of course I was not in danger of overdoing this highly evolved metaphor but there was enough in the association to know that without doubt, despite all the traffic and travel to the Bedouin city of Mecca, the Indonesians were still drawing on a region in themselves where Plato himself found the source which started him on his dialogue with Socrates.

This dynamic memory of Indonesia's Hindu past, which was so dramatically expressed in the landscape where the mountains carried the names of Hindu gods like that of the greatest, Ardjuno, was also reflected in the theatre in which I joined those tensely-watching Javanese faces. It was their version of perhaps the greatest mythological love story ever told, the *Ramayana*, where the reincarnation of the deity as Krishna is so movingly anticipated in the story of Rama, his Sita, the monkey god and the squirrel, and their victory over the evil king of Ceylon.

I was joined as much to that moment in Java as I was to moments in my youth when I learned from Indian friends in Port Natal of the sacred books and mythology of India, and heard on a scratchy gramophone Rama's lament. Strange as the idiom of Indian music was to me, this lament nonetheless echoed a chord deep within myself, and I grieved with Rama as he sat on the rock furthest out to sea at the pointed end of the peninsula of the sub-continent of India nearest to Ceylon, where the evil king had imprisoned his beloved Sita. I remember vividly the moment when the god-hero himself feels abandoned and utterly alone, and this aloneness so communicates itself to the natural world around him that a squirrel comes as its ambassador to sit beside him and commiserate with him. As a result the god is stirred, and strokes the back of the squirrel and, in stroking it, the course of his fingers is made visible on either side of the squirrel's spine. That is why the Indian squirrel to this day has white lines along his back, to remind everyone of this show of compassion in the generous little animal heart over the loss and desolation in the god himself.

So, all in all, when the time came and I had to face going back to Batavia, I felt like an astronaut who, after weeks in space exposed to the darkness and the mere light of stars in the expanding universe, must turn his face to where the earth for so long has glowed like a jewel of amber, and see it go pedestrian under his feet.

CHAPTER TWELVE

End in Beginning

I ARRIVED BACK in Batavia in the late afternoon and went straight to
my office to see what awaited me. I found Gilbert MacKereth still at
work and, as I walked into his office and he looked up and saw me,
it seemed that, for a trifle of a moment, I appeared a stranger to him.
And then, of course, he was his immediate warm and welcoming self.
He stopped work at once and invited me to spend the evening with
Muriel and himself. Those two dear people knew instinctively, I
suspect, that I still needed time to emerge emotionally from wherever
I had been, and could do so best in their company.

And I remember later, as I said goodnight, how Muriel came over
and kissed me on both cheeks, almost as if it was meant to be both a
hail and a farewell, and said in her lovely, caring voice: 'It's good to
have you back.'

I did not know the meaning of the fragile impediment that had
preceded Gilbert MacKereth's welcome, or of the sense of delicate
ambivalence in Muriel's goodnight, until several years later. They
then told me that one of the reasons they were so happy to see me
back was that a look which they feared had become an abiding look
on my face and a something else in my person when I was in relative
repose, which had distressed them both deeply because it suggested
a deep hurt of the past still alive in me, had utterly gone. Typically,
they had recognized this resolution in myself before I was totally
aware of it.

Yet there was something else to explain what had happened so
subtly between us that evening. Next morning MacKereth told me

that in my absence he had been informed by the Foreign Office that he was being recalled as soon as he could wind up the British occupation and when he felt that the valid contribution of his own presence in Batavia was no longer needed. He said that of course his appointment had always been a special and not a permanent one, and he had to do as his masters in the Foreign Office ordered, but he was greatly concerned about me. What did I truly feel about his going? Did I not perhaps feel that the time had come when I myself should go? I had done, he said, far more than the call of duty had demanded of me. In fact, he said (and I remember his words so clearly because they were to be a great comfort to me in the days to come) I had done freely, in a most impressive way, a great service to Britain and I had more than earned the right to go whenever I felt I had to. He felt this so strongly that he was prepared, if I wished, to recommend that the Foreign Office take up the matter with the War Office and arrange for me to go at once.

He himself would hate me to go. He was certain he could not do what he still had to do half so well if I went, yet he felt that he, let alone our remote masters had no right to expect more of me.

I was very moved by his concern and by the way in which he spoke to me, but I told him I would never have considered leaving him alone at the end of his official mission. I would not do so simply because of the regard I had for him and Muriel and the immense importance of our friendship to me. In my diminished wartime physical state I knew that I could not have come through in the way I had done without their immense understanding and the extraordinary coincidence of our tastes and interests. But whatever it was that made me stay on in Java was not yet satisfied that I had accomplished what it had inspired me to do.

In the interior I had had a chance to think about all that had happened since the Japanese surrender. In those calm transcendent days in that lovely country I had recognized more than ever that we were in great danger from a totally unlived history at work in the spirit of the Dutch. There had been that 'moment of innocence' after the war, which I had encountered in Holland, a moment of freedom from the past in the sense of having to begin again. It had been expressed for me in the liberal Schermerhorn government, and it was by instinct and nature the Holland that had never been interested in, nor had identified closely with, colonial affairs.

But the Linggadjati agreement had not yet been ratified. The Dutch forces were still being built up in Indonesia, and there had always been – as Gilbert and I knew to our cost – a keen school of thought among the Indonesians and close watchers of the Indonesian scene that the Dutch had a secret agenda of their own and were just using this appearance of honourable negotiations with the Indonesians to hide their intention of imposing their will on Indonesia by force. They believed that the Dutch had never had any other solution than the unconditional abdication of all nationalist demands, dressed with a few cosmetic concessions, and that they would make certain that they were ultimately in complete military and civilian control of Indonesia. And so the time in which the other, liberal Holland might assert itself was running out fast.

In a sense time was also running out for the Indonesians. One of the things that had surprised me most in the interior was the sense of order, and the control which the Sjahrir government had acquired during the period in which we had held the fort. There seemed a readiness to give the new form of leadership which Sjahrir and his supporters represented a proper chance. But even they, if they did not in the end agree some sort of settlement with the Dutch which satisfied this great reawakening of the Indonesian peoples, would not remain in power for long. Potentially there were forces of unlived history at work in the peoples of Indonesia too, after some three centuries of suppression, which would come out by fair means or foul. At the moment there was a chance that they would come out by fair means, but that depended on a quick response now from the Dutch. If, however, the Dutch failed to respond then I was sure that the violence in the Indonesians that had exploded at the time of the Japanese surrender would recur relentlessly, and on an increasing scale. The Dutch, I was certain, would not be able to suppress it by force. They might try but they would not succeed and I did not think that the world would allow them to succeed. The new United Nations, the Americans and, ultimately, the British would not condone a backdoor reconquest of a colonial kind.

The nature of my own contribution to MacKereth's heroic effort to alert London to what was urgently needed in Dutch policy towards Indonesia now changed somewhat. I had found that writing my report had reawakened the long-suppressed writer in me. Writing, after all, was my main vocation, and so now I continued to get up earlier than I had usually done and wrote special memos for MacKereth on things which had matured within my imagination in the night. I found that the special interest I had developed in the Far East and South-east Asia through my confrontation with the awakening Japan in 1926 had given me insights and perceptions that enabled me to put the situation in Indonesia into its legitimate context within the world. MacKereth said he found that extra dimension of great help.

I wrote too, in that hour, letters to all sorts of people who could be of help in promoting what we were trying to do in Indonesia. I wrote at length to Christie, to the Admiral, and to the various people in high positions with whom I had had contact and discussions in Singapore and at other conferences in the Far East, and kept them informed of what we were doing. I thought that I could perhaps start a kind of whispering campaign. I had great faith in whispering campaigns. I had seen how in villages it was the most powerful weapon that the village could use to defeat those that threatened it. And this village that was Indonesia, in the tumultuous and impetuous new world that was emerging, needed all the whispering forces that could be summoned.

One country above all I thought it important to keep fully informed, and that, as MacKereth agreed, was Australia. The war had been a rude awakening for the Australians. Hitherto preoccupied with Britain and Europe, they now became aware of the need to reappraise their situation in the Pacific and, through the Pacific, the world. Part of this awakening had been the discovery that their neighbour, the Dutch empire, which stretched from Sumatra to New Guinea, was not the idyllic empire they had taken it to be. The Australians had found, for instance, that in liberating the islands between Australia and Java from the Japanese, they were also liberating many hundreds of Indonesian political exiles who, like Soekarno and Hatta, had been banished to these islands without trial merely because the Dutch Governor-General of Java had ruled that it was in the public interest to silence them and keep them out of sight.

Already in the course of the British occupation the Australians had sent a senior judge of the Australian Federal Court of Arbitration on an exploratory mission to Indonesia. His name was Richard Clarence Kirby and he was a remarkable person in every way and most unusual for someone in so exalted a legal position. He had a great capacity for looking at the totality of things and appeared to me to have no inclination to make points in life. I developed a firm friendship with him and frequently, with MacKereth's consent, sent him copies of the special memos I had written. As a result Judge Kirby was unusually well informed on the subject of Indonesia; and in 1948, during the truce imposed by the United Nations on the war in Java (which had broken out within weeks of my departure and which the Dutch euphemistically called a 'police action'), he became a member of the Australian mission sent to promote Australian policy in Indonesia.

MacKereth and I were aware that there was less and less to be accomplished in Indonesia through the Dutch government in Batavia. Gilbert in particular felt that, in this regard, we still had to reinforce as much as possible what Dr van Mook professed to be doing. The fact that Dr van Mook was still there as Governor-General in Indonesia was, in itself, something not only to his credit but potentially vital for the solution still in suspense. The temptation for van Mook to resign, as he had announced so often he would, had been tremendous, and the pressures to which he was subjected both in The Hague and in Indonesia were unimaginable.

I believed that MacKereth's emphasis on the need to support Dr van Mook was the correct one. We had no other choice, as the Dutch government of the day had no one else with whom to replace him. Yet I had reservations, and a growing feeling that this approach, inevitable as it was, could not work. Gradually I came to doubt whether Dr van Mook himself, in his heart of hearts, still believed that agreement was possible, and to wonder whether he was not slowly becoming reconciled, as many people with hindsight believed he must have been, to the suppression of the Indonesian nationalist movement by force and the establishment of full control over greater Indonesia, as had started to happen in the outer islands.

As a result of all our work, the day for MacKereth's departure approached with incredible swiftness. Then, just a few days before he left, a new member of what was to be a regular consulate-general in Batavia arrived as Passport Officer. One of the first things he did was to see MacKereth, and an embarrassed MacKereth then came to me and said that the Passport Officer had been instructed to have a special conversation with me. He begged me not to take it amiss and said it was the sort of thing that happened to everyone in the course of their foreign service.

Accordingly the Passport Officer and I had a meeting and it was not long before I realized that he was subjecting me to a screening. He had an abnormal interest in what might be my political convictions and background. It was not difficult to deal with that sort of probing, but it depressed me more than almost anything that had happened to me in Java. In these last weeks with MacKereth the preposterous

Dutch campaign against me had not diminished and I had learned to live with it. But the fact that the Foreign Office, for whom I had done work of such importance for so long, should feel the need to have me screened was hard to bear. I went back to my mess in low spirits. But then Sybil came to me with a letter from Group Captain Nichols, written towards the end of March 1947. In it he summed up what the prisoners had felt after their homecoming, and his own experience of more than a year in so-called peacetime Britain.

The letter began with an account of an RAF officer whom he had found a major problem in prison, and who was still proving something of a problem in peace. The officer, he wrote, 'was a bit like Saul of Tarsus. Through his association with you he saw a great light upon the way, which took him completely by surprise. When he came home it went out! But he has never forgotten it and it changed him – for the better – quite considerably.'

And from the particular the letter went on to the general:

We had some splendid people with us in the bag, didn't we? By and large, a nicer crowd of chaps it would be hard to find. They compare very favourably indeed with those who remained outside. I have come to the conclusion that they became like that in prison, and that is why we liked them so much more at the end than at the beginning.

We were quite different from people who had not been POW, and different from all other POWs. The POWs ex Germany and Italy were most of them unbalanced, talking broken English, suffering from nervous disorders, hitting the booze, and letting themselves go. The other POWs, ex Far East, were generally in a bad state physically, mad keen to have a good time, and inclined to overtax their strength. Large numbers of them, after a first burst of freedom, returned to the rehabilitation centres and hospitals for long periods of care and rest!

We chaps from Java upset all calculations. For one thing, we seemed quite well, which rather snubbed the elaborate organisation of well-wishers who were so keen to look after us. Instead of being wild mentally and uncontrolled, we were frightfully controlled and quiet, tightly in hand, and independent. Instead of bursting into tears on the bosom of our families, and wanting to be fussed over, we were inclined to regard the people at home as the ones in need of succour and guidance, and to be rather critical, and not very impressed with their morale and general behaviour. To them, we appeared constipated, sanctimonious, ceremonious, and humourless. And the peculiar understanding we had with each other drove them wild.

Altogether we were a great puzzle to everyone, and they weren't comfortable with us, and didn't like us very much.

He then went on at some length to say how people thought we were like a lot of little Jesus Christs; then he asked if all this were news to me. 'Because, of course,' he wrote, 'it was caused very largely by the extraordinarily high morale achieved in our camps, for which you were 80% responsible.'

His letter instantly took me back to all we had endured and found in our three and a half years of imprisonment, and the Passport Officer and the antics and villainies of the Dutch fell from me as if totally unreal. What is more, the healing effect of this letter lasted to the end of my days in Indonesia. As I finished reading it I had in my mind one of my favourite characters in Dickens, Mr Toots, the great fool in *Dombey and Son*, and his remark in the face of all frustrations and disappointments: 'It is of no consequence.' And then I went straight to my piano and began to play, starting with *Finlandia*. I went on playing, finishing with a Chopin Nocturne which started – as Chopin often does – calmly and easily, but then suddenly got (as I put it in my mind) too 'trilly' for my prison-bound fingers. I stopped playing, shut the piano with a bang, and went to bed.

The parting with Gilbert and Muriel was for me an undiluted misery. They had decided, after all they had endured in Java, to give themselves a break and go back by sea, and I went to see them off at the harbour. Of all the ways of saying farewell to people who are about to leave one on a journey which may take them out of one's life for good, I do not know any that can express the emotions that go with those occasions more deeply and symbolically than saying goodbye to people waving handkerchiefs from the rails of a ship going out to sea. No doubt those waving also feel it very deeply, but they have the immunity that a real voyage at sea confers on the traveller that those who are left on land to continue their humdrum daily life do not possess, and which is so vividly summed up in a proverb that my French great-grandmother would quote: '*Partir c'est mourir un peu*'.

I stood watching the ship take on the immensity of the sky over the ocean, looking like a setting devised by the hand of Fate itself.

The weeks that followed were made more dismal by the change which seemed subtly to come over 'Dul. He had been so staunch in his stand that neither the Dutch nor the Indonesians should resort to violence, and MacKereth and I could never have done what we did without his unwavering support. Yet there were signs now that the strain of being one of the few real influences at the Palace, and on the Dutch, was beginning to tell upon him. Even before the MacKereths left there was a certain friction developing between him and Sri. She bitterly resented the fact that the majority of his own countrymen seemed to regard him as nothing but a Dutch stooge. She herself was increasingly dependent for companionship on those in the Palace circles and spent a great deal of time there, and now a change of mood came over her whenever she heard 'Dul and me discussing the situation in Indonesia.

Then one evening I was resting in a side room off the main room in my mess when I heard Sri and 'Dul come home. Before entering the house, they sat on the wall of the veranda outside, Sri talking to 'Dul in Dutch. The fact that they spoke in Dutch seemed somewhat ominous because they only did that when they did not want to be understood by any of the staff inside, who all spoke only Javanese. Sri concluded with what almost sounded like a concealed ultimatum, that 'Dul must now see how the Dutch had been more than patient with the Indonesians and that it was clear that the Indonesians would not learn the decent way but would have to be, as she put it, 'clobbered' into seeing reason. Unless he saw that, she could not bear to think of the consequences for them both.

'Dul listened and responded quietly, as if to contain what was extreme in her language. At the end he did not reply immediately but then, in a voice which seemed to come from very far away, said: 'I fear, Sri, that after all you are right. We have no other course any longer.'

It was a voice that seemed very old and very tired, the voice of a spirit overcome with fatigue not of the body but of the soul. I believe that Sri too was almost overcome by what she had done. Immediately her tone changed and became all that was maternal in her and part of her normal caring and supportive self, as if possessed of some doubt over this reversal of the feminine values which she had in abundance. For instead of taking the drawn *kris* – the Indonesian dagger – from her husband and putting it back in its sheath, as the ancient cultural tradition of Java demanded, she had, as it were, drawn it from its sheath and handed it to her husband to use.

I lay awake for hours realizing what a frontier had been crossed in that moment, not only in 'Dul but in all of us. Finally I fell asleep, on a couch by the door of my front room which was also my study. I could not have been asleep long when a sharp mechanical 'Click!' made me sit up with a start. I always slept with my pistol beside me and by reflex I grasped it now. Then I saw in the window the blurred shape of a man climbing out. As I called out he dropped down over the wall. In the first glimmer of morning light I could see the outline of my typewriter, which had produced the sound that had awakened me when it was deposited on the window sill. I ran outside and just saw his slight, rather tattered shape darting out of the gate and disappearing down the street.

The timing of this attempt to deprive me of the typewriter on which I had typed all those urgent dispatches and signals and reports for so long, with the impact of what I had overheard the night before still fresh in my mind, seemed to me a significant omen that the time might have come for me to go.

A few days later there was another sign. Sjahrir unexpectedly asked me to see him one afternoon, when Batavia tends to have a kind of siesta atmosphere. I was talking with him in the front room of his house when – in one of those trembling silences of a Javanese afternoon charged with incipient thunder – we heard the unmistakable noise of a military truck coming down the street at great speed. It pulled up sharply, its brakes screaming. As I heard a scramble of men and the sound of feet coming through the gate, I jumped up and said to Sjahrir: 'You stay there. I'll see what it is.'

I saw what looked like a section of Ambonese infantry coming fast towards the house. I went instantly to the edge of the veranda and called out sharply: 'What are you doing here without an officer? You know it is forbidden!' They looked amazed because although I wore a British uniform I had spoken in Dutch.

The warrant officer who was at the head of the group stopped and looked bewildered. I said: 'Go back and fetch an officer and bring him to me immediately.' He hesitated for a moment, and I said: 'If you do not go immediately I'll report you myself on the telephone to your general.' With that, they all rather sheepishly turned about, got back into their truck and drove away as fast as they had come, and we did not see them again.

I do not want to make too much of this incident, but it had all the elements of something extremely serious considering that Kenneth Pope, my staff captain, had stopped a group of Ambonese from shooting Sjahrir some time before. It may be that I had prevented a repeat of that performance.

The impact of this disturbing incident did not finish with that afternoon. It went on for days because it seemed to have become part of a process which had been sparked off by my overhearing the conversation between 'Dul and Sri. The tendency I had after Gilbert and Muriel had gone to feel desperately alone, if not abandoned, and helpless to exercise some kind of active control over events now that our army had withdrawn, was greatly increased by 'Dul's failing in all that he and I had fought so hard for over the preceding eighteen months. It added not only to the aloneness but to a sense of vulnerability, as if my last support had been knocked from under me.

All I learned in the next few days from my many sources of intelligence seemed to suggest the worst. For instance, our Passport Officer, who was also our security officer, came to ask me if I knew anything about strange rumours circulating amongst the Dutch concerning something serious that was due to happen towards the end of June, or in July. I knew of the extraordinary inability of the Dutch to keep anything absolutely secret, and I had no doubt what these rumours meant. I just thanked him and said I would be most grateful if he could let me know if he heard anything more because I too had been wondering what was causing these rumours.

Gradually I had to accept that the thing I had always feared was about to happen: the Dutch were planning to reassert themselves in Indonesia by force. I did not of course disclose to anyone how I had come to my conclusion and I continued to take 'Dul totally into my confidence, as before. I took no trouble to pass on information to Gilbert MacKereth's successor but I went more frequently to report to my General in Singapore. He was Neil Ritchie, whom I had last seen at El Agheila on the Mediterranean coast in December 1941. He and his Chief of Staff, Dixie Redman, a rifleman in the First World War with a distinguished career as a brigadier in the Second, had become real friends of mine and I found that by far the best means of conveying my intelligence was to get Dixie Redman to include it in his dispatches to the War Office in London where I was certain it would be passed on to the right quarters in the British government.

I spent more time than ever before with the friends I had made among the Indonesians. My circle of Indonesian friends by now had gone far beyond the political leaders with whom I had dealt for more than a year, and included all sorts of young intellectuals who were among the most ardent of Sjahrir's supporters, men of prominent Indonesian families like the Boediardjos, and in particular Ali Boediardjo and his sisters. Although they had had access to a radio all through the war, unlike the internees and prisoners, they were surprisingly ill-informed about what had happened outside Indonesia and the south-east Pacific. I told them all I knew about the new sort of world that was coming into being and about the new United Nations, so that they realized there was something more effective than the old League of Nations to turn to if ever violence was used against them in Indonesia.

I also spoke to them about the emerging Australia, using it as an example of how it was possible for a country to pass through all the phases of evolution of empire, from penal colonies to protectorates, to crown colonies, and ultimately to dominion, and empire transformed into commonwealth. I described the Australians with whom I had come in contact since 1946, and in particular recommended Richard Clarence Kirby, as I had already recommended them to him.

In this manner I think I did perhaps some of the most valuable work of the whole of my time since the Japanese capitulation. Though all I had done since was work of immense tactical importance and immediacy, somehow I managed, in the last weeks, to do something of lasting value, I felt, for the future of the human spirit in Indonesia.

There were, of course, moments when I wished that 'Dul would resign, and I came very near to begging him to do so. It seemed to me that if he and Dr van Mook, both native Indonesians and, as far as I was concerned, the outstanding personalities on the scene, resigned, it would so shake even the Dutch that they might break out of what amounted to a sleep of history and come to reappraise themselves in a truly contemporary way. But, alas, I realized that as far as the Palace was concerned it would be a futile exercise to suggest it and that it would merely confirm the view of me already held there; and if I tried to add to the argument that was raging night and day in 'Dul I would be abusing love and friendship. The history of our collaboration and our friendship would be by far the most eloquent advocate. If anything could help at that moment, it was the trust and the affection that nothing could shake in a threatening world.

Finally there came a morning when I realized that it was indeed time for me to go and that if I stayed any longer I would diminish rather than add to what I had helped to create in Java. Accordingly, on one of my regular visits to Singapore, I informed Neil Ritchie and Dixie Redman that I feared the worst and could almost give them the week, if not the day, when the Dutch would present the Indonesians with an ultimatum which they could not accept and which would inevitably lead to war. I told them also that I would like to be relieved of my post immediately and thought it was in everyone's interests that I remove myself from the scene. I had already on previous occasions told them I would not be staying on indefinitely and had asked them to alert the Foreign Office and get them to think about a replacement for me. Nonetheless they both seemed surprised and, in the General's case, also somewhat shocked: 'But if something so grave is going to happen we shall need you more than ever. We can't let you go.'

I explained that I would be the last person who could be of any use to them if it came to a war in Indonesia. They would want an experienced senior British officer whose impartiality could not be questioned by Dutch or Indonesians. The sooner I could go the better, and therefore I asked if he could please give the matter the utmost priority.

The General turned to Dixie Redman and said: 'Well, I could grant him leave almost at once on compassionate grounds.'

'Sir, please, you cannot do that!' I protested.

'But why not?'

'Because it would not be true. You know as far as I am concerned, that is not the reason.'

Dixie Redman exclaimed: 'Compassionate grounds my foot, sir! If anybody has earned the right to go, he has!'

It was not until the end of May that the all-clear came: I could leave my post and a senior officer would soon be on his way to take my place.

In those last days I had some of my most meaningful meetings with the Indonesian leaders. At first they tried to get me to stay on and said that it was in the interests of the Dutch, themselves and the British that I should do so, but I said that the real power bases in this matter had moved from Indonesia to The Hague and London. In the end Sjahrir assembled all the original Indonesian leaders who had been at my first meeting with them in Batavia, with the exception of one. Significantly, he was the leader of what had become a militant and potentially dangerous fundamentalist youth movement and the most critical and difficult of Sjahrir's colleagues. We had a five-hour meeting and went through an immense reappraisal of what had been done, what could still be done, and what could be done if the worst came to the worst.

The meeting ended with Sjahrir saying to me that, if I had to go, they would all like to give me a special present as a sign of their gratitude and as something to be remembered by. I said that the relationship which had evolved between us all had been gift enough. Besides, it was an absolute rule of the British services that we could not receive presents. And then Amir Sjarifoeddin looked from one to the other with an expression on his face that I knew so well and never failed to warm to: 'Surely you would not mind if perhaps we gave you something like a book to remember us by?'

I said there was nothing I would like better than a book from them.

Some days later Abdul Ghani and Sjarifoeddin came to see me. Sjarifoeddin carried a substantial roll of ancient batik manufactured by the Sultan of Djokja's own craftsmen, with a note from Soekarno saying, among other things, that he felt he had the right, as someone who loved his mother as much as I loved mine, to send my mother on behalf of his mother a roll of authentic batik, in gratitude for lending her son for so long to Indonesia.

Abdul Ghani himself then produced two volumes. They were first editions of Stamford Raffles's *History of Java*, personally inscribed by him on behalf of the others. I could not have had anything I appreciated more than those two presents. When they had gone I opened the Stamford Raffles history and showed it to Sybil, and I read out to her the first few lines:

> As it is possible that, in the many severe strictures passed, in the course of this work, upon the Dutch Administration in Java, some of the observations may, for want of a careful restriction in the words employed, appear to extend to the Dutch nation and character generally, I think it proper explicitly to declare, that such observations are intended exclusively to apply to the Colonial Government and its Officers. The orders of the Dutch Government in Holland to the Authorities at Batavia, as far as my information extends, breathe a spirit of liberality and benevolence; and I have reason to believe, that the tyranny and rapacity of its colonial officers, created no less indignation in Holland than in other countries of Europe.

I stopped there because suddenly I heard Sybil beginning to cry. I tried to comfort her, not knowing what was wrong. Finally she wiped the tears away and declared how she resented all the many unfairnesses that had been heaped on me.

'It's so awful!' she cried. 'Don't people ever learn, and know how to change properly? Raffles wrote that more than a hundred years ago, and he is saying exactly the same things about the Dutch and the Indonesians as you have been saying and we have all been trying to put right. I can't bear it!' and she started to cry again.

I believe that this present of these two peerless books of history was a recognition of the fact that the British army of occupation had briefly brought to their minds all that Great Britain had given them in those years, more than a century ago, when Raffles reformed the colonial services of Java and gave them an act of recognition and affection that they had never received from any other foreign power before or since.

And then, hardest of all, I spoke to 'Dul about my leaving. He knew that it was going to happen and took it very calmly, simply saying that he felt it was right for me to go, and that I could do far more for them all in London than I now could in Java. I was aware, too, that in a sense he was deeply relieved that I would go before whatever was going to happen happened. Our meeting ended with him asking: 'When would you like me to arrange for you to say goodbye to Dr van Mook?' When I said I had no intention of saying goodbye to him because it seemed utterly unwanted and irrelevant he insisted that I should do so. I could see it was a profound part of his concept of good manners, crucial at times of crisis and potential chaos. He concluded his protests with a phrase he had often used in the past when something was demanded of us both, saying: 'It is for the honour of the house!' – the house being my mess. As a result, because he wanted it so badly, I put all my own considerations aside and, at eleven o'clock on a cloudless Indonesian morning, I went to bid Dr van Mook a formal farewell.

I was expected, and was shown almost immediately into the Governor's library. Dr van Mook did not return my 'Good morning, sir,' but just said: 'Drink?'

When I replied with a polite, 'No, thank you', still without a word he turned his back on me, went to a cupboard, opened it and filled a large cut-glass tumbler full of gin and drank it down like water. After the last gulp he called again over his shoulder: 'Drink?'

Again I replied with a 'No, thank you', marvelling at the unfailing talent of Fate for inflicting elements of farce as relief to its predetermined design.

Thereupon he filled another glass, drank it down, filled a third, turned and came to face me across his desk, uttering a peremptory command and not an invitation: 'Sit!'

I declined, saying, 'I won't stay. I have just come to say goodbye. I am very sorry that I should have to leave you like this.'

He said nothing and merely began sipping his gin, looking somewhere above my head. So I just uttered 'Goodbye', turned about, and made my way out of the room and out of the Palace into the sun, as if I had gone from the dark night not only of the imperial spirit but also of whatever soul Dr van Mook still had in himself – and I could have wept.

I could also have wept for 'Dul when I saw him anxiously waiting in my mess for my return. He asked me how my visit had gone and I told him, surprised by what I found was a note of near despair in my voice: 'It was a proper formal farewell, 'Dul, and I hope you'll feel that the honour of the house has now been satisfied.'

From that moment onwards in the time that was left me, the memory of the old 'Dul was still so powerful that at odd moments, when one of the old phrases or observations fell from his lips, I could not help hoping he might still snap out of it and be his whole self. But alas, it was not to happen.

Only some weeks before that fatal conversation, 'Dul had at my instigation written a summing-up for the Dutch, in which he reasserted the importance of avoiding any form of further conflict. This had ended with a remarkable paragraph in which he told the Dutch that it would be far better if necessary to let the Indonesians go, because better a stranger who was a friend than a lot of rebellious and sullen subjects. But that was the end of it, and I felt even more unhappy for 'Dul because the distance between himself and his countrymen was increasing, and I would not be there to bridge it for him through Sjahrir and my other friends.

That distance was almost lethally increased when the Dutch imposed what to me was the ultimate depravity on him, shamelessly using him for a transparent piece of window-dressing. To prove to the world how much the Indonesians were part of the Dutch plan for the future, van Mook persuaded the Dutch to appoint 'Dul Acting Governor-General of Indonesia. The 'Dul I had known would never have accepted the appointment. He would have said something to the effect of: 'Gentlemen, I will help you all I can because I believe it is in the interests of us all, not least the interests of my countrymen, which I have most at heart. But I cannot ever rule my country on your behalf and prescription.'

But he accepted, and therefore when the time came for the Dutch to yield to the Indonesian demands for independence, 'Dul had to withdraw because his life would no longer have been safe in the new Indonesia. He then endured years of what was at heart exile in Europe. I have often thought that it was as a result of such an outcome that Sri died at a comparatively young age soon afterwards. I was to see 'Dul in London, and he no doubt contributed a great deal to the future relationship between Holland and Indonesia, but it was many years before he could set foot again safely in a country he loved before all else and for which he had, despite this loss of heart, done so much. His country owes him a great deal and ultimately has nothing to forgive because the damage that was done was not to them but to 'Dul himself and no one else.

On the afternoon of the day before I left Batavia, I took myself in my jeep to the far edge of the perimeter which the Dutch had enlarged around the capital. And there, on the edge of the marshes, I found a quiet place to draw up and to look once more at the interior and those blue, blue hills, and the unblurred blue-pencil line where they drew themselves up to their full height. In front of me there were those wonderful paddy fields with the last of the women, in their wide-brimmed hats, going home to their hamlets and villages. And in the water in which they had planted, tended and harvested the miracle of rice all together in one all-embracing moment, the clouds were reflected as they too built up to their daily rehearsal of their own version of a *Götterdämmerung*, a twilight of all the gods from the island's aboriginal past, of the *Bhagavadgita*, of the *Mahabharata*, the *Ramayana*, the Boroboedoer of the Buddha, and all the mystery of the earth combined in a new phase of creation itself.

I sat there for some hours, not thinking about the past or analysing the years of war behind me and the five and a half years since my arrival in Java. I just sat there and let something happen between me and the day as it passed so dramatically into night. All my journey, without definition or concept, was present with me there, from my first view of Krakatoa with a feather of smoke in its crooked hat as usual; my look across the Sunda Strait, on to Bandoeng; and Lembang, clinging to the flanks of the sleeping Tangkoeboehan-Praauw, 'the Ship Turned Upside Down'; and from there, where I had been on so many reconnaissances, over the island of Java itself, to Soekaboemi, 'the Desired Earth', clinging to the slopes of the twin peaks of the Raja and Goenoeng Gedeh; and then south to Palem Boehan Ratoe, the 'Dropping Anchor Bay' of the Malays and the 'Wine Purchase Bay' of the Dutch; on to Tjikotok and its little mine of ancient gold where Paul Vogt walked out of the jungle at night and into my life as if predestined; to Lebaksembada, 'the Valley That Was Well Made'; and Djaja Sempoer, 'the Mountain of the Arrow', where the Japanese had finally captured me. And so on and back at last to the citadel, the Krak des Chevaliers that the mountain of Malabar had become for me, on to Ardjuno, Merapi 'the fire mountain', and the centre of it all, in the Boroboedoer.

And in the process it was as if I was looking with a strange feeling of finality on what had become native country, as if I had had a kind of second birth there and, with the two births behind me, was being sent to make my way into a new world for the first time. Yet there was also an extraordinary feeling, that I have experienced on other occasions too, a special nostalgia which was a kind of homesickness, a real sickness for the future, as if I had been there before.

All these feelings somehow came together. I did not dare to interrupt them; I just sat and sat and looked, until the last of the dragonflies that provided the diamond glitter of those days withdrew as the long level light vanished, and the fireflies, all lamp-lit, and the glowworms, phosphorescent as if fresh out of the sea of darkness, took over. I heard the first of the bamboo gongs of the watchers of the night in every hamlet, and I withdrew quietly and gently as from a candlelit cathedral. I recalled Walter de la Mare, so special a poet to me, and his exhortation to us in our brief and brittle lives to 'Look on all things lovely always as if for the last time' – and I could add, as I had in this eucharist with earth and sunset land, to re-see all also as though for a first time, and first and last made one and immediate.

On my way back I passed an old military barracks of the Dutch, and the sound coming from it made me stop, because to me that sound was imperative. The street was empty and I could draw up without any feeling of intrusion and listen to the sound that had come to me as a timely reminder of the clash of opposites that is the raw material either of the tragedy or of the glory of men on earth. I had heard it so very often. It was that hymn with which the Ambonese and Menadonese, out of their Christian hearts, always ended their days. They were singing in Dutch, in their deep, natural baritone voices, 'Abide with Me', and the sound of it made me remember all that was good as well within them.

Not until it came to an end did I continue on my way back to my mess, to a final supper with 'Dul and his Sri, Sybil and Colin McLaren.

In the morning they all came to the airport with me; they and no one else. I had decided to take Sybil with me to Singapore. She had served me so faithfully without ever taking a day off, and I thought it would be something of a long-overdue holiday for her. Also, if I found any impediment to my going, she could then take down any confidential writing I might have to do.

When the last moment came, Sri embraced me warmly and kept saying in that moving Malay farewell, 'Go in peace!' And with a rather wet face she repeated: 'Thank you, Lawrie! And oh! Lawrie! Go in peace. Go in peace!' She uttered this in a manner which seemed as if it might become almost hysterical, and I found myself saying, 'I shall, little Sri, I shall – but it's going to be difficult without your cooking to help me!'

That, as I had intended, brought all the sense of the mother in life alive in Sri and she immediately began to wipe her tears away, retaliating in a much more rational way: 'Oh, you men! Always thinking of your stomachs – even at a time like this!'

Then I turned to 'Dul. He instantly came to attention and saluted me. For the second and last time in my life I was in trouble over this business of exchanging salutes. It was not that I failed in the exchange of salutes as Ian Lauder had done – it would not have been understood if I had not returned his salute immediately – but it felt so hopelessly inadequate for the occasion. I quickly went up to him. I would have liked to embrace him but I knew that that would be too much, even if not for him with his aristocratic upbringing then because of the number of spectators around. I just put my hands on his shoulders, looked at him, and said: ''Dul, you know I can't thank you enough, and I shan't try to. But I hope you know how grateful I and all of us will always be for the honour you brought to our house.'

And then I added what always comes to my mind at all farewells that truly matter, the Japanese '*Sayonara*'. Most people do not know the innate symbolism of the word and think of it in a sentimental way; but it comes from the deepest area of the Japanese spirit, so full of a sense of what they call '*shikataganai*' – 'it cannot be helped'. My rendering of it in the urgency of the emotions that were passing between us was a rough: 'Bless you, old 'Dul. I'm afraid it has to be, for a while. Bless you and thank you.' And this time I saluted him.

And then there was Colin, dear Colin, who had served so well and was to go on doing so for many months to come. I said goodbye to him, and he joked: 'I cannot tell you how relieved we are that you are ending your occupation of Indonesia without any need for us to signal Singapore to have you poured out of the 'plane!'

Only Sybil knew the context of the signal to which he referred, and I heard her behind me trying her best not to laugh. She was still giggling when I sat down beside her in the aircraft, shaking her head and saying, 'That Colin . . !'

At the end of some days of conferences and consultations in Singapore with the General, Dixie Redman and others, I took Sybil out for what used to be called 'a real spree', the first in her life which had been so brutally interrupted by three years of internment. I have never enjoyed three days in South-east Asia more. They were full of fun, and the expression on Sybil's face, the glow of new light and life in her eyes and of general happiness as if she were caught up in a fairy tale were a joy and immense comfort to me. And when I finally said goodbye to her, and left her standing alone on the quay at Singapore, waving at me as I waved back to her from a launch carrying me out fast towards my flying boat, if waving could have reduced the growing distance and sense of separation between us, this waving would have done so. Not only had she served me, MacKereth, our office and our cause so loyally without a break for nearly two years but, above all, she had passed with honour through the finishing school of fate which internment and imprisonment under the Japanese had been. She had come to me in a lottery of chance from a pool of suitable young women, and I have always blessed Providence for giving me her help in the special idiom and values shared only by those who had been in the same school with the Japanese. That picture of her standing there in the light of morning, so clear-cut a person in her own right, is the one that remains uppermost in my mind. It was just as well that neither she nor I knew then that we would never meet again.

The flying-boat flew first to Rangoon. There I was joined in the cabin by three young civil servants from Burma, now already fully independent. We flew on to Karachi in what is today Pakistan and, after a night there, on to an RAF station on the Persian Gulf. The next day we continued to Alexandria. And on that day, when we were flying across the desert of Saudi Arabia, tossed about on the currents of hot air rising from the burning sands below, the Captain suddenly came into the cabin and told us, in the most English of voices, that the Derby was being run in England that day, and he proposed a sweepstake among all the people on board. To make it worthwhile it was important that we all join in.

I was not prepared for the boost that this incident was to give to my spirit. It was a major boost, too, to my three Burmese companions:

two of them instantly responded to the Captain's invitation by saying they would gladly buy two tickets in his sweepstake; but the third and the youngest, an extremely good-looking young man with a shaven head and refined features, utterly refused to participate, ending his refusal by saying: 'I believe that all human beings have a portion of good fortune meted out to them at birth. That and no more. We are going to Washington on an extremely important mission for our country, the first time our nation has initiated such a mission. I prepared myself, as you can see from my shaven head, in a monastery for weeks before we left. I know we shall need all that we have of good fortune for our mission and – I am sorry – I am not going to spend any of mine on a gamble.'

His two companions looked at one another, and then at me and the Captain, with dismay, obviously feeling that they were losing face before foreigners. I hastened to reassure them, saying I was so notoriously unlucky in these little gambles that I was in any case hoping to be allowed an extra ticket; and that we all understood and respected their companion for his devotion to his duty.

This extra ticket in due course was to draw a horse called *Pearl Diver*, but before that happened my memory took me back to the first sweepstake in which I had ever taken part – a sweepstake on the Derby. I was barely eighteen, and working in Durban under the direction of a remarkable editor who had been trained by Scott of the *Guardian*. All his staff were English; there was not even an English-speaking South African on the staff. But he had decided to take me on, he said, because he welcomed the idea of having a 'back-veld boy' in the office, though my appointment nearly caused a rebellion amongst the staff.

I had not been there long when Derby Day came round. I knew the Derby remotely as part of the history of my time, but I had never experienced it before among English people. It was one of those intense focal points of all English people, wherever they were in an empire on which the sun never set. There were several focal points like that, but none which seemed so joyous and exciting a recovery of their Englishness as the day of the Derby. The whole newspaper had been in a fever of the most elaborate precautions to see that the cables came through in time for us to include the result of the Derby in the 'Stop Press' of our final edition. A sweepstake had been organized in which everybody, from the editor to fathers of chapels and printers' devils, printers, lino-typists and all, took part. To my amazement I drew a horse. The horse was called *Blenheim*, and the year was 1925.

As we all sat crowded round the news editor's desk waiting for the cable to come, the excitement was immense. When it arrived and *Blenheim* emerged as the winner, they all turned to me as one and gave me such a cheer of unadulterated delight that the roof might have flown away. I can still hear the vibration, almost before the cheers had died away, of the rumble of the presses going into action, like the sound of a ship going out to sea.

There was another important association I had with the Derby. The year was about 1932 and I was lunching in Soho with Lilian Bowes-Lyon the poet and cousin of the present Queen Mother. All around us was talk of nothing but the Derby. The newspapers had been full of it too, and much of the talk was about a horse called *Hyperion*. It was the smallest horse that had ever run in the Derby, and what made it even more controversial was the fact that it had three white hocks. There was an old horse-copers' saying: 'One white hock, fight shy; two white hocks, don't buy.' This horse had stretched even the horse-copers' limit. And yet, in spite of it all, I had a feeling that *Hyperion* was going to win the Derby. I told Lilian about this extraordinary certainty I felt, and said if I had £100 I would not hesitate to back it. Without saying a word she opened her bag and counted out twenty of those wonderful black-and-white 'fivers' that were not notes so much as cheques drawn on the Bank of England.

'I had to go to the bank this morning,' she said. 'Here is £100 – go and back *Hyperion!*'

I protested, appalled, and said: 'But suppose it doesn't win? I'm very hard up at the moment – God knows when I would be able to pay you back!'

'Please, I have great faith in your hunch!' she urged me. 'Back *Hyperion* without delay!'

I got up and asked the owner of the restaurant if he could place £100 on *Hyperion*, to win. Then Lilian and I sat talking for two of the longest hours of my life until, just after three, the news-boys outside started shouting. The result of the Derby was through – and *Hyperion* had won.

And here, now, in a flying-boat in mid-air over one of the vast deserts of the earth, it was as if I was being caught up once again in an abiding pattern of my own moments of good fortune in life, of which the Derby and the horses I have mentioned were such striking omens. Suddenly I was incredibly happy, and not at all surprised when the Captain came down and announced that *Pearl Diver* was the winner.

The face of the young Burmese was transfigured with joy, and he said again and again: 'You see? If I had taken that ticket I would have won, and that would have used up some of the good fortune we shall need in Washington!'

I was invited by the Captain to join them in the cockpit to have a sip of the champagne I had ordered, as tradition demanded. There I looked down on this world of horrendous burning sand but, way up in front, on the far horizon, the light was softening and the world of Homer's Mediterranean was beginning to calm the day and slowly become more defined and precise, introducing us to what was to be landfall at the city of Alexandria.

That view completed a process which broke the obsession of my mind and heart with Java. I had left Java physically, but until then I had not left it in spirit. Indeed I had been quite a long way down the road towards 'going native', a well-known phenomenon among Europeans in the days of empire, until the question of the Derby and *Pearl Diver* arose. I have told the stories of the Derby in some detail because each one of them marked the end of a phase in my life and the beginning of an important new one. *Hyperion*, for instance, provided me with sufficient money to withdraw from Fleet Street and concentrate on finishing my first book. Now as I stood there looking west I realized that all that had happened in Indonesia had begun to be a memory. It was as if *Pearl Diver* recalled the end of *The Tempest* and Ariel's release from the spell Prospero had cast over him, and the end of his song came to me:

> Full fathom five thy father lies;
> Of his bones are coral made:
> Those are pearls that were his eyes:
> Nothing of him that doth fade,
> But doth suffer a sea-change
> Into something rich and strange.

And that 'strange' was indeed prophetic, because if it had not been for the reminder of those strange synchronicities in my life, I would not have been so ready to confront one of the strangest of all synchronicities awaiting me in Alexandria, and another illustration of the way in which my life has been shaped in so great a measure by chance. There, at the military airstrip, was another aircraft that had landed just before us. It was a South African military 'plane, and three South African officers in uniform were standing by it talking while it was being refuelled. As I went walking towards them, one of the officers saw me, looked hard at me for a moment, and then broke away, calling: 'My God, Blitz, you're supposed to be dead! What are you doing here?' (Blitz was my nickname at school.) I instantly answered, calling him by his nickname: 'My little old Gogga-tjie, I knew the Germans would never be able to put you down!'*

The words, the associations, everything then attacked me with a feeling of homesickness which I'd never allowed into my conscious self in Java. When I told him, he said: 'But it's simple. Jump in, man, and come home with us.'

Without hesitation I went to the transport officer and signalled Singapore and the War Office, telling them that I had to break my journey and would write a full explanation of why I'd done so from the Cape of Good Hope. Then I went back to the 'plane and jumped in.

---

*Gogga means insect and is derived from the Bushman. 'Little old' is one of the extreme ways of expressing endearment in Afrikaans, and the diminutive I added to the word 'gogga' raised that endearment to its ultimate height.

CHAPTER THIRTEEN

In a Glass Brightly

I HAVE NEVER been back to Java. I have on many occasions since flown over it, been near it, and have been in Singapore many times and could easily have gone back. But my own life had become as exacting as any life could be, and I had more than enough to deal with on my private, personal and public plate. In due course I received from Java all the papers from my office, including the report, complete with that of MacKereth, and Sharman's commercial report which accompanied it. They arrived at my home in Aldeburgh just as Sybil had sent them to me and there, in the coastguard's tower in which I worked, I placed them unopened with all the other things from my past.

And it was there, nearly fifty years later, when I wound up our home in Aldeburgh and, inevitably, had to consider what to do with such a mound of papers from spent years, that I opened Sybil's parcel, still with the scent of my office in Batavia in it, and saw all my most confidential signals, my 'Most Immediate' messages to Mountbatten, to the Admiral in *Cumberland* and to the ALFSEA Commander-in-Chief in Singapore. All were neatly there, but crumbling and yellow because of the inferior quality of the paper and their increasing age. Only my report, retyped at the Foreign Office on their special paper, remained fresh and unblemished.

In a strange way this moment made me stop and look deeply into the question of why I had never been back to Java. Why did I not want to go back to a country in which I had experienced such a heightening of perception as that raised in people by war and suffering, and how could it have come to mean so little consciously to me? I started to read my own report, at first reluctantly and then not so much with emotion as with fascination at its singular objectivity. Indeed the determination of the writer of the report to be objective was carried in one way to an extreme which made the report incomplete. There is almost no reference whatsoever in it to all the work that was done before the arrival of *Cumberland* and up to the arrival of the British forces or (as I have described in what I have now written) to the process of hard and indispensable re-education of those in command of the British forces, both military and political – because the whole of that missing story was really about the author.

When I finished reading the report it was as if it was written by someone other than myself. To this day I remember how through those years of war, imprisonment and solitary confinement, this 'more-ness' of things, this elemental 'other-ness' of events in life, was kept alive in me by the companionship of all that I had read and heard and seen in art and literature and, of course, most of all in the area regarded as singularly religious. Somewhere in that area is this feeling of 'other-ness' allotted to each individual, always there waiting, if our rational selves are defeated.

This was something so complete that I had a physical vision of the author, across the fifty years in between, as an ageless and fresh young face; not a face directly observed so much as the face of someone who had come silently up behind me and was looking over my shoulder into a mirror where his reflection joined my confrontation in that quicksilver surface. I had a feeling then, which I have always had but which has grown much more profound, that everything on earth, from the first moment when the cold day was warmed and the moss was stirred to cling to stone, every natural and living thing from the last and smallest, everything is much more at a given moment than it appears to be and than we can conceive.

In regard to this 'other' self I could think of all sorts of high-minded motivations for his actions – a sense of duty, a sense of what he owed to all the people who had suffered with him in the war and under the Japanese, all such fine-sounding reasons and motivations – but they would not have answered this questioning in myself roused by confrontation with this 'other' of fifty years ago.

Not only was the happening in Indonesia itself unique, but the human qualities demanded for it had to be equally unique. I believe the person in the mirror, with his history and at that time and that place, was the only person in the world who matched the challenge.

All the past – not only my past but the past which is in what I have labelled 'the great memory' – was suddenly there as a 'now', and as a point in which all that followed in the future was fulfilled in that reflection in the glass.

We are all born and go through life wrapped in a mystery which, no matter how much we explore it or how much we discover and rediscover it, remains infinite. We are entrusted by Creation with a role in a drama within the theatre of the master-pattern, enfolded in our own little portion of time. We are armed only with the sense of wonder which it provokes in our deepest hearts and which makes us see all the horizons, physical and non-physical, which confront us not as the limitations they purport to be in the totality of our vision but as an invitation to go on beyond.

There, on the last horizon of our ultimate awareness and senses, it is as if this mystery in some unforeseeable way has a relevant eventfulness of its own. It shows itself in perhaps the most mysterious way of all in its imponderable workings in the phenomenon of chance. This phenomenon seems to behave beyond any laws of cause and effect as if it were the purest of happenings and in a dimension where there is no dividing line between mind and matter. We know it only as a meaningful experience and more and more as we grow older through the synchronicities which accompany it. These synchronicities I am certain are what the Chinese have in mind when they talk about 'signs of confirmation' and are part of what they call 'the meaning which has always existed through itself'.

Across this Grand Canyon of time that divides me today from the man in the mirror, it seems to me that his life was shaped and could not have been fulfilled in the manner in which it was fulfilled had it not been for an unrecognized alliance with chance. I could give many examples of how, over and over again, chance and its synchronicities intruded to save my life and the lives of others under my command, and helped me in many moments of transition.

One of the most striking illustrations of this, of course, was what I have already referred to as 'The Parable of the Two Cups of Coffee'. With an act of kindness in 1926 to two lost and bewildered Japanese journalists, that man in the mirror was saving his life in the jungles of Java in 1942. What is more, in between had come a memorable voyage to Japan, and in the time spent there learning the language he had acquired an insight into the mind and spirit of the people, gaining not only an understanding but also a love of what is best in their culture which I believe worked unseen and unrecognized in his spirit all through those years in prison, to create a positive rather than a negative atmosphere between us and the Japanese.

It was there to such an extent that when the last of the great synchronicities which confronted him took place in a flying-boat in a paradoxical storm of heat and sand over the Arabian desert, the special pattern for which his life had so uniquely predisposed him was utterly fulfilled.

And it is when I come to this point that it is as if I have done what needed to be done in regard to him. He himself recorded the humanity of so many of the people who served with him and worked with him during the British occupation of Indonesia. He recorded it all in the many reports he wrote and dispatches he sent, summed up in what MacKereth called his 'inspired and masterful report' to the Secretary of State. But in his own life, his spirit existed before and went on after the event.

He was larger than the history he not only recorded but also helped to make. But there was another thing for which perhaps he had been uniquely born, which was lived out in those days in Java in such a way that it was no longer a purely subjective element, but objective and of meaning to his fellow men.

I felt this with increasing confidence as I came towards the end of his story. The pattern which he lived in Indonesia is a pattern in every man, a pattern which had compelled Joseph Conrad, for instance, to write his book *Lord Jim*, a book which this man in the mirror loved from the time it was given to him at the age of 14. He had read it over and over again with an extraordinary sense of premonition, and when he arrived in Indonesia (Jim's Insulinda), it was as if he'd been there before because of this book, although he had not known that the immense challenge to live this pattern truly to its appointed end was coming, as it had to Jim, 'veiled like an oriental bride'.

Conrad felt compelled to write his story of Tuan Jim because Jim was (as Conrad put it) 'one of us'. And this man in the mirror was not some cold product of duty and predetermined intellect, he too was one of us. He was one of us as all the leaves of a tree are part of the thing to which they owe their shape, their colour and the sound they make in the wind. They belong, one and all, to the same tree yet they are all different from one another.

As well as belonging at one and the same time to the heart of human creation, the life-giving importance of this difference is to fulfil to the utmost what one was born to be; as Leonardo da Vinci said so confidently, 'I am what Nature has predisposed me to be.'

Perhaps the greatest example of this is in the source of the Christian extension of the Hebraic myth, when the individual is free to be in bondage forever to the end for which he has been born.

It is also so movingly expressed by Dante when, in the final act of his great journey as he is about to move into the presence of the ultimate light, he sees the whole of heaven stacked with all the souls that have ever been and is amazed that each soul is there because it has been its individual self.

I believe this is the pattern which the whole life of the young man in the mirror had fulfilled in Indonesia, and in such a manner that he became truly one of us. When I reached this point an extraordinary feeling overcame me. I am a writer and my business is with words, and as I dragged their meaning out of the silence which accompanied them into the world of vision and sound, the face I saw so brightly in the mirror suddenly withdrew. The glass was empty and the quick had left the silver. It was as if I saw a young figure resolving into a charged and meaningful day of cloud and thunder and finally blessed rain, there in Indonesia, and I knew that in making his meaning known I had added the final dimension to fulfilment.

So there was nothing left for me to do. All I owed him now was a decent farewell and a proper thank you, and I found myself instinctively doing it in the way the first people of Africa do on a momentous moment of separation. They call after the vanishing person: 'We have seen you, we praise you, and we thank you.'

So now there is no need for me ever to look back. But I shall always remember how, once upon a time, among those thousand and one islands of Insulinda that are strung along the Equator like emeralds on an ancient necklace, there was a land called Java. And on the slopes of a great sleeping volcano, in a city called Bandoeng, a soldier stood under the light of the rising full moon watching his officers and men go down the street on their way to the sea and home. And when the last of them had disappeared into the night he turned about and walked away alone in the opposite direction to begin the story of his own 'Once upon a time . . . .'.

Index

INDEX

NOTE: Place names are given in the form used in the text, but modern Indonesian names are generally added in brackets, with cross-references where appropriate. LP signifies Laurens van der Post.

p. 72

p. 156 "The light within"

p. 290 ! The journey of the spirit

p. 318 – 319